FIFTY KEY CHRISTIAN THINKERS

*Peter McEnhill
and George Newlands*

Routledge
Taylor & Francis Group

LONDON AND NEW YORK

First published 2004
by Routledge
2 Park Square, Milton Park, Abingdon, Oxfordshire, OX14 4RN

Simultaneously published in the USA and Canada
by Routledge
29 West 35th Street, New York, NY 10001

Routledge is an imprint of the Taylor & Francis Group

© 2004 Peter McEnhill and George Newlands

Typeset in Bembo by Taylor & Francis Books Ltd
Printed and bound in Great Britain by TJ International Ltd, Padstow, Cornwall

British Library Cataloguing-in-Publication Data
A catalogue record for this book is available from the British Library

Library of Congress Cataloging in Publication Data
McEnhill, Peter.
Fifty key Christian thinkers / Peter McEnhill and George Newlands.
p. cm. — (Routledge key guides)
Includes bibliographical references and index.
1. Theology, Doctrinal—Popular works. 2. Theologians. I. Newlands, G. M., 1941-
II. Title. III. Series.
BT77.M159 2004
230'092'2—dc22
2004000796

ISBN 0–415–17049–4 (hbk)
ISBN 0–415–17050–8 (pbk)

FIFTY KEY CHRISTIAN THINKERS

Fifty Key Christian Thinkers introduces the lives and ideas of some of the most influential figures in Christian history. Providing a comprehensive overview of the development of Christian thought from its roots to the present day, the work includes entries on:

- Thomas Aquinas
- Arius
- Augustine of Hippo
- John Calvin
- Ludwig Feuerbach
- John Hick
- Immanuel Kant
- Martin Luther
- Paul
- Hermann Reimarus.

Fully cross-referenced and featuring a handy glossary of key terms, this book is an invaluable resource for all those interested in the history of Christianity over the past two millennia.

Peter McEnhill holds the Barbour Chair in Systematic Theology at Westminster College, Cambridge. **George Newlands** is Professor of Divinity at Glasgow University.

You may also be interested in the following Routledge Student Reference titles:

Religion: The Basics
Malory Nye

Fifty Key Christian Thinkers
Peter McEnhill and George Newlands

Fifty Key Jewish Thinkers
Dan Cohn-Sherbok

Fifty Key Medieval Thinkers
G. R. Evans

Gurdjieff: The Key Concepts
Sophia Wellbeloved

Eastern Philosophy: Key Readings
Oliver Leaman

Key Concepts in Eastern Philosophy
Oliver Leaman

Fifty Eastern Thinkers
Diané Collinson, Kathryn Plant and Robert Wilkinson

Who's Who in Christianity
Lavinia Cohn-Sherbok

Who's Who in Jewish History
Joan Comay, new edition revised by Lavinia Cohn-Sherbok

Who's Who in the New Testament
Ronald Brownrigg

Who's Who in the Old Testament
Joan Comay

ALPHABETICAL LIST OF CONTENTS

Chronological list of contents   vii
Preface   ix

Abelard   3
Anselm   9
Aquinas   16
Arius   25
Athanasius   32
Augustine   38
Baillie, John and Donald   48
Barth   58
Boethius   67
Bonhoeffer   70
Brunner   80
Bultmann   85
Calvin   91
Cappadocian Fathers – Basil of Caesarea, Gregory of Nyssa
    and Gregory Nazianzen   102
Duns Scotus   109
Edwards   112
Feuerbach   116
Forsyth   121
Gutiérrez   127
Harnack   131
Hegel   135
Hick   141
Irenaeus   149
John of Damascus   154
Justin Martyr   158
Kant   161

Kierkegaard	168
Küng	174
Luther	180
Moltmann	190
Newman	195
Niebuhr	198
Origen	203
Pannenberg	207
Paul	214
Rahner	221
Reimarus	226
Ritschl	229
Ruether	233
Schleiermacher	236
Schüssler-Fiorenza	240
Strauss	244
Tertullian	249
Tillich	255
Tracy	263
Troeltsch	266
Zwingli	269
Glossary	278
Index	286

CHRONOLOGICAL LIST OF
CONTENTS

Paul (?–c.64)	214
Justin Martyr (c.100–65)	158
Irenaeus (c.130–200)	149
Tertullian, Quintus Septimius Florens (c.160–c.225)	249
Origen (c.185–254)	203
Arius (c.270–336)	25
Athanasius (c.295–373)	32
The Cappadocian Fathers: Basil of Caesarea (330–79); Gregory of Nyssa (335–95); Gregory Nazianzen (329–90)	102
Augustine of Hippo (354–430)	38
Boethius, Anicius Manlius Torquatus Severinus (c.480–525)	67
John of Damascus (c.675–749)	154
Anselm of Canterbury (1033–1109)	9
Abelard, Peter (1079–1142)	3
Aquinas, Thomas (1225–74)	16
Duns Scotus, John (c.1265–1308)	109
Luther, Martin (1483–1546)	180
Zwingli, Huldrych (1484–1531)	269
Calvin, John (1509–64)	91
Reimarus, Hermann Samuel (1694–1768)	226
Edwards, Jonathan (1703–58)	112
Kant, Immanuel (1724–1804)	161
Schleiermacher, Friedrich Daniel Ernst (1768–1834)	236
Hegel, Georg Wilhelm Friedrich (1770–1831)	135
Newman, John Henry (1801–90)	195
Feuerbach, Ludwig (1804–72)	116
Strauss, David Friedrich (1808–74)	244
Kierkegaard, Søren (1813–55)	168
Ritschl, Albrecht (1822–89)	229
Forsyth, Peter Taylor (1848–1921)	121

Harnack, Adolf von (1851–1930)	131
Troeltsch, Ernst (1865–1923)	266
Bultmann, Rudolf (1884–1976)	85
Baillie, John (1886–1960) and Baillie, Donald (1887–1954)	48
Barth, Karl (1886–1968)	58
Tillich, Paul (1886–1965)	255
Brunner, Emil (1889–1966)	80
Niebuhr, Reinhold (1892–1971)	198
Rahner, Karl (1904–84)	221
Bonhoeffer, Dietrich (1906–45)	70
Hick, John Harwood (1922–)	141
Moltmann, Jürgen (1926–)	190
Pannenberg, Wolfhart (1928–)	207
Küng, Hans (1928–)	174
Gutiérrez, Gustavo (1928–)	127
Ruether, Rosemary Radford (1936–)	233
Schüssler-Fiorenza, Elisabeth (1938–)	240
Tracy, David (1939–)	263

PREFACE

Christians think – at least sometimes. They do not think alike. The fifty Christian thinkers discussed here represent very different styles of thought. They reflect the language and cultures of very different times and cultures. They contradict each other. But they also echo basic beliefs and affirmations, which arise from reflection upon and engagement with the Christian gospel. They echo the influence of the Bible and Church traditions. They interact, in dialogue or in lack of dialogue, with non-Christian traditions, whether from other religions or from secular sources. This is a dynamic dialogue, for the process of interaction is thousands of years old, embracing material from pre-Christian cultures in various parts of the world. It is a thought process shaped too by ever-changing perspectives on the nature of humanity and divinity, selves and societies.

In this reflective process the dialogue partners change in what are often surprising ways. For example, ancient figures such as Augustine and Aquinas come to figure centrally in postmodern debates around the millennium about truth, reality and desire. Kierkegaard, hardly noticed outside his native country in the nineteenth century, becomes a catalyst for theological revolution in the early twentieth century. We have not attempted to categorise our selection of Christian thinkers, but have simply put them in alphabetical order. In this way we leave readers free to juxtapose their own selections, as an invitation to further revolutions in Christian thinking.

Something should be said about the choice of entries. Needless to say this has not been an easy matter. What after all constitutes a Christian thinker? Here we have tended to interpret that to mean theologians who have self-consciously and explicitly attempted to re-think the Christian faith for their context and time. We are of course aware that not all Christian thinkers have been theologians but some principle of selection is necessary and that is one which we have applied. We have also tried to include a balanced selection of writers from the ancient, medieval and modern period. Certain thinkers, such as Athanasius, Augustine, Anselm, Aquinas, Luther, Calvin, Kant, Hegel, Schleiermacher, Barth, Rahner etc., suggest themselves as canonical figures for the tradition and would appear on any list of important Christian thinkers, but there are many significant figures who do not find themselves included, even though the scale and importance of their contribution would fully merit a place. Unfortunately (or fortunately) there have been many more than fifty major Christian thinkers!

As it stands, the selection is heavily weighted to the Northern (European and American) hemisphere and is overwhelmingly male. To some extent this simply reflects accurately the history of the subject up until the relatively modern period. (For comparison see a similar preponderance in *Fifty Major Philosophers*.) The relative paucity of female thinkers reflects the historical exclusion of female voices from the arena of theological discourse. Therefore only Ruether and Schüssler-Fiorenza find a place here, but undoubtedly future volumes of this type will do more to reflect the rich and diverse contributions being made by feminist theologians today. However, it is difficult to assess the long-term and ongoing value of many bodies of work that are still being actively added to and assessed as we write. Similarly, one might say something similar concerning those thinkers who would represent the many fine emancipatory and contextual theologies that are emerging today. Of these the prime example considered here is Gustavo Gutiérrez.

Thus, the selection of thinkers seeks to be reflective of the historic development of the subject in that we have tried to include those thinkers who have made important and far-reaching contributions to the theological debate and who have moved it in a different and new direction. To some extent the selection is also pragmatic in that this volume is intended as an aid for those students undertaking courses in academic theology in English-speaking countries. Many of the figures encountered herein still tend to dominate the courses taught in the academic institutions of the English-speaking world. This pedagogical stress also accounts for the preponderance of Continental thinkers of the nineteenth and twentieth centuries. For the themes and preoccupations of the great nineteenth-century thinkers set the agenda for how the giants of the twentieth century were to perceive the theological task. It was an extraordinarily productive and critical period that produced impressive re-thinkings of the faith as well as profound attempts at revision. Strauss and Feuerbach stand here to show how heterodox and radical those criticisms could be – they represent as it were the borderlands of nineteenth-century religious thought.

We have thus attempted to include the centrally significant figures in Christianity, and people representative of particular traditions. But lists are by nature contestable, and we might have excluded some of those who are here and included others. It may well be, too, that the fifty most significant Christian thinkers of the next two millennia will be even more interesting than the ones we have selected here.

Peter McEnhill and George Newlands

FIFTY KEY CHRISTIAN THINKERS

ABELARD, PETER (1079–1142)

A brilliant and acute philosopher who was famed for his learning, his powers of rhetoric and for his determination to pursue all matters, including matters of faith, to their logical outcome no matter the consequences. As such he has been fêted as a rationalist before his time and although this may be an over-exaggeration there is no doubt that Abelard is one of the glowing figures of the early scholastic period, that period which was most determined to pursue the relationship between faith and reason

The chief source for Abelard's early life is his own work *Historia Calamitum* (History of My Troubles, c.1133) wherein Abelard tells us that he was born in 1079 at Le Pallet in Brittany, the eldest son of a local knight. Eschewing a career as a knight-errant he decided to become a philosopher. Abelard was trained by Roscelin (c.1095) in the methods of dialectical argumentation and he quickly became a proficient and skilled practitioner of this art. Possessed of a brilliant mind and powerful debating skills he explored issues, including vital issues of faith, to the fullest degree possible, not content simply to accept matters on received authority. Arriving in Paris around 1100, Abelard was at the centre of the controversy between his current teacher, William of Champeaux, and his former teacher, Roscelin, on the nature of *universals*. Much medieval philosophy was to be dominated by this question. Briefly, the disagreement resolves into two positions which are usually termed *realist* and *nominalist*. The realist position holds that when we perceive that two or more objects share a common property it is because the objects are embodying a universal property which exists apart from the objects themselves. For example, two red objects embody the universal concept of 'redness', two tigers embody the universal property of 'tigerness' and two individual human beings embody the universal property of 'humanness', etc. The nominalist position on the other hand states that there is no universal property of 'redness', 'tigerness' or 'humanness'. For the nominalist position we simply have two or more particular objects that are red or whatever, and there is no reason to posit a universal concept that they both share.

Although the question of universal categories might seem to be the prime example of the type of rational nit-picking for which the scholastics were to become infamous, there are important issues at stake. Issues of truth, knowledge and being – for it is the case that we do speak of universal qualities and we do have concepts of species and the like. How then do we give account of the commonality that we clearly believe exists between human beings, tigers and red objects?

Roscelin advocated the extreme nominalist position that universals do not exist apart from their embodiment in individual things, as opposed to the realists who believed, in a platonic fashion, that universals do have a separate existence apart from the individuals that embody them. However, Roscelin's stance suffered from the classical weakness of nominalism in that it becomes extremely difficult thereby to give an account of what it was that the individual members of a species or genus shared in common. Roscelin's response to this objection – which was to maintain that there was in fact no unity to a species – led him into deep and troubled waters in relation to the doctrine of the *Trinity*. (Not the first time that an originally purely philosophical disagreement has had profound and unforeseen implications for Christian belief.) For the logical outcome of Roscelin's position seemed to imply tri-theism in that there could be no universal property of 'divinity or Godness' that bound the three persons of the Trinity together as God. Since classical Trinitarian theology did speak of the Father, Son and Spirit as sharing the one divine substance this was problematic, and Roscelin's views were thus extremely suspect in the eyes of many.

Abelard modified Roscelin's extreme position, but he also rejected the position of his then teacher William of Champeaux, who taught the real existence of universals. Abelard brilliantly refuted William's views (or so he himself tells us) and forced him to retreat from his strongly realist position towards an acceptance of some sort of modified nominalism. Abelard's mediating position was to argue that although universal ideas do not exist independently of the individuals that embody them, nevertheless they are necessary creations of the mind and they enable us to establish and speak of the resemblances between individual things in a way that leads to real knowledge. These resemblances are not things (*res*) as such, but they have an existence as *vox* or *nomen*, conceptual abstractions that are adequate representations of the things referred to and which enable us to speak of the universal properties that unite a particular species.

Abelard's mastery in the debate with William enhanced his growing reputation and attracted many students to his cause. He turned his attention to commentating upon the Bible and began to lecture on Ezekiel. According to his own judgement he did not follow received authority but relied on his own ability – and as he was by popular repute an attractive and powerful speaker, he pleased everyone who heard him. The motivation for this work, however, was not as noble as the manner of its delivery. Abelard had been spurred to take it on by the dull reputation and methods of another of his teachers, Anselm of Laon. Abelard's habit of making powerful enemies by intellectually humiliating former teachers (Roscelin and William for example) was to prove costly to him in the future.

It was around this time that Abelard met the woman with whom he would be forever associated – Héloïse. Héloïse became Abelard's secret lover until they were forcefully separated in 1119. The separation was more than emotionally painful: Héloïse's uncle had Abelard forcibly castrated and made Héloïse take the veil and become a nun. Abelard retreated first to the monastery at St Denis, and then afterwards to a place of his own near Nogent-sur-Seine, where he established an oratory dedicated to the Holy Spirit and lived as a monk without a monastery.

In the intervening period at St Denis, Abelard had published his first explicitly theological work the *Theologia Summi Boni*. In this work Abelard sought to establish that the doctrine of the Trinity could be found among the platonists as well as being attested in the Bible. Citing **Augustine** as a support in this matter, Abelard wanted to establish that the Trinity was not an absolute mystery – that is, a matter which only could be known because God had revealed it in the scriptures and the teaching of the Church – but was something that could be arrived at by the application of reason alone. According to Abelard there is only one God: a simple, undivided substance existing in three persons, co-eternal and co-equal. These persons differ not in number but only in characteristics or attributes. God the Father denotes the divine power, the Son denotes the wisdom of God and the Holy Spirit denotes the goodness of God. The work of the three persons is one as power is always guided by wisdom and established in goodness. Although Abelard's very precise and careful elaboration of the relations between the persons tries hard to (and probably does) maintain the unity of the divine substance, to his opponents Abelard had so identified the persons with these abstract characteristics that he implicitly denied their co-equality. Failing that it could also seem that by so stressing these traditional appropriations of power, wisdom and goodness he simply made them aspects of the one undifferentiated Godhead. This would have made Abelard guilty of the heresy of Sabellianism, which taught that there were not three eternal and co-equal persons in the Godhead, but one God successively known as Father, Son and Spirit. Abelard was called to defend his views at the Council of Soissons in 1121 where his views were condemned and he was forced to burn his own book.

Abelard continued to defend his Trinitarian position in later works such as the *Theologia Christiana* and the *Theologia Scholarum*. The *Theologia Christiana* introduced the term theology as a technical term for Christian doctrine. In relation to other matters of the faith Abelard's keen intellect and bold manner of expression led him into other areas of controversy. He suggested that in the act of the incarnation the human nature of Christ was nothing to the divine person and was merely a garment that the divine Son assumed. This did not take seriously enough what had been the traditional interpretation of the Church since the Council of Chalcedon in 451 (see **Chalcedon**) that the Son of God had personally united himself with the human nature of Christ.

In relation to the *atonement* (theories that explain how Christ's death on the cross saves human beings from sin), Abelard is, of course, famously associated with his commentary on Romans 3:19–26, where he stressed the exemplary nature of Christ's death on the cross. He rejected the classical 'ransom' theory of the atonement which taught that Christ's death was a ransom paid to the devil to secure the release of human beings from sin. This theory had already been rejected by **Anselm** of Canterbury but Abelard also questioned the adequacy of Anselm's own satisfaction theory. Anselm had felt that the deficiency in the ransom theory was that it seemed to give the devil rights in relation to God such that he had to be paid to release humanity from sin. Anselm argued that it was God's honour that had been wronged when human beings sinned and that Christ's death was not a payment to the devil, but the price of satisfying God's offended honour. Abelard, however, preferred to focus upon the effect of Christ's death evoking a response of love in gratitude in the heart of the believer. Thus in his commentary on Romans 3 Abelard writes:

> [N]ow it seems to us that we have been justified by the blood of Christ and reconciled to God in this way: through his singular act of grace made known in us (in that his Son has taken our nature on himself, and persevered in this nature, and taught us both by his word and example, even to the point of death) he has more fully bound us to himself by love. As a result, our hearts should be set on fire by such a gift of divine grace, and true love should not hold back from suffering anything for his sake ... Therefore, our redemption through the suffering of Christ is that deeper love within us which not only frees us from slavery to sin, but also secures for us the true liberty of the children of God, in order that we might do all

things out of love rather than out of fear – love for him who has shown us such grace that no greater can be found.

This theory has been dubbed the 'moral influence' or subjectivist account of the atonement. However, it now seems to be generally agreed that too much cannot be read into this rather brief passage in Abelard's writings as elsewhere he was perfectly capable of using the traditional language of sacrifice and of Christ bearing the punishment for our sins. Nevertheless, Abelard's theory does fulfil a useful function in enabling theologians to give some account of what the act of atonement might mean in the subjective experience of the believer as against the more 'objective' accounts which sometimes seem to present it as a transaction carried out behind the backs of human beings.

In addition to these major works Abelard also produced *Sic et Non* (Yes and No) and *Scito te ipsum* (Know thyself). *Sic et Non* reveals Abelard's method most clearly. He considers some 150 or so theological points with related scriptural texts. The texts are drawn from the Bible and seem almost mutually contradictory. In resolving some of these contradictions Abelard begins to develop his procedure of methodological doubt and exemplifies what was to become the normative method of the scholastic period. In order to understand one must first begin by questioning, for it 'is by doubting we come to questioning, and by questioning we perceive the truth'. For Abelard we must understand in order to believe whereas for Anselm of Canterbury we must believe in order to understand.

Scito te ipsum is an ethical work in which Abelard begins to argue that the moral value of any act must be found in the intention and will of the agent. Contemporary accounts tended to understand morality in terms of obedience to a known divine command or law. Abelard argues that a person acts rightly when they act in accordance with their conscience – but their action is most fully right when their conscience is in accord with the moral law of God. Sinful or evil actions are thus those actions which follow from an evil intention or willing. However, in outlining this view Abelard chose the unfortunate example of those who crucified Christ, arguing for their innocence as they did not understand the full implications of their actions. This shocked the sensibilities of his contemporaries and led many to reject his position, although in general terms moral theory was later to move in the direction that Abelard suggested.

Abelard's later life was not without incident. He left his oratory to become Abbot of the monastic community of St Gildas (transferring ownership of the property of the oratory to Héloïse and her community of nuns). However, Abelard found that his new monks were hostile to him and his reforms – hostile to the point of trying to poison him according to Abelard. This unhappy situation could not continue forever and Abelard left them in 1132 to take up teaching in Paris again. However, his later works once again fell under suspicion of heresy and Abelard found this time that he had an extremely powerful foe in the person of Bernard of Clairvaux. He was condemned at the Council of Sens in 1141. Abelard appealed to the Pope but was advised to retract that which was objectionable in his writings. This he did and he was allowed to live in peace at Cluny where he died in 1142.

Abelard is a difficult figure to assess in terms of his influence. Taken up by later figures he was portrayed as the first rationalist, but this is almost certainly anachronistic as he knew what it meant to rely on the authority of the teaching of the Church and the traditions of the Fathers. As he wrote to Héloïse in 1141: 'I will never be a philosopher, if this is to speak against Paul; I would not be an Aristotle, if this were to separate me from Christ … I have set my building on the corner stone on which Christ has built his Church … if the tempest rises, I am not shaken; if the winds rave, I am not fearful … I rest upon the rock that cannot be moved'.

See also: **Anselm; Aquinas; Augustine; Duns Scotus**

Glossary: *Atonement; Chalcedon; nominalism; realism; scholastic; Trinity; universals*

Major writings

Historia Calamitatum, ed. J.T. Muckle, Medieval Studies, 1950
Opera Theologica, Vol. 2, ed. E.M. Buytaert, *Corpus Christianorum, Continuatio Mediaevalis*, Vol. 12, Turnholti: Typographi Brepols Editores Pontificii, 1969
The Letters of Abelard and Heloise, trans. B. Radice, Harmondsworth: Penguin, 1974

Further reading

M.T. Clanchy, *Abelard: A Medieval Life*, Oxford: Blackwell, 1997
L.O. Nielsen, 'Abelard and Gilbert of Poitiers' in G.R. Evans (ed.), *The Medieval Theologians*, Oxford: Blackwell, 2001

ANSELM OF CANTERBURY (1033–1109)

Theologian and Archbishop of Canterbury and one of the most outstanding thinkers of the medieval period, Anselm was certainly the most profound theologian (at least in the Western Church) between the age of **Augustine** and that of **Aquinas**. He differed from most of his contemporaries by relying on the appropriate use of reason rather than the current practice of citing recognised authorities as the proper way of approaching theological problems. But this stress on the appropriate use of reason is not to suggest that Anselm employed an arid rationalism, nor is it to say that he placed reason above revealed faith. Reason is always subject to faith, and some of the most famous of Anselm's works are cast in the form of a prayer to God. Anselm's famous phrase '*fides quaerens intellectum*' ('faith seeking to understand') shows that he recognised that faith is the basic precondition for the right use of our reason. That minds enlightened by God could employ reason to arrive at truths concerning the deepest mysteries of faith was a conviction that was to remain with him throughout his life.

Anselm was born in Aosta in 1033, the son of a well-to-do landowner. He left Italy for France in 1056 and embarked upon a period of peripatetic wandering, seeking a mentor to further his education in accordance with the practice of the times. In 1059 he eventually settled in the Benedictine monastery at Bec, which was then gaining a considerable reputation as a monastic school of some quality under the direction and guidance of Anselm's fellow country-man Lanfranc. Bec was unusual at this juncture in taking pupils from the children of the local nobility who were not exclusively headed for the monastic life. Anselm himself had desired intensely to become a monk as the result of a youthful dream but had been discouraged from joining his local monastery.

A year later, under the stimulation of intellectual and personal contact with Lanfranc, Anselm decided to fulfil his childhood ambition and take monastic vows. He was to replace his mentor Lanfranc as Prior of the abbey three years later. Succeeding his mentor was to become something of a habit for Anselm as he was later to follow Lanfranc as Archbishop of Canterbury in 1093. As Prior, Anselm soon displayed his considerable intellectual and teaching gifts by developing a new style of teaching his monks which involved a dialogical question and answer session between pupil and master. Utilising this method, Anselm's pupils were encouraged to move from the rational examination of questions such as truth and goodness in ordinary everyday human affairs to God as the source of all goodness and truth. Thus, in his first work, *Monologion* (1077), subtitled 'faith seeking understanding', a work prompted by requests from Anselm's pupils to record his teaching style, we catch a glimpse of Anselm's method. Anselm begins the work with the proposition that 'There is something that is the best, the greatest, the highest of all existing things'. This one thing cannot be known directly because God is beyond all knowing and understanding, but some clearer picture of God can emerge by clarifying the concepts that we use in relation to God such as goodness, love, justice, etc.

Anselm proceeds to offer an analysis of goodness, arguing that all things that are deemed 'good' must share some common property which makes them good. This common property, however, since it makes all things that are good good, must be a greater or higher good as it is the source of goodness in all things. This greater or higher good is one thing above all others and is the highest of existing things and therefore we can say something about God (who is the highest of all existing things) through an analysis of goodness.

> But who could doubt that that through which all goods are good is itself a great good? Therefore, it is good through itself since every good is good through it. So it follows that all other goods are good through something other than what they are and that this other alone is good through itself. But no good which is good through another is equal to or greater than that good which is good through itself. Hence, only that good which alone is good through itself is supremely good; for that is supreme which so excels others that it has neither an equal nor a superior. Now, what is supremely good is also supremely great. Therefore, there is one thing which is supremely good and supremely great – i.e., which is the highest of all existing things.[1]

Anselm's method is clearly evident at this point; he proceeds via the rigorous analysis of concepts to show what they must necessarily entail. Having established that there is one supreme being, Anselm continues to argue from the concept of being that all particular beings must find their origin in one supreme being; since to posit a manifold cause of the plurality of beings would end in hopeless contradiction. Such a supreme being must be self-caused and itself be the cause of all other things through an act of creation out of nothing. Eventually, after the consideration of some 80 or so propositions Anselm has established, (at least to his own satisfaction and) on the basis of rational arguments alone, the existence of the one, simple, although *Trinitarian*, creative God of the Christian faith.

Whatever one may think of the merits of this type of argument, Anselm himself was not satisfied with it, as it was, in his own words, 'composed of a chain of many arguments',[ii] and he sought to find a single argument that would prove that God truly exists and that he is the supreme good. The argument that Anselm finally came up with proved to be that rarest of creatures – a wholly original argument – and is one that has intrigued and infuriated subsequent philosophers down to the present day. It is contained in the *Proslogion* (1078) and is often referred to as the 'ontological argument'. It argues from a basic definition of God as 'that than which nothing greater can be thought' to the actual existence of God. On the face of it acceptance of this definition seems uncontroversial as presumably it simply unpacks what we usually mean when we use the term God – we intend to refer to the most supreme form of being that there could possibly be. However, in Anselm's outlining of the argument, accepting such a definition necessarily leads to accepting the real or true existence of such a being.

Anselm's argument – which is cast in the form of a prayer and is a deep meditation on the faith, thereby conforming to the axiom of 'faith seeking understanding' – considers the case of the 'fool' who says in his heart that God does not exist. But the fool can understand and accept Anselm's definition of God as 'that than which nothing greater can be thought', even if he does not consider it to exist. But, Anselm counters, if 'that than which nothing greater can be thought' exists in the understanding of the fool alone then it is not 'that than which nothing greater can be thought'. For, Anselm argues, 'that than which nothing greater can be thought' existing in reality would be greater than 'that than which nothing greater can be thought' existing in the understanding of the fool alone, and therefore 'that than which a greater cannot be thought exists both in the understanding and reality'.[iii]

Not satisfied with simply showing that God exists in reality, Anselm moves on to argue that God exists necessarily, or, in Anselm's words, 'cannot be thought not to exist'. Anselm proceeds again from his basic definition of God as 'that than which nothing greater can be thought' and argues that if it is conceivable that this being can be thought not to exist then it is not truly that 'than which nothing greater can be thought'.

11

For there can be thought to exist something whose non-existence is inconceivable; and this thing is greater than anything whose non-existence is conceivable. Therefore, if that than which a greater cannot be thought could be thought not to exist, then that than which a greater cannot be thought would not be that than which a greater cannot be thought – a contradiction. Hence, something than which a greater cannot be thought exists so truly that it cannot even be thought not to exist.[iv]

This argument proved as controversial to as many of Anselm's contemporaries as it has to contemporary philosophers, and one of them, Gaunilo, a fellow monk, was swift to offer a counter-argument. Gaunilo went to the heart of the matter by positing a 'Lost Island', that is, the most excellent of all islands, and argued that according to Anselm's logic such an island must therefore exist. Such a conclusion is entailed, according to Gaunilo, if we follow Anselm's logic that existence in reality is greater than simply existing in the under-standing.[v] To his credit Anselm was so impressed by the quality of this criticism that he ordered future editions of the *Proslogion* to include Gaunilo's criticisms. He may have been less generous if he had not had a ready-made reply. Anselm's reply was to argue that the logic of his argument applied only to 'that than which nothing greater can be thought', that is, God, and not to the greatest conceivable example of any contingent entity. It applies only to God because any contingent reality, no matter how great, can be thought not to exist without inherent contradiction. But this is precisely the force of Anselm's second argument – 'that than which a greater cannot be thought' must exist so truly that it cannot even be thought not to exist – for to do so is to necessarily involve oneself in a logical contradiction.[vi]

Whatever one thinks of the validity of the presuppositions that Anselm used in constructing this argument, there is no doubting the intellectual power and rigour of his analytical abilities. As such the argument has engaged the attention of many of the greatest minds in the history of ideas: Aquinas, Descartes, **Kant**, Leibniz and **Hegel** (although not all were in favour). Up to and including the twentieth century, Anselm's argument has continued to provoke rigorous debate. Bertrand Russell and F.C. Copleston had a celebrated disagreement on the question as to whether the concept of a 'necessary being' was in any way meaningful. Anselm's argument has been subjected to rigorous reformulations by 'Christian' philosophers as diverse as Alvin

Plantinga and Charles Hartshorne. Plantinga's reformulation of Anselm's argument slightly modifies it by showing, not that God necessarily exists, but that if God exists then God must do so necessarily!

It would be fair to say that the general consensus is that the argument doesn't work, but that showing that it doesn't work leads one into some of the deepest issues in philosophy, for example the nature of the term 'existence', and considers whether or not this term is a predicate or attribute or property of things such that it would have to be included in any exhaustive definition of the thing under consideration. If it were a property that was part of the definition of something then the argument would work, but it is not usually conceded that 'existence' is a property in this sense. For to list the defining properties of what it is to be a cow, say, and then to say that a creature bearing those properties 'exists', does not add anything at all to the original concept of the cow, but merely says that there is an instantiation of the cow so described in the actual world of things.

As if developing an original argument for the existence of God wasn't enough, Anselm also made a significant contribution to the development of Christian atonement theology in his celebrated work *Cur Deus Homo* (Why God became Man, 1098). Dissatisfied with existing accounts of how Christ's death procures salvation for humankind (theories of **atonement**), Anselm recast the whole account in terms of the legal, social and feudal relations of medieval Northern and Western Europe. These relations involved notions of order, honour, debt and obligation, and all these categories find their way into Anselm's theory. Previous atonement theories (deriving from the period of the early Church) had tended to focus on Christ's death as a ransom paid by God to the devil for the souls of humankind. Due to the fall, humankind had fallen under the sway of the devil and it was merely just that God should pay a ransom to redeem them. Variations on this theory sometimes portrayed the resurrection as a trick played by God on the devil to cheat the devil of his ransom.

Anselm felt that such notions were detrimental to God and his honour as they implied that God owed something to the devil or that the devil had rights *vis-à-vis* God. He sought to purge atonement theology of such distortions by arguing that the fall of Adam and Eve had offended God's honour. This act of disobedience had violated the correct order of things and put humankind under the dominion of sin. God could not simply forgive humankind because his honour had been violated and he required satisfaction. Here Anselm is drawing directly upon feudal lord and vassal relations as a way of understanding the divine human relationship. What could be done? A debt was owed, but who could pay it? God himself could not pay it as he was not the debtor. A human being should pay it, but as all human beings were tainted by sin and, as creatures, already owed God the full obedience of their lives, they literally had no resources with which to pay this infinite debt of obligation towards the offended honour of God. The plight of humankind seemed hopeless; only humans should pay, but no human being could possibly pay the debt owed to God.

The solution is provided by God himself in the incarnation of God the Son who took on humanity in order to pay the debt owed by humanity As this was a real humanity it was a fully human paying of the debt that was owed. Moreover, as the sinless Son of God, Jesus was not bound to the penalty of death and therefore his death, freely sacrificed upon the cross for his brethren, had infinite merit as a sacrifice and truly satisfied God's honour. Similarly, his free and willing obedience to the Father restored the proper relationship between God and humankind which had been violated by the disobedience of Adam.

Although we may now concede that Anselm too readily regarded categories that were inextricably bound up with his time and context as constant and fixed features of the divine human relationship there is no doubting that his theory constituted an advance upon earlier models that granted the devil rights in relation to God. The negative aspects of his position would be explored fully in the subsequent development of medieval Catholic penitential theology (the sacramental and confessional system of the medieval Church whereby believers confessed their sins and received absolution based on the stored merits of Christ's sacrifice). And again, in a different fashion, in the related and structurally similar penal substitutionary theology of later Protestantism. In this account the penalty of death due to humans on account of sin was transferred to Christ on the cross who acted as our substitute in receiving the penalty demanded by God's justice.

As well as the writings mentioned here, Anselm made a significant contribution to the Western clarification of the doctrine of the Trinity at the Council of Bari (1098), where he was asked by the Pope to defend the *filioque* clause in the Nicene creed. The filioque addition to the Nicene creed asserted that the Holy Spirit proceeds from the Father and the Son rather than from the Father alone, as was the position in Eastern Christianity. Disagreement on this issue was one of the great fault lines between Latin or Roman Catholic Christianity and Eastern Orthodox Christianity because the Western Church had inserted the clause, which expressly affirmed the double procession of the Spirit, into the ancient creed. Anselm subtly defended the position of the Western Church and the results of this defence are contained in his *On the procession of the Holy Spirit*. In addition Anselm wrote notable works on grammar, the nature of truth, the freedom of the will, the incarnation of the Word and the fall of the devil.

His output is all the more noteworthy when one remembers that the later works at least were produced when Anselm was an active Archbishop of Canterbury much involved with the care of his church. His tenure as Archbishop was not without conflict as he wrestled with King William II over the issue of the royal seizing of lands belonging to the Church and also over Anselm's recognition of Pope Urban II as the proper Pope. (The English king had not formally recognised Urban during a period of schism when Urban was challenged by an 'anti-pope', Clement III. Although William was later to recognise Pope Urban he also at the same time asked him to depose Anselm.) Anselm's resistance to William resulted in a period of exile in Rome. Matters did not change under William's successor Henry I, as Anselm, following papal decrees against the practice of the lay appointment of bishops by monarchs, refused to renew the homage he had paid to William II or to recognise the bishops that Henry had appointed. The disagreement between them meant a further period of exile in Rome from 1103 until 1107, when Anselm was able to return to England. He died in 1109.

Although Anselm claimed to offer no advance upon the theology of St Augustine and believed that virtually everything he taught could be derived from Augustine, it is nevertheless the case that he established a place for himself as one of the great thinkers of the Christian tradition. Precise and analytic, he explored concepts with considerable sophistication and intellectual power and it is for this reason that Anselm continues to exert an influence today in the works of both theologians and philosophers.

Notes

i   *Anselm of Canterbury,* Vol. One, *Monologion, Proslogion, Debate with Gaunilo and a Meditation on Human Redemption,* ed. and trans. J. Hopkins and H.W. Richardson, London: SCM Press, 1974, pp.6 and 7

ii   *Ibid.*, *Proslogion,* p.89

iii   *Ibid.*, *Proslogion,* p.94

iv   *Ibid.*

v   *Ibid.*, *Proslogion,* p.119

vi   *Ibid.*, *Proslogion,* p.125

See also: **Augustine**

Glossary: **Atonement; filioque; Trinity**

Major writings

The major works of Anselm referred to in this article can be found in *The Major works/Anselm of Canterbury,* ed. with an intro. by Brian Davies and G.R. Evans, Oxford: OUP, 1998

Further reading

G.R. Evans, *Anselm,* London: Geoffrey Chapman, 1989
J. Hopkins, *A Companion to the Study of St. Anselm,* Minneapolis: University of Minnesota Press, 1972
D.E. Luscombe and G.R. Evans (eds), *Anselm: Aosta, Bec and Canterbury,* papers in commemoration of the 900th anniversary of Anselm's enthronement as archbishop, 25 September 1093, Sheffield: Sheffield Academic Press, 1996

AQUINAS, THOMAS (1225–74)

St Thomas Aquinas was the most distinguished of medieval Christians and enormously influential on the future of Christian thought. Building on the work of Aristotle and of his own teacher Albert the Great, Thomas denied the basic platonic thesis that man has an intuitive knowledge of God's nature. For Thomas, there can be true knowledge of God gained through disciplined reflection and deduction from our sense-experience of the created world. Such knowledge, although available, is only accessible to a small number who have both the aptitude and the leisure to reflect upon such matters, and so God has also made himself known through **revelation**. This revealing of God occurs within the created order itself but pre-eminently knowledge of God is gained from study of the Bible, the Creeds and through the teaching authority of the Church. Knowledge of God gained as the product of rational critical reflection is therefore possible, and it is real knowledge, but it can never be complete or exhaustive, and such is the nature of human existence that it is always commingled with error. For Thomas then, we can know that God exists simply as a result of reflecting upon the world, but to know that God is **Trinitarian** or that Jesus Christ is divine can only be known through the scriptures and the teaching office of the Church.

Thomas was born in 1225 at Roccasecca near Aquino in Italy, to a comfortable upper-class family. After schooling at Monte Cassino

Abbey he spent five years at the University of Naples and, age 19, became a Dominican friar. Thereafter he went to Paris, where he spent much of the rest of his life teaching theology. This was not a time when an atmosphere of undisturbed calm reigned in the city but was a period of endless warring parties – between the secular diocesan clergy and the friars, between those who promoted the introduction of the philosophy of Aristotle and those who opposed it (which effectively meant between the arts faculty and the theology faculty, Thomas often being held in more favour by the former than the latter), between the university and the papacy. Thomas taught therefore in a time of intellectual and theological turbulence partly occasioned by the introduction of Aristotelian philosophy which was impacting widely throughout Western European intellectual culture due to the encounter with the then far more advanced civilisation of Islam. Thomas's own reasoned response to this crisis and the synthesis he achieved between Christian thought and Aristotelian philosophy was not (and never has been) uncontroversial. His later elevation to the place of foremost thinker and defender of Catholic doctrine dates mainly from the modern development of Thomism, a systematised version of his thought dating from the nineteenth century.

In the period of the early Church, theology was largely the exposition and interpretation of the scriptures. It has been suggested that Thomas was also an essentially biblically oriented theologian, and there is some justice in this claim. Apart from the Bible, **Augustine** was the dominating influence in the West, and by 1200 students would work from the standard theological introduction of Peter Lombard, consisting of his selections from the 'early Church Fathers' and his comments on particular passages. But the new philosophy of Aristotle was gradually filtering into the West to challenge Augustinian *neo-platonism*. For Augustine the ultimate referents for theology are God and the soul. The soul finds fulfilment through the knowledge of God, which comes by divine illumination of the mind by the divine ideas inherent in things. This is essentially a platonic understanding of knowledge whereby all knowledge is possible only because we have an innate capacity for recognising certain things, because 'ideas', 'forms' and 'concepts' are present already within our minds as impressions. All learning and knowledge therefore is an act of recollection or recognition. Where Augustine broke with earlier forms of platonism was in his assertion that the recollection and understanding of concepts such as goodness, wisdom, love, justice, etc., is achieved only through an act of divine illumination on the part of Christ the teacher whereby we come to understand and comprehend that which we previously did not know. For Aristotle, however, knowledge comes from reflection on our experience of the world of empirical reality, that is to say, by making deductions on the basis of that which we observe and experience happening around us through the use of our senses. Thus God is conceived not as the divine lover of the human soul illuminating our minds via a set of innate categories which are hard-wired into our physical make-up, but is instead the ultimate cause which holds the universe in being and who can be known and reasoned about from the effects of his action in the world.

Thomas synthesised the less systematic work of his teacher Albert of Cologne, forging a brilliant and original system which created a new balance between these Augustinian and Aristotelian strands of thought. The condemnations which followed his death illustrated the perils of diverging from Augustine. Aristotelian philosophy and its usefulness for theology was still a matter that was widely suspect in the Church and after Thomas's death many theses directly derivable from his work were condemned by Church authorities in Oxford and Paris. The traditional teaching practice of the Church and its inherent conservatism, coupled with the fact that Augustine's understanding of the divine illumination of the human intellect seemed much closer to the illumination by the Spirit of which the scriptures speak than the empirical approach to knowledge of Thomas, meant that the Augustinian method was preferred for some time longer. This should not surprise us as it is a problem which haunts theology in every age. How far are the biblical parabolic images to be taken as providing a literally correct description of God as the object of theological reflection? Or is such an attempted parallelism a confusion of descriptions of two separate though inter-related processes, the coming of the grace of God and the mundane conceptual homework which is our duty as users of ordinary human language?

What for Thomas was theology about? At the beginning of his great work the *Summa Theologiæ* (paradoxically, given its profundity and complexity, a work that was to be used in the 'education of beginners' and not to be confused with the *Summa Contra Gentiles* or 'the truth of the Catholic faith' which many find a gentler and less exacting introduction to his thought), the subject matter of faith, and indeed of theology, is said to be revealed by God. Revelation is necessary because human reason cannot by its own power recognise certain truths about God. For example, the truth that although God is one he nevertheless exists in the Trinitarian form of Father, Son and Holy Spirit. Revelation also includes matters which human nature might learn concerning God simply through the process of reflection. But as these things would be learned only slowly and gradually, and only by some, and always with the likelihood of error due to human dullness and sin, and without the certainty that revelation affords, God has chosen to disclose true knowledge to them by means of the scriptures and the teaching authority of the Church.

This immediately tells us the sources of revelation according to Thomas. Knowledge of God is contained in the scriptures which come from God. He has imparted to the prophets by inspiration 'certain definite pieces of information, by means of transient impressions' and has confirmed the divine inspiration of the scriptural authors by miracles and signs. This revelation can be systematised as a doctrine, whose centre is the first truth, God, upon which all else, e.g. Christology, sacraments, Church, depend. Through these things we are directed towards God, and we assent to them also on account of the divine truth that they contain.[i] This is a theology centred on God from first to last.

But Thomas is aware that it is not always clear how scripture is to be interpreted for it is certain that over time heretics have introduced many false interpretations. Therefore, he argues, it was necessary for the correct interpretation to be enshrined in Creeds and in the deliverances of Church councils. Ultimately, the final arbiter of the correct interpretation of scripture is him 'by whose authority a council is assembled and his opinion confirmed, the Pope'. [ii]

The teachings of the Church and of scripture are assumed by Thomas to be in harmony. But the role of the authority of the Church in determining which interpretation of scripture shall be regarded as correct is crucial. The crisis of Church versus scripture in the shape of the problem as it arose in the later Protestant reformation was not yet for Thomas, as indeed it had not been for the early Church Fathers, a live issue.

Ultimately, revelation is understood and accepted not by reason but through faith. This knowledge which comes through faith is not contrary to reason but is above reason. Faith in this life can only achieve an imperfect knowledge of God and the true goal of faith comes in the life which is to come after death when the faithful believer will gain perfect knowledge of God. Reason, then, does not prove the truth of revelation which faith believes, but reasons are a kind of persuasion, showing that the things which are presented in the faith are not impossible.[iii] Yet such things as theology does know of through revelation are more certain knowledge than all of the other sciences, because they are derived from the principles of revelation, which come from God himself. The scope of reason is limited in relation to what it can know of the things of faith, but its partial results are assured because of their dependence on a higher set of principles based on the faithful reception of scriptural and Church teaching that comes from God. Reason properly applied will never contradict the revealed truths of faith for they constitute one harmonious whole. Any contradictions that would seem to emerge from the application of reason to the revealed faith of the Church would point to a flaw in the reasoning process rather than in the teachings of scripture or Church.

Thomas thus was confident that reason has a limited but entirely reliable role to play in relation to revelation. This derives ultimately from Aristotle and in the first instance from Thomas's position on the central medieval problem of the status of universal categories. That was the dispute as to whether universal concepts such as 'humanity', 'redness' or 'fishness' actually existed as realities in the world. On one view individual human beings or red things or fish existed in that particular way because they individually realised the appropriate universal category of humanity, redness or fishness. In this view the universal category is in a fundamental sense more real than any particular example of it. The opposing view argued that universal categories such as 'humanity' or 'redness' did not truly exist, but were simply useful abstractions that enabled us to speak about the commonality between particular human beings or red things. In a famous phrase in the *Summa Theologiæ* Thomas says: 'Nothing is in the intellect which was not in the sense'. [iv] Man perceives external objects by means of the senses. For the present we cannot know (*cognoscere*) God except through material effects.[v] The universal does not exist as a general idea, but it is in the objects that we perceive with our senses under certain conditions (*universale in re*). The original type is seen in the ideas of God (*universalia ante rem*). Thus the essential nature of things is itself dependent on the divine idea. But the general conceptions of God, or anything else, that we conceive are always merely derivative from our sense perceptions (*universalia post rem*). But now revelation supplies the defect, adding to our knowledge of the particulars a true knowledge (*in via*) of the universal. And so the knowledge of this world in its cause and effects, its detailed particulars, becomes a source of knowledge of God. (We may contrast **Anselm**, on the one hand, for whom we may obtain by reasoning alone a true knowledge of the universal, i.e. God, which is a more optimistic platonic theory of knowledge, and on the other hand Augustine, where faith produces its own intuitive knowledge of God in the mind of the believer by effective spiritual signs, a neo-platonic influence, as in Augustine's *On Christian Doctrine*. It must be remembered that all these distinctions are themselves crude and may overlap).

Thomas is not a perfectly consistent theologian. But he does display an astonishing degree of consistency. This is at once one of the great virtues and one of the great faults of his system. It may simply not be appropriate to deal with numerous moral and metaphysical issues in exactly the same way. Likewise, his methodological introductions are not always his first thoughts on the subject, being already moulded by his understanding of the nature of the underlying subject matter.

Thomas is a God-centred theologian *par excellence*, concentrating on the divine essence. Everything comes from God and goes to God. God is the subject of Trinitarian doctrine. God for Thomas, as indeed for Aristotle, is the supremely existent one, the prime mover, and as such is not simply another creature, even the most powerful and awesome creature in the world. God stands outside all the categories of the created order and is not describable by them. There is a real sense in which it is inappropriate to say even that God exists, for God is that reality which all things that do exist depend upon for their very existence. This raises acute problems for our understanding when we try to speak of the unique way that God exists or, better, 'is', in contrast to all forms of creaturely existence. As Thomas has it: 'We cannot consider concerning God how he is, but rather how he is not'.[vi]

God's hiddenness is thus important as it witnesses the 'otherness' of God – the ways in which God cannot be thought or spoken about as a creature among other creatures or as the highest aspect of the created order. Nevertheless, God is a thinking, willing being. As the prime mover he is pure action, without any unrealised potentiality. In thinking and willing he realises a goal, which is related to the nature of God himself. Since he is supreme goodness, he wills only in accordance with goodness and love. He acts in the world in love and he loves the world. His love could perfect the world in various ways, but he chooses to operate in love supremely through the incarnation in Jesus Christ. The doctrine of God is theologically fundamental and prior to everything else, and determines what can be said about the incarnation. (This contrasts strongly with **Barth**, for example, for whom the doctrine of God is based on Christology, or **Luther**, for whom everything is unfolded from the experience of personal salvation.) If there is a weakness in Thomas's thought here it is perhaps that there is not a sufficiently concentrated attempt to integrate the doctrine of God with Christology. Thomas outlines the tradition about the nature of God as it was inherited from the early Christian Fathers and as such it is heavily influenced by the classical Greek philosophical understanding of the divine which so characterised the thought of the early Fathers. Thomas then adds to this an account of the Trinity which is essentially a reworking of that offered by Augustine. Only then does Thomas introduce the subject of Christology, and this is a representation of the classic Christology of the Council of Chalcedon of 451.

In faithfulness to the **Chalcedonian** statement as to the union of God and man in Christ, the centre of Christology is found in the hypostatic union. This is a union between the person of God the Son and Jesus of Nazareth that does not compromise or diminish either the divine or human nature by altering them or changing them into a third hybrid substance or nature. Divine and human natures remain unchanged in the union. The union of divine and human consists in the relation of the divine and human natures to the person of God the Son. God the Son adds to his unique way of existing as God the Son, the human life of Jesus of Nazareth. The union is more real in the human nature than in the divine in that the divine life is not directly affected by the act of incarnation. This assumption of a human nature does not lead to a duality in the incarnate figure of Christ as the human nature of Jesus does not constitute an independent person. Only in the act of incarnation does the human nature achieve personhood through the personhood of God the Son. Thus there is essentially only one being in Christ, since there is no distinctive personal centre in the human nature of Christ other than that of God the Son.

The consequences of this Christology are worked through in the understanding of redemption. The human nature of Christ is not 'mere' human nature, but has in consequence of its union with Christ a certain efficacy or virtue. Christ is the head of the human race and of the Church. From the head flows virtue upon the members of the Church. By his teaching, acts and suffering Christ has become the pattern and teacher for the new humanity. Thomas takes up the question of whether Christ had to die to satisfy God's righteous anger or wrath.[vii] This is not absolutely necessary (a departure from, say, Anselm's view) because God could even without such satisfaction forgive sin. The passion of Christ was not only a sufficient but also a superabundant satisfaction, meriting salvation not only for himself but for all his members, and continuing to intercede for us in his state of exaltation. The result is the forgiveness of sins.

Human beings are sinful creatures. They have lost their original righteousness due to the Fall and their natures have been debased in certain respects; only reason, which is sufficient to convict of sin, remains intact. Thomas commits himself to what is effectively an Augustinian account of the origins of sin when he says that in the act of conception the soul itself becomes sinful. As sin is thus so deep-seated and so prior and fundamental an aspect of human existence human beings are entirely dependent upon God's grace.

Grace is at one and the same time both the free movement of God towards the individual and also the effect of the divine act. The gift of grace creates an infused condition in the soul which transforms the sinner and makes them more righteous. By the same act God both grants grace and remits guilt. Without grace there can be no merit and thus no release from the sinful condition. But further special grace can be earned by acts of contrition and the faithful desire and intention to perform good works. In this way room is left for the development of human initiative. The works of God and man may be seen to complement each other in the process of salvation. Grace thus heals and completes nature.

The salvation of man is dependent on the passion of Christ, and that of the individual believer is dependent on the sacraments. For Thomas there are seven sacraments (Holy Orders, marriage, extreme unction, penance, confirmation, baptism and the mass), all immediately instituted by Christ. The physical elements constitute the material of the sacrament, and the words of institution of the Last Supper constitute its form, which is to say its determining principle or inner intention. The result of the consecration of the elements by a properly ordained priest, with the right intention, saying the prescribed and authorised formula of words is the presence of the true body and blood of Christ. The celebration of the liturgy takes place within the Church which is the community of the faithful. The pope presides over bishops, priests and people.

The methodology of theology includes an important distinction between philosophical and doctrinal theology. Theology has both theoretical and practical dimensions. Doctrinal theology is based on revelation, which yields a knowledge of God in faith, real but limited in this life. There is a road from nature to grace, but only God can lead a man along it. The Bible is central to faith, but needs to be interpreted, according to the teaching of the Church, taking account both of literal and spiritual meanings.

Thomas was a brilliant interpreter of the work of Aristotle, in criticism of the tradition based on Plato (neo-platonism) that had prevailed in the West from Augustine to Anselm. But he was not afraid to criticise Aristotle when necessary. A classic example of his theological adaptation of Aristotle's philosophy is in his doctrine of analogy, often misinterpreted but worked out with great subtlety. Thomas's views on analogy can be overstated, but simply put he argues that the words we apply to God neither mean exactly the same as when we use them in relation to things in the world, nor do they mean something completely different. When we say that God is good, or wise or loving, we are speaking of a quality in God which is appropriate to God's own self of which our own experiences of love, goodness, wisdom, etc., are but pale reflections. Nevertheless we can gain some understanding of what we mean when we speak of God as loving by an analogical inference from what we mean when we talk of human love.

In his excellent study of the subject Victor Preller concluded that whenever Thomas uses the language of intrinsic attribution (speaking of attributes or qualities that apply truly to God's own internal nature), he is speaking hypothetically from God's point of view – at these moments he is being most radically a theologian. When he uses the language of extrinsic attribution (speaking of attributes or qualities that are inferred from our experience in the world and that only 'virtually' apply to God) he is emphasising that we do not have access to the language of God. This is in sharp contrast to the traditional tendency to unite everything in a single doctrine. The doctrine of analogy is then not a means of knowing God, but an analysis of the words we use to name God. There is an analogy of being from God's side, but our proofs for the existence of God are our way of confessing our ignorance of its true nature. The famous proofs that Thomas offers for the existence of God prove the existence of a prime mover, first-cause, Necessary Being, etc., but at the end of these arguments Thomas acknowledges that we still have not truly arrived at the reality of God by saying of each one 'and that we call God'.

Thomas produced brilliant reinterpretations of the central concepts of divine being, action and causality, and a careful reappraisal of traditional Christology. His direct influence on Catholic thought has varied over time but the intensity of focus, depth of insight and logical precision of his detailed analysis of the Christian faith has meant that his work is a resource that has been returned to time and time again. At the end of his life Thomas had a mystical experience which so profoundly moved him that he declared that in contrast to what he had glimpsed all his life's work seemed as straw. However, whatever his own opinion and no matter how later generations may judge the particular shape of his work, there is no doubt that he was an intellectual genius of the first rank.

Notes

i   *Summa Theologiæ* (hereafter referred to as *S.T.*) 2.2. q.1a,1
ii   S.T. 2.2. q.1a, 9
iii   S.T. 2.2 q.1a, 5
iv   S.T. 1. q.85a, 3 and 7
v   S.T. 1. q.86a, 2 and 1
vi   S.T. 1. q.2a, 3.
vii   S.T. 3. q.46a, 3

See also: **Anselm; Augustine; Barth; Luther**

Glossary: Neo-platonism; revelation; Trinity

Major writings

Selections in Basic Writings, ed. A.C. Pegis, New York: Random House, 1945
Philosophical Texts, ed. T. Gilby, London: OUP, 1951
Theological Texts, ed. T. Gilby, London: OUP, 1955
Summa Theologiæ, 61 vols, ed. T. Gilby *et al.*, London: Blackfriars in conjunction with Eyre & Spottiswoode, and McGraw-Hill: New York, 1964–81
Summa Contra Gentiles, Indiana: University of Notre Dame Press, 1975

Further reading

M.D. Chenu, *Towards Understanding St Thomas*, Chicago: Regnery, 1964
B. Davies, *The Thought of Thomas Aquinas*, Oxford: Clarendon Press, 1992
A. Kenny, *Aquinas*, Oxford: OUP, 1980 (reprinted 1997)
F. Kerr, *After Aquinas: Versions of Thomism*, Oxford: Blackwell, 2002
J. Milbank and C. Pickstock (eds), *Truth in Aquinas*, London: Routledge, 2000
P.E. Persson, *Sacra Doctrina*, Oxford: Blackwell, 1970
V. Preller, *Divine Science and the Scence of God*, Princeton: PUP, 1967
E.F. Rogers, *Thomas Aquinas and Karl Barth: sacred doctrine and the natural knowledge of God*, Notre Dame, IN and London: University of Notre Dame Press, 1995

ARIUS (c.270–336)

Arius was a distinguished fourth-century theologian from Alexandria in Egypt of very considerable talent whose views on the precise relationship between God the Father and God the Son in the Christian conception of God were condemned at the Council of Nicaea in 325. Arius has been remembered ever since as the archetypal arch-heretic. However, he deserves attention because the issues he raised remain central to the discussion of Christian doctrine and in particular to Christology and the nature of God.

The controversy that Arius occasioned lasted approximately from 318 to 381 and developed mainly in the churches of the East that is to say churches in what we would now call Egypt, Greece, Turkey and Asia Minor. It involved central issues such as the precise understanding that was to be given to the divinity and the pre-existence of Christ. It arose from earlier debates between followers of **Origen** and his opponents, who viewed his doctrine with suspicion, notably Bishop Alexander of Alexandria. It should be realised that at this time there was a wide variety of understandings of the nature of God within the Church, particularly in relation to the precise relationships between Father, Son and Holy Spirit. The issue had not yet been precisely defined and Origen, a third-century theologian of significant influence, had taught a hierarchical understanding of the *Trinity* with the Son and Spirit definitely subordinated to the Father who alone was the source of the divine life. However, Origen also seemed to teach that the Son or *Logos* (meaning Word, both terms are derived from the gospels and refer to the same second person of the Trinity who became incarnate in Christ) shared in some way in the divine nature. Therefore we find in Origen language that implies that the Son is a subordinate and 'second God' after the Father as well as language that seems to imply that the Son is 'eternally generated' (that is, produced without a beginning in time) by the Father and shares in the Father's nature. It seems that the philosophical and theological terminology employed by Origen was not yet sufficiently technically clarified for him to give a precise and distinct meaning to his understanding of the divine nature. This lack of sufficient technical and conceptual clarification in the theological legacy of Origen meant that he could be, and was, understood in a number of different ways. Consequently much confusion remained and the possibility of disagreement and misunderstanding between various Christian scholars and thinkers of the period was an ever-present danger.

Even before the specific controversy began that led to the Council of Nicaea, Arius, who was a priest of strongly ascetic lifestyle and a pupil of Lucian of Antioch, had been engaged in controversy with his own Bishop, Alexander of Alexandria, when he protested against Alexander's understanding of the relationship of the Son (the second person of the Trinity) to the Father. Arius was a strong-willed and truculent priest who was not afraid to disagree with his own Bishop and the consequence of his protest was that he was excommunicated by Alexander at the synod of Alexandria in 318. However, as we have already seen, there was a considerable variety of views on this question within the Church at large and Arius was able to seek refuge with Bishop Eusebius of Nicomedia. He was also to be supported then and subsequently by the Western Bishop Eusebius of Caesarea. The emerging controversy took on wider political dimensions when the Emperor Constantine, who wanted a religiously unified Church throughout his empire, called the bishops to a Church council at Nicaea to resolve the issue. Thus it was that supporters and opponents of Arius met at the Council of Nicaea in what is regarded as the first ecumenical council of the Church and the first to set the not altogether happy precedent of a secular emperor calling together a council of the Church.

Although it is often said that Arius denied the divinity of Christ, that is a gross over-simplification. Arius maintained that Jesus was God (in the sense of sharing in the divine nature) and not fully man, that he was a created God who only derivatively could be said to share in God's divine nature. The incarnation in Jesus of Nazareth was the incarnation of the Logos (Word of God), but not of God the Creator. There is, according to Arius, a gulf at the most fundamental level of being between the Father and the Son. Arius could not see the Logos as a kind of second divine principle perfectly reflecting the transcendent Father. Like his opponents, he was concerned to distinguish God from all else. But he assigned the Logos to the creaturely side of the gulf. The Logos is created *ex nihilo* (out of nothing), hence the famous phrase attributed to Arius – 'There was a time when the Logos was not'. The divine essence of God, on the other hand, is simple, eternal and indivisible. The Logos or Son participates in the grace, but not the essence of the Father. Only the Father is unoriginate in the sense of having no source or beginning in anything else. Only the Father is the source of his own independent eternal self-existence. The Son finds his origin and beginning in the creative will of the Father and as such can be said to be the highest and first-born of creation, the most exalted and glorious creature, but still, nevertheless, most definitely a member of the creaturely realm.

For Arius there simply cannot be two unoriginate principles in the sense of two beings that are the explanation and origin of their own self-caused existence. This is what it means to be God and it is an attribute of the Father alone, and in this important sense the Father is superior to the Son. For the Son was created by an act of the Father's will before time, but not by an eternal act of generation. Unlike the Father, the Son had a beginning. Arius is therefore willing to confess to one God, eternal and unchangeable, who begat the only-begotten Son before all time, in reality, as a perfect creature, 'but not as one of the creatures'. His insistence upon this distinction between Father and Son was born of a desire to protect the unity of the divine nature. For if the divine substance were divided, the immutable changeless God would become mutable and changing.

Obviously, as was the case with everyone else involved in this disagreement, Arius was heavily influenced by concepts of the divine that were inherited from classical Greek philosophy. It was simply taken for granted that God was one, perfect and unchanging. Everyone in the debate agreed to this, but Arius allied this Greek conception of the divine to what he understood to be the plain meaning of scripture. Therein Jesus is described as the only-begotten Son of the Father. For Arius this language of being begotten by the Father implied derivation from the Father in time and nature. Therefore, Jesus as the only-begotten Son of the Father might be very closely related to the Father as an act of his will and purpose, but in the most fundamental sense possible he is not the same as the Father. Obviously, this account of the scriptural language of Jesus' sonship rules out the crudest implications of physical generation of the Son on the part of the Father. The brunt of Arius' attack therefore was that on both the shared Greek understanding of the nature of God and the most straightforward reading of the scriptural texts his description of the relationship between God the Father and the Son seemed the most plausible explanation that was available.

The Alexandrian opponents of Arius attempted to counter his arguments by suggesting that the existence of an eternal Father implies an eternal Son. (For the Father could not be the Father without a Son and therefore although the Son was generated by the Father he was generated 'eternally', that is without a beginning in time). But that logic proved too much, the Arians replied, for one could just as well argue that the eternal Father might also imply eternal creatures and an eternal creation.

Thus Arius' own work entitled *Thalia*, or Short Summary of Theology, stresses that God originally was alone. The Son is changeable (and thus not truly God, who is unchanging) though made morally perfect by grace. In this way he was able to withstand temptation. The implication of this view – and an implication clearly seen by Arius' opponents – was that there is little place here for a human soul and will in Christ.

The Arians had themselves suggested that the claim that the Son was **homoousios** (of one substance or consubstantial) with the Father was clearly wrong. Arius' opponents at Nicaea picked up this expression and used it to firmly reject Arius' position by consciously declaring that the Son is of the same substance with the Father. The adoption of the expression *homoousios* was hugely controversial to many in the Church at this time, including many of those who were not disposed towards Arius, as it was hard to see how the notion of two beings sharing the same substance did not effectively produce an unwanted duality in the divine nature. For many, *homoousios* could not help but imply two Gods. Alternatively, two beings of identical substance could be understood as repetitions of the same substance in which case Father and Son would not be distinguishable at all in reality save under the guise of appearance.

As such the adoption of the *homoousion* formula effectively closed one debate for the time being, but opened up another – the possibility of monism and Sabellianism. (The latter term refers to the teaching of one Sabellius, eventually declared heretical, which stated that the differences between the persons of the Trinity were not real, but were mere names or conventions that referred to differing appearances of the one undivided reality that is God. Thus the terms Father, Son and Spirit name different temporal and succeeding manifestations of the one God.)

It could also be claimed that *homoousios* understood in this sense was clearly unscriptural in that Jesus is clearly distinct from the Father to whom he prayed and to whom he was obedient. (A Sabellian understanding effectively meant that Jesus was praying to himself.) In response to this it was argued that the term was necessary to safeguard the truths in scripture, and that *homoousios* does imply distinction of a sort – for one thing can only be consubstantial with another, not with itself. Eusebius of Caesarea assured his diocese that to be consubstantial means the Son is of the Father, but not 'part of his substance', and that there was no change in the Father's power. The Son was perfectly similar to the Father, and potentially in the Father, without being begotten, before he was actually begotten.

In any event the Nicene creed finally and explicitly ruled out Arius' position when it asserted: 'We believe in one God, the Father Almighty, maker of heaven and earth, and of all things visible and invisible. And in one Lord Jesus Christ, the only begotten Son of God, and born of the Father before all ages. God of God, light of light, true God of true God. Begotten not made, consubstantial with the Father, by whom all things were made'.

But many Eastern bishops were displeased with this rendition, and continued to oppose the Nicene solution, which became identified with the new Bishop of Alexandria, **Athanasius**. This testifies to the fact that there were many in the Church at that time who held views that were close to Arius, and they did not simply disappear overnight. There were many variations of Arius' views, often called 'semi-Arian' positions, and the question of when differences in degree become differences in kind is one which has exercised Christians to the present day. Athanasius, Arius' bitter opponent and champion of orthodoxy whose name is forever linked with this controversy, always thought of the Logos-Son as one with the creator, not with the created order, whereas Arius thought of Christ as belonging to the world of created things. Athanasius too had his own hesitations about the Nicene *homoousios* formula, but he eventually supported it fully as being a better guardian of the mystery of the incarnation than the contrary position of *homoiousios*, which argued that the Son was only of like substance with the Father.

Although the decision of the Council of Nicaea may have gone against him, Arius continued to have a significant level of support. Subsequent to the council Arius managed to persuade the Emperor Constantine of his orthodoxy and, after signing a declaration of faith that was acceptable to the Emperor, Constantine asked Athanasius, who had succeeded Alexander as Bishop of Alexandria, to receive Arius back into communion with the Alexandrian church. However, this declaration did not contain the key term *homoousios* and Athanasius, recognising that this was crucial, refused to accept Arius back into fellowship.

Arius died in 336, out of fellowship with the Church, but his great opponent Athanasius was to find himself exiled by various 'Arian' emperors such as the Emperor Constantius who ruled against Athanasius at the Synod of Milan in 355, and the opponents of Arius did not finally triumph until the Synod of Constantinople in 381. The controversy in the end thus involved imperial politics and local nationalism as much as purely theological matters. Arius had been finally disowned, but the questions that he raised remained, as part of the paradox of the faith.

Although the Nicene declaration of the Son's substantial unity with the Father is decisive for the future direction of Christian faith and theology, the Council of Nicaea did not attempt to explain the working of the divine unity in the incarnate figure of Jesus of Nazareth. The main question remaining was to explain what it meant to say that Jesus Christ was *homoousios* with God. This was to be the main task of the councils of the next hundred years. Arius himself received support late in life through Eusebius of Nicomedia, and he would probably have been restored to office had he not died suddenly in 336. The Nicene victory was not finally achieved until the Council of Constantinople of 381, and even then Arianism flourished among the Teutonic tribes of Germany well into the sixth century. Although the Nicene solution was probably the best available for the articulation of classical Christian faith, it should be recalled that flourishing Christian communities continued without accepting Nicaea, and that the intolerance displayed by the victors in the dispute could serve to detract from the value of their affirmations.

One of the reasons for the triumph of Arius' opponents at Nicaea was that those Western bishops who were there had long been accustomed to using the terminology of 'one substance' (una substantia) to describe the relationship of Father and Son in the Godhead. Thus, in the West decisive support was given to the Athanasian position by Hilary of Poitiers in his De Trinitate, although he too had initial hesitations about the homoousios formula. Hilary realised that this was in no sense a blueprint of the nature of God, but an expression that safeguarded what needed to be affirmed better than the available alternatives – 'Of what we cannot speak, we dare not be silent'.

The long-term importance of the Arian controversy was that it gave urgency and definition to the further development of the doctrine of the Trinity, especially in light of the later participation of the **Cappadocian Fathers**, Gregory of Nyssa, Gregory of Nazianzen and Basil of Caesarea.

One of the difficulties about knowing what people deemed to be heretical really thought is that their works were often destroyed, or preserved only in supposedly incriminating fragments which give a one-sided impression of their thought. Arius may have suffered from this. However, he does not appear to have written a great deal. His work *Thalia* (Banquet), was a verse composition which contained his central ideas. There is also a statement of his views in a letter to Bishop Alexander, and a letter asking for support addressed to Eusebius of Nicomedia.

See also: **Athanasius; Cappadocian Fathers; Origen**

Glossary: **Homoousios; *Logos*; *Trinity***

Major writings

Thalia (Banquet). Fragments only in works of Athanasius and other opponents.

Further reading

M.R. Barnes and D.H. Williams, *Arianism after Arius*, Edinburgh: T & T Clarke, 1993
R.C. Gregg and D.E. Groh, *Early Arianism, a View of Salvation*, Philadelphia: Fortress Press, 1981

C. Kannengiesser, *Arius and Athanasius: Two Alexandrian Theologians*, Aldershot: Variorum, 1991

G.C. Stead, *Doctrine and Philosophy in Early Christianity: Arius, Athanasius, Augustine*, Aldershot: Ashgate Press, 2000

M.F. Wiles, *Archetypal Heresy, Arianism after Arius*, Oxford: OUP, 1996

R. Williams, *Arius: heresy and tradition*, London: Darton, Longman & Todd, 1987; 2nd edn, London: SCM Press, 2001

ATHANASIUS (295–373)

Bishop of Alexandria from 328 to 373 and one of the most influential theologians of the early Church. Forever associated with the struggle against Arianism, Athanasius also made other important contributions to the development of theology that are wider than the strict parameters of that debate. Not much is known about Athanasius' early life but it is clear that he served as deacon and secretary to Bishop Alexander of Alexandria from 318 onwards and that he travelled with Alexander to the famous Council of Nicaea in 325. This council, called by the Emperor Constantine to resolve the dispute over the Arian controversy (see **Arius** for more on this), made the landmark decision that the Son of God was '*homoousios*' (of one substance or consubstantial) with the Father. This term, which avowed the full divinity of the Son, explicitly contradicted the Arian claim that the Son was a lesser being than the Father and was simply a created intermediary between the Father and the world. It is doubtful that Athanasius spoke or participated in the proceedings as he was only a deacon at this point in time, but he seems to have been active behind the scenes on Alexander's behalf. For the rest of his life, however, Athanasius was to prove a staunch defender of Nicene orthodoxy.

Decisive as Nicaea was it would nevertheless be a gross mistake to assume that the issue was settled there and then. Arius and his followers commanded a significant level of support both in the Church and in the political arena and for a considerable time there was a continuing struggle for supremacy between the two factions. Thus it was that Athanasius, who succeeded Alexander as Bishop of Alexandria in 328, was requested by Constantine to receive Arius back into communion with the Alexandrian church after Arius had signed a declaration of faith which was acceptable to the Emperor. However, this declaration did not contain the key term *homoousios* and Athanasius, recognising that this was crucial refused to accept Arius back into communion.

Athanasius' authority was already weakened at this point due to the fact that he was embroiled in a local controversy with a group of schismatic Christians who refused to accept the validity of his consecration as Bishop. The schismatics were followers of Melitus, who had taken a rigorous position as to whether Christians who had lapsed into apostasy by denying the faith during the time of the Diocletian persecution should be allowed back into the fellowship of the Church. This was a live issue as the Church had undergone a period of significant persecution instigated by the Roman Emperor Diocletian and many Christians had offered worship to the Roman Gods and denied Christ for fear of torture and imprisonment. The original disagreement between Peter, Bishop of Alexandria at that time, and Melitus resulted in the creation of a parallel schismatic church to that of the Alexandrian church. Over time a compromise solution had been reached and the two groups lived in an uneasy and tense relationship. However, on the death of Alexander and the imminent consecration of Athanasius, these tensions were fostered and renewed by Eusebius, Bishop of Nicomedia, a virulent opponent of Athanasius and a friend of Arius.

The level of enmity and the degree to which Athanasius' opponents would stoop to remove him from office is seen in the fact that they accused Athanasius of murdering Arsenius, Bishop of Hypsele, who sympathised with the Meletian cause (Athanasius did seem to be guilty of encouraging aggressive and high-handed behaviour towards the schismatic Meletian priests). This charge was fortunately proved to be false when Athanasius managed to find Arsenius alive and well and in hiding. The fact that Athanasius could find and produce Arsenius suggests that he was no mean schemer and plotter himself. It would be fair to say that such political intriguing and subterfuge does not reflect well on the Church and the sheer fact of its existence should disconcert those who would view this period of the Church's life through rose-tinted spectacles.

Nevertheless, Athanasius' refusal to obey the Emperor's command to accept Arius, combined with the questions surrounding his consecration and the further charge (not, it seems, wholly unfounded) that Athanasius had threatened to interfere with the Empire's corn supply from Egypt, led to his deposition and banishment into exile in Trier in 336. Thus began a chaotic period for Athanasius which was to result in him being recalled and banished on no fewer than a further four occasions depending upon the success of his cause and the favourable opinion (and poor health!) of various Emperors.

Thus, Athanasius returned from exile upon Constantine's death in 337, but was forced to flee to Rome in 339 due to the growing power and influence in the Imperial court of his old foe Eusebius of Nicomedia. Restored to office by the Emperor Constans in 346, he was then driven into hiding in the desert in 356 by the Emperor Constantius who sided with the Arianising faction within the Church. Athanasius remained in hiding until the accession of the Emperor Julian in 361 who recalled Athanasius in 362 upon the murder of George, Athanasius' replacement as Bishop of Alexandria. However, Athanasius' troublesome personality soon offended Julian and Athanasius found himself ordered to leave Egypt again in 363. Recalled after Julian's death, Athanasius was to be banished once again by an Arianising Emperor in the figure of Valens, who commanded all bishops previously exiled by Constantius to leave their posts. However, this time the ban was short-lived and Athanasius returned to Alexandria in 366 and lived in relative peace until his death in 373.

Given this turbulent history it is surprising that Athanasius managed to write at all but write he did. He wrote a notable biography of the Egyptian St Anthony entitled the *The Life of Anthony*. This did much to foster an interest in Eastern monasticism in the Western church, but also helped to create a self-confident and sometimes insular sense of identity within the Egyptian church that persists to this day. Athanasius' principal theological works are his *Against the Pagans* (*Oratio Contra Gentes*), and *On the Incarnation of the Word* (*De Incarnatione Verbi*). These two are sometimes thought to be a single work, and are supplemented by Athanasius' *Orations against the Arians* (*Oratio Contra Arianos*). *Contra Gentes* focuses upon the irrationality of idolatry (to worship something other than God as God), and polytheism (the worship of many Gods), arguing that human beings were originally created to live their lives in an unblemished contemplation of God but instead . . .

> . . . they turned their minds away from intelligible reality and began to consider themselves. And by considering themselves and cleaving to the body and the other senses, deceived as it were in their own interests, they fell into selfish desires and preferred their own good to the contemplation of the divine. Wasting their time thus and being unwilling to turn away from things close at hand, they imprisoned in the pleasures of their body their souls which had become disordered and defiled by all kinds of desires, and in the end they forgot the power they had received from God in the beginning.[1]

This turning from God to the self leads human beings into the prime delusion that is the source of idolatry and polytheism, namely, the worship of created things in place of the Creator. Fairly traditional arguments drawn from the Bible, but also platonic philosophy, are then used to demonstrate the fundamental irrationality of idolatry. However, serious as this fall into ignorance is, it is not the only consequence of the fall of human beings. For human beings as creatures are always threatened by non-existence and this was only forestalled by the fact that God gave human beings a share in immortality through their contemplation of, and participation in, his image. In turning to themselves and no longer contemplating God human beings had defaced the image of God and lost their share in immortality.

The resolution of this problem is the subject matter of *De Incarnatione*, in which Athanasius argues:

> None other could restore a corruptible being to incorruption but the Saviour who in the beginning made everything out of nothing. None other could re-create man according to the image, but he who is the Father's image. None other could make a mortal being immortal, but he who is life itself, our Lord Jesus Christ.[ii]

The incarnation of the Word of God in Jesus of Nazareth accomplishes the complete salvation of humankind in a number of distinct though related ways according to Athanasius. By dying on the cross and experiencing as his own the death which is humanity's due, the debt owed to God's honour is thus repaid and death itself is put to death. Furthermore, human nature is re-created as incorruptible or not subject to death and dissolution of the body because the Word, in the resurrection of Jesus, was raised into incorruptibility and is no longer subject to death. Furthermore, the Word as the image of God restores the image of God that was lost in the fall of Adam to humankind. Human beings were originally created as immortal and incorruptible and in becoming human the Word restores these gifts to humanity through the life and death of Jesus Christ. A favourite metaphor in relation to this aspect of salvation is that of a coin where the original image stamped upon it has become defaced. Through the fall humanity has defaced and lost the image of God, but in the act of assuming human nature as Jesus the Word has once again stamped the divine image upon human nature.

The role of the incarnate Word in the **salvation** of humanity is central to Athanasius' refutation of Arianism in his *Orations against the Arians*. If, as Arius maintained, the Word was himself a created being, no matter how exalted, then the very salvation of humankind was threatened. For a true revelation of God (and therefore a renewed contemplation of God) was not possible if the Word was not God. Similarly the re-creation of human nature in the divine image could only be achieved by God himself and death itself could only be overcome by the Lord of life himself dying and rising to eternal life.

The first two volumes of *Orations against the Arians* provide a detailed summary of Arius' teaching, at least as Athanasius understood it. The third volume contains Athanasius' positive argument that the Word is naturally and eternally generated by the Father and clearly states that the Word is *homoousios* (of one substance) with the Father. Athanasius' other writings do not substantially add to the theology of these works. In his letters to Bishop Serapion he uses the same structure of argument that he used in establishing the divinity of the Word to maintain the divinity of the Holy Spirit. That is to say he argues that, since our salvation depends upon our participation in the Spirit, the Spirit too must therefore be of one substance with God the Father or our salvation is again threatened. Athanasius' Easter letter 39 (367) to his diocese is of interest in that it contains the earliest reference to the twenty-seven books of the New Testament canon as we currently have them.

The underlying question concerning Athanasius' Christology is whether or not it is docetic. Does it present a truly human figure in Jesus Christ or does the Word incarnate as Jesus only appear to be human? Many scholars have asked if Athanasius truly has a place for a rational soul or human mind in the figure of Christ? Much of Athanasius' language can be read to imply that his understanding of the incarnation is that the Word took the place of a rational soul (a mind in today's terms) in the incarnate figure of Christ. Athanasius seems to have confronted this problem for the first time in his *Tomus ad Antiochenos* written in 362, and here, at least on a surface level, he seems to argue that our salvation requires that the Word was incarnate in a body with a soul. However, scholars of this period remain sceptical as to what this meant for Athanasius, and it is clear that his system does not require, nor did he make any distinctive use of, the idea that the incarnate figure of Christ possessed a human rational soul or mind.

Athanasius then is a theologian drawing upon the wellsprings of platonic and **neo-platonic** philosophy to fashion a theology that has the salvation of human beings as its principal concern. His Christological concerns and formulations were to prove normative for the Alexandrian understanding of the incarnation from thenceforth, and as this tradition, through the work of Cyril of Alexandria, was to prove decisive in formulating the Chalcedonian definition of the person of Christ (i.e. the definition arrived at the Council of Chalcedon in 451, namely that Jesus of Nazareth is one person with two natures – fully human and fully divine), Athanasius' work can clearly be seen to be seminal. Lionised by the early Church soon after his death, he seems to have been a much more irascible and intractable figure in real life, more than capable of bullying and traducing friend and foe alike. This is not to gainsay his contribution but perhaps to enter a note of caution as to his presentation of the Arian position which is receiving a much more sympathetic reception in the writings of contemporary scholars. Nevertheless, his recognition of the importance of the Nicene *homoousios*, with its clear affirmation of an identity of substance between the Son and the Father, is an affirmation that the Christian Church has never gone back on, and on this issue Athanasius' insights have proved pivotal.

Notes

i   *Contra Gentes*, par. 3
ii   *De Incarnatione*, par. 20

See also: **Arius**

Glossary: **Homoousios; neo-platonic/neo-platonism; salvation**

Major writings

Contra Gentes and De Incarnatione, ed. and trans. R.W. Thomson, Oxford: Clarendon Press, 1971
St. Athanasius: Select Works and Letters, Select Library of Nicene and Post-Nicene Fathers, Ser. 2., Vol. 4, ed., with prolegomena, indices, and tables, A. Robinson, Grand Rapids, MI: 1971
The Life of Anthony, and, the Letter to Marcellinus, trans. and intro. R.C. Gregg, London: SPCK, 1980
On the Incarnation: the treatise de incarnatione verbi Dei, trans. and ed. Sister Penelope Lawson, New York: MacMillan, 1981

Further reading

T.D. Barnes, *Athanasius and Constantius: theology and politics in the Constantinian Empire*, Cambridge, MA and London: Harvard University Press, 1993

D. Brakke, *Athanasius and the Politics of Asceticism*, Baltimore, MD and London: Johns Hopkins University Press, 1998

A. Pettersen, *Athanasius*, London: Geoffrey Chapman, 1995

G.C. Stead, *Doctrine and Philosophy in Early Christianity: Arius, Athanasius, Augustine*, Aldershot: Ashgate Press, 2000

AUGUSTINE OF HIPPO (354–430)

Augustine can lay claim to being perhaps the most influential theologian of the entire Christian tradition. If, as is often said, philosophy is nothing other than footnotes to Plato then much of theology is similarly footnotes to Augustine. He made original and far-reaching contributions to the doctrine of the *Trinity*, and to the understanding of grace, *predestination* and free will. He is infamously associated with the doctrine of original sin and in the course of his controversy with the Donatists (see p. 45) he made significant contributions to the developing doctrine of the Church. If that were not enough he developed a theological interpretation of history in his magnum opus *The City of God* (413–26) which mapped out an understanding of the relationship between Church and civil society that survived into the relatively modern era. This book, written as a response to the catastrophe that was the fall of the Roman Empire in 411 (the book offers a response to those who blamed Rome's adoption of the Christian faith for the cause of its fall), interpreted that terrible event for Christians in a way which gave them hope for the future.

Augustine was born in present-day Algeria in North Africa. His mother Monica was already a Christian, and her influence on his life was to be great. She desired that her bright and intelligent son should be a Christian also. After a standard education in the humanities Augustine devoted himself to the study of literature and was seeking to find 'wisdom' in the study of the classical authors of antiquity. As someone who was associated with the Christian community, Christ and the Christian religion would have been presented to the young Augustine as the 'true wisdom' of the world. Augustine – given this background – naturally turned to reading the Bible to find this wisdom; unfortunately he was horrified by what he found there. The biblical stories seemed grammatically and stylistically crude when compared with the classical authors he had become accustomed to reading. Moreover the God presented therein seemed overly anthropomorphic and overly concerned with animal sacrifice. During this period Augustine encountered disciples of the Manichees (a severe heretical sect that stressed a primeval and ongoing conflict between the forces of light and darkness as the explanation for evil in the world and that regarded the material world as evil). They taxed the already doubting would-be Christian with the question of the problem of evil – where does evil come from if God is good? Augustine had no answer, and for a time he accepted the answer of the Manichees. He became an adherent of the sect and one of their more skilful debaters.

Augustine became a professor of rhetoric in Rome (382) and then in Milan (384). Gradually he became more of a **neo-platonist** in philosophy and grew more interested in Christianity, partly under the influence of Bishop Ambrose of Milan. Augustine came to believe that he was only held back from faith by what he now regarded as a sinful physical relationship with his mistress. (He also wanted to make a 'better' marriage to a woman of higher class. It was an accepted social practice in the ancient world for a young man to take on a long-term sexual partner – usually of a lower class – without committing himself to marriage.) After a dramatic conversion experience which Augustine recounts for us as taking place in the context of the reading of the Bible he spent a period of retreat at Cassiacum (386), finally returning to Africa in 388 to establish a sort of monastery with a group of friends. He abandoned his mistress and desired to devote himself to a life of philosophical reflection. The relation between faith and sexuality remained a source of profound tension in his life, his thought and his legacy to the Church. He was baptised in 387 and became a priest in 391, becoming Bishop of Hippo in 395; he was to remain in that position until his death on 28 August 430.

Augustine was the most influential theologian in the West during the period between St **Paul** and Martin **Luther**. He was deeply influenced by Pauline thought, and Luther was steeped in the Augustinian tradition throughout his life. His influence was exercised through his voluminous writings, not least in connection with three central theological disputes – with the Manichees, with the Donatists and with Pelagius. He had an abiding influence on political theory through his magisterial reflection in *The City of God*. But his most frequently read book was undoubtedly his *Confessions* (397), which moulded the spiritual life of Western Christendom for a thousand years.

Right from the beginning of the *Confessions* the keynote is the soul's search for God, 'because you have made us for yourself, and our hearts are restless till they find rest in you'. God is addressed in praise, penitence and faith, through reflection on the human condition. The work owes a great deal to the classical educational tradition yet is steeped in biblical quotations and centres on a profound spiritual encounter. Classical education had aimed at the creation of a higher type of humanity which was the purpose of all human effort. We find comparable autobiographical reflection in the Greek writer Isocrates, in Cicero's letters and speeches and in historians such as Tacitus and later Libanius.

Religious self-portrayal was characteristic of the age of Augustine, whether in terms of conversion to philosophy as in Synesius' confession of sin and of praise in the verse of **Gregory Nazianzen**, the rhetoric of Ennodius or the pure devotion of Paulinus of Nola. There seemed to be a universal desire for mystical union with God, typified in the *Enneads* of Plotinus, to which Augustine often makes reference.[i]

Yet Augustine's work is not a simple outpouring of mystical piety. It is a highly disciplined exercise. Already he had treated of his conversion in the objective form of philosophical dialogue, in which God was not directly addressed, and prayer is made in the rather formal manner of Plato's dialogues. In the *Confessions* he turned to the form of continuous prayer, characterised by a spiritual humility which, by attributing all to the grace of God, avoids the self-consciousness of others such as St Patrick, his near contemporary, but which none the less was moulded by all the accomplishments of his classical education.

In the *Confessions* Augustine tells us of his early education, of his difficulties learning Greek (his studies were almost all in Latin) and arithmetic, his sufferings at school, his journeys further afield to Madaura for lessons in grammar and rhetoric, and to Carthage. He was, as he said himself, largely a self-made man, with the limitations of a provincial education, yet clearly he was extremely well educated. Despite his frequent criticism of the classics, he uses all the literary categories of the rhetorical schools.

What deeper influence did classical culture have on his thought? He confessed to having been much influenced by Cicero's dialogue, *Hortensius*. Through Cicero's Tusculan dissertations and his work on *Ethics* (*De Finibus*) Augustine was deeply imbued with Cicero's ideal of *humanitas*. But Cicero was a theological sceptic, and secular Latin literature was to produce no solution to the urgent problem of the reality of God.

Fortuitous acquaintance led Augustine to Manichaeism, with its cosmology based on the ancient Persian dualism of light and darkness, and a materialistic pessimism based on its conception of evil being embedded in the material world. Ultimately however the Manichees could provide no satisfactory solution to his problems.[ii] Augustine had also read Aristotle's philosophy, but the classification of traditional logic was of little value for understanding that which is unique such as God.[iii] Even contact with the famous and influential Bishop Ambrose of Milan brought no immediate answers, although it taught him to understand the place of authority in the realm of thought.[iv]

A further decisive step was the acquisition of the famous 'certain books of the platonists', translated from the Greek into Latin, in which he found ideas and sentiments that were similar to the first if not the second half of the Johannine prologue ('In the beginning was the Word and the Word was with God ... All things were made by him and without him nothing was made'). With platonism came the answer to the problem which had forced Cicero into scepticism and had bedevilled Manichaeism, the affirmative answer to the possibility of non-material reality in the concept of the Forms. The late platonists considered Forms not as solid objects but as non-material existent things, the total corpus of which is in some sense fused with the divine mind that created them, and the reminiscence of which, and thus knowledge of God, is possible by direct perception.

Augustine was now sure of the existence of an incorporeal reality that was God, but was unaware of the next step, until he found that pearl of great price – the Bible.[v] He now turned with greater understanding to that book, which he must have handled as an adherent of the Manichees. Now an awakened awareness of the power of evil paved the way for an increasing understanding of sin. He was to find an answer in the Genesis creation sagas to the neo-platonic problem of the fusion of creator and created (i.e. the problem of associating the perfection of the eternal creator with the flawed, decaying, transient world of matter).

In the famous account of his conversion, which Augustine himself provides, a copy of Paul's letters was on his desk when his friend Alypius called, and it is in the context of reading this piece of scripture that the major turning point of his pilgrimage occurred. The suggestion that he should turn to St Paul is ascribed by Augustine to the voice of a child calling in a nearby house 'Pick up and read, pick up and read'.[vi]Augustine picks up the copy of the scriptures and reads these words: 'Not in riots and drunken parties, not in eroticism and indecencies, not in strife and rivalry, but put on the Lord Jesus Christ and make no provision for the flesh in its lusts'.[vii] He asserts: 'I neither wished nor needed to read further. At once with the last words of this sentence, it was as if a light of relief from all anxiety flooded into my heart. All the shadows of doubt were dispelled'. The philosopher had become a Christian and the impact on all subsequent Christian theology was to be profound.

Augustine could now add the second part of the Johannine prologue to his previous platonic understanding of the divine. 'Again, I read there that the Word, God, is "born not of the flesh, nor of blood, nor of the will of man nor of the will of the flesh, but of God". But that "the word was made flesh and dwelt among us" I did not read there'[viii] ('there' being the writings of the platonists).

Yet he still had some way to go. Even in the first work, the *Soliloquies*, the way to God cannot be completely articulated in Christian terms as the retention of the platonic concept of memory suggests. Only after 395, with the transformative role of grace, as distinct from conversion to the faith, can a comprehensively Christian theology be said to be achieved.

What is now distinctive about the Christian education which for Augustine replaces the classical one? The reception of the gist of faith is followed by a renewed search for understanding in the examination of the work of creation (the last books of *Confessions*). Augustine asked of God the question – 'Where did I find you?' The answer was that God was working in him throughout his life, and revealed himself specifically in the occasion of reading the scriptures in the garden. The question then arose – 'How did I remember my life story, and how do I remember God?' In the *Soliloquies*, that involved the concept of memory. The learning of specific facts is a reminiscence from the time when we learned the facts. But how do we remember God now?[ix] Augustine's answer is that God alone provides illumination by his grace, by implication the grace of the incarnate word in the context of the reading of scripture.

Augustine is quite prepared to use platonic imagery and, if need be, to disregard some of its implications. For example, his descriptions of the transience of human life, or of chaos in creation, or of God's transcendence and immanence, employ Plato's philosophy and have direct parallels in his dialogues. God is paradoxically most present when he is most hidden. Yet there is no necessary connection between God and man of the sort suggested by Plato. The question of the Christian assertion of the total separation of God from his creation arises most acutely in his consideration of questions arising from Genesis, i.e. what God was doing before creation, and leads Augustine into a long discussion on the nature of time. Above all Augustine had to combat the equation of time with eternity and the resulting conception of God as part of a non-created ever-recurrent cycle. Although he has used the cyclic concept readily to express the fleeting nature of human life, now he uses the Aristotelian notion of the divine life as a movement complete in each minute. Time of course passes and involves change, but time only begins with God's act of creation.[x]

Even throughout these more 'technical' passages of the *Confessions*, however, the influence of the Bible is still apparent.[xi] Quotations from the Psalms are very numerous. Yet unlike many of the Psalms there is little sense in the *Confessions* of a complete separation of God and man. The sense of the divine presence is always very real to Augustine, and the relationship is of a very close communion. This evocation of the one who is most hidden and yet most present plays a considerable role in transforming the work from a collection of scattered biblical quotations and philosophical fragments within an autobiographical framework into a living prayer of adoration.[xii]

From the above analysis (and this could be paralleled from other works such as *The City of God* or *On the Trinity*) it would seem to be clear that Augustine's thought is integrally and simultaneously related both to ancient classical education and to the Bible, as he exploits all available means in pursuance of his task of praising God and exhorting men to follow in the way. His thoughts were indeed moulded by the concepts of his time, but this added greatly to his apologetic powers, and we have seen that he had no difficulty in rejecting concepts that he did not want.

It could be argued that Augustine never quite attained the breadth and minute erudition that we find in the writings of his Cappadocian counterparts. Yet he grasped the basic tendencies of the classical mind and could apply these methods to the problems of his time. To this, the new educational programme of the Bible added what was lacking, as God met him in the context of his Word. 'For who shall liberate me from this body of death, except your grace in Jesus Christ our Lord? This the Greek writings did not contain. No one there sings, "Shall not my heart be devoted to God, from whence comes my salvation".'[xiii] Finding here peace, in complete trust and obedience he was impelled to communicate the secret to his fellow men: 'From you [God] it is sought, from you it is asked, to you we are drawn, Thus, thus it will be received thus found and thus opened'.[xiv]

While the technical issues concerning for example the nature of time, of knowledge and of memory are still expressed with the aid of philosophical concepts, the influence of the Bible in the *Confessions* is everywhere clear: 'I can do everything through him who comforts me. Therefore Christ died for all, that those who live may not live for themselves alone, but for him who died for all'. The book is saturated in the piety of the Psalms, and therefore of the sense of God as a living presence. God, most secret and most present, is the source of adoration. The new *paideia* or education of the Bible adds to the old what was lacking. Thus he can say: 'Give what you command, and command what you will'. Everything is asked for from God, moves towards God, and is accepted, found and opened up in God.

This is a radically God-centred theology. It is also Christ-centred, but not perhaps as consistently as it might at first seem. Critics have sometimes thought to detect a strongly Stoic framework of determinism, softened by the language of Christological imagery. Certainly in the treatment of the problem of evil we have a sense that the framework, and therefore the solution, in the form of the non-reality of evil as being the absence of Good, is influenced by the platonic insistence that since everything that is is created by God, it must therefore be good. For Augustine the Manichee God might be pictured as a realm divided against itself, including good and evil. This was now seen by Augustine to be 'a shocking and detestable profanity'. There could be no possibility of evil in God himself. Being is good. The created world is good, created out of nothing by God. Evil is only the absence of Good. The source of evil is lost in the mystery of human freedom and is ultimately inexplicable. Augustine came to believe that 'Free will is the cause of our doing evil, and thy just judgement is the cause of our having to suffer from its consequences'.[xv] The primary sin of men and angels is a turning away from the highest good, that is God, to a lesser good, his creatures. The angels fall, human beings fall, the universe itself is beautiful, and our awareness of death and decay is due only to our mortal frailty which does not perceive the larger harmony that exists.

Evil arises because of human sin. In a fateful linkage for the subsequent treatment of sex in the Christian tradition Augustine linked the mechanical transmission of sin down through the generations to the act of procreation. Though the act of conception is not evil, the physical desire that makes it possible *is* evil. Hence human sin, based on lust, is at the heart of suffering and disaster in the cosmos. We are all born into the condition of original sin in this manner. Baptism into the Church deals with the stain of this sin but its effects continue in our daily lives. This understanding of sin as essentially an individual matter in the context of intimate human relationships has had incalculable consequences, often adverse, in the Christian world. For example, apart from hugely complicating the development of personal relationships in society, it has led to an underestimation of the corporate and social dimensions of sin, not least in the economic sphere.

Augustine was one of the seminal figures in the history of Christian thought and life. His virtues and achievements, and his mistakes, were to have great influence in the West. His polemical writings against the Donatists were to influence the understanding of the Church as a broad Church, full of the sheep and the goats until the Second Coming. The Donatist church was a church that existed alongside the Catholic church in North Africa and was numerically superior in many areas. The Donatists took a rigorous position in relation to Church discipline and in particular to the validity of the Church's ministry and sacraments. During the persecution instituted by the Emperor Diocletian (303–5) many Bishops and priests had, as demanded, handed over copies of the scriptures to be burned by the civil authorities. In the view of the Donatists such people had deprived themselves of spiritual power by their actions and they refused to follow bishops and priests who had themselves betrayed the Church or to accept the validity of bishops and priests who been ordained by such people. The Donatists therefore preached a doctrine of a 'pure and perfected Church' made up of the holy and the pious. Augustine argued that the Church was a mixed community (hence the sheep and goats analogy) made up of the truly pious, but also of the wicked and unfaithful. Its holiness did not lie in the holiness of its members but in its participation in Christ. Augustine conceived of the Church as both visible and invisible. The visible Church is the empirical and sociological reality that we can see and this is a mixed community. The invisible Church is known only to God and consists of those who are truly elect. The sacraments that are distributed to everybody belong to Christ and do not depend upon the holiness or perfection of the priest or bishop for their effectiveness. Everyone in the visible Church may be baptised and receive communion but the spiritual effects of the sacraments only truly apply to those who are the 'elect' of God – who are members of the invisible Church. By means of these distinctions Augustine gave the Catholic church a theology that enabled them to be an inclusive community rather than a separated sect for the morally perfect.

The Pelagian controversy arose out of a dispute with the British monk Pelagius around 411. Pelagius took issue with certain teachings of Augustine about sin, baptism and the way that grace functions in the life of the believer. The debate was to last until the end of Augustine's life and Augustine was gradually to harden his position over time. Pelagius taught a form of moral perfectionism that stressed the freedom of the human will and therefore intensified an individual's responsibility for his or her own wrongdoing. Pelagius felt that human beings could co-operate with the grace of God as received through the sacraments and the teaching of Christ and could perfect themselves morally. The importance of human free will was stressed and the understanding of infant baptism as dealing with original sin was denied because babies, having no free will, could not sin. In response Augustine outlined his notion of original sin. He argued that sin originated in the transgression of Adam and that it has been ingrained into human nature by physical heredity. We are born therefore with a sinful taint or quality. This original sin is involuntarily acquired but it brings with it original guilt. By virtue of this taint of sin and guilt the human race is a mass of sin (*massa peccati*). Human beings are free and responsible for their actions but their freedom in their sinful state invariably leads to further acts of sin.

Part of the seriousness inherent in Adam's fall is that Augustine stressed the perfection and original righteousness of Adam. Adam was free in his ability not to sin (*posse non peccare*) – he did not yet possess the *non posse peccare* – the inability to sin which is our future state in heaven. He was, however, good and disposed to virtue. Yet Adam fell – through a mysterious unintelligible misuse of his free will he turned from the highest good which is God to a lower good. This possibility of choosing was inherent in his freedom and was part of his changeable creaturely nature. The source and ground of this choice Augustine considered to be pride – the desire to be God in God's place. If pride had not already resided in Adam's soul he would never have listened to the tempting words of Eve. Nevertheless, this fall has affected the whole human race, which is a 'mass of sin' out of which God has elected some souls for salvation. The manner by which God exercises this choice is through his 'irresistible grace'. This does not destroy human freedom because true freedom is willing the good that God desires whereas fallen human beings can only choose what is evil. Infants need to be baptised because this deals with the taint of original sin and removes the guilt acquired. Babies who are not baptised will therefore go to hell, albeit a less severe form of hell than those who have deliberately and wilfully exercised sinful choices as adults. It is a hard and severe doctrine that has influenced both Catholic and Protestant (particularly that of John **Calvin**) accounts of the condition of human beings before God in different ways. In its entirety Augustine's teaching on this matter has never been formally declared orthodox by a council of the Church and it may be that the Church has in fact tended towards a modified form of Pelagius' position on this matter. However, it may be that Augustine's robust presentation of the matter defined the thinking about nature and grace which was to be the framework of the Reformation controversies a thousand years later. His massive work *The City of God* affected political theory over an even longer period. His work *On the Trinity* (399–420) offered an understanding of the triune nature of God which is still massively influential. Drawing upon contemporary understandings of the mind Augustine drew an analogy between the activities of the mind and the threefold person of God. Thus we can distinguish mind, knowledge and love, yet one self; memory, thinking and willing, yet one self. Elsewhere Augustine speaks of relations of love when he says that the Father loves the Son and the Son loves the Father and the Spirit is love by which the Father loves the Son and the Son loves the Father. Some have argued that this does not offer a third person in the form of the Spirit, but simply an abstract relation. Augustine was aware of the profoundly mysterious nature of the **Trinitarian** personhood of God and did not in fact want to use the term 'person' in relation to the three members of the Trinity as it could introduce unwanted implications of three separate individuals. Nevertheless it was better to use the term than to say nothing. Some contemporary accounts of the matter regard Augustine's mental analogy as never breaking free from a unitary understanding of God and would look to his near contemporaries, the **Cappadocian Fathers**, for a more nuanced account of the matter. However, Augustine's faith remains one of the absolutely classical paradigms of Christian faith.

Notes

i   *Confessions* 4:8.1; 6:7.10
ii   *Ibid.* 5:7; 6:4
iii *Ibid.* 4:16.28
iv   *Ibid.* 6:5f.
v   *Ibid.* 8:1; Cf. 9:1
vi   *Ibid.* 8:12
vii *Ibid.* 8:12; Romans 13:13–14
viii *Confessions* 7:14; John 1:13–14
ix   *Confessions* 10:20.28
x   *Ibid.* 12:5; 12:11
xi   *Ibid.* 11:13
xii *Ibid.* 10:27
xiii *Ibid.* 7:21
xiv *Ibid.* 13:30
xv   *Ibid.* 7:3.5

See also: **Aquinas; Calvin; Cappadocian Fathers; Luther; Paul**

Glossary: **Neo-platonism; predestination; Trinity**

Major writings

Augustine: earlier writings, trans. John H.S. Burleigh, London: SCM Press, 1953
The City of God, trans. H. Bettenson, Harmondsworth: Pelican, 1972
Confessions, trans. H. Chadwick, Oxford: OUP, 1992
Works against the Pelagians and the Manichees, Commentaries and sermons in *Augustine: major writings*, ed. Benedict J. Groeschel, New York: Crossroad Pub. Co., 1995

Further reading

Peter Brown, *Augustine of Hippo*, London: Faber & Faber, 1967
Henry Chadwick, *Augustine: a very short introduction*, Oxford: OUP, 2001
Mary T. Clark, *Augustine*, London: Continuum, 2000 (c.1994)
Gillian Evans, *Augustine on Evil*, Cambridge: CUP, 1990
J.M. Rist, *Augustine: ancient thought baptised*, Cambridge: CUP, 1994

BAILLIE, JOHN (1886–1960) and DONALD (1887–1954)

John and Donald Baillie were among the most significant Scottish theologians of the twentieth century. They were outstanding among a series of distinguished scholars of their generation and stood for an approach to theology that was at once sympathetic to the traditional teachings of the Church and at the same time questioning of anything that was not intimately connected to the living heart of religious faith. This sympathetic but questioning approach to faith has been termed 'liberal-evangelicalism' and it well describes the approach of both Baillies, neither of whom were prepared simply to repeat the theological truisms of past generations but who instead attempted to think and re-think the faith in terms of the challenges posed by the secular and humanistic reason of the modern period. In the writings of the Baillies the Scottish theological tradition reached a peak and a new maturity.

John and Donald Baillie were born in the Free Church of Scotland manse of Gairloch in 1886 and 1887 respectively. The Free Church had come into being as a result of a split in the established Church of Scotland in 1843 over the rights and role of the state in relation to the internal affairs of the Church. The Free Church took the rigorous view that the state should support the Church but should have no say in its internal deliberation of doctrine, nor in matters such as the settlement of ministers in parishes. Theologically, the Free Church was evangelical and reflected the 'Calvinistic' theology that was dominant in Scotland at that time. However, although the Free Church was in many respects a conservative institution, it was also committed to the ideal of truth and valued an educated ministry. It encouraged many of its ministers and the professors of its theological colleges to spend time studying in Germany, at that time the leading centre of new and radical approaches to theology and to biblical criticism. Paradoxically, it was through this type of cultural exchange that the professors of the Free Church colleges – nominally more conservative institutions than the faculties of divinity of the universities – became the primary conduit for the new theological ideas that were filtering into Britain from Germany. Thus it was that John Baillie could later recall his Christian development in terms of 'a rigorously Calvinistic upbring-ing' at the hands of his mother (she was widowed very early), but also in terms of the astonishingly liberal and humanistic strands that were present in nineteenth-century Free Church culture. Specifically, he recalled the influence of the huge respect for learning in the Free Church tradition which drove both brothers through brilliant academic careers, first in school at Inverness then University at Edinburgh, both graduating with Firsts in Philosophy, a Distinction in Divinity and winning every possible prize, medal and fellowship in sight. The impact of this secular and liberal learning was not always wholly positive however, causing both brothers a certain difficulty in reconciling faith with the demands of reason. Donald in particular seems to have wrestled with real doubts throughout his relatively short life. Yet, both brothers refused simply to acquiesce in the face of the secular attack on Christian faith and attempted instead to answer the attack of humanistic reason on its own terms.

Both brothers became assistants in the philosophy department at Edinburgh. Both spent some time working with the Young Men's Christian Association in France during the First World War rather than serving as combatants in the trenches. Both brothers, like many churchmen, had studied in Germany before the conflict and were not so ready as many of their countrymen to heed the bellicose cries. Donald, whose health was always fragile, was invalided home quite quickly, but John gave educational lectures to the troops.

Thereafter their paths diverge. John married in 1919 and immediately went off to Auburn Theological Seminary, New York State, being ordained in the Presbyterian Church there in 1920. This was followed by six years of intensive teaching and research in theology, culminating in *The Roots of Religion in the Human Soul* (1926) and a large-scale work, *The Interpretation of Religion*, completed in 1925 but not published until 1929.

These books reflect an extraordinarily wide cultural and theological experience: the Calvinist manse; the liberal tradition of arts and divinity in Edinburgh before the First World War; the impact of four years with the YMCA in France; immersion in American culture – its poetry and politics; the polarisation of Church politics in the *Fundamentalist* debate; and participation in conferences on the *social gospel* in New York during the early 1920s, all long before such issues came to centre stage in Church circles elsewhere.

John's writings of the 1920s, and in particular *The Interpretation of Religion*, betray everywhere the influence of **Kant**, but Kant as had been interpreted by his philosophy teachers at Edinburgh. Thus the traditional philosophical proofs for the existence of God were regarded as misguided and wrong. The true source of religious feeling derives from our experience of moral value. Like Kant, John was impressed by the unconditional nature of the moral demand that is placed on human beings. This demand is not something that we invent, nor is it simply the by-product of the forces and pressures of social life, but is a deep apprehension of the nature of ultimate reality. This ultimate reality must be personal, argues John, as we cannot believe in, and experience as an obligation, such matters as the sanctity of personal life without also believing that the source of that sanctity is also personal. Religion, however, although intimately related to moral experience is not simply identical with moral experience but arises from it. Religious practice and its concomitant symbolism extends and completes our experience of the reality disclosed through our experience of moral obligation. In the fashion of **Hegel** Christianity is regarded as the crowning point of human religious development. And again like Hegel, John argues that the classical affirmations of the Christian faith are to be respected and believed in for the insights that they refer to, but in their original formulations they are no longer intelligible and have to be reinterpreted. In this sense he follows the classic strategy of all forms of liberal theology in deriving the sense of God from arguments drawn from what he believed to be general and universal features of human experience in the world.[i]

John moved to Toronto in 1927, partly perhaps to be near old friends from Scotland (his wife was in sanatoria with TB from 1923 until 1930, and looking after their only son was not an easy task so any support was welcome), partly too because of the challenge of a new *ecumenical* college in the newly formed United Church of Canada. Gospel and culture, social issues and ecumenical concern were to be the focal points of much of his later work. He returned to America, to the Roosevelt Chair at Union Theological Seminary in New York, then arguably the world's greatest theological seminary, and provided a forum for theology from which, along with Henry Sloane Coffin,

Reinhold **Niebuhr** and Henry Van Dusen, he was to have a major impact on Western theology for the next two decades.

In fact John returned to Edinburgh in 1934. But the transatlantic links remained very strong, and through visits and letters Baillie, Coffin, Niebuhr and Van Dusen exerted huge influence on the new World Council of Churches, along with their friend Bishop Henry Sherrill and others. The four men differed in emphasis in several ways but they agreed on a middle path between an extreme liberalism which all but abandoned or substantially reinterpreted in purely rational terms distinctively Christian claims about the world and God, which they regarded as an unacceptable dilution of the gospel, and a narrower theology based on the approach of **Barth**, which they regarded as an over-reaction to the over-reaction that was the liberal theology of the nineteenth century.

The overarching theme of the presence of God was central to John's next three books, *And the Life Everlasting* (1934), *Our Knowledge of God* (1939) and *Invitation to Pilgrimage* (1942), while the emphasis on spirituality was manifested in *A Diary of Private Prayer* (1936) which sold (and is still in print) tens of thousands of copies, the latter a devotional work combining honest self-examination with concentration on God's reconciling grace. *Our Knowledge of God* revealed the most significant change from John's earlier work of the 1920s and seemed to derive from an engagement with the theology of Barth. The impact of Barth's ferocious attack on the practices and forms of liberal theology seemed to lead John to think that his earlier approach to theology was a dead end. Nevertheless, he took up his theological cudgel and outlined the idea with which he is most famously associated – namely, the idea that our knowledge of God is neither direct nor inferred but is always given 'in, with and under' other forms, something John termed 'mediated immediacy'. The various ways in which knowledge of God is mediated to us are: (i) the natural world in its beauty and order reveals something of God to us (albeit not as a proof, for 'Nature is not an argument for God, but is a sacrament of Him'); (ii) our service of other people in love leads to an apprehension of the God who is love (a refinement of John's earlier arguments from moral obligation); (iii) that all knowledge of God is mediated within a specific history, tradition and culture; and (iv) the medium of God's presence in the history of Israel brings us to Jesus Christ and to the mediation of God once and for all in a human life. Furthermore, the knowledge of God gained here controls and constrains what we know of God through the other more diffuse media.[ii]

The Christological emphasis clearly betrays the impact of Barth, but the willingness to countenance a genuine knowledge of God outside the Christian proclamation of Christ shows that John never lost his original liberal instincts – hence the appellation 'liberal-evangelical'.

The next major development was exemplified by John's increasing impact and influence in Church affairs. In 1940, when the Nazi threat was at its height and the prospects for British life were at their very bleakest, he was asked to chair an important Church commission for the interpretation of 'God's Will in the Present Crisis'. It was to begin issuing its reports in 1942 and the following year he was made Moderator of the General Assembly of the Church of Scotland. (The Church of Scotland has no formal individual leader as such, but each year elects a Moderator who chairs its annual assembly and acts as a spokesperson throughout the rest of the year.) The reports of the committee that John chaired were gathered together in a volume entitled *God's Will For Church and Nation* (1946).

This report combined critique of the Nazis with a programme for social reconstruction in Britain after the war, a programme echoed in the government-sponsored Beveridge Reports which were to be the foundation of the postwar health service and welfare systems. The report recognised the difficulty in applying Christian principles in society, and took the route of 'middle axioms', which should 'exhibit the relevance of the ruling principles to the particular field of action in which guidance is needed'. An example is that '[e]conomic power must be made objectively responsible to the community as a whole'. The result is 'the clear declaration that the common interest demands a far greater measure of public control of capital resources and means of production than our tradition has in the past envisaged'.[iii]

In his introductory remarks on the report John acknowledged its key realisation that the Britain which emerged after the war would not, and could not, be the same Britain that entered into it. Church and society were being changed in the cauldron of war, and the divisions and inequalities that existed in prewar Britain would have to be combated vigorously. Thus the report stressed that extreme inequalities of wealth were dangerous to the common interest and that steps should be taken to control them. Furthermore, people were to be given the opportunity of engaging in purposeful activity and to be paid a living wage for it. Such opinions may be more or less the common fare of contemporary Church reports on society, but in 1940s Scotland the expression of such views by a Church of Scotland committee almost bordered on the revolutionary.

The subject matter of the report echoed visits to Germany during the 1930s and conversations with both sides of the German Church struggle (that is, the struggle between those churches that opposed Hitler's regime and tried to maintain independence and those who were more or less supportive of Hitler's attempts to co-opt the Church into the sphere of state control), numerous Church of England and ecumenical gatherings, not to mention the Moot, an influential forum which met in Oxford during the late 1930s and early 1940s. Members of the Moot regularly included J.H. Oldham, its founder, John Baillie himself, Karl Mannheim, Walter Moberley and Alec Vidler, but there were others, including T.S. Eliot, H.H. Farmer, Donald Mackinnon and John Middleton Murry.

Against John's formidable public international career in theology and the Church it may seem that the work of Donald Baillie is but a pale shadow. Donald suffered from poor health all his life, was shy, modest to a fault and always self-deprecating. Yet his books demonstrated a keenness of intellect and imaginative capacity which some have thought to be better than anything in John's writings, and his letters to his brother, always a great source of counsel, reveal a penetrating and often devastating capacity to sum up people and situations in the sharpest possible focus. John, the dominant figure on the world stage during their lives, is remembered only faintly now whereas Donald's original contribution to Christology is still referred to frequently.

After being invalided out of the YMCA in France in 1917 Donald became a parish minister in Bervie in Kincardineshire in 1919, moving to Cupar in Fife in 1923, Kilmacolm in Renfrewshire in 1930 and then to a Chair of Systematic Theology at St Mary's College, St Andrews in 1934, where he remained until his death in 1954.

Like John, Donald had spent semesters as a student in Germany, in his case in Marburg and Heidelberg, and his fluency in German led to contributions to the translation of **Schleiermacher**'s *The Christian Faith*. His first book, *Faith In God* (1927), was a study of the anatomy of faith and it established Donald as a serious contributor to theological debate. It attempted to provide an apologetic for faith in the existence of God based on human moral commitment. However, apart from some articles and works for Church publications, the only other major book published during his lifetime was *God was in Christ* (1948), a book at once hailed for its clarity and elegance of exposition of the central issues of Christology and one of a few British theological books to be translated into German (in 1954). The posthumous *Theology of the Sacraments* (1957), together with two volumes of simple but profound sermons – *To Whom Shall We Go?* (1955) and *Out of Nazareth* (1958) – served to confirm Donald's reputation as a major theologian. In addition he edited the 1952 *Intercommunion* volume of the World Council of Churches Commission on the subject which he chaired, and produced a splendidly evocative *Memoir* of David Cairns.

It may be said that while John was at his best on the larger public stage, as theological lecturer or church politician, Donald was most effective in small groups, where his humour and the warmth of his personality inspired generations of students, notably at Student Christian Movement gatherings with which he was constantly involved from the early 1930s. The Baillie brothers were very close throughout their lives, and very sympathetic critics of each other's work.

Though John's writing more often dealt with matters of method and Donald's with substance, both were concerned to maintain a proper balance between faith and culture, the gospel and society, in which extremes of liberalism or conservatism were avoided. They were sensitive to theology in context, and when it seemed right, could deploy arguments from the Barthian theology which came to have such an influence from the early 1930s. But both deplored any sort of exclusive or dogmatic narrowness, either from Fundamentalism or from liberal illusions of finality.

When we turn to John Baillie's last book, published as *The Sense of the Presence of God* (1962), we find his characteristic combination of an appeal to human experience in the world with an exploration of rational grounds for belief in God. A brief synopsis should perhaps indicate the flavour of the argument. Chapter One, 'Knowledge and Certitude', deals with some of the most basic problems in the philosophy of religion. Knowledge seems to imply certainty or it could not properly be called knowledge. Yet, even in some of our most rigorous disciplines knowledge in fact often does not go beyond probabilities. The concept of faith always contains both the idea of knowing and the idea of not knowing fully: 'No Christian, then, can say that he knows nothing'. But equally, 'all human thinking is defectible'. There are indeed certainties, in the natural sciences, in moral and especially in our religious convictions. A distinction is drawn between knowledge of truth and knowledge of reality. Our knowledge of the realities is primary, and our knowledge of truths concerning them secondary

But does it work? Turn to Chapter Two, 'The Really Real'. John argues that many have doubted our knowledge of any reality, certainly any beyond what can be verified by the methods of natural science. But what about the conviction that honesty and loyalty are required of us all? Moral convictions are central. Here reality presents itself to us, requiring concern for others. This phenomenon is described further in a chapter on 'The Range of Our Experience'.

Early man felt himself to be at one with nature, not alien from it: 'Our total experience of reality presents itself to us as a single experience'. Analysis of individual elements comes later. This is especially true of moral convictions. The point of this train of argument becomes clear by the time we reach Chapter Four, 'The Epistemological Status of Faith': 'How do we 'reason things out?' Procedures for verification and falsification are discussed. 'A faith that is consistent with everything possible is not a faith in anything actual.' Complete agnosticism is less frequent than we often imagine. For John, the ultimate refutation of doubts is theological and incarnational: the claim made upon me by the presence of my neighbour is made by unconditioned being, by God. It now becomes possible to consider 'The Nature and Office of Theological Statements' (Chapter Five). Faith is 'an awareness of the divine presence itself, however hidden behind the veils of sense'. God reveals himself within a tradition and a community. The indirectness of faith's apprehension of God is explored through the Bible, **Aquinas** and Kant. Hegel and others from the nineteenth century are now invoked, then those from the twentieth. The result of this indirect apprehension of God is that theological language is characterised as analogical or symbolic. Our language cannot directly refer to God unproblematically given the indirectness of our apprehension of God and the necessary partiality of all forms of knowledge.

Chapter Six explores the role of 'analogy and symbol' further. 'In the widest sense of the term all language may be said to be symbolic.' But not all theological statements are analogical. Despite being known in, with and under other realities, yet there is a certain directness in the apprehension of God. However, this two-way communication is in the nature of the case internal to the mind of the believer, and is always open to doubt on the part of the non-believer.

Chapter Seven, 'The Framework of Reference', seeks to relate theory to practice. Christianity is a way of living. Love of God is always related to love of neighbour, and beyond this to a new humanity. This leads on to Chapter Eight, 'Meaning and Reference'. The gospel needs to be translated into the language of the present. Otherwise it is inevitably dismissed as irrelevant to contemporary life. In particular, it is important not to confuse dogmas with the primary perceptions of faith. Chapter Nine raises the wider issue of 'Faith and the Faiths'. The Greeks and the Romans developed philosophies of religion. Did they have a true knowledge of God? What does it mean to speak of salvation in a name? For John, there is some awareness of God in 'the pagan religions', but the Way of Christ is decisive: 'It is Christ himself who has created the world's desire for him'.

Chapter Eleven deals with providence. Scientific and religious accounts of the world complement one another. Through modern physics, 'contradiction has been turned into complementarity'. What others may see as coincidence, Christians will read as providential. This naturally brings John to Chapter Twelve, 'Grace and Gratitude': 'He lov'd us from the first of time, He loves us to the last'.

'Gratitude is not only the dominant note of Christian piety but equally the dominant motive of Christian action in the world.' This is the imitation of Christ. We should also recognise vestigial forms of gratitude in those who are not explicitly Christian. The final chapter (Thirteen), titled 'Retrospect', reconsiders the argument. Faith is trust and propositions about God are necessary, but not sufficient. We have to do with 'a God whose living and active presence among us can be perceived by faith in a large variety of human contexts and situations'. John ends characteristically with Vaughan's prayer, 'Abide with us, O most blessed and merciful saviour, for it is towards evening and the day is far spent...'

Donald's enduring work *God was in Christ* (which echoes in many respects John's *The Place of Jesus Christ in Modern Christianity* (1929) stands with John McLeod Campbell's *The Nature of the Atonement* and HR Mackintosh's *The Person of Jesus Christ* as representing the best of Scottish Christology in the modern era. Donald Baillie was concerned to stress that God was really, concretely, involved in all the risks and uncertainties of particular occasions in human history. This led him to emphasise the individual and complete humanity of Jesus, despite the theoretical advantages offered by concepts of impersonal humanity. He focuses on the fatherhood and the Love of God, and on Jesus' spiritual struggle as involving the conflict between divine love and evil. He underlined the paradox of grace, the relation of the cross to the life of Jesus, and the balance of subjective and objective in **atonement**. John Macquarrie, the renowned Scottish-Anglican theologian who in many ways stands in the same succession as the Baillies, summed it up in this way – 'It is not surprising that this book of Baillie's has attained to the status of a modern classic, for it combines the post-Enlightenment approach to Christology "from below" with a deep spiritual sensitivity'.[iv]

Certainly Donald's attempt to maintain a strong hold on the historical Jesus as being fundamental to the doctrine of the incarnation was a pivotal insight. Similarly, his appeal to the experience of grace in the life of the believer as providing a distant analogy for how we might understand the nature of God's incarnation in Jesus Christ gave his Christology a warmth and humanity often lacking in many accounts. Although written in 1948 Donald's concerns were prescient and anticipated the developments in Christology that would later emerge in the writings of figures as diverse as Wolfhart **Pannenberg**, the celebrated Bishop of Woolwich John Robinson and the contributors to the 'Myth of God Incarnate' debate of the mid-1970s.

What if anything may be learned from the Baillies? Both John and Donald were concerned with theology in context, and with looking to the future. They would not be interested in a repristination of their own detailed arguments, which were fashioned for their time. Indeed, John notes already by 1939 that references to the debates of the 1920s have disappeared from his work, since the students of today − of his day − face new challenges.

John and Donald's work would appear to point to a theology and a church which remains both resolutely liberal and resolutely evangelical. This would mean resistance to an easy assimilation with the prevailing culture, in the name of the vulnerable Christ who is the judge of all exploitation and domination which is so common both in State and in Church. It would also mean resistance to a complacent retreat to the calm of paradise the blessed, in a Church and theological framework in which all answers are known in advance and all nonconformists are excluded.

In the face of pluralism and fragmentation in the modern world there is an attraction in various forms of totalitarianism − we saw at least two forms of this in the twentieth century. John insisted that we should not attempt to respond to these movements with a form of Christian totalitarianism. Donald was if anything even more insistent. There may be a promising path for the future in the direction of what can be programmatically described as a liberal, engaged, agonistic, Christological multiculturalism. This is the direction which is suggested by the Baillies, and by their friends Niebuhr, Coffin and Van Dusen.

Notes

i For more on this see David Fergusson's article 'John Baillie: orthodox liberal' in *Christ, Church and Society*, p.133

ii Again I am indebted here to Fergusson's article, *ibid.*, p.143

iii D. Forrester, 'God's Will in A Time of Crisis: John Baillie as a social theologian' in Fergusson *op cit.*, p.229

iv J. Macquarrie, *Jesus Christ In Modern Thought*, London: SCM, 1990, p.329

See also: **Barth; Kant; Niebuhr**

Glossary: atonement; Ecumenical; epistemology/epistemological; fundamentalist; social gospel

Major writings

John Baillie

The Roots of Religion in the Human Soul, London: Hodder & Stoughton, 1926
The Interpretation of Religion, Edinburgh: T & T Clark, 1929
The Place of Jesus Christ in Modern Thought, Edinburgh: T & T Clark, 1929
And the Life Everlasting, London: Scribners, 1934
A Diary of Private Prayer, London: OUP, 1936
Our Knowledge of God, London: OUP, 1939
Invitation to Pilgrimage, London: OUP, 1942
What is Christian Civilisation? London: OUP, 1945
The Sense of the Presence of God, London: OUP, 1962

Donald Baillie

Faith in God and its Christian Consummation, Edinburgh: T & T Clark, 1927
God was in Christ, London: Faber & Faber, 1948
To Whom Shall We Go, Edinburgh: St Andrew Press, 1955
Theology of the Sacraments, London: Faber & Faber, 1957
Out of Nazareth, Edinburgh: St Andrew Press, 1958

Further reading

David Fergusson (ed.), *Christ, Church and Society*, Edinburgh: T & T Clark, 1993
G.W. Newlands, *John and Donald Baillie: transatlantic theology*, Oxford: Peter Lang, 2002

BARTH, KARL (1886–1968)

Swiss-German theologian who was probably the single most influential theologian of the twentieth century. Barth is famous for transforming the shape of Protestant theology by rejecting the nineteenth-century liberal tradition of theology in which he himself had been schooled. Barth came to see that this approach to theology had entered into what he believed to be an unacceptable compromise with the methods and presuppositions of **Enlightenment** philosophy. The result was a fatal dilution of the unique and distinctive message of the gospel of God's gift of himself in Jesus Christ. Barth's whole project was to let ring out the single truth that God had given himself to the world in Jesus Christ. It was the determining norm of his entire theological programme and one which stressed the surprising, unmerited sheer otherness of God's action. According to Barth, liberal theology had replaced authentic speech about God with nothing more than talk about human religious experience – albeit with a 'loud voice'. Barth's whole programme was to replace this talk about human beings and their various religious apprehensions with nothing other than talk about God's self-revelation in Jesus Christ

Barth was born in Basle 10 May 1886; he died in the same city in December 1968. Between these two dates the secure world of the nineteenth century fell apart, wracked by two world wars. Barth's whole body of work is in some sense a response to the crisis of the end of modernity typified by the dissolution of high European culture as a result of these events. He himself was personally caught up in the tumult. First as a pastor in Switzerland, observing the impact of the collapse of Germany and the economies of Europe on the people of his parish, and second as an academic theologian banished from Nazi Germany due to his opposition to Hitler's regime.

The crises of the times were matched by a crisis in theology and Barth's programme, which self-consciously attempted to break the easy association and collusion of liberal theology with secular reason and culture, is sometimes termed 'crisis' or 'dialectical theology'. Barth refused the attempt to justify theology by external norms and standards, be they derived from science or philosophy. God's word was self-authenticating and the Church's first task was not to show the inherent reasonableness of its faith to a secular audience, but to be faithful to the proclamation of its *kerygma* (the message of the gospel) – that God was in Jesus Christ reconciling the world to himself. This stress upon the Church's attentiveness to its basic message provides the third name often given to Barth's theology in this early period – kerygmatic theology.

Barth wrote many works but his lifetime achievement and that which he laboured over more than any other is his multi-volume *Church Dogmatics*. Begun in 1933 and consisting of thirteen volumes (some six million words), it was still incomplete when he died. A flavour of Barth's radical approach can be caught in his famous saying – 'A good theologian does not live in a house of ideas, principles and methods. He walks right through all such buildings and always comes out into the fresh air again. He remains on the way' (Barth to Heiko Miskotte, 12 July 1956).

Barth was educated in Bern, Berlin, Tübingen and Marburg, in the liberal Protestant school of **Ritschl**, Herrmann and Rade. For Karl Barth, the Swiss pastor, it was the German theologians' glorification of the First World War that sparked off his rebellion and break with the liberal theology that they represented. Barth was horrified to find that many of his most esteemed and best-loved professors of the great German universities had signed a letter in support of the Kaiser's war. Barth had already been struggling towards a new conception of theology, but this event finally convinced him that liberal Protestantism's naïve accommodation with the European culture of the day (which had led the theologians to 'baptise' the Kaiser's actions) was both morally and spiritually bankrupt.

The God that Barth believed he found in the gospels was not simply the summation of human moral and spiritual achievement. Barth's God is the 'wholly other'; he is the Lord who is not simply accessible to human beings and their pious imaginings, but is rather the God who in Christ reveals himself as and when he wishes. This portrayal of a God who judges humanity and who is not at the disposal of humanity in their religious searchings or in their philosophising is developed in Barth's revolutionary *Commentary on the Epistle to the Romans* (1919, 2nd edn 1922). This work was much influenced by **Kierkegaard**, the nineteenth-century Danish thinker, who had similarly rebelled against the Hegelian synthesis that dominated the theology of his time (see **Hegel**) and who in protest stressed the irrational and unreasonable aspect of religious faith. Barth adopts a method that is intended to bring about a transformation in his reader by affirming and negating statements often in the same sentence. Hence the term 'dialectical theology'. Therefore Barth says such things as: God's No to us is complete, but in its completion it is also his Yes to us. God is known as the unknown. Religion is – as liberal theology had said – the highest possibility of humanity and its greatest flowering, for it is the quest for that which alone can fulfil us. Yet precisely because it is this, it is also our attempt to use eternity for our own purposes and thus ultimately it is an attempt to evade who God really is by constructing a false God with whom we would much rather deal. Barth himself said that the message of the *Epistle to the Romans* was Kierkegaard's 'infinite qualitative difference between "time and eternity", or between God and humanity'. This book and his later book on **Anselm**, *Fides Quaerens Intellectum* (Faith Seeking Understanding, 1931), were decisive for his development. Barth said of this later book that it was a 'farewell to the last remnants of a philosophical, i.e., anthropological foundation and exposition of

Christian doctrine'.[1] After pastorates in Geneva and Safenwil, Barth was called to academic posts in the universities of Göttingen, Münster, Bonn and Basle.

Barth's thought, perfected in his magnum opus *Church Dogmatics*, is a penetrating and brilliantly insightful exploration into the fact of God's *revelation* in Jesus Christ. Jesus Christ is a unity, a single word of revelation. Because of Barth's commitment to the idea that act and being are united in the figure of Jesus of Nazareth he refused to allow the separation between the 'Jesus of history' and the 'Christ of faith' that had become a staple of liberal theology. That is to say, he refused to separate the historical figure of Jesus and the Christ who was proclaimed in the teaching and preaching of the Church. As such we cannot begin with supposedly objective facts about the historical Jesus – discoverable to the believer and non-believer alike – and then move from such facts about Jesus to the Christ of faith. We cannot as it were build up enough historical evidence to make the move from the man Jesus to the divine Christ. Jesus is who the scriptures say he is, he is God's self-revelation and the fulfilment of God's promises to Israel. In Jesus the old covenant promise to Israel, that God chooses to be with his people, is fulfilled. This Jewish background is essential (an important point that Barth never lost sight of in face of Nazi anti-Semitism). But Jesus is not just the hope of Israel. He is God's only Son. 'Either in Jesus we have to do with God or a creature, and if with God, we have to affirm what Nicaea affirmed.'

Jesus Christ is also the *man*, the measure of all human being. As God's revelation Jesus shows us the meaning of divinity, but he also shows us the meaning of true humanity before God. For Barth Jesus is the measure of all things human and divine. This truth does not depend on our acknowledging it as such and indeed is known only through an act of revelation by God. Incarnate by the Holy Ghost and born of the Virgin Mary, Jesus lived a life of obedience as the Son of God and the Son of Man. Humiliated, murdered by the judiciary, he is exalted by the empty tomb to be the eternal source of salvation. Barth's grand symphony is clearly not the only music in theology, but its intrinsic merit already makes it a classic.

In principle Barth accepted the modern critical approach to the Bible. In practice he often ignored its implications and rarely engaged in questions about the historicity or factual nature of biblical events. Other scholars, aware that we have only a very limited number of the actual words of Jesus, have produced rather different Christologies, building on what are taken to be the reflections and liturgies of the early communities. Where Barth saw lineaments of the classical

Christology of **Chalcedon** in the Bible, others have drawn very different conclusions.

Barth laid great stress on his own understanding of realism in theology. God is hidden to human beings and is available only through grace which creates faith. The nature of God in his revelation itself imposes limits on our concepts. The concept of 'God' is to be filled out through his revelation in Jesus Christ. We should not confuse our doctrine with the reality of God himself. 'Dogma is an **eschatological** idea, to which each particular dogmatic statement is only an approximation, which can neither anticipate nor conceal it.... This door especially must not be bolted.'[ii]

Karl Barth's concept of God is based not on the abstract philosophical possibility of there being a God, but on the Christian tradition of the reality of God as creator, sustainer and saviour of the universe. God is known only through grace, mediated through his revelation in Jesus Christ. He is not a solitary being with added attributes in relation to creation such as omniscience, omnipotence, etc. He is thoroughly personal, in the threefold personhood of Father, Son and Holy Spirit.

God is a living God, dependent on nothing, free and self-existent. His attributes (Barth's term for the classical attributes of God is 'perfections') can only be understood as perfections of the divine love. Barth rethinks the traditional attributes of God in terms of these perfections. As perfect love God is forever constant, faithful, concerned without end or limit. The perfection of eternity does not, as it did for much of the classical Christian tradition, mean that God is outside of time, but rather involves God constantly in involvement in temporality, rather than solitude and **immutability**. These are paradoxical affirmations, arising out of the nature of the unique subject that is God, but paradoxes which we just have to live with, while always seeking a deeper understanding.

God is being and is personal. He is transcendent (that is, not simply identified with his creation, nor exhausted by it, but exceeding it) and immanent (at the same time completely involved at every point in his creation.). God is self-giving love and is self-sufficient, requiring none other to be complete. God cannot be known through rational theology, but his revelation can be discussed rationally. We may think here that God's grace works in, with and under the human response, not instead of transcendent action but as part of it, overcoming human frailty because it is sheer grace. This thought does not alter the substance of the concept of God, but opens up the way to wider searching for rational grounds for faith, as well as to a sympathetic approach to non-Christian reflection on God as the source of creation and salvation.

God is the one who loves in freedom. For Barth, God's being and action are integrally related. Being involves becoming and vice versa, for it is precisely the being of self-giving love. Such a love is self-sufficient and can produce true freedom in the creatures that it supports, creating uniquely free independent beings (a view stressed also by Karl **Rahner**). The traditional attributes of God become the perfections of the divine love in freedom; because the living God, in the death of Jesus, has taken death into his own being from all eternity, grace is effective beyond evil and death to all eternity. This understanding of divine love in action is formally articulated in the doctrine of God outlined in the early volumes of the *Church Dogmatics*. It is symbolically developed in Volume 4, in the Christology built on the parable of the prodigal son, on rejection and consummation.

Feuerbach's famous critique of all human religious experience as the projection of human wishes led Karl Barth to abandon the field of human experience to the secular moralist and philosopher. Inevitably Barth came back to this area, regarding our experience of divine presence as the special gift of the Holy Spirit. The Holy Spirit is the most intimate friend of a proper human understanding of man, but by that stage a framework has been created in which the full force of the significance of God as active in, with and under human activity could not always be taken up. This is in a way all the more surprising, since no one has offered such a detailed appreciation of God as creator and man as creature as has Barth. For **Augustine** and **Aquinas** the role of Christology, albeit central, is limited. For Barth, fear of anthropomorphism and neglect of historical consciousness leads to a failure to grasp the nettle of immanence.

The coming of dialectical theology brought a watershed in thinking about creation, as in all else in Christian doctrine. Emil **Brunner** has a long and careful chapter in his *Dogmatics* (Vol. 1) about the creator and his creation. For Barth the doctrine of creation is an article of faith. It is not self-evident that this world has its origin in God. We 'know' this only in Jesus Christ in whom we see by faith the union of God with man and the world, as his own creation and possession. Creation provides a basis for the covenant of grace. It is itself historical, in the sense of being a temporal event. Creation is also God's time in his primal turning towards the creature in eternity. We can comprehend this time and the event of creation when viewed in the light of the time of grace in Jesus Christ. But we cannot describe it in terms of creaturely time.

Barth and Brunner also famously disagreed as to whether there was a neutral point of contact between human beings and God. Brunner had suggested that the concept of human beings being created in the image of God suggested that human beings had some innate capacity to receive God's revelation. Barth vehemently rejected this suggestion with a resounding *Nein!* (No!). God's revelation could only be apprehended through the work of the Holy Spirit, who is the subjective possibility of revelation. There is no innate human capacity for God, no neutral point of departure for faith. Here Barth radicalises the Reformed's insistence that salvation was wholly a work of God in its inception and completion in *epistemological* terms.

One of the most powerful parts of the *Dogmatics* is found in Volume 4, where Barth outlines the doctrine of reconciliation in terms drawn from the gospel story of the prodigal son. Barth describes the path of the Son of God into the 'far country' in terms of humiliation and exaltation. He sees the humiliation of the Son of God and the exaltation of the Son of Man as two forms of the one reconciling action of Jesus Christ. Humiliation demonstrates the glory of his deity and exaltation restores his true humanity: 'That Jesus Christ is very God is shown in his way into the far country in which he the Lord became a servant. Made sin for us, he stands in our place'.[iii]

The very heart of the *atonement* is the overcoming of sin: sin in its character as the rebellion of man against God, and in its character as the ground of man's hopeless destiny in death. It was to fulfil this judgement on sin that the Son of God took our place as sinners. He took our place as judge but he also took our place as judged: 'He was judged in our place and he acted justly in our place'.

But the real significance of the *for us* is consummated in the resurrection. Here is the new creation: 'In him man is made the new man, reconciled with God'.[iv] This is tied in eternity to election: 'The true humanity of Jesus Christ was and is and will be the primary context of God's eternal election'. The whole reason for creation and the whole of human history is God's decision to be for us in Jesus Christ. This is what Barth means by election – God has decided to be for humanity in Jesus Christ. Through the 'wondrous exchange' between human and divine, disrupted existence is restored and peace with God is achieved for all through Christ, by individuals appropriated through the Holy Spirit.

Barth's understanding of the Bible is an interesting development in Calvinist orthodoxy. Following **Calvin**, Barth held that Christ does not actually make himself present from within the text, but that God reveals himself in the history of Jesus Christ as testified in the scriptures, through the seal in the heart of the believer of the testimony of the Holy Spirit. Scripture is not then for Barth the words of God written on the page, but it becomes the Word of God to us in the act of proclamation and reading as the Holy Spirit opens our hearts and minds to what God has to say. The unintelligibility of scripture to modern man is part of the general problem of man's anthropocentric rather than God-centred way of thinking. What is required is not a new hermeneutic of scripture that supposedly relates a difficult and remote past culture to our present culture, as in the manner of **Bultmann**. Rather, the Holy Spirit reorients a person's whole life in the context of the proclamation of the Word, within the ongoing life of the community of faith.

Barth can often surprise us with his radical and novel approach to ethical issues, unafraid often to challenge tradition. Barth's ethics is everywhere an ethics of grace. As we have seen, he had been highly critical of many of his teachers in their support for war in 1914: 'The absolute ideas of the gospel are being simply suspended until further notice, and German war theology is put in their place, christianised with a lot of talk about "Sacrifice" and the like' (letter to Thurneysen, September 1914). He continued to criticise traditional theologies of the 'Just War'. 'The problem of avoiding war is present and always has to be tackled during every time of peace.' Pacifism has 'almost everything to be said for it, and it is almost overwhelmingly convincing'. 'The normal, the crucial condition is that of peace.' Radical pacifism however is a mistake because 'man can only take a relative decision'.[v] There might be an extreme case in which a people has serious grounds for not allowing the loss of its independence. The decision must be one in a given case rather than a decision in principle.

Barth was a great churchman, yet he could be extremely sceptical about doctrines of the Church: 'For about two hundred years the Protestant Church has largely ceased to be interesting', as he wrote in 1932. Not the human organisation but divine grace is prior. As he said in a searching critique against Nazism in 1933, 'The gospel means, purely and simply, not men for God but God for men'. And as the Barmen Declaration of the Confessing Church, in which he had a major hand, was to put it: 'The church is the community of brothers, in which Jesus Christ is at work through the Holy Spirit in Word and sacrament'.

Barth, like **Schleiermacher**, did not have a high doctrine of the sacraments. He spoke of the birth of Christ as the one sacrament, and of the human nature of Christ as the first sacrament. In Book 4 of

Volume 4 of *Church Dogmatics* Barth was to advocate, again against tradition, adult rather than infant baptism. Barth saw water baptism as above all the authentically human response to God's baptism of people through the Holy Spirit in Jesus Christ. This view was to gain widespread influence in Reformed churches throughout continental Europe and was to be taken up later by another Reformed theologian, Jürgen **Moltmann**.

It may be thought that in the Europe of the mid-twentieth century the Barthian theology which had provided such a wonderful basis for resistance to Nazism had proven peculiarly helpless in the face of the need for reconstruction and for Christian leadership in pointing to the structures of a new society. Nevertheless, however one may judge his specific theological proposals, Barth was a man of quite astonishing gifts of character and intellect. He never gave way to the temptation to follow fashion for its own sake, He was above all his own man. That is why his work still commands the critical attention of professional theologians, and has been taken forward in a flexible and critical manner by such independent thinkers as **Moltmann**, **Küng** and **Pannenberg**.

Notes

i   *How I Changed My Mind*, ed. J. Godsey, Richmond, VA: John Knox Press, 1966, p.42
ii   *Church Dogmatics* (hereafter *C.D.*) 1.2, Edinburgh: T & T Clark, 1956, p.895
iii *C.D.* 4.1, Edinburgh: T & T Clark, 1956, p.241
iv   *C.D.* 4.2, Edinburgh: T & T Clark, 1958, p.2
v   *C.D.* 3.4, Edinburgh: T & T Clark, 1961, pp.450ff

See also: **Bonhoeffer; Brunner; Bultmann; Calvin; Feuerbach; Küng; Moltmann; Pannenberg; Rahner; Schleiermacher; Tillich**

Glossary: Atonement; Chalcedon; eschatological; enlightenment; immutability; revelation

Major writings

The Epistle to the Romans, trans. E.C. Hoskyns, Oxford: OUP, 1933
Church Dogmatics, trans. T.F. Torrance, G. Bromiley, *et al.*, Edinburgh: T & T Clark, 1936–68.
Anselm: Fides Quaerens Intellectum, trans. I.W. Robertson, London: SCM, 1960
The Humanity of God, Richmond, VA: John Knox Press, 1960
Protestant Theology in the 19th Century, trans. B. Cozens and J. Bowden: London: SCM Press, 2001

Further reading

Hans Urs von Balthasar, *The Theology of Karl Barth*, trans. John Drury, New York: Holt, Rinehart & Winston, 1971

T. Gorringe, *Karl Barth: against hegemony*, Oxford: OUP, 1999

G. Hunsinger, *How to Read Karl Barth*, Oxford: OUP, 1991

G. Hunsinger, *Disruptive Grace Studies in the Theology of Karl Barth*, Grand Rapids, MI and Cambridge: W.B. Eerdmans, c.2000

E. Jüngel, *Karl Barth, a Theological Legacy*, Philadelphia: Westminster Press, 1986

B.L. McCormack, *Karl Barth's Critically Realistic Dialectical Theology: its genesis and development, 1909–1936*, Oxford: Clarendon Press, 1995

J. Webster (ed.), *The Cambridge Companion to Karl Barth*, Cambridge: CUP, 2000

BOETHIUS, ANICIUS MANLIUS TORQUATUS SEVERINUS (c.480– c.525)

Undoubtedly one of the greatest scholars in the period between **Augustine** and **Aquinas**, Boethius was a tragic figure. There is uncertainty about the dating of events in his life. He was probably born around 480 in Rome and died in 525 or 526. Born into an ancient noble family, the son of a consul, after the death of his father Boethius was taken into the family of another immensely powerful family, that of Quintus Aurelius Memmius Symmachus. He was highly educated, able to read Greek, and may have studied in Athens. His talents were prodigious, stretching to mathematics and musical theory, logic and philosophy. He became consul in 510, and his two sons were consuls in 522. In that year (522) he himself achieved the high civil service rank of Master of the Offices to King Theoderic. However, within a short time he was in prison, under sentence of death for high treason. The charge: that he plotted to restore 'Roman liberty' and that he practised astrology, which was sacrilege. While imprisoned he wrote, over a period of months, his famous work *The Consolation of Philosophy*, in which he argued the complete injustice of his fate. There is no overt reference to the Christian faith in this work, and since Boethius was facing almost certain death some have questioned his allegiance to it. It seems clear however that he opposed corruption in the state at every level, thereby making himself enemies – when he defended a senator, Albinus, who was accused of treason on behalf of the Eastern Emperor Justin, Boethius was implicated in the scandal and condemned, unheard, with Albinus. It is said also that he was tortured before execution. How could this have happened? By 522 Theoderic was deeply embroiled in political problems which divided Goths and Romans, Christians and non-Christians, Catholics and Arians (see

Arius; Athanasius). Although an Arian, Theoderic ruled his Catholic subjects for three decades with no great difficulty. But there was always the possibility of renewed instability. It has been suggested that the Emperor Justin may have deliberately sacrificed Boethius, Albinus and also Symmachus for long-term political gain. Boethius was clearly not a pragmatic politician.

Boethius produced important translations of the work of Aristotle, especially the work on logic, and translated Porphyry's introduction to the philosopher. He also produced philosophical commentaries on Aristotle and on Cicero. He wrote his own studies of music and arithmetic. Although he wrote five short pieces on Christian doctrine, because of a lack of overt reference to the Christian faith in his *Consolation* some have doubted the authenticity of his authorship of these works. However, scholars have shown that Boethius was steeped in the thought of Augustine and that there are many similarities between his philosophical and doctrinal work, and thus have concluded there is nothing incompatible with Boethius having written both.

These short pieces on Christian doctrine deal with the unity of the **Trinity** (conceived in broadly Augustinian terms), the consubstantiality of Father, Son and Holy Spirit (see **homoousion**), the importance of Substance, and the Catholic Faith, and include a work against Eutyches and Nestorius. In this work Boethius defends the **Chalcedonian** 'two natures in one person' account of Christ. His work *On Catholic Faith* gives a short and precise account of Augustine's doctrine of redemption, stressing the uniqueness of the Christian gospel as a challenge to the philosopher. He is perhaps most known for his famous definition of a person – 'a person is the individual substance of a rational nature'.

In his *Consolation* Boethius developed a somewhat austere understanding of God as the ultimately unknown mystery, drawing heavily on Aristotle. This inheritance enabled him to make an influential contribution to thought about God's nature and action – notably in the issues of free will and **universals**. God foresees the free acts of the free will, but this does not destroy their freedom and contingency, for foreknowledge of an act does not imply the necessitation of an act. God sees all things concurrently and eternally, even though they take place through the succession of time in the created world. Boethius draws too on Augustine and Plato in developing an argument for the existence of God as the supreme good, beyond the varying degrees of goodness in human beings. This concept of God, than whom nothing

BOETHIUS, ANICIUS MANLIUS TORQUATUS SEVERINUS

better can be conceived, was to be taken up in **Anselm**'s famous ontological argument.

From Aristotle too came Boethius' solution to the problem of universals, raised in his commentary on Porphyry's *Isagoge*: the universal subsists in material things, although it is itself immaterial. This neat judgement between Aristotle's and Plato's accounts of universals was influential both for eucharistic controversy and the later twelfth-century debate on theological method. For Boethius too, however, there was an indispensable connection between theory and practice. It has been argued that it was precisely his awareness of this connection that probably drove him to strive after the greatest possible formal precision.

In Book One of *Consolation* Boethius is composing mournful verse when a vision of the lady Philosophy appears, to guide him in his hour of need. 'Then was the dark night dispelled, the shadows fell away, and my eyes received returning power as before ... he who has calmly reconciled his life to fate, and set proud death beneath his feet, can look fortune in the face, unbending to good and bad.'

Book Two brings on Rhetoric, to persuade him not to let his happiness depend on anything that Fortune can give or take away. 'Nothing is to be sought in her, and it is plain she has no innate good, for she is not always joined with good men, nor does she make good those with whom she is joined.'

Book Three then raises the issue of the nature of the Supreme Good. God is the supreme good. 'Have we not shown that complete satisfaction exists in true happiness, and we have agreed that God is happiness itself, have we not?'

Why then, asks Book Four, do the wicked flourish – Job's question? Good and bad deeds will produce their own eternal rewards. 'A man who lacks good cannot justly be described as a good man; therefore we may say that good habits never miss their rewards. As honesty itself is the reward of the honest, so wickedness is itself the punishment of the wicked.'

Book Five asks whether, then, there is such a thing as Chance. All is under the providence of God, and man must live remembering that he is always in the presence of God. 'Hopes are not put vainly in God, nor prayers in vain offered: if these are right, they cannot but be answered.'

Throughout the work there is stress on the unreality of earthly greatness, and the superiority of things of the mind. There is no overt reference to Christianity – perhaps at this point Boethius wished to distract himself with pure philosophy; we simply do not know.

Boethius' *Consolation* was one of the most influential books of the Middle Ages. It was translated into Old German and Anglo-Saxon, and influenced a range of writers from Chaucer to Dante. His specifically Christian writings and the themes raised therein were to be much discussed and commented upon by Aquinas and others during the later Middle Ages. Boethius was executed by an Arian King and this has resulted in his veneration as a martyr saint of the Catholic church – St Severinus.

See also: **Anselm; Aquinas; Arius; Athanasius; Augustine**

Glossary: **Chalcedonian; Trinity; universals**

Major writings

The Consolation of Philosophy, trans. with intro. and explanatory notes by P.G. Walsh, Oxford: OUP, 2000

Further reading

Henry Chadwick, *Boethius: the consolations of music, logic, theology, and philosophy*, Oxford: Clarendon Press, 1981

Margaret Gibson (ed.), *Boethius: his life, thought and influence*, Oxford: Blackwell, 1981

John Marenbon, *Boethius*, Oxford and New York: OUP, 2003

BONHOEFFER, DIETRICH (1906–45)

A German Lutheran theologian who became actively involved in the German Resistance movement against Hitler during the Second World War and who was hanged for high treason during the closing months of that war. Bonhoeffer was born into an affluent and privileged upper middle-class family in Breslau on 4 February 1906. His father Karl was a successful neurologist who became Professor of Psychiatry at the University of Berlin, moving the family there in 1912 to take up his new post. Cultured and sophisticated, the Bonhoeffer family was not particularly religious in terms of their diligent attendance to Christian worship, but they shared in the general German middle-class identification with its cultural Protestant heritage. Despite the family's fairly nominal allegiance to the Christian faith there had been a number of notable theologians and ministers in the family history. On his mother's side Bonhoeffer could boast of having as a great-grandfather one Karl August Van Hase, a prominent Church historian of the previous century, as well as a grandfather who had been chaplain to the emperor. However, despite this notable family lineage there was still much dismay at the young Bonhoeffer's decision to pursue a religious career, with his elder brothers in particular viewing the Church as a backward, bourgeois and stuffy institution.

Bonhoeffer, however, was not to be dissuaded, and at the age of 17 he went to Tübingen to begin his study of theology. In 1924 he returned to Berlin to study under some of the leading figures of German liberal theology, including Adolf von **Harnack**, Reinhold Seeberg and Adolf Schlatter. Under the guidance of Seeberg, Bonhoeffer completed his doctoral dissertation entitled *Sanctorum Communio* in 1927. He was aged just 21. Bonhoeffer then had a short break from purely academic studies when he served as curate to a German-speaking congregation in Barcelona. However, he returned to Berlin in 1929 to begin work on his habilitation thesis (a second higher postdoctoral thesis) *Act and Being* (finished in 1931); in the traditional German manner, this was intended to pave the way towards an academic career. His thesis was accepted and the young Bonhoeffer had obviously greatly impressed his eminent teachers as he was invited to join the faculty at Berlin. Before taking up his post as lecturer, however, Bonhoeffer went to Union Theological Seminary in New York in 1930 for a period of postdoctoral study. Here he was influenced through the friendship and teaching of Reinhold **Niebuhr** to take seriously the demand to relate the gospel to the needs of the poor in the form of social action. Student friends also took the young Bonhoeffer to witness the conditions of black Americans in nearby Harlem. Bonhoeffer visited and worshipped in the black churches on a regular basis and in the spring of 1931 taught Sunday school at the Abyssinian Baptist church in Harlem. The one disappointing feature of this visit to America, according to Bonhoeffer, was his perception that American students lacked any interest in rigorous academic theology and were satisfied with what he described as a very 'thin' theology.

Bonhoeffer returned to Berlin in 1931 and immediately began teaching. The content of some of his lecture courses has been preserved in the posthumous publications *Creation and Fall* (1960) and *Christology* (1966). Back in Germany the young Bonhoeffer was to forge links that were to prove decisive for his future activity as a member of the Resistance when he became increasingly involved in the emerging *ecumenical* movement as a regional secretary for the youth commission of the World Alliance for Promoting International Friendship through the Churches. During this period Bonhoeffer was becoming increasingly attracted to, but not entirely uncritical of, the new approach to theology emanating from the pen of Karl **Barth**.

Ominous events were, of course, taking shape elsewhere and the early 1930s saw the rise to power of the Nazi party and the consolidation of that power in Hitler's appointment as Chancellor of Germany in 1933. Bonhoeffer, who had already begun publicly to oppose the prevailing Nazi philosophy, started to feel increasingly disenchanted with the response of the churches and gave up academic teaching in October 1933 to travel to London where he became pastor to two German-speaking congregations. Bonhoeffer's presence in London at this time brought a stinging rebuke from Barth who strongly urged him to return as the 'house of your [Bonhoeffer's] church is on fire'. However, this period was significant in that Bonhoeffer renewed his friendship with the Bishop of Chichester, G.K.A. Bell, who was to be a key conduit of information between Bonhoeffer, representing the Resistance movement in Germany, and the Allied political leadership. Bonhoeffer's presence in London meant that he was not present at the founding of the Confessing Church in Barmen in 1934. The Confessing Church comprised those groups of German evangelical Christians who opposed the Nazi-sponsored 'German-Christian' movement which attempted to co-opt the churches of Germany into the state-sponsored programme of Nazi pro-Aryan propaganda. They produced the famous Barmen Declaration (1934) which proclaimed the sole Lordship of Christ over the Church and insisted upon the freedom of the gospel from all outside interference. However, a year earlier, in his drafting of the *Bethel Confession*, Bonhoeffer had already articulated some of the key theological responses and insights that were to form the basis of the Confessing Church's resistance to Hitler. In particular, he questioned the Nazi teaching that the Jews had been replaced in God's divine plan of election by a new master race.

Bonhoeffer could not stay disengaged from the situation in Germany forever and he returned in 1935 at the behest of the Confessing Church to lead an illegal and underground seminary eventually based at Finkenwalde, the purpose of which was to train ministers for the Confessing Church. The residents of this seminary came under strong suspicion from the Gestapo and were ceaselessly harassed until the seminary was eventually forced to close with all its members being called up to some form of military service. This was no period of seclusion in a cloistered community and Bonhoeffer remained engaged with the struggle against the claims of the Nazi party. He utilised his contacts with the ecumenical movement to make the worldwide church more aware of the crisis in Germany, even going so far as to refuse to participate in a conference if the German

Christians were allowed to send a representative alongside that of the Confessing Church. He also continued to speak out on the 'Jewish Question' and was involved during some of his trips in the smuggling of Jews into Switzerland. Bonhoeffer's major writings during this period were *The Cost of Discipleship* (1937) and *Life Together* (1939). It was also during his time at Finkenwalde that Bonhoeffer met Maria von Wedemeyer, to whom he would later become engaged.

As war clouds gathered over Europe in 1939 Bonhoeffer left Germany for America. He seems to have been particularly disillusioned by the lack of response of church leaders to the events of a year earlier, when, in the horrific happenings of 'Crystal Night', thousands of Jewish shops and synagogues were attacked throughout Germany and many Jews were arrested and taken to concentration camps. This was followed by the failure of the Church, including ministers of the Confessing Church, to speak out when, on the occasion of Hitler's fiftieth birthday, the Minister for Church affairs called upon all German pastors to swear an oath of unswerving loyalty to Hitler. Many in fact complied. Disillusioned and worried Bonhoeffer left Germany for America but had no sooner arrived than he realised that he was making a terrible mistake. In a letter to Niebuhr he explained his decision to return to Germany, saying: 'I will have no right to participate in the reconstruction of Christian life in Germany after the war if I do not share the trials of this time with my people'.

On his return, through family contacts, he gained a post in military counter-intelligence (the Abwehr) and thus was introduced to some of the central figures in the German Resistance movement such as Admiral Canaris and General Oster. Bonhoeffer at this point effectively became a double agent as the Abwehr explained his usefulness to the Gestapo (and thus secured permission for his travels abroad) by arguing that through his ecumenical contacts Bonhoeffer could secure vital intelligence from the Allied countries. In fact, through these contacts Bonhoeffer was able to communicate the intentions and hopes of the Resistance movement within Germany to the outside world. Increasingly Bonhoeffer was being drawn into a dangerous and compromised position as he eventually came to see the need to assassinate Hitler. However, the Gestapo became aware of the Resistance's plans to kill the German leader and Bonhoeffer was arrested on 5 April 1943 and sent to Tegel prison near Berlin. He was never to be a free man again. The later attempt on Hitler's life served only to redouble the efforts of the Gestapo to incriminate the conspirators and eventually damning evidence was found linking Bonhoeffer and his friends directly with the attempt on Hitler's life. In the closing months of the war Bonhoeffer was taken first to Buchenwald concentration camp and then finally to Flossenbürg, always keeping just one step ahead of the advancing Allied forces. After a cursory trial the conspirators were convicted of high treason and Bonhoeffer was hanged on the 'grey dawn of Monday' (9 April 1945).

It was during his time as a prisoner in Tegel that Bonhoeffer wrote and reflected upon the nature of Christian faith in the modern world. His thoughts were put down in letter and note form which he managed to smuggle out to friends and relatives. These moving and often profound documents, although admittedly fragmented and often underdeveloped, are combined in *Letters and Papers from Prison* to make a work shot through with rich and suggestive insights that have earned them their rightful place as one of the classic religious documents of the twentieth century – the musings of a martyr for the faith.

In *Letters* (1953) Bonhoeffer made tantalising suggestions as to a new direction for theology in a world which had come of age. Writing to his friend Eberhard Bethge he asked:

> What is bothering me incessantly is the question what Christianity really is, or indeed who Christ really is for us today? The time when people could be told everything by means of words, whether theological or pious, is over, and so is the time of inwardness and conscience – and that means the time of religion in general. We are moving towards a completely religionless time; people as they are simply cannot be religious any more.
>
> [. . .] How can Christ become the Lord of the religionless as well? Are there religionless Christians? . . . then what is religionless Christianity? Barth, who is the only one to have started along this line of thought, did not carry it to completion, but arrived at a positivism of revelation which in the last analysis is essentially a restoration. For the religionless working man (or any other man) nothing decisive is gained here. The questions to be answered would surely be: What do a church, a community, a sermon, a liturgy, and a Christian life mean in a religionless world?
>
> [. . .] How do we speak (or perhaps we cannot now even 'speak' as we used to) in a 'secular' way about 'God'? In what way are we the ecclesia, those who are called forth, not regarding ourselves from a religious point of view as specially favoured, but rather as belonging wholly to the world? In that

case Christ is no longer an object of religion, but something quite different, really the Lord of the world. But what does that mean? What is the place of worship and prayer in a religionless situation?[i]

These and other remarks remain in an undeveloped form and we do not know in what direction Bonhoeffer himself would have taken them had he lived. But he was certainly calling for something new to deal with the sheer scope of the crisis facing Western culture. Human beings now had to live 'as though God were not there'. Bonhoeffer was searching for a secular or worldly interpretation of key biblical concepts such as repentance, faith, *justification* and *sanctification*, but was unable under the circumstances (and might never have been able despite his best intentions) to complete them for himself.

What seems clear is that Bonhoeffer (in common with the earlier works of Barth) was rejecting any attempt to ground or locate talk of God in religious interiority, in human weakness or in a God who was simply called in to explain the gaps in human knowledge. Along with Barth, **Bultmann** and neo-orthodox theologians in general, Bonhoeffer resisted any attempt to establish a neutral point of contact between God and humanity in some innate human religious capacity. However, neither could he accept either the sheer 'positivism' of Barth's account of *revelation* which seemed to empty human time and history of any real meaning.

In contrast with Barth, Bonhoeffer focused upon what he termed the 'world come of age', by which he meant the maturity of the secular world in its ability to give an account of itself without reference to God. This 'world come of age' had no recourse to God as a cipher for filling in blanks in its self-understanding. Instead, Bonhoeffer argued that:

> God is no stop-gap; he must be recognised at the centre of life, not when we are at the end of our resources; it is his will to be recognized in life, and not only when death comes; in health and vigour, and not only in suffering; in our activities, and not only in sin. The ground for this lies in the revelation of God in Jesus Christ.[ii]

Paradoxically, this banishment of God by the movement towards autonomy in the world's self-understanding was mirrored, according to Bonhoeffer, in the life of Christ who 'allows himself to be edged out of the world and onto the cross'. The abandonment of God and the religionlessness of human beings is paralleled by the humiliation and forsakeness of Christ. Thus the starting point of the secular non-religious interpretation of the Bible is to take with utmost seriousness John 1:14, 'The Word became flesh and dwelt among us'. Only by focusing upon the humiliated Christ can we properly reject as false a human religiosity that focuses upon God as an all-powerful figure whom we invoke to meet our needs (*deus ex machina*). This is the sharp point of contrast between Christian faith and all other forms of religion. True Christian faith points towards the impotence and the suffering of God, knowing that 'Only the suffering God can help'.

Radical as such suggestions might look it is now conceded by most scholars that they share a deep structural continuity with Bonhoeffer's earlier thought. The continuity is found in the concentration upon the person of Christ. 'Who is Christ for us today?' is a central theme that runs through all of Bonhoeffer's writings. His early Berlin lectures on Christology (which we have only in the form of notes made by students in the class and even these are incomplete) ask the same question and refuse to place the 'how' of the incarnation before the question 'who is Christ for us today?'. This Christ is the humiliated Christ, the crucified Christ who is the man for others. Bonhoeffer stresses the complete humanity of Jesus and the hiddenness of God's presence in him.

> That means that the form of the scandal is the very one which makes belief in Christ possible. In other words, the form of the humiliation is the form of the *Christus pro nobis* ... There is only faith where a man so surrenders himself to the humiliated God-man as to stake his life on him, even when this seems against all sense. Faith is where the attempt to have security from something visible is rejected.[iii]

Bonhoeffer's stress begins to become clear, and it is that God himself has undergone our abandonment by God in the world and has taken it upon himself. As God entered the world and suffered in it, so Christians should not attempt to live in a separate 'religious sphere', but are to enter into the world as Christ did and to live for others. In so doing they will encounter the transcendent God, not in the sense of having a 'religious relationship with God', but precisely in this living for others. To encounter God in this way is to know God as 'the beyond in the midst of life'. In this 'living for others' we will become fully human, which is what Christianity actually seeks to make us as opposed to making us religious.

> To be a Christian does not mean to be religious in a particular way ... but to be a man – not a type of man, but the man that Christ creates in us. It is not the religious act that makes the Christian, but participation in the sufferings of God in the secular life ... Jesus calls men, not to a new religion, but to life.[iv]

With this stress upon true Christian discipleship as comprising living wholly for others and thus becoming truly and fully human, it is easy to see why Bonhoeffer was a source of inspiration to the secular theologies that were so prominent in the 1960s. The reasons for this are partly accidental, in that it was *Letters and Papers from Prison* that first brought Bonhoeffer to the attention of English and American theologians. The brief and suggestive fragments were originally interpreted without reference to the larger corpus of his works and thus Bonhoeffer was used to justify positions that he almost certainly would never have espoused. Thus, in the writings of others, phrases such as 'religionless Christianity' became popular slogans that lost the vital connection to the humiliation of Christ on the cross that Bonhoeffer was so keen to stress. Similarly, the 'death of God' was pronounced and the 'coming of age of the world' was celebrated in the abandonment of any form of religious or spiritual discipline, something that is hard to square with Bonhoeffer's thought as expressed in *Life Together* where he sought to describe how Christian faith might be concretely expressed in community.

Gradually, as Bonhoeffer's work has been collected and translated, the deep continuities of Bonhoeffer's earlier and later writings have become more and more apparent and the underlying link is fundamentally Christological. As early as his first doctoral thesis, *Sanctorum Communio*, Bonhoeffer had defined the Church as 'Christ existing in community'. In his later *Ethics* (1955) he repeats that 'The Church is nothing but the part of humanity in which Christ has really taken form'. This strongly concrete understanding of the nature of the Church and its importance for Christian discipleship in the world has meant that Bonhoeffer continues to be a rich resource for contemporary political and *liberationist* theologies.

One of Bonhoeffer's most famous contrasts is the contrast between 'cheap grace' and 'costly grace' which is developed in *The Cost of*

Discipleship. This attempt to resolve the famous Lutheran dilemma (see **Luther**) over the relationship of grace to law attempts to do so by linking belief integrally with the practice of obedience. Focusing upon Jesus' teaching in the Sermon on the Mount, Bonhoeffer attempts to show the extraordinary and radical nature of Christian discipleship in the demands that it places on the believer. This demand is severe in that the call to follow is to follow in the way of the cross, but this is the only way to true joy and peace. True discipleship is the type of discipleship that leads the Christian back into the world following in the footsteps of Christ. It is a discipleship that remembers that salvation is costly and demands obedience and discipline. Cheap grace on the other hand 'is the preaching of forgiveness without requiring repentance, baptism without Church discipline, communion without confession, absolution without contrition'.[v] Cheap grace is universalised grace, a grace that is automatically accessible to human beings. Bonhoeffer will not allow a 'cheap' form of grace that lessens the demand to follow Christ in absolute obedience. As such this work is (as it was almost certainly intended to be in the context of the times in which it was written) a powerful refutation of all other claims to absolute obedience in the name of the call of Christ who is the 'One beyond any Other'.

Bonhoeffer's other major work, *Ethics*, is also a fragmentary and unfinished collection published after his death. Here again Bonhoeffer seeks to engage profoundly with what it means to follow the path of Christ in the world. The Christian cannot wholly reject the world, which is a penultimate reality, but neither can s/he completely sanction it either. Bonhoeffer had a profound distaste for a false Christian piousness which minimised the proper enjoyment of God's created order and he sought to redefine the relationship between Christianity and the world, not as two opposing spheres, but as one single reality unified in the figure of the incarnate Christ. The whole world is therefore related to Christ and the Christian is called to engage in this penultimate reality, to engage in the life of the world, as it is infused and given meaning by the ultimate reality that is God. Bonhoeffer attempted to rethink the four traditional Lutheran mandates (he rejected the nomenclature 'orders of creation') of work, marriage, government and church in terms of this revelational reality of Jesus Christ. Thus Christian service in the world is itself 'participation in the encounter of Christ with the world'. The implication of the rejection of two spheres of reality is that there is no secular reality outside the reality of Jesus Christ and thus the Church's mission cannot be to exist for its own sake but to live as Christ himself lived for the sake of the world.

Bonhoeffer died at the age of 39 and we have no real idea what the mature theologian might have made of some of the radical suggestions of his wartime musings. Would the radical and religionless Bonhoeffer have moved back in the direction of the more conservative Bonhoeffer of *The Cost of Discipleship* and *Life Together*? Hopefully, we have managed to show that such a sharp polarity between the two Bonhoeffers is ultimately mistaken and that the underlying general trend of his thought can be clearly discerned. It is to be regretted that Bonhoeffer became associated with the type of glib optimism concerning the human condition that was so much a feature of the secular theologies of the 1960s. Works such as John Robinson's *Honest to God* and Harvey Cox's *The Secular City* might have served to introduce Bonhoeffer's thought to a wider, non-specialist audience but only at the expense of considerable distortion. It has become increasingly clear that Bonhoeffer's critique of religion has its roots in a much more profoundly theological critique of the equation of gospel and culture that was so prominent a feature of nineteenth-century liberal theology. It is also clear that his Christological focus upon the suffering of God and the centrality of the cross for Christian faith was to become a dominant (if not *the* dominant) theme of late twentieth-century theology as it sought to come to terms with the impasse to all theological thinking and believing that is the Holocaust and Hiroshima. One only has to ponder how central these key themes of Bonhoeffer have been to the theology of Jürgen **Moltmann** to realise just how significant his thought remains for today.

Notes

i   *Letter and Papers from Prison*, pp.279–82, various letters to E. Bethge.
ii   *Ibid.*, p.312
iii *Christology*, pp.114/115
iv   *Letters and Papers from Prison*, pp.361–2
v   *The Cost of Discipleship*, 1948, p.38

See also: **Barth; Brunner; Bultmann; Luther; Moltmann; Niebuhr; Harnack**

Glossary: **Ecumenical; justification; liberationist theology; revelation; sanctification**

Major writings

Letter and Papers from Prison, ed. E. Bethge, London: SCM, 1986 (1953)
Life Together, London: Collins, 1954

The Cost of Discipleship, London: SCM (New York: Macmillan, (1948, 1959)
Sanctorum Communio, London: Collins, 1963
No Rusty Swords, London: Collins, 1965
Christology London: Collins, 1966
The Way to Freedom, London: Collins, 1966
Ethics, London: Collins, 1968

Further reading

E. Bethge, *Bonhoeffer, Exile and Martyr*, London: SCM, 1975
J. De Gruchy, *Dietrich Bonhoeffer: Witness to Jesus Christ*, London: Collins, 1988
J. De Gruchy (ed.), *The Cambridge Companion to Dietrich Bonhoeffer*, Cambridge: CUP, 1999
C. Marsh, *Reclaiming Dietrich Bonhoeffer: the promise of his theology*, Oxford: OUP, 1994

BRUNNER, EMIL (1889–1966)

Swiss Reformed theologian and leading member of the early dialectical theology movement along with Karl **Barth**, Rudolf **Bultmann** and Friedrich Gogarten. Brunner was born at Winterhur near Zurich on 23 December 1889. He studied at the University of Zurich and then served as a pastor before returning to Zurich in 1924 as Professor of Systematic and Pastoral Theology.

Although often overshadowed by the figures of Barth and Bultmann, Brunner made his own distinctive contribution to the break with nineteenth-century liberalism that dialectical theology represented. Brunner was as critical as Barth was (and even more critical than **Schleiermacher**) of liberalism's prevailing tendency to assert a continuity between some innate human capacity for religious experience and a genuine knowledge of God.

Brunner tried to be faithful to what he understood to be the classic approach of Reformed theology to the question of *revelation*. He was as convinced as Barth that Christian knowledge of God is dependent upon God's self-revelation and that this self-revelation is given in encounter with Christ. However, in order to give an account of how this revelation operated, Brunner was more willing than Barth to draw upon prevailing philosophical systems to clarify the situation. Thus Brunner drew heavily upon the I–Thou philosophies of Ferdinand Ebner and Martin Buber. These thinkers regarded the I–Thou relationship as fundamental to what it means to be human in the world. Following these thinkers Brunner developed an anthropology which understood human existence as defined and made real by the presence of the Thou – the other before me. Paradigmatically, the Thou before the individual is God.

With respect to a theory of knowledge Brunner utilised this schema to overcome what he believed to be the fatal imprisonment of theology in a subject–object dualism. Consequently, he distinguished between 'I–It' forms of knowledge, which is knowledge of the world of impersonal objects, and 'I–Thou' knowledge, which is knowledge gained from personal encounter. Because the encounter with God is always an encounter between persons, the 'I–It' form of knowledge is never the appropriate way of dealing with knowledge of God. Only the 'I–Thou' form of knowledge is appropriate to the personal encounter between God and the believer.

The problem with much theology (especially philosophical and metaphysical theology) is that it attempts to deal with God as a neutral object in the world and it remains therefore steadfastly in the realm of 'I–It' knowledge. Even biblical theology, for as long as it concentrates upon the objectivity of the 'truths' given as an object of belief, remains within the objective realm of 'I–It' knowledge.

In developing this personalist approach to knowledge Brunner is attempting to overcome the classical subject–object dichotomy that bedevils most attempts to give an account of revelation. God, according to Brunner, does not communicate words about himself, he communicates himself in the act of revelation.

> In his Word God does not deliver me a course of lectures in dogmatic theology, he does not submit to me or interpret for me the content of a confession of faith, but he makes himself accessible to me ... he does not communicate 'something' to me, but 'himself'.[i]

This self-giving of God occurs historically in the event of Jesus Christ and is made a present reality to the believer here and now by the internal witness of the Holy Spirit. This movement in God is matched by a response from the human side as human beings respond in faith and trust to God's gracious encounter. This responsiveness to God is developed by Brunner using the category of 'personal correspondence', which implies that the individual is drawn into a relationship that mirrors God's prior movement of love towards him. This 'personal correspondence' of the individual to God links both knowledge of God and fellowship with God in an overcoming of the subject–object dichotomy, for to know God means to be one with him.

Due to his rejection of 'I–It' forms of knowledge as appropriate forms of knowledge for God, Brunner was driven to reject the idea that the words of scripture were themselves inspired or infallible. He was indeed scathingly critical of his more conservative colleagues who taught just this very thing. Scripture and the word about Christ is necessary of course, but it is necessary not because it is itself the revelation of God but because it is an indirect witness to the revelation of God.

Here again Brunner would have argued that he was being faithful to the witness and impetus of the Reformers. For they never simply identified the words on the pages of the Bible as the words of God in a simple and direct fashion, but always appealed to the internal illumination of the Holy Spirit as necessary in making these words the word of God to us.

> The Scripture – first of all the testimony of the Apostles to Christ – is the 'crib wherein Christ lieth' (Luther). It is a 'word' inspired by the Spirit of God; yet at the same time it is a human message; its 'human character' means that it is coloured by the frailty and imperfection of all that is human.[ii]

The Bible then for Brunner is an indispensable source of doctrine and faith as it contains the original apostolic witness to Christ. But the guarantee of its truthworthiness and authority as a source is not bound to the words themselves being infallibly correct, but in the present activity of the Spirit in witnessing to Christ through them.

In 1934 Brunner explicitly distanced himself from Barth's position on the question of natural theology with the publication of *Nature and Grace*. Barth had regarded these categories as mutually exclusive and therefore firmly rejected any concept of a natural knowledge of God. Brunner sought to recover the classical Reformed approach to this matter which he felt delineated a 'proper Christian natural theology'. He appealed to the biblical notion of creation as bearing the imprint of God and thus – as the object of God's creative activity – as a source of revelation. It is true that human beings immediately distort this revelation due to sin, but this does not diminish the fact that the biblical (and classically Reformed) witness is that there is some natural knowledge of God.

Brunner further appealed to the 'image of God' in human beings as the subjective corollary of what was the case in the created order. Brunner argued from the fact that we were created in the 'image of

God' that there is therefore 'a point of contact' for divine grace. He was very careful not to give this point of contact any positive content in and of itself, nor to say that it constituted an independent place from which to begin the religious search after God. This would simply be a repeat of the errors of liberalism. Brunner was quite clear that human beings are fallen and thus the image of God is fatally marred. Nevertheless, we still formally retain the image inasmuch as we remain human beings capable of speech and reason. Brunner contends that only beings so endowed can be described as ethically responsible in any real sense. Only beings who have the powers of speech and reason can have any conception of themselves as sinners. This formal capacity of human beings is the presupposition of revelation in that it is the ability to speak and listen, and thus to possess the capability of being addressed, that is the basis for hearing the divine word of revelation. But this is only a formal bare capacity, a point of contact; the fact that human beings do hear a word of revelation is solely due to the gracious revelatory activity of God.

Despite Brunner's careful qualifications surrounding this bare 'point of contact' it occasioned an immediate and resounding No! from the pen of Barth that was heard around the world. So sharp was Barth's reply that contact between the two theologians was formally broken off until Brunner's final illness. It would be true to say that Brunner never really recovered and was from then on constantly attempting to justify his position in relation to Barth's criticisms.

Today, many commentators feel that Brunner was contending for something that is vitally important to theology. Although he may have lost the battle in the crisis of those times, it is increasingly recognised that he probably had the truer insights into the matter. The sharpness of Barth's response (though not unusual for him) was partly due to the situation he confronted in Germany and his belief that Brunner's bare point of contact negated the gospel of grace. In his later writings Barth was to acknowledge that he had not paid sufficient attention to the human dimension of the faith. But this was only after he had been phenomenally successful in changing the direction of theology so that the whole of human existence – fallen and redeemed – was viewed from a Christological perspective. With this safeguard achieved he was quite capable of speaking insightfully about the human reception of faith and the practice of Christian life in the world.

A year after the Nature and Grace controversy Brunner published a full-scale theological anthropology entitled *Man in Revolt*. Again the concept of 'I–Thou' relationships is utilised to illuminate what it means to be human. For it is only in the context of a relationship with another person – with a Thou – that I can know myself as a person. The individual has thus to live in responsibility before this other – this Thou – and 'true responsibility is the same as true humanity'. Brunner distinguishes between the 'true man', who has his origin in the word of God, and the 'real man', who also has his origin in the word of God, but who denies it and is thus 'man in revolt'. Brunner portrays man in revolt as being caught in an inevitable contradiction that marks his entire existence. Man lives in rebellion but even this rebellion points to the God against whom he is rebelling. Everywhere he looks man finds evidence of his dislocation from God and the consequent distortion of his existence. The very idea of God, the perfection for which he longs, the moral consciousness which stands before him, the striving after truth, all point to man's origin in God but also at the same time to his perverted denial of God. Only by faith in the revelation of God given in Jesus Christ can man win back his true human nature.

Brunner was contending for this bare point of contact in the light of his commitment to what he termed 'eristic theology'. This approach was marked by strongly apologetic concerns in its attempts to engage with those inside and outside the Church. By calling his approach an 'eristic theology' Brunner wanted to stress the importance of debating with contemporary philosophy and social thought in order to expose its weak points and to show how effectively the gospel meets those deficiencies. Brunner's later works such as *Truth as Encounter* and his three-volume *Dogmatics* are further attempts to carry out this programme by overcoming the subject–object dualism so predominant in Western thought.

Since his death Brunner's theology has gone into a virtual eclipse. He is now largely referred to simply as a footnote in the development of dialectical theology or as a useful foil in explaining Barth's rejection of natural theology. This was not always so; Brunner received a far earlier and far wider reception in the English-speaking world than Barth. However, he has since suffered considerably in comparison with Barth who is generally thought to be more creative, more radical and more insightful. All this may be true but it is to be hoped that Brunner's more open and apologetic style, along with his avowal of certain key themes of Reformed theology that Barth may have too readily neglected, will one day merit a return to prominence for this important thinker.

Notes

i   Brunner, *The Misunderstanding of the Church*, London: Lutterworth Press, 1953, p.1
ii   *Dogmatics, The Christian Doctrine of God*, Vol. 1, p.34

See also: **Barth; Bultmann; Luther**

Glossary: **Revelation**

Major writings

The Mediator, trans. O. Wyon, London: Lutterworth Press, 1952 (1934)
The Divine Imperative, trans. O. Wyon, London: Lutterworth Press, 1949 (1937)
Man in Revolt, trans. O. Wyon, London: Lutterworth Press, 1962 (1939)
Christianity and Civilisation, 2 vols, London: Nisbet & Co., 1948
Dogmatics, The Christian Doctrine of God, Vols 1–3, London: Lutterworth Press, 1949, 1952, 1962
The Scandal of Christianity, London: SCM, 1951

Further reading

J.E. Humphrey, *Emil Brunner: makers of the modern theological mind*, Waco, TX, 1977
C.W. Kegley (ed.), *The Theology of Emil Brunner. The Library of Living Theology*, vol. 3, New York and London: Macmillan Co., 1962
Mark G. McKim, *Emil Brunner: a bibliography*, London: Scarecrow Press, 1996
Paul G. Schrotenboer, *A New Apologetics: an analysis and appraisal of the eristic theology of Emil Brunner*, Kok Pharos: Kampen, 1955

BULTMANN, RUDOLF (1884–1976)

Rudolf Bultmann was born in Wiefelstedt in Germany in 1884. He studied in Marburg and was a professor in Marburg from 1921 to 1951. To some extent he is someone who could be viewed as having lived the quiet life of an intellectual scholar spending most of his adult life in Marburg. He was, however, a member of the Confessing Church (see **Barth**) during the Nazi period and he lost a brother in the concentration camps of Germany and another in the battlefields of the First World War. In other words he was not untroubled by the catastrophic events of this century. Moreover, he is generally regarded as one of the greatest – if perhaps one of the most radical – New Testament scholars of his generation. His views were to spark controversy and excitement in equal measure and he continues to be a much debated thinker.

His first major book on *The History of the Synoptic Tradition* (1921) took up the work of Johannes Weiss in demonstrating that the synoptic tradition (the gospels of Mark, Luke and Matthew) represented the thoughts, beliefs and interests of the early Christian communities rather than being accurate records of the entire original and authentic words of Jesus himself. At this time Bultmann was allied with Karl Barth in his attack on the form of liberal Christianity that had dominated German theology throughout the nineteenth century. This liberal theology (with its focus on the personality of the Jesus of history and a stress upon the teaching and example of Jesus who taught a simple gospel about the Fatherhood of God and the brotherhood of men and the universal value of the human soul) had, in the opinion of Bultmann and others, downplayed the radical otherness of Jesus as an *eschatological* prophet who challenged our religious and moral categories with the demand of God. Bultmann countered this rather cosy and comforting portrayal of Jesus in his ground breaking book *Jesus* (1926)

Perhaps his most famous large scale work was his *Commentary on the Fourth Gospel* (1941), in which he analysed the central concepts of the gospel in relation to the current religious culture, showing similarities to Gnostic and other belief systems. (The Gnostics were a contemporary and parallel, if inchoate, religious movement to early Christianity which laid special emphasis upon secret and esoteric knowledge (Gnosis) about God as the path to salvation. The beliefs that they held are not fully known nor were they fully systematised but are generally held to include something like the following: The material world is evil and a prison to the fallen human soul. Human beings are akin to the divine and are in effect a spark of heavenly light imprisoned in a material body. Possession of this knowledge and perhaps of secret formulas enables the individual to traverse through the many heavenly levels of reality back to the divine. (See **Irenaeus** and **Tertullian** for more.) Bultmann believed that some of these Gnostic ideas and in particular what he termed the 'Gnostic redeemer myth' had influenced the early development of Christian accounts of Christ. At the same time, partly through the influence of the philosopher Heidegger, with whom he conducted joint seminars in the twenties, Bultmann developed his own '*existential*' interpretation of Christianity, which is also expressed powerfully in the Johannine commentary. An 'existential' interpretation of the gospel message means interpreting the text in terms of the possibilities and decisions inherent in human existence in the world. This existential stress continues an emphasis begun in *Jesus*. Whereas liberal theology had focused upon the personality and words of Jesus, Bultmann's existential theology was less interested in trying to penetrate the personality of the historical Jesus than it was in allowing his message to meet us with the question of how we are to interpret our own existence before the demand of God today.

Bultmann's thoughts on the relation of gospel to myth found formal expression in his 1943 essay on 'The New Testament and Mythology'. This was to create strains with former allies, notably Barth and his followers in the Confessing Church, because it appeared to undermine their view of *revelation* through the biblical Word. Yet **Bonhoeffer** for example welcomed the essay as a liberation. Bultmann shared Barth's concern for a theology of the Word. (The Word here primarily refers to Christ as the Word of God who is present in the Bible and the proclamation of the Church.) However, unlike Barth, Bultmann was a New Testament scholar and an advocate of the historical critical method of interpreting the scriptures. Whereas Barth preferred to indulge in a theological exegesis of the biblical texts, only rarely referring to matters such as the sources behind the texts, or the cultural influences upon the text, Bultmann, as a professional historical scholar, was much more attentive to such matters. For both men the message of the gospel and the scandal of the cross was an offence to modern minds (indeed an offence to all forms of human religiosity over time – *á la* the apostle **Paul**). But for Bultmann it was clear that modern people must be presented with the authentic scandal of the gospel message, and not simply a scandal of interpretation due to the fact that the gospel was inevitably conveyed within and through the concepts of an ancient culture. Such concepts, Bultmann believed, were no longer meaningful for people in the then twentieth century and thus he wanted to reinterpret the gospel accounts of a world where heaven was just beyond the clouds and hell just below the ground, a world where demons were the cause of illness and disease – all this was myth and had to be reinterpreted. It is important to realise that Bultmann did not simply wish to jettison the ancient thought forms. It was necessary first to demythologise them, in order to understand their true message, then to remythologise them, in order to bring the biblical passages to bear on contemporary issues. Bultmann stressed the Word as much as Barth, but in a different form. Through the act of preaching the Word becomes a Christ-event (an encounter with the risen Christ in the act of faith), which calls us to faith and creates the faith to which we are invited.

Bultmann was to be much criticised. His extremely radical position that we had virtually none of the original sayings of Jesus combined with his desire to reinterpret the mythical elements of the New Testament world-view were simply too far-reaching for many to accept. He was denounced in some Church circles as a heretic. His existential philosophy – with its stress upon the importance of individual decision in the face of the gospel – was attacked as inadequate. Perversely, from other perspectives he was attacked as not going far enough and not being sufficiently faithful to the radical impact of his basic insights. For instance, Bultmann remained focused upon Christ and his death and resurrection as the central event of God's saving action towards the world. But this keeps his approach wholly within the realm of Christology and the Christian scriptures. But, it was asked, isn't the notion of a Christ or Messiah itself a mythical concept that requires reinterpretation?

We might sum up the main themes of Bultmann's programme like this. Nineteenth century scholarship had interested itself in the self-consciousness, the personality of Jesus. About this we know next to nothing, This did not interest the gospel writers and need not interest us. What matters are Jesus' words and actions, and his purposes within the concrete situation in which he lived. Jesus' words tell us how he understood himself, and approached the world as it confronted him. But our life too confronts us with the question of our own self-understanding. Who are we, and what are we doing? Who we are, our very existence, depends on the decisions we take from moment to moment.

Now Jesus too worked in this kind of situation, and his words give us answers to the questions that confront us. When Jesus says 'I am the way and the truth and the life', this shows us how he understood himself. When he says 'forgive one another', this shows how he behaved to others and demands that we should do likewise. We then have an historical encounter with Jesus only when we take his words seriously, as we take his word as the decisive word in our lives. Many people refuse to do this, because obedience is a costly thing. In that we decide to act according to Jesus' will, we decide for the person of Jesus.

Here the critic might well ask whether we can be sure that we have any of the exact words of Jesus, since the material of the gospels was compiled twenty to fifty years after the events. Bultmann suggests that even if the earliest strand of the tradition did not stem from Jesus, this is not decisive. So long as a person takes the words of the gospel tradition seriously, as decisive for his own existence, that is enough for an encounter with the Jesus of history.

It could be asked whether the words themselves need some connection with the actual situation of the earthly Jesus to preserve their meaning. Is the situation of the early Christian community the same as that of Jesus himself? Is Bultmann suggesting that the words and thoughts have an eternal validity quite apart from each concrete situation – as if the questions of existence were the same at all times, and knowledge of one's own existence were without any reference to the situation of the individual. If so, what has become of the historical particularity of the coming of God into history? Is Bultmann's own solution just as abstract and metaphysical as the older classical Christology which he rejects? It would not then be easy to show reasonable grounds for belief that the death of one man 2000 years ago should be of crucial significance for people today without something approaching in effect, if not in intention, the position that the life and death of Jesus are of central importance today because within the particularity of this life there was the presence of God, who is distinguished from creation precisely in his transcendence of the bounds of creaturely finitude.

Bultmann's *Jesus* appeared fairly early in his career and later he was to develop and broaden his position in various directions – both through his work as a New Testament exegete and as a systematic theologian. Central to Bultmann's thought is the category of faith. He wrote the famous article on *pistis* in Kittel's *Woerterbuch*. Faith is a constant theme too in the great commentary on the Fourth Gospel.[i] Faith is true faith when it is without objective security. Although his famous insistence on the non-objectifiability of faith is traced by critics to **Kant**, and criticised as *fideism*, yet it is also firmly in the tradition of **Luther** and central to Christian theology. For a rounded picture of his contribution the rather sceptical posture of some of his critical scholarship must be balanced by the deep piety of his sermons (translated as *This World and Beyond*) especially in the war period, e.g. those given in December 1939.

Bultmann was a member of the Confessing Church circle in the Marburg area, which included Hans von Soden and other theologians. In his sermons and his writings he was a critic of the Nazi government. In particular he was one of twenty-one scholars at the University of Marburg who issued a statement saying that in accordance with the witness of the New Testament both Jewish and Gentile Christians were equally fitted for office in the Church. Attempts were made in the 1930s to support him by international recognition, e.g. in the award of an honorary DD by the University of St Andrews in 1935.

For Karl Barth, Bultmann was much too concerned with man's subjective experience. God's saving act in Christ has been reduced to a secondary position, in being understood primarily as a reflection in the mirror of Christian existence. For Barth the cross and resurrection have an inherent meaning of their own, and are not to be understood primarily in their meaning 'for us'. Faith as an existentialist reinterpretation of a demythologised 'kerygma' or gospel message has no anchorage in actual history, but is a timeless speculation akin to Gnostic speculation. Christology is reduced to anthropology and faith to existentialist speculation.

On the other hand, critics such as the philosopher Karl Jaspers attacked Bultmann's insistence that, although the biblical message needed to be demythologised, it was unique in that it alone witnessed the central saving act of God. For Jaspers this was typical theological exclusiveness. All myths, he insisted, are potential witnesses to transcendence. This process of 'dekerygmatising' was to be taken further by the Swiss theologian Fritz Buri. The centre is a mythological symbol which assists man to realise his own capacity for authentic existence. For Bultmann man has no such innate capacity, but receives it of grace. For Friedrich Gogarten faith was concerned not so much with individual response to the gospel as with working out its implications in secular society, an issue also taken up by Bonhoeffer, who was much impressed by Bultmann's famous essay on demythologising of 1942.

More recently, literary and sociological analysis of the New Testament and its period has questioned many of Bultmann's specific conclusions and proposed new methods of research. But scholarship is always an ongoing process, and theology is greatly indebted to Rudolf Bultmann for giving a huge stimulus to New Testament study.

Note

i   *The Gospel of John*, John 15:1–10, p.412

See also: **Barth; Bonhoeffer; Irenaeus; Luther; Paul; Tertullian**

Glossary: ***Eschatological; existentialist; fideism; revelation***

Major writings

The History of the Synoptic Tradition, Oxford: Blackwell, 1963 (1921)
Jesus and the Word, trans. from 2nd edn by L.P. Smith & E. Huntress Lantero, London and New York: Scribner's Sons, 1935
The Gospel of John: a commentary, trans. G.R. Beasley-Murray, R.W.N. Hoare & J.K. Riches, Oxford: Blackwell, 1971 (1941)
Theology of the New Testament, 2 vols, trans. K. Grobel, London: SCM, 1952–5
Primitive Christianity in its Contemporary Setting, Edinburgh: Fontana, 1956
History and Eschatology, Edinburgh: The University Press, 1957
Jesus Christ and Mythology, New York: Charles Scribner's Sons, 1958

Existence and Faith, London: Meridian Books, 1960
Faith and Understanding, ed. with intro. R.W. Funk, trans. L.P. Smith, London: SCM, 1969

Further reading

D.A.S. Fergusson, *Bultmann*, London: Chapman, 1992
R. Johnson, *Rudolf Bultmann: interpreting faith for the modern era*, London: Collins, 1987
G.J. Jones, *Bultmann, towards a critical theology*, Cambridge: Polity Press, 1991
J. Macquarrie, *An Existentialist Theology: a comparison of Heidegger and Bultmann*, Harmondsworth: Penguin, 1980

CALVIN, JOHN (1509–64)

French Protestant reformer and theologian who gave the emerging Protestant movement its first great systematic theological expression in his *Institutes of the Christian Religion* (1536–59), a work which set the standard for all subsequent Reformed systematic theologies until the modern period.

Calvin was born in the Cathedral city of Noyon, 10 July 1509. His family had recently risen to the rank of the petty bourgeois when Calvin's father became notary and solicitor to the Bishop and Cathedral chapter at Noyon. Calvin's father intended Calvin and his two brothers for the priesthood and he managed to use his influence with the bishop to secure chaplaincies and benefices for them.

In 1523 Calvin was sent to Paris to continue his education in the arts and theology at the university there. It is unlikely that Calvin formally studied theology at any point during his stay in Paris and it is not known if he was taught directly by the great Scottish philosopher and theologian John Mair (Major) who was at the height of his teaching fame in Paris at this time. The direction of Calvin's studies changed abruptly sometime between 1526 and 1528 when Calvin left Paris to begin studying law at the University of Orléans. We do not know the reasons for this abrupt change but his period of study at Orléans and later at the University of Bourges brought him into close contact with humanist philosophy and introduced him to a circle of friends that were sympathetic to the aims and ideals of reform, including some who had already decisively identified themselves with the Reformation such as Pierre Robert and Melchior Wolmar. The humanist approach to texts that Calvin learned during this period was to prove influential for the rest of his life in determining his approach to scripture.

After his father's death in 1531 Calvin returned to Paris to continue his literary studies and it was during this period that he published his first work – a commentary on Seneca's *De Clementia* (1532). The choice of this work reveals Calvin's emerging interest in, and indebtedness to, the humanist tradition as the work is an attempt to improve upon Erasmus' own treatment of this text. It is not clear, however, precisely when Calvin moved from being a humanistically inclined Catholic, with moderate intentions to reform the Church, to being someone who was wholeheartedly identified with the Protestant cause. Calvin is notoriously coy on the question of his conversion, referring to it only once in the preface to his *Commentary on the Psalms* (1537), where he refers to himself as 'someone obstinate in their attachment to the Church of Rome until God made his heart teachable'. It is clear that upon his return to Paris Calvin quickly became part of a 'reform'-minded group gathered around the figure of Nicholas Cop, as he had to flee Paris when Cop's rectorial address to the University of Paris on All Saints Day 1533 provoked a vigorous reaction from the authorities. Thus Calvin began a period of peripatetic wandering. He returned to Noyon in 1534 to resign his ecclesiastical benefices and this date is usually taken as the limiting date for Calvin's conversion and final break with Rome.

Eventually returning to Paris Calvin was forced to flee again in 1534 when the French authorities initiated a fresh bout of persecution of those suspected of Reformed sympathies. Calvin became an itinerant scholar eventually settling in the Swiss city of Basle where he was to publish the first edition of his celebrated *Institutes* in 1536.

Intending to visit Strasbourg Calvin was forced by the hostilities between Charles V and Frances I to take the roundabout route via Geneva and so had his fateful first encounter with Guillaume Farel in the city with which he was to become forever associated. Farel, who had already embarked upon the process of reform in Geneva, challenged the young author of *Institutes* to stay and further the work of reform there. Initially hesitant, Calvin eventually responded to Farel's strong imprecations and took the fateful decision to stay and become a Reader in the Holy Scriptures in Geneva.

Calvin and Farel swiftly set about organising the ecclesial affairs of Geneva and in 1537 Calvin submitted to the city authorities his *Articles on Ecclesiastical Organisation*. This involved the submission of a formal confession of faith to all the inhabitants of Geneva, not all of whom were yet converted to the Protestant cause. It also contained a radical proposal to put discipline, and more formally the power of excommunication, under the control of Church authorities. This proposal was resisted by the civil magistrates who, after freeing themselves from the control of the Catholic prince bishop of Geneva, had no wish to submit themselves once again to the control of ecclesial authority. They argued that the supervision of public morals and the enforcement of excommunication were the proper remit of the civil authorities of Geneva. This disagreement, and a refusal to accommodate themselves to the religious and liturgical practices of Geneva's more powerful neighbour Berne, reveal the weakness and the political ineptitude of Calvin and Farel at this time. The result of their intransigence was that Calvin and Farel were forbidden to preach by the civil authorities and when they refused to heed this injunction they were banished from Geneva in 1538.

Calvin settled in Strasbourg where he became minister to the French Protestant refugees in that city. He went there at the invitation of another great figure of the Reformation, Martin Bucer. Bucer's influence was to prove decisive on many aspects of Calvin's later mature theology as can be seen in the revised edition of the *Institutes* produced in Strasbourg in 1539. Bucer was also a player in the international arena of Church affairs and he included Calvin in the conferences at Frankfurt (1539), Worms (1540) and Ratisbon (1541) which attempted to unite the riven Church. During these encounters Calvin came into friendly and mutually respectful contact with Melancthon who thereafter was to refer to Calvin simply as 'the Theologian'.

It was therefore a grander and more authoritative Calvin who responded to the request of the Geneva authorities that he return to the city in 1541 and once again take up the process of reforming that city according to the principles of Holy Scripture. Much of the legend concerning Calvin as the virtual dictator of Geneva stems from the fact that the invitation to return bestowed upon Calvin great moral and personal authority. However, it should be noted that Calvin's authority was always personal and moral and never official, and he was not even a citizen of Geneva until 1559. Calvin's authority such as it was depended upon persuading the civil authorities of the justness and rightness of his cause, and his ability to do that depended upon the precise make-up of the city council at any particular time. Calvin was often successfully opposed and never succeeded in persuading the authorities to adopt certain practices such as the monthly celebration of communion which he expressly favoured.

Nevertheless, Calvin was undoubtedly a formidable figure and the most influential individual in Genevan life after his return. He quickly reintroduced revised regulations for the conduct of ecclesial affairs in

1541. This document identified four categories of ministry: pastors, doctors, elders and deacons. Church government was placed in the hands of a consistory (Church council) comprised of the pastors and twelve elders. Once again the question of responsibility for excommunication was a vexed issue. Calvin understood this power to be central in underpinning the Church's authority in relation to the moral and spiritual life of Geneva. The civil authorities were no less resistant to the idea than they had been before. Eventually, a compromise and ambiguous formulation was devised that was to be the source of endless disputation as it allowed the consistory to decide upon a matter and advise excommunication to the civil authorities. From the consistory's perspective they were merely handing over the offender to the civil arm for the carrying out of the punishment that they had determined. From the civil authorities' viewpoint they were merely receiving a recommendation from the consistory that they could decide to enforce or not to enforce as the case may be. Endless opportunities for disagreement were thus created and it wasn't until 1555 that Calvin finally won a definitive victory for his understanding of the relationship between the two bodies.

From his return until his death in 1564 Calvin was an industrious and energetic advocate of the Reformed cause. He preached and taught regularly, writing extensive and detailed commentaries on every book of the New Testament except the book of Revelation as well as commenting upon many of the books of the Old Testament. He engaged in correspondence with the major figures of the day from religious contemporaries such as Cardinal Sadoleto to political figures such as Edward VI. Calvin founded the Genevan Academy in 1559 for the training of ministers for Geneva, but also for the French Protestant Huguenots. Genevan influence on the French Protestant church was massive due to the substantial number of refugees who came to the city during periods of intense persecution, many of whom returned to France after training as Protestant pastors, bolstered by the theology of the *Institutes* which was now widely available in French translation.

Undoubtedly the incident that has served most to foster Calvin's reputation as the intolerant despotic dictator of Geneva was the burning of Michael Servetus as a heretic in 1553. Servetus was a brilliant if idiosyncratic character who had for some time been engaged in disputatious and abusive correspondence with Calvin. His views on the Trinity, the divinity of Christ and the practice of infant baptism had brought him into conflict with both Roman Catholic and Protestant authorities in various European cities. It is unclear why he came to Geneva when he did as it must have been obvious that his previous contact with Calvin and his reputation as an arch-heretic would ensure a hostile reception. Nevertheless he did come and he was duly arrested and Calvin did act in his capacity as a theologian-cum-prosecutor to advise the magistrates upon the nature of Servetus' heretical beliefs. He was found guilty and although Calvin advocated death by beheading Servetus was burned at the stake. The severity of the punishment, although not unusual by the standards of the time, led to demands for the abolition of the death penalty for heretics. Calvin's role in the proceedings certainly cast him in a poor light although he would have understood himself to be acting in the only way appropriate to stem the chaos that unchallenged heresy would undoubtedly bring. And with this assessment most of his contemporaries, both Protestant and Catholic, would have readily concurred.

It is also pertinent to point out that the Servetus affair took place when Calvin's opponents – the Perrinists or libertines – had full control of the civil authority and thus were the effective judges of the case. Calvin could not be excluded from a case where heresy was the central issue and it was he who had initiated charges but it would be gross calumny to imagine that he could have forced through a decision against the wishes of the civil authorities at this point in time. It was only after the fall of the Perrinists in 1555 due to the failure of a half-hearted attempt at a violent takeover of Geneva directed against Calvin and French influence in general that Calvin could be said to have unhindered sway in Genevan affairs.

Calvin continued to minister to Geneva and the wider Reformed cause until his death in 1564. A practical minister of the Word of God rather than an armchair theologian, he knew personal loss through the death of his child (1542) and his wife (1549). He battled with failing health and constant pain to write the final and definitive version of the *Institutes of the Christian Religion* in 1559 and this has to be taken as the clearest expression of his theological system.

The 1559 edition is sub-divided into four books dealing with: (i) the knowledge of God the Creator; (ii) the knowledge of God the Redeemer in Christ; (iii) the way in which we receive the grace of Christ; and (iv) the external means or aids by which God invites us into the society of Christ and holds us therein – the Church, sacraments and civil society.

In Book One Calvin proceeds to state what we can know of God. A surprising and rather modern assertion is made that knowledge of God and knowledge of self are inextricably inter-related: 'The sum of sacred doctrine is contained almost entirely in these two parts: the knowledge of God and of ourselves'.[i] For Calvin, however, the proper method for proceeding is to inquire what we can know of God and then to understand ourselves in the light of that knowledge. According to Calvin knowledge of God is never abstract or neutral but should issue forth in piety – the life of faith.

> Properly speaking we cannot say that God is known where there is no religion or piety ... the effect of our knowledge of God ought to be, first to teach us reverence and fear; and second, to induce us, under its guidance and teaching to ask every good thing from Him, and, when it is received ascribe it to him.[ii]

In the opening chapters of the *Institutes* Calvin asserts that humankind possesses a natural knowledge of God implanted within and can also gain knowledge of God from the evidence of God's works in the created order. Nevertheless, due to the dullness of our faculties, our tendency towards idolatry and superstition and the continuing effects of sin, this knowledge is of no avail. Into this desperate situation God has revealed himself clearly in the scriptures which are an accommodation to our weakness and sinfulness: 'No-one can have even the least taste of sound doctrine and know that it is of God, unless he has been to this school, to be taught by the Holy Scriptures'.[iii] In another favourite metaphor Calvin describes the scriptures as the 'spectacles' through which we see God.

God, who is incomprehensible, has revealed himself to us in the language of scripture and the source of the authority of scripture is not the Church nor its councils but the Holy Spirit.

> Though indeed God alone is sufficient witness to himself in his word, nevertheless that word will obtain no credence in the heart of man if it be not sealed by the interior witness of faith ... Wherefore it is necessary that the same Spirit who spoke by the mouth of the prophets must enter our own hearts and touch them to the quick, in order to persuade them that the prophets have faithfully set forth that which was commanded them on high.[iv]

It is the same Spirit then who inspired the scriptures that authenticates them in the life of the believer. This doctrine of the internal illumination of the Spirit has been massively influential in Reformed theology, inspiring even Karl Barth's approach to scripture which was in many respects a retrieval of Calvin's position. It has long been debated whether this account commits Calvin to the later view that scripture is inerrant and infallible. In some respects this is an anachronistic question as the problem had not posed itself in that way during Calvin's lifetime. It is true to say that, although his commentaries reveal an ability to offer a critique of scripture and to acknowledge that at times scripture accommodates itself to the simple images and metaphors appropriate to a primitive people, nevertheless, the strong impression is given that for Calvin scripture is ultimately trustworthy in relation to what it has to say about God and humankind.

Book Two concerns itself with knowledge of God the Redeemer and begins with an account of the human condition subsequent to the fall of Adam. This fall in which every human being is included in Adam has had disastrous consequences for the human condition which is radically and thoroughly impaired by the fall and subject constantly to sin. Free will remains but it is powerless to resist sin.[v] Calvin then proceeds to outline the manner of God's preparation for the coming of Christ by the giving of the law to the people of Israel. This law is part of God's one covenant of grace with humankind. In distinction from **Luther** Calvin argues for three uses of the law: (i) to reveal human sinfulness; (ii) to restrain the chaotic elements and forces within society from having unhindered free reign (thus far in accord with Luther); and (iii) to guide believers in that form of living which is pleasing to God. The introduction of this third category led many to accuse Calvin of confusing gospel and law but Calvin was careful to distinguish the law of the Old Testament from that law which is given in Christ.[vi]

Calvin's Christology is essentially traditional. Jesus Christ is both God and man incarnate for our salvation. 'Who could have done this had not the self-same Son of God become the Son of Man, and had not so taken what was ours as to impart what was his to us, and to make what was his by nature ours by grace.'[vii] This account of Christ's person is intimately linked to his work in that Christ as our mediator offers himself on the cross in an act of obedience that pays the penalty for our sinful transgression.[viii]

This saving work of Christ is further elaborated by use of the threefold imagery of prophet, priest and king. Christ is the one who proclaims the message of grace, who is Lord and rules over all that God has given into his hand and who is himself the priestly sacrifice paying the debt for our sins. Thus Calvin manages to interpret the great offices of the Old Testament in a way that understands them as finding their summation and fulfilment in Christ. In a discussion of how the two natures of Christ co-exist in one person Calvin argues that the *Logos* exists independently of the human nature which he assumed. That is to say that there is not a complete identification of attributes between the two natures of Christ and it is possible to say that the Logos remained in heaven whilst incarnate in Christ.[ix] This concept, known as the *extra-calvinisticum*, was to become central to Calvin's understanding of the presence of Christ in the eucharist.

Book Three of the *Institutes* concerns itself with the way of coming to the grace of Christ, and the benefits that derive to us from it. Here Calvin sounds for the first time in this work that central theme of Lutheran theology '*justification* by faith'.

> ... we must consider at greater length this point of justification by faith, and consider it in such a way as to keep well in mind that this is the principle article of the Christian religion, in order that everyone may take great pains and diligence to know the resolution of it.[x]

Some commentators feel that justification by faith is a lot less central to Calvin's thought than it was to Luther's but there is no doubting its fundamental importance to him. Any lessening of its centrality may very well be due to the fact that the idea had already established itself as the principal theological principle of the Reformed cause and no longer needed to be contested so vigorously as the focus of debate had shifted to other issues.

It is in this section that Calvin outlines his doctrine of the believer's mystical union with Christ and it is clear that this idea is central to his thought. Here Calvin argues that it is in spiritual union with Christ that the believer receives both justification and *sanctification*. Through this union all that Christ himself is becomes ours through faith. It is to be regretted that this rich imagery of salvation fundamentally construed as incorporation into the life of Christ has not received the same profile within reformed theology as that of the doctrines of penal substitutionary **atonement** or **predestination**.

It is of course in Book Three that Calvin deals with the issue of predestination, which is by no means the central doctrine of the *Institutes* but with which Calvin's name has forever since been associated – we might even say blackened. Calvin did not invent the doctrine of predestination and the idea can be found in the writings of many of his predecessors including Luther and **Aquinas**. Calvin himself thought he was simply spelling out what was clearly contained in scripture and the writings of **Augustine**.

It is also true that for Calvin the purpose of the doctrine was to provide assurance to those who were saved and also to explain why there were those who did not respond to the gospel. Was this because God's purpose for them was being thwarted? Nevertheless, Calvin spelled out what he termed this 'terrible decree' and profound mystery in clinical and precise fashion:

> Now, that the covenant of life is not preached equally to everyone, and even where it is preached is not equally received by all – in this diversity there appears a wonderful secret of the judgement of God. For there is no doubt that this variety serves to his good pleasure. But, if it is evident that this takes place by the will of God, that salvation should be offered to some and the rest be excluded from it, from this there arise great and high questions which cannot be resolved otherwise than by instructing the faithful as to what they should hold concerning election and predestination by God.[xi]

In Book Four Calvin addresses the Church and civil society as a means of grace. In relation to the Church Calvin is attempting to tread a narrow path that legitimates the Reformed break from the Church of Rome but which militates against those tendencies of the radical reformers towards schism and even in some cases to dispense with the Church completely. Thus he is able to argue that the Church is a necessity even using the Cyprian favoured image of the Church as the believer's Mother.[xii] It is necessary for eternal life to remain within the bosom of this Church for outside the Church there is no hope of remission of sins or salvation.[xiii]

Following Augustine Calvin makes a distinction between the visible and the invisible Church. The invisible Church is the elect called out by God comprising all people in all times and known only to God. The visible church is the social and cultural reality which we have to deal with and it is this church that is Calvin's primary concern. Against the radical reformers' tendency to create churches for a spiritual elite Calvin argues that the visible church is a mixed community and that it is not for believers here to judge who ultimately is a member of the true church. Obviously there is discipline for those who are in gross error with respect to belief or conduct of life but in general Calvin's position calls for a generous estimation of the members of the visible church.

But not all churches are true churches and Calvin offers this definition as a way of determining whether a true church of God exists in a particular place – 'Whenever we see the Word of God purely preached and heard, and sacraments administered according to Christ's institution, there it is not to be doubted, a church of God exists'.[xiv] Where these marks are present one should not separate oneself from the Church on frivolous grounds for it is always dangerous to separate oneself from the Church. These marks of course would exclude most Roman Catholic churches but Calvin does not exclude the possibility that a Catholic congregation could exhibit these marks. However, the marks operate negatively as well as positively and where these marks are not present then separation from such a so-called church is both legitimate and necessary.

In accordance with his original ecclesiastical reconstruction of the life of the Genevan church Calvin argues for a fourfold pattern of ministry of pastors, teachers, elders and deacons. In relation to the sacraments Calvin argues vigorously that there are only two: baptism and the Lord's Supper. Sacraments are 'signs and seals' of God's grace. They are accommodations towards our weak and finite capacities whereby God gives us visible pictures of an invisible grace. Calvin engages in an extensive attempt to legitimate the practice of infant baptism in the face of the compelling arguments of those sects advocating adult or believer's baptism in opposition to this practice. He draws a parallel between the role and function of circumcision in the Old Testament and infant baptism in the New.

In relation to the Lord's Supper Calvin tries to maintain a 'real presence' in the eucharistic over against the Zwinglian position (see **Zwingli**) without identifying the presence of Christ exactly with the elements in a local and corporeal manner. Believers truly receive the body and blood of Christ in their partaking of the Lord's supper but they do this spiritually and in faith through the power of the Spirit. Against Lutheran ubiquity Calvin maintains that the ascended Christ is present at the right hand of God and therefore cannot be identified locally in the elements. Instead, in language which is never wholly clear, Calvin seems to imagine a twofold operation of the Spirit whereby Christ is made truly present to the believer in the act of reception and the believer is raised heavenward to the ascended Christ.

The concluding section of the *Institutes* deals with the relationship between the Church and the civil magistrates. Calvin envisaged a complementary rather than a competing relationship in that the magistrates have their position from God and a rightful obedience is owed to them although they are to support the work of the Church and not try and usurp its work. In cases of tyrannous magistrates Calvin allows for the proper right of resistance but only on the part of lesser magistrates or figures in authority; he did not seem to envisage a role for the individual in resisting tyrannous rule in the way that the later Scots Confession of 1560 clearly does.

In summing up, Calvin was a clear and precise thinker who did much to articulate an intellectually defensible Reformed system of doctrine. His contribution and legacy have been massive. Churches inspired by his theology were by far the most vigorous and active exponents of the Reformed faith in the years following his death. Theologians of the faith were to follow the tramlines set down in the *Institutes* until well into the nineteenth century and the beginnings of the modern theological period, and even then figures such as **Schleiermacher** and **Barth** owed much more to Calvin than is usually realised. The clarity and elegance of his style in the successive French translations of the *Institutes* impacted upon the development of the French language itself. And although the thesis that Calvinism produced capitalism is wholly overstated in that there were clearly discernible tendencies towards capitalism in Europe pre-Calvin, nevertheless there was a profound and undeniable synergy between those societies which were to adopt the Calvinist version of religion and the emerging capitalist economies. Similarly, Calvin did not invent modern democratic government (indeed there is something autocratic about his views) but it cannot be denied that his preference for conciliar forms of church government and his conception of the complementary roles of Church and civil society operating with distinct spheres of responsibility was a template that was to be used in the development of forms of government in those areas of the world most influenced by Calvinist religion, most notably in the United States.

Notes

All footnotes are from *The Institutes of the Christian Religion*
i 1.1.1
ii 1.2.1 –2
iii 1.6.2
iv 1.7.4
v 2.3.5
vi 2.7.2f.

vii   2.12.2
viii   2.12.3 –2.16.5
ix   2.13.4
x   3.2.10
xi   3.21.10
xii   4.1.1
xiii   4.1.4
xiv   4.1.9

See also: **Aquinas; Augustine; Barth; Luther; Schleiermacher; Zwingli**

Glossary: *Atonement; justification; predestination; sanctification*

Major writings

Commentaries/Calvin, trans. & ed. by Joseph Haroutunian, in collaboration with Louise Pettibone Smith, London: SCM, 1958

Calvin's New Testament Commentaries, 12 vols, ed. D.W. Torrance, Grand Rapids, MI, 1959–72

The Institutes of the Christian Religion, ed. J.T. McNeill, trans. F.L. Battles, Philadelphia: The Westminster Press, 1960

The Bondage and Liberation of the Will: a defence of the orthodox doctrine of human choice against Pighius, ed. A.N.S. Lane, trans. G.I. Davies, Carlisle: Paternoster and Grand Rapids, MI: Baker Books, 1996

Further reading

W.J. Bouwsma, *John Calvin: a sixteenth century portrait*, Oxford: OUP, 1988

B. Cottret, *Calvin: a biography*, Grand Rapids, MI: W.B. Eerdmans, 2000

A.E. McGrath, *A Life of John Calvin*, Oxford: Blackwell, 1990

E. Stickelberger, *John Calvin*, Cambridge: James Clarke, 1959

F. Wendel, *Calvin*, London: Collins, 1963

CAPPADOCIAN FATHERS, THE

The Cappadocian Fathers is a term usually used to describe three celebrated thinkers of the Eastern Church who were pivotal in the development of **Trinitarian** orthodoxy. They are Basil of Caesarea (330–79), Gregory of Nyssa (335–95) and Gregory Nazianzen (329–90). Basil and Gregory of Nyssa were brothers and Nazianzen a life-long friend. Basil, also known as Basil the Great, was the senior and most influential figure of the three during their lifetimes, although he was not the greatest in terms of theological insight or philosophical subtlety. All three were educated in the philosophical, literary and cultural norms of their day. Theologically they were influenced by

Origen, but also by **Athanasius** in his attempts to argue for the legitimacy of the *homoousion* as a description of the Son's relation to the Father. However, the Church in Cappadocia and its environs contained many Christians, sometimes misleadingly referred to as semi-Arians, who were suspicious of the *homoousion* and who preferred the term *homoiousion* (that is, they were happier saying that the Son is 'like substance' to the Father rather than that the Son is of 'one substance' with the Father. The insertion of the 'i' is all important. (See **Arius** and **Athanasius**). A large part of the significance of the Cappadocian Fathers is that their conceptual articulation of Trinitarian terms enabled this group to remain within Catholic orthodoxy by detailing an account of the divine relations within the Godhead that they could accept.

Basil was born into a wealthy Christian family in Caesarea (in modern-day Turkey) and he retained forever afterwards something of the authoritarian and dictatorial habits of the landed and aristocratic classes of the day. He was a proud patrician figure, often given to temperamental outbursts but also capable of great kindness. Basil was educated at Constantinople and at the University of Athens where he rekindled his earlier friendship with Gregory of Nazianzus, whom he had known in Caesarea.

Basil's education in the classical philosophy and literature of the ancient world fitted him for the career of a professor of rhetoric and that is what he duly became at the school of rhetoric in his home town. However, Basil was to be shaken from his comfortable existence by the sudden and unexpected death of his younger brother, and under the influence of his saintly and somewhat ascetic sister Macrina he abandoned his career as a rhetor and embraced the monastic life. He prepared himself for this vocation by visiting the anchorites and hermits of Egypt, Syria and Palestine, but he was not impressed by the waywardness and lack of discipline of many of the hermits and so he purposed to found a monastic community that would be governed by a set of rules. These rules and regulations for governing the monastic life were principally set out in two works: the *Moralia* and the *Asceticon*. The Rule of St Basil continues to govern the life of orthodox monastic communities to this day, although in its present from it is a work of the sixth century containing many later additions to the original precepts.

Following the example of his sister who had already set up a community for women, Basil set up his monastery at Ibora near Annessi in 358. He was joined there for a period by his friend Gregory Nazianzen. Basil was not to remain a monk for long however. He was made priest against his will in 364 by Bishop Eusebius, whom he eventually succeeded as Bishop of Caesarea in 370. This made Basil bishop of a large and significant diocese and he energetically threw himself into organising and structuring its life, particularly in relation to its care of the poor. However, these were not propitious times for bishops who were proponents of Nicene orthodoxy and Basil found himself opposed by the Arian Emperor Valens. The settlement of the Council of Nicaea in 325 had announced that the Son who was incarnate in Jesus Christ was of one substance (*homoousios*) with the Father. This meant that what the Father in essence was, the Son also was. This was a controversial decision and many in the Church who adhered to the position of Arius (that the Son was an exalted creature but essentially a creature of the Father) found it difficult to accept. Arius' position was supported by many and, occasionally, even by emperors such as Valens. Valens ordered that Basil's diocese be split in half and in the struggle to reorganise and find new leaders for the depleted churches left under his control Basil turned to his family and friends, making his brother Gregory, Bishop of Nyssa, and his friend Gregory, Bishop of Sasima, although Nazianzen never took up residence there.

It is against the context of the Arianising tendencies of the age and the related tendency of many in the Church to deny the full divinity of the Holy Spirit that we have to understand the significance of the contribution of the Cappadocian Fathers. It was widely agreed that the Spirit was not a creature and was given to us by the Father, but there were many – known as Spirit-fighters or *Pneumatomachians* – who denied the full divinity of the Spirit. The wide variety of views concerning the Spirit at this time is actually recounted for us by Gregory Nazianzen in one of his theological orations. He acknowledges that the subject is difficult and that there are those who consider the Spirit as a force or activity, those who consider the Spirit to be a creature and those who consider the Spirit to be God. The problem as it presented itself to these early Christians was that scripture was not definitively clear on the matter. Furthermore, the settlement of Nicene orthodoxy nicely articulated a twofold understanding of God as the Father without origin in anything other than himself and as the Son whose sole origin was the Father – but how could the Spirit be divine without postulating thereby 'two sons' or 'two inoriginate first principles'?

Basil's tactic in relation to dealing with the Spirit-fighters was to proceed with great caution. In his public preaching he preferred simply to deny that the Spirit was a creature and he never actively affirmed the divinity or consubstantiality of the Spirit to the Father in his preaching. He was castigated by many for his reserve, although Athanasius defended his tactic of not offending the weaker parties in the Church who were not yet ready to make such a decisive move. It is also possible that this reserve may be related to the fact that at that time in Christian churches there were sections of the liturgy that were reserved mysteries for the faithful members of the Church alone, and that therefore Basil did not feel himself at liberty in the proclamation section of the service to develop what were mysteries of the faith.

However, in his work *On the Holy Spirit* (375), Basil did argue that the Spirit was to be recognised as holy by nature and inseparable from the Father and the Son: '[T]he natural goodness and the inherent holiness and the royal dignity extended from the Father through the Only Begotten to the Spirit'. The basis of this argument was founded on two sources – scripture and the liturgical life of the Church. Scripture in that it describes the operations and activities of the Spirit in terms of operations that properly belong to God. Liturgy and worship in that the formula of baptism clearly links Father, Son and Spirit inseparably together. The Spirit, however, is neither ungenerate (having no generation outside himself) nor generate (being generated from the Father) as these are properly the attributes of the Father and the Son. Rather we are to say that the Spirit is from the Father.

Basil also introduced the important technical distinction between *ousia* and *hypostasis*, arguing that we should speak of God as one *ousia* existing in three *hypostases*. This was an important distinction in that *ousia* and *hypostasis* were synonyms for substance or essence and could be taken to mean essentially the same thing. Indeed, Athanasius stated that *ousia* and *hypostasis* were essentially the same. However, the Cappadocians began the process of interpreting *ousia* in terms of substance or essence and *hypostasis* in terms of a concrete and particular embodiment of a substance. This distinction gave Christian theology the linguistic and technical tools to maintain the unity of God while at the same time speaking meaningfully of a threefold diversity within that overarching unity.

> *Ousia* has the same relation to *hypostasis* as the common has to the particular. Every one of us both shares an existence by the common term *ousia* and is such or such a one by his own properties. In the same manner, in the matter in question, the term *ousia* is common, like goodness or Godhead or any

similar attribute, while *hypostasis* is contemplated in the special property of Fatherhood, Sonship or the power to sanctify.

(Epistle 214)

However, Basil's tendency to use as an analogy for the *ousia–hypostasis* distinction the notion of three individual human beings sharing a common human nature could definitely be taken to imply tri-theism despite his best intentions.

Basil's insights would be developed by his brother Gregory of Nyssa and his friend Nazianzen. Gregory of Nyssa, who was by nature more contemplative than his brother, did not seem to have been provided with the same level of formal education that his elder brother was privileged to have received. However, although the details of his formal education are obscure it is nevertheless clear that he possessed a greater degree of philosophical acuity than his famous elder brother. Often portrayed as being, at least initially, a reluctant Christian, he was almost certainly a reluctant Bishop of Nyssa. Pressed into a role for which he was unsuited, he was eventually to find himself deposed on charges of financial irregularity, although admittedly the deposition was carried out by a synod of hostile and largely Arian bishops.

Gregory's most significant work in relation to the Trinity is *On not saying that there are three Gods*, in which he builds on the distinctions already suggested by Basil. Gregory argues that the unity of the Trinity is maintained by the fact that every action or operation of God is one in which all three persons share. The external operations or activities of the one God are indivisible in that they are operations of the Father, through the Son in the Spirit. There is a sense, of course, in which the operations are conceptually distinguishable, and this would give rise to the later doctrine of the appropriate attribution of certain operations to the Father, Son and Spirit, but in all essential respects the external operations of God are one.

Since then the Holy Trinity fulfils every operation in a manner similar to that of which I have spoken, not by separate action according to the number of the Persons, but so that there is one motion and disposition of the good will, which is communicated from the Father through the Son to the Spirit, so neither can be called those who exercise this Divine and Superintending power and operation towards ourselves and all creation, and inseparably, by their mutual action, three Gods.

(On not saying that there are three Gods).

Gregory also makes the important distinction that the persons of the Trinity can be distinguished from one another only by virtue of their internal relations of First Cause, Only Begotten and the Spirit mediated through the Son from the Father. Nevertheless, despite these careful qualifications Gregory still perceived the dangerous implications of the human nature/individual people analogy and he was moved to deny, in a platonic fashion, the propriety of speaking of many men sharing a common human nature, instead suggesting that it would be more correct to speak of one man in all. These qualifications were allied with Gregory's strong stress upon the incomprehensibility and mystery of God, which meant that he was prepared to concede that, although we call God Father, strictly speaking we do not apply gender to God, and, although we call God three and one, we do not apply the concept of number to God. Taken together this forms the basis of Gregory's argument for the unity of God's being, which for all their commitment to the Trinity was an absolute fundamental for all three Cappadocians.

Gregory Nazianzen, who was to be called 'the Theologian', did not leave a large body of extant written work dealing with the controversies of the day. His reputation as a thinker and defender of the Christian faith stems from his orations and it is certain from these that he was an orator of considerable ability. Of most interest here are the five theological orations delivered in Constantinople in 380. In these Gregory clearly teaches the complete identity of the divine persons apart from their relations of origin. In this treatment Gregory Nazianzen also clearly defines the specific attribute of the Spirit as that of proceeding and he was aware that he was minting this word afresh.

> The Father is Father and Unoriginate, for He is of no-one, the Son is Son, and is not unoriginate, for He is of the Father ... The Holy Ghost is truly Spirit, coming forth from the Father indeed, but not after the manner of the Son, for it is not by generation but by procession since I must coin a word for the sake of clearness;
>
> (*Theological Orations* (*Or.*) 39.12)

Gregory was also much more forceful than Basil had been on affirming the full divinity of the Holy Spirit. He declares: 'Is the Spirit God? Most certainly. Well then, is He consubstantial? Yes, if He is God' (*Or.* 31.10). However, as mentioned earlier Gregory was aware that such a teaching was not clearly set forth in scripture, nor could it claim to have been the clear and common mind of the Church since apostolic times, and so he was forced to offer a defence of it via a developmental view of doctrine and tradition.

> The Old Testament proclaimed the Father clearly, but the Son more darkly; the New Testament plainly revealed the Son, but only indicated the deity of the Spirit. Now the Holy Spirit lives among us and makes the manifestation of Himself more certain to us, it was not safe, so long as the divinity of the Father was still unrecognised, to proclaim openly that of the Son; and so long as this was still not accepted, to impose the burden of the Spirit, if so bold a phrase may be allowed.
>
> (*Or.* 31.26).

In relation to Christology Gregory Nazianzen was a powerful advocate of a form of two-nature Christology. He was convinced that Christ possessed a fully human nature, including a rational mind and soul, and fully divine nature. Furthermore, he argued that the union of the two natures was by essence and not grace. He opposed the Christological teaching of Apollinarius that Christ did not possess a rational soul or mind with the powerful adage: 'What is not assumed is not healed'.

The Cappadocian position in relation to the full deity of the Holy Spirit was to be affirmed at the Council of Constantinople in 381. Their account of Trinitarian relations was to provide the framework for the Eastern understanding of the Trinity from then onward, although Augustine's model would emerge as the primary vehicle for Latin Trinitarian thought (see **Augustine**). In recent years the Cappadocian model of the Trinity has been revived as a source for contemporary 'social doctrines' of the Trinity, although many of these fail to demonstrate the restraint, and the essential commitment to the fundamental unity of the divine being, that was so characteristic of Cappadocian thought and as a result are indistinguishable from tri-theism.

The Cappadocians wrote widely on topics other than those of strictly Trinitarian concern, but their most abiding influence has been in relation to that doctrine. Basil and Nazianzen probably put together the *Philokalia*, a collection of the works of Origen. Basil's earliest work was *Against Eunomius*, an anti-Arian tract expounded largely in Athanasian terms. He also produced the *Hexameron* (The Six Days of Creation), a collection of homilies in which he attempts to reconcile and expound the biblical account of creation in terms of the Aristotelian science of the day. It is a work of considerable poise and beauty. Besides these we have the rules governing monastic life and many, many letters which reveal the thought of an active and vigorous Christian leader. His brother Gregory of Nyssa was also, after Basil's death, to take up the literary cudgel against Eunomius, but he also wrote significant works on virginity and the monastic ideal, although he was the only one of the three to marry. Commenting posthumously on his brother's work was to become something of a habit for Gregory of Nyssa as he also composed a work on creation that attempted to correct mistaken readings of Basil's *Hexameron*. Gregory was also to suggest, following Origen, that there would be a universal restoration of all things in the eschaton. Interestingly, he also suggested that the mutable nature of human beings was useful in that eternal life would consist in a never-ending exploration of the mystery of the divine life.

The scale and breadth of the Cappadocian contribution to Trinitarian and Christological thought is hard to overestimate. In their own time they were probably crucial to maintaining a place in the Church for those of semi-Arian tendencies. In articulating a doctrine of the Holy Spirit which asserted his full and consubstantial divinity, while at the same time maintaining the strict unity of God's essential nature, they provided a framework for Christian Trinitarian theology not only in their own time but for all subsequent generations.

See also: **Athanasius; Augustine; Origen**

Glossary: HOMOOUSIOS; *Trinity/Trinitarian*

Major writings

The major writings of Basil, Gregory of Nyssa and Gregory Nazianzen can be found in *A Select Library of the Nicene and Post-Nicene Fathers of the Christian Church*, First Series, 14 vols, ed. P. Schaff, New York; Second Series, 14 vols, ed. H. Wace & P. Schaff, New York, 1890–1900; new edn, Grand Rapids, MI: 1980. Volumes 8, 5 and 7 of the second series respectively.

Further reading

A. Meredith, *The Cappadocians*, New York: Crestwood, 1995

DUNS SCOTUS, JOHN (c.1265–1308)

Born near Duns in Berwickshire in Scotland, he became a Franciscan, and probably studied and taught in Oxford around 1300. He may have spent some time in Paris, moving in 1308 to Cologne where he died on 8 November 1308. His main work is the commentary on the *Sentences* of Peter Lombard. He also wrote on Aristotle and Porphyry.

In the work of John Duns Scotus the Augustinian concentration on God's will, especially against Pelagius (see **Augustine**), again comes to the fore. As a result confidence in reason as a way of knowledge of God wanes. We must learn simply to obey God's will. Duns's work was to be carried forward in a creative and original manner by William of Ockham, for whom the entire rational framework has now become suspect. We can say nothing of the divine attributes of God as he is in himself. We can only obey his will. God is infinitely transcendent.

This line of thought was to lead to a new stress on the authority of the Church as the source for knowledge of the will of God, and a stress in Duns on Mary as the mediator (mediatrix) of salvation between the mystery of God and humanity. In this schema Christ is the supreme manifestation of God's love, and Christ's coming was not conditioned by any other events such as the fall into sin. The incarnation of God in Christ would have taken place even without the fall.

Much medieval philosophy was dominated by the strife between broadly realist and broadly nominalist positions on the question of universal categories. At stake were basic issues of truth, knowledge and being. Put succinctly, *realism* was the doctrine that abstract concepts such as *universals* have a real existence apart from the individuals or particulars that they embody. **Anselm** was in this sense a realist. Thomas **Aquinas** was a modified realist; he rejected the view that universals exists apart from the individuals (*universalia ante res*) and upheld a doctrine of modified realism (*universalia in rebus*). Nominalism on the other hand was a theory of knowledge that denied reality to universal concepts. **Abelard** called universals 'names' (*nomina, voces*), rather than entities (*res*), which were however useful to describe similar objects. William of Ockham appears to have held that universals were not in reality but only in the *nomina*: every substance is radically individual. This was to have many consequences for theology. For example, on this basis Gabriel Biel denied the plurality of divine attributes, such as God's omnipotence and mercy – all attributes are ultimately one in God. The reality of the three persons of the Trinity cannot thus be proven but be accepted only in faith. Reason with its inherent limitation in relation to matters pertaining to the divine cannot demonstrate that the First Cause is God.

In the fourteenth century nominalism appeared to have won the day. Yet both Duns and his opponent William of Ockham combined elements of earlier realist and nominalist positions. The basic issue is how much reason can know of faith. Both men laid stress on the concept of God as sheer will rather than as the source of rationality. You cannot understand the nature of God by reasoning. True knowledge of God is found in understand and obeying the will of God. All this was to be stressed again during the Reformation. If reason cannot decide what is correct theology, this must be replaced by an appeal to authority, in the first instance to ecclesiastical authority. Hence we find in Duns a new emphasis on the importance of papal and conciliar decisions. But here too there were changes. Man is no longer thought of in terms of the corporate concept of humanity. Humanity is rather the sum of all the individuals in the community. The individual self-consciousness becomes increasingly important as the arbiter of theological judgement.

Duns's writings are full of precise, technical argument, and are not always easy to read. For example we may look at his treatise *On God as First Principle*. The final section deals with 'the simplicity, infinity and intellectuality of the First Being'. Yet the technical argument can easily be cast, as in Anselm, in the form of a kind of doxology, addressed to God:

> O Lord our God, Catholics can infer most of the perfections which philosophers knew of you from what has been said....
> you are happy, indeed you are by nature happiness, because you are in possession of yourself. You are the clear vision of yourself and the most joyful love, and though you are most self-sufficient and happy in yourself alone, you still understand in a single act everything that can be known.
>
> (4.84) (abbey.apana.org.au/Theology/Scotus/04.htm)

Major writings

On First Philosophy, A.B. Wolter, Chicago: OFM, 1966
Philosophical Writings, trans. with intro. & notes, A.B. Wolter, Indianapolis: Hackett Pub. Co., 1987

Further reading

E.H. Gilson, *Jean Duns Scot*, Etudes de philosophie médiévale, tom. 42, Paris, 1952
G. Leff, *Medieval Thought*, London: Penguin, 1958
Marilyn McCord Adams (ed.). *The Philosophical Theology of John Duns Scotus*, Ithaca, NY: Cornell University Press, 1990

EDWARDS, JONATHAN (1703–58)

American theologian in the puritan and Calvinistic tradition who is increasingly regarded as America's greatest theologian and a thinker whose depth of insight and philosophical subtlety fully merit him a place alongside the great European thinkers such as Locke, **Hegel** and **Schleiermacher**. Edwards, the fifth son of Timothy Edwards, a pastor in East Windsor, Connecticut, was born on 5 October 1703. His mother Esther was the daughter of the Rev. Samuel Stoddart, minister of Northampton Church, Massachusetts. Samuel Stoddart was to be an influential figure in the life of the young Edwards as Edwards would eventually act as his assistant at Northampton before following his grandfather as full minister of that church.

Edwards was schooled by his father before proceeding in 1716 to study at what was later to become Yale University. There he studied philosophy and science and was profoundly influenced by the writings of John Locke and Isaac Newton. He graduated in 1720 and two years later was licensed to preach the gospel at a Presbyterian church in New York. He then exercised a further short period of ministry as pastor at Bolton, Connecticut, before becoming a tutor at Yale in 1724. He left Yale to become assistant to his grandfather at Northampton in 1726 and three years later became the sole minister in charge of that church.

At Northampton Edwards was to exercise a powerful and intense preaching ministry and many of his sermons from that period are still read to this day. The tenor and tone of his preaching can best be discerned in this extract from one of his most famous sermons 'Sinners in the Hands of an Angry God' (1741)

> O sinner! Consider the fearful danger you are in: it is a great furnace of wrath, a wide and bottomless pit, full of the fire of wrath, that you are held over in the hand of that God, whose wrath is provoked and incensed as much against you, as against many of the damned in hell. You hang by a slender thread, with the flames of divine wrath flashing about it, and ready every moment to singe it, and burn it asunder; and you have no interest in any Mediator, and nothing to lay hold of to save yourself, nothing to keep off the flames of wrath, nothing of your own, nothing that you ever have done, nothing that you can do, to induce God to spare you one moment.

During his time in Northampton, and apparently as a result of his preaching, there was an outbreak of religious revival and enthusiasm between 1734 and 1735 which Edwards carefully documented and examined. This outbreak of religious fervour slightly predated, but was similar in tone and content to, the evangelical revivals in England that we associate with John Wesley and George Whitfield. To his great regret the revival proved to be relatively short-lived but long enough for Edwards to reflect on its nature in a number of treatises, but most famously in his 'Concerning Religious Affections' (1746) which is still regarded as an insightful and pertinent discussion of such matters. In contrast to those who were suspicious of the religious experiences of the 'enthusiasts' of the revivals, Edwards stressed the importance of the role of the heart and the affections in religious life. For Edwards true religion involves rationality; it includes the intellect and understanding. Yet that is not the end of the matter for it must also include the will and it is the affections which motivate the heart towards that which the will chooses. The greatest of these affections is love. Moreover, in his discussion of the genuine signs of Christian piety Edwards argued that Christian practice in conformity to Christian rules is the principal sign of true religion.

However, despite this great success, Edwards was to become embroiled in a dispute with the leading figures of his church when he insisted that members of his church should make a basic profession of faith before being admitted to communion. His predecessor (his grandfather) had pursued a more lax policy by issuing an open invitation to the communion table and Edwards's more hardline position was much resisted. Eventually, in 1750, Edwards was dismissed as minister.

In 1751 he accepted a call to become pastor at a frontier station at Stockbridge, Massachusetts, where the majority of inhabitants were native Americans, but despite the rigours of this form of frontier life he still found time to write and think. In 1757 Edwards's growing intellectual stature was recognised in his call to become President of the College of New Jersey (later Princeton University). Edwards travelled to Princeton to take up his post and as smallpox was rife in the area at that time he agreed to be inoculated against the disease. It appears that the vaccine was insufficiently treated as Edwards quickly succumbed to the disease and died in February 1758.

Edwards's most famous work is perhaps his treatise 'A Careful and Strict Enquiry into the Prevailing Notions of the Freedom of the Will' (1754), written to counter Arminian understandings of the nature of salvation which stressed the individual's freedom of decision against the Calvinistic understanding of God's **predestination** of the individual to salvation. Edwards, favouring what he took to be the biblical teaching of predestination, engaged in a profoundly philosophical discussion of matters such as causation, necessity, contingency, will and motivation. He stressed that human beings are free in so far as they have the power to do as they choose. However, these choices are in fact determined and necessitated by the will, which is always controlled by motives. Edwards was keen to argue that everything has a cause both in terms of the physical operations of the world and also in the moral and religious realm of human action. For Edwards God alone is the cause of all things and famously he argued that the 'liberty of self-determination' must be denied to the world or else God must be excluded from his creation. In relation to our moral choices these too have a cause for they are determined by our natures. If this were not the case our actions would be utterly random and inexplicable. And as our human natures are sinful then our choices are likewise sinful. Thus in relation to salvation sinful human beings are totally dependent upon God's grace for their salvation.

Edwards turned to defend the traditional doctrine of original sin in the treatise 'The Great Christian Doctrine of Original Sin Defended' (1758). Edwards's approach is in many ways more similar to the traditional Catholic understanding of the nature of sin than his own Reformed and Calvinist tradition in that he argued that the fall of Adam was a fall from a higher state of 'original righteousness', where Adam possessed a supernatural experience of grace and was governed by the love of God, to an inferior or 'natural righteousness' where Adam was controlled by the impulses of the flesh. In the state of original innocence Adam (and presumably all other human beings) would have followed the path of our higher more spiritual nature where love of God would dominate. However, because of the disobedient choice of Adam, God withdrew himself from Adam and left him at the mercy of his natural and fleshly impulses, and consequently 'Man did immediately set up himself, and the objects of his private affections and appetites, as supreme; and so they took the place of God'. The point of this account of the matter is to preserve God against the charge of being the author of sin. For on this account God simply withdraws himself from Adam and from his posterity and thus leaves humanity at the mercy of its natural and fleshly impulses. God in this sense permits sin but is not the author of it. However, Edwards then proceeded to outline a fairly rigorous account of how God deals with Adam and his posterity (i.e. the whole human race) as one, and includes the whole of humanity in Adam's guilt. The inclusion of humanity in Adam is based on the divine decree, but also on a metaphysical understanding of God as the source and continuing maintainer of all created being: 'I am persuaded no solid reason can be given, why God, who constitutes all other created union or oneness according to his pleasure, . . . may not establish a constitution whereby the natural posterity of Adam . . . should be treated as one with him'. Edwards was unrelenting in his conviction that the just reward for sin was the punishment of hell and that hell served ultimately to glorify God.

Harsh and uncompromising as such views might seem, Edwards was not without an appreciation of beauty and virtue and a more expansive account of the divine. The entire scope of his theological and metaphysical system did not become clear until the posthumous publication of two works – 'The End for Which God Created the World' and 'The Nature of True Virtue'. These works reveal a deeply *neo-platonic* influence on Edwards's thought. Virtue is defined as a love and benevolence towards being and, as ultimate being is God itself, then true virtue is firstly love for God and thereafter love for other beings in so far as they partake in the true being of God. In 'The End for Which God Created the World', Edwards offers an account of infinite being and its tendency to communicate itself via an emanation of its own being. Thus the world was not created out of nothing, but is an emanation of the divine being. God is thus infused throughout the whole of creation, which itself partakes of the divine reality. The goal of this entire process is the glory of God.

> In the creature's knowing, esteeming, loving, rejoicing in, and praising God, the glory of God is both exhibited and acknowledged; his fullness is received and returned. Here is both emanation and remanation. The refulgence shines upon and into the creature, and is reflected back into the luminary. The beams of glory come from God, and are something of God, and are refunded back again to their original. So that the whole is *of* God, and *in* God, and *to* God, and God is the beginning, middle and end of this affair.

Edwards thus in a powerful and robust way combined his basically Calvinist theological heritage with that great neo-platonic tradition which so influenced the development of normative Christian doctrine in the early period of the Church's history. This, combined with his utilisation of, and creative response to, the philosophical systems of

Locke and Berkeley makes him an interesting and original thinker in his own right. Edwards was not to be followed in his doctrine of sin by mainstream American religious thought – indeed for large parts of that tradition he lay neglected and forgotten. The late twentieth century, however, brought a rediscovery and re-estimation of Edwards's thought and importance such that he was hailed as America's greatest and most original theologian.

See also: **Calvin; Hegel; Schleiermacher**

Glossary: Neo-platonic; predestination

Major writings

The Works of Jonathan Edwards, ed. P. Miller & J.E. Smith; New Haven: Yale University Press, 1957

Further reading

S.R. Holmes, *God of Grace and God of Glory: an account of the theology of Jonathan Edwards*, Edinburgh: T & T Clark, 2000
R.W. Jenson, *America's Theologian: a recommendation of Jonathan Edwards*, New York and Oxford: OUP, 1988
J.E. Smith, *Jonathan Edwards: puritan, preacher, philosopher*, London: Chapman, 1992

FEUERBACH, LUDWIG (1804–72)

German philosopher and famous anti-theologian, Feuerbach was first a disciple and then an arch critic of the philosopher **Hegel**. Born in 1804, the son of a successful and influential lawyer, Feuerbach received the full benefits of the high German culture of his day. He studied theology at Heidelberg and then went to Berlin in 1824 in order to study under the great giants of German thought at that time, **Schleiermacher** and Hegel. It seems to have been during this period that Feuerbach abandoned any thought of a career in theology and decided to devote himself to the study of philosophy.

Due to financial problems Feuerbach completed his studies at the University of Erlangen, eventually becoming an occasional junior lecturer there. However, his academic career was stalled upon the anonymous publication of *Thoughts on Death and Immortality* in 1830. In this work Feuerbach clearly denies the traditional Christian affirmation of the immortality of the soul. In contrast he argues that if there is any sense of immortality at all it is in the transmission of human culture as it carries on from generation to generation.

Disappointed with his lack of prospects at Erlangen, Feuerbach attempted to kick-start a career in philosophy elsewhere by publishing a *History of Modern Philosophy from Bacon to Spinoza* in 1833, followed by a critique of Leibniz's philosophy in 1837 and a work on Pierre Bayle in 1838. These works were well received and earned Feuerbach a sound reputation as an emerging philosopher in the Hegelian school, but unfortunately his prospects of a university career had been fatally damaged by *Thoughts on Death and Immortality*. A series of attempts to find Feuerbach an academic post failed on the grounds of his reputation as an atheist and dangerous thinker and by 1836 Feuerbach had effectively abandoned any lingering hopes of an academic career. In 1837 he married Bertha Löw, a woman of modest but independent means through her inheritance of a share in a porcelain factory. From this point onwards Feuerbach lived and worked as an independent free and radical thinker albeit of diminishing financial means as the years progressed.

In 1839 Feuerbach announced his decisive break with the philosophy of Hegel with the publication of his *Critique of Hegelian Philosophy*. If Feuerbach was later to conclude that theology was a veiled anthropology then Hegel's philosophy was a veiled theology. One of the central reasons for Feuerbach's break with Hegel was his insistence on the primacy of the material over consciousness. For Hegel 'the rational is the real and the real rational' whereas for Feuerbach nature and the material is the presupposition of all consciousness. Therefore, it is not the case, as Hegel taught, that objects are generated from thought but rather thought is generated from objects. This materialist basis to his thought is a significant link between Feuerbach and the later existential tradition. Feuerbach develops a form of sensuous materialism in which people and their material needs become the very foundation of social and political thought. This stress upon the concrete sensuous nature of what it is to be a human being led to the famous aphorism and pun 'Man is what he eats'. This insistence upon the importance of the material was to prove a key influence in the later development of historical materialism in Marxist ideology which owes a great deal to some of the key insights of Feuerbach, including the idea that religion is fundamentally an illusion, as well as the important notion that the criticism of religion is the beginning of human liberation.

The scale and depth of the break with his former master is revealed most clearly, however, in Feuerbach's most famous work, *The Essence of Christianity*, published in 1841. In this work Feuerbach radically departs from the thought of Hegel. He now regards Hegel's work as essentially duplicitous in its assertion of the identity of human being with divine being. Feuerbach begins to call Hegel's system the Old Testament of philosophy and regards his own work as the correction of Hegel's enterprise. In an inversion of Hegel's famous assertion of a divine human unity, Feuerbach argues that the notion of the divine is itself an objectification of what is in fact human. Famously, Feuerbach was to assert, 'I deny God', but for him this meant that he denied 'the negation of man'. For Feuerbach the question of God was really the question of man and what the religious consciousness has expressed as God is really humanity's own sense of itself as perfect, complete and infinite. This sense of itself, which is a sense of the species rather than the individual, is not recognised as such, but is projected and reified as the divine object.

> Religion, at least the Christian, is the relation of man to himself, or more correctly to his own nature (i.e. his subjective nature); but a relation to it, viewed as a nature apart from his own. The divine being is nothing else than the human being, or rather, the human nature purified, freed from the limits of the individual man, made objective – i.e. contemplated and revered as another, a distinct being. All the attributes of the divine nature are, therefore, attributes of the human nature.[i]

From this one can readily understand the meaning of one of Feuerbach's most celebrated phrases – 'the secret of theology is anthropology' – meaning the highest being is the human being. But if human beings are truly the subject of religion then religion is fundamentally an illusion in its projection of the qualities that truly belong to the human species as a whole onto the figure of a divine being. Thus Feuerbach can say that 'the consciousness of the infinite is nothing less than the consciousness of the infinity of the consciousness'. But the fact that these qualities are projected onto an illusory divine being means that human beings are themselves diminished in their understanding of their own true nature and this makes religion a form of alienation. In contradistinction from Hegel who presented the world and its history as the self-alienation of Absolute Spirit, Feuerbach presents God as the self-alienation of the human species.

The radical character of Feuerbach's ideas meant that he very quickly became infamous throughout Europe as an atheist – replacing D.F. **Strauss** as the great enemy of Christianity – although Feuerbach understood himself to be 'the dot on the *i* which Strauss had already delineated'. However, the impact of *The Essence of Christianity* along with the swiftly following *Preliminary Theses for the Reform of Philosophy* (1842) was such as to make Feuerbach the leading figure among the radical thinkers of the age. Strauss was to repay Feuerbach's compliment by asserting that 'To-day, and perhaps for some time to come, the field belongs to him. His theory is the truth for this age'. And it was during this period that Karl Marx was to state: 'You have no other way to truth and freedom than through the fire-brook (Feuerbach)'. George Eliot translated *The Essence of Christianity* into English in 1854. Despite these high estimations Feuerbach's fame and the impact of his work were soon to go into a rapid decline in fortunes that mirrored the rapidity of his rise to prominence. Partly, this was due to the collapse of the revolution in Germany and a change in the philosophical climate, but also this was due to the eventual rise to prominence of the thought of Marx himself whose materialist philosophy seemed to say everything that Feuerbach said but in a more comprehensive and expansive fashion.

Feuerbach was later to return to the subject of religion in *The Essence of Religion* (1845) and in his Heidelberg *Lectures on the Essence of Religion* (1851). In this broader account of religion Feuerbach continues to maintain that fundamentally religion is an illusion and a form of wish-fulfilment. It still arises out of the consciousness of human beings of themselves as a species which distinguishes them from animals who can only be said to be conscious of themselves as individuals. However, human beings sense themselves to be dependent creatures – dependent upon nature and upon other people. Religion is the attempt to overcome this sense of dependence through an act of imaginative projection and Feuerbach gives an account of key religious concepts on this basis. For example, sacrifice, which he holds to be a central religious theme, expresses dependence in the sensed need to propitiate another, but also represents the overcoming of dependence in the acceptance of the sacrifice.

In these later works Feuerbach outlined a developmental view of religion in its progression as an expression of the various forms of human self-consciousness in relation to nature. Early forms of religion were polytheistic and primitive as human beings felt themselves to be fundamentally part of nature and subject to nature. Subconsciously aware of this dependence human beings worship the powers of nature in the form of polytheistic gods. These gods are often represented by natural objects such as planets, trees, rivers or even animals as human beings project their dependence upon nature onto the realm of the gods. Monotheism, however, emerges as human beings begin to gain some control and mastery over nature and project their own internal qualities onto the figure of a transcendent divine being. But this magnifying of the divine leads to a diminishing of the human as humanity is alienated from its own highest qualities: 'To enrich God, man must become poor; that God may be all, man must be nothing'. This transposition most clearly takes place in Christianity which, in this sense, Hegel was right to call the 'absolute religion'. Here in the doctrine of the incarnation we have a veiled confession of the true reality of the situation – God is a human being. The positive aspect of Feuerbach's philosophy was that the true heart of religion was revealed and no longer was God to be regarded as the perfect expression of love, morality and suffering but rather that the human qualities of love, morality and suffering were understood themselves to be divine. Religious symbolism, understood as a veiled anthropology, when subjected to the critique of Feuerbach turns out to be a positive expression of human worth and value. And so we understand why Feuerbach said of his own work: 'God was my first thought; Reason my second; Man my third and last thought'.

Feuerbach's critique of religion had an immediate and devastating effect upon the young radical thinkers of the age, but as we have seen his influence upon his contemporaries was not to prove of lasting duration. Marx's materialism was to transcend and overshadow Feuerbach's contribution and later Freud was to develop a theory of religion that would also argue that at root it was an illusion, a form of projection, a neurosis whose origins lay in the desire to have unconscious needs, desires and wishes fulfilled. However, in the latter part of the twentieth century when Freudian theories and Marxist ideology seem to be in permanent decline Feuerbach's influence can still be detected in the writings of radical non-realist accounts of the Christian faith such as that offered by Don Cupitt and the Sea of Faith movement.

Note

i   *The Essence of Christianity*, p.14

See also: **Hegel; Schleiermacher; Strauss**

Major writings

The Essence of Christianity, trans. G. Eliot, New York: Harper & Row, 1957
Gesammelte Werke, Ludwig Feuerbach; herausgegeben von Werner Schuffenhauer, Berlin: Akademie-Verlag, 1967

Lectures on the Essence of Religion, trans. R. Manheim, New York: Harper & Row, 1967

Thoughts on death and immortality: from the papers of a thinker, along with an appendix of theological-satirical epigrams, edited by one of his friends, trans. with intro. & notes by James A. Massey, Berkeley & London: University of California Press, 1980

Further reading

E. Kamenka, *The Philosophy of Ludwig Feuerbach*, London: Routledge & Kegan Paul, 1970

A. Van Harvey, *Feuerbach and the Interpretation of Religion*, Cambridge: CUP, 1995

M.W. Wartofsky, *Feuerbach*, Cambridge: CUP, 1977 (reprinted 1982)

FORSYTH, PETER TAYLOR (1848–1921)

Scottish Congregational theologian and minister of the late nineteenth and early twentieth centuries whose thought is proving increasingly durable in the modern period. In his rejection of liberal theology and his affirmation of a kerygmatic centre to the Christian faith that was not based on an infallible and literalist reading of the scriptures, Forsyth has often been described as a Barthian before **Barth**. However, it is becoming increasingly clear that Forsyth deserves recognition as an original thinker in his own right. No less a figure than Emil **Brunner** has described Forsyth as the greatest British theologian of the twentieth century. Like Barth, the young Forsyth drank deeply from the wells of liberal theology, but again in similar fashion to Barth, he found that this theology was not adequate to the task of proclaiming a meaningful gospel to the working men of Shipley in Yorkshire, where Forsyth began his ministerial career in 1876. During his ministry in Shipley, Forsyth discovered the power of the biblical message of grace and he described his discovery in the classical language of conversion.

> There was a time when I was interested in the first degree with purely scientific criticism. Bred among academic scholarship of the classics and philosophy, I carried these habits to the Bible, and I found in the subject a huge fascination, in proportion as the stakes were much higher. But, fortunately for me, I was not condemned to the mere scholar's cloistered life ... It pleased God also by the revelation of his holiness and grace, which the great theologians taught me to find in the Bible, to bring home to me my sin in a way which submerged all the school

questions in weight, urgency and poignancy. I was turned
from a Christian to a believer, from a lover of love to an object
of grace.[i]

Born and educated in Aberdeen, Forsyth was of relatively humble
origins but distinguished himself in the arts faculty of the university
there by taking a first in classics. Following the advice of the great
Scottish biblical scholar, Robertson Smith, Forsyth went to study
under Albrecht **Ritschl** at Göttingen in Germany and thus began a
life-long interest in German theology and an initial infatuation with
liberal theology. He returned from Germany to enter New College in
London to begin his training for the congregational ministry.
Although allowed to leave early in 1874 due to ill health, Forsyth
was to return to academic life in 1901 as Principal of Hackney College
and later to be Dean of the Faculty of Theology of the University of
London.

Forsyth ministered in Shipley, Hackney, Manchester, Leicester and
Cambridge and in each place he threw himself into the pressing social
needs and concerns of the people to whom he ministered. The
importance Forsyth placed on relating the gospel to the pressing needs
of the day was captured in his chairman's address to the Congregational Union in 1905.

Do not take my arm and lead me away to the dwellings of the
pound-a-weeks and the nothing-a-weeks and tell me if I want
realities to consider there ... Long ago I was there, and
worked there, and considered there, and have been considering ever since.[ii]

Forsyth was a prolific author, producing original works on topics as
varied as preaching, Christology, *atonement* theory, *theodicy*, ecclesiology, the sacraments and Church and State relations. His style of
writing was epigrammatic and aphoristic and this has often led to the
accusation that he was not a sufficiently technical theologian to be
considered among the great systematic thinkers. It would be true to
say that his style at times obscures rather than reveals his meaning, and
that deeper analysis of some of his central insights would have yielded
greater results. Nevertheless, there are rich and profound insights to be
quarried from most of his works and this is testified to by the
resurgence of interest in his thought shown by a number of present-
day theologians.

Forsyth's central theme that pervades so much of his writing is the holiness of God conceived in personal and relational terms. It was the discovery of the holiness of God, so eloquently described in his famous sermon to the Congregational Union entitled 'Holy Father', that drove Forsyth to see the inadequacies of the liberalism in which he had previously indulged. From the point of this sermon, delivered in 1896, the central themes of all of Forsyth's subsequent theology are clear and present – the holiness and majesty of God, the power of his holy and gracious love, the sinfulness of human beings and the gracious gift of the cross of Christ as a redemption from sin.

In his first full-length work *Positive Preaching and the Modern Mind* (1907) Forsyth touched base with the Reformed roots of his own theological tradition and argued that 'with its preaching Christianity stands or falls'. Forsyth's account of preaching is virtually sacramental in that it is a divine/human encounter in which the real presence of Christ is made known as the power of the gospel. The similarities with Barth are obvious but both are drinking deeply from Calvin's well at this point (see **Calvin**).

The next three major publications that Forsyth produced centred on the person and work of Christ and it is for his contributions in these areas that he is rightly famous. Thus *The Person and Place of Jesus Christ* (1909) offers an account of the divine presence in Christ in moral and personal terms. Although Forsyth had broken with the liberalism of Ritschl, and was an ardent critic of R.J. Campbell's attempts to devise a reductionist 'new theology' based on Hegelian and Ritschlian categories, he remained a sufficient child of his times to reject the language (although not the substance) of classical metaphysical and philosophical categories for describing God's presence in Christ in favour of moral, relational and personal concepts.

The central move that Forsyth makes is to argue for a complementary two-stage movement of *kenōsis* and *plērōsis* in the life of Christ. In becoming man the divine person engaged in a voluntary act of self-humiliation whereby there was a real self-limitation of powers (*kenōsis*). Forsyth's theory anticipates and deals with the objection, already lodged against other kenotic theories, that an immutable being cannot divest itself of its powers by arguing that the divine powers were reduced from the actual to the potential by a voluntary self-abasement on the part of Christ to the form of a servant. But this kenotic act (which implies a strong commitment to the pre-existence of Christ) is matched by a corresponding *plērōsis* or self-fulfilment in the human life of Christ. That is to say, Forsyth acknowledges a certain validity to the classical liberal idea of a 'progressive incarnation' in the life of Christ. However, here the 'progressive incarnation' in the life of Christ is firmly based on a prior act of *kenōsis* so that Christ's growth in moral and spiritual terms is a gradual realisation of that which he had previously voluntarily laid down. Forsyth refuses the false option of choosing between the violent intrusion of a divine stranger from above, or the moral achievement of the first perfect man, in favour of a double movement in the life of Christ whereby an act from the divine side is mirrored by an act from the human side so that Christ's human life of growth is the gradual recovery of Christ's prior mode of being as Son.

In *The Cruciality of the Cross* (1909) and *The Work of Christ* (1910) Forsyth focused upon that central act of God which dominated his entire approach to theology – the cross of Christ. For Forsyth the holiness of God is crucial, and as holy, God cannot simply overlook sin or treat it with less than utmost seriousness. Therefore, judgement was a key category for Forsyth and he vigorously rejected all sentimental and purely moral and subjective models of atonement that were current in the liberal theology of his day. Forsyth's account of the cross is actual and objective; God has effected our redemption on the cross and it is not simply the **revelation** of his prior disposition as love. Forsyth's model, related to his concept of a progressive realisation of the will of God in the life of Christ, is that Christ's life of obedience develops until upon the cross we have 'the offering of a holy self to a holy God'. Therefore the cross involves God's judgement on sin and Christ's acceptance of that judgement as our representative who confesses God's holiness and the justice of God's judgement. But this should not be read as simply repeating classic penal substitutionary theories of atonement, although there may be a superficial resemblance. The emphasis for Forsyth is upon Christ's obedience unto death rather than the idea of Christ offering an equivalent for our punishment – there is no transfer of guilt from us to him. Judgement takes place to be sure, and there is punishment – God's punishment on sin – but 'God did not punish Christ, but Christ entered the dark shadow of God's penalty upon sin'.[iii]

Such insights are provocative indeed, and his model of atonement shares a certain structural similarity with that of his famous fellow countryman, McLeod Campbell. Although Forsyth may have struggled to fully express what he was attempting to say the general consensus is that his model of atonement might still have much to say now.

As for the times in which he lived and the estimation that Forsyth was more or less neglected by his contemporaries, this claim has to be carefully nuanced. For it would have to take account of his various successful ministries, the call to be Principal of a denominational theological college, his period of tenure as Dean of the Faculty of Theology of London University and his chairing of the Congregational Union in 1905.

However, once all that is said, it is the case that Forsyth was moving against the tenor of the liberal theological climate of his times. In this he resembled another prophetic figure, **Kierkegaard**, whom he greatly admired (another touching point with Barth). Like Kierkegaard, and later Barth, Forsyth railed against a liberalism that proclaimed an all-too comfortable accommodation of God to humankind. For Forsyth human beings, even in their religion, were preoccupied with themselves rather than with God. The crisis of the cross and the fact of sin were too central for Forsyth to be comfortable with such an easy accommodation of the human to the divine.

> Without such a cross and its atonement we come to a religion of much point but no atmosphere, much sympathy and no imagination, much kindness and no greatness, much charm and no force ... religion becomes too aesthetic, too exclusively sympathetic, too bland, too naturalistic. Our very Christmas becomes the festival of babyhood, Good Friday the worship of grief, and Easter of spring and renewal instead of regeneration.[iv]

With such sentiments, so forcibly expressed, in an age when liberal theology was in the ascendant, it is no surprise that Forsyth's theology went into a virtual eclipse soon after his death and even less of a surprise that interest in it would be re-ignited after the Barthian revolution had taken place.

Today, Forsyth's work is being appraised afresh in many quarters. For some he is a prophetic voice warning against any return to those forms of anthropocentric religion which are a constant temptation to the Church. For others he is a moderating figure who manages to maintain an evangelical commitment to the gospel and to the essential truth of the biblical story without denying the proper claims of modern historical criticism of the Bible. It is true that he found historical criticism's mere *Historie* – the recording of the events of the life of Christ – an insufficient method for getting to the heart of the gospel story. Instead (once again showing himself to be an heir to the school of Ritschl) he argued that in the texts of the New Testament we have to deal not only with *historie* but with *Geschichte* –

the events as they are interpreted through the apostolic witness, made present to us now through the preaching and worship of the Church by the power of the Holy Spirit.

Whether the current interest in Forsyth's theology will last is a moot point. The exclusivity of his focus upon Christ and the sheer concentration upon the cross makes much of his thought uncongenial to those wrestling with the issues of religious pluralism. From the other side of the religious divide he may find that the oft-noted similarity with Barth counts against him too. For while there is no doubt that Forsyth anticipated some of the central thrusts of the Barthian programme, there is little doubt either that Barth offers the more systematic and sustained development of the consequences of that programme for Christian faith. However, Forsyth's account of revelation never loses touch with the realities of human existence in the way that Barth's more positivistic account often threatens so to do. Consequently, it may be that Forsyth's theology will continue to speak to succeeding generations of Christians.

Notes

i   *Positive Preaching and the Modern Mind*, p.281
ii   P.T. Forsyth, 'The Grace of the Gospel as the Moral Authority of the Church' in *The Church, the Gospel and Society*, London: Independent Press, 1962, p. 87
iii   *Positive Preaching and the Modern Mind*, p.154
iv   Rodgers, *The Theology of P.T. Forsyth*, p.19

See also: **Barth; Brunner; Calvin; Kierkegaard; Ritschl**

Glossary: ***Atonement; KENŌSIS; PLĒRŌSIS; revelation; theodicy***

Major writings

The Church and the Sacraments, London: Independent Press, 1955
The Cruciality of the Cross, London: Independent Press, 1955
Faith, Freedom and the Future, London: Independent Press, 1955
The Person and Place of Jesus Christ, London; Independent Press, 1955
Positive Preaching and the Modern Mind, London: Independent Press, 1955
God the Holy Father, London: Independent Press, 1957
The Justification of God, London Independent Press, 1957
The Work of Christ, London: Independent Press, 1958

Further reading

T. Hart (ed.), *Justice the True and Only Mercy: essays on the life and theology of Peter Taylor Forsyth*, Edinburgh: T & T Clark, 1955

L. McCurdy, *Attributes and Atonement: the holy love of God in the theology of P.T. Forsyth*, Carlisle: Paternoster, 1999
J.H. Rodgers, *The Theology of P.T. Forsyth: the cross of Christ and the revelation of God*, London: Independent Press, 1965

GUTIÉRREZ, GUSTAVO (1928–)

Peruvian priest and theologian and crucial figure in the development of Latin American liberation theology. Born in Lima in 1928 Gutiérrez abandoned an early intention to train as a medical doctor in order to train as a priest. From 1951 to 1959 Gutiérrez studied in Europe at the Universities of Louvain, Lyon and the Gregorian University in Rome. He was ordained in 1959 and the following year began teaching at the Pontifical Catholic University of Peru.

Gutiérrez quickly found himself being used as a theological resource person by the Peruvian episcopate. This role and the position of influence that it gave to Gutiérrez was to have decisive results at the Second General Meeting of the Latin American Episcopate at Medellín, Colombia, in 1968. This meeting is often regarded as the pivotal point in the recognition of a new priority for the poor in Latin America on the part of the Catholic church, and Gutiérrez's briefings and papers are seen as crucial to this.

Gutiérrez's own fully fledged description of liberation theology would emerge in 1971 with the publication of *A Theology of Liberation*. In this work Gutiérrez combined a rudimentary Marxist philosophy of history with an emerging social analysis of the Latin American situation and allied these to traditional theological themes of liberation, exodus, redemption and spirituality to produce a startling and potent new way of doing theology.

One of the key concepts that Gutiérrez took over from the emerging analysis of the true situation facing the Latin American continent in relation to the rest of the world was that of dependency. The classic developmental model of the economy of Latin America (and the rest of the third world) assumed that its markets and financial systems could be structured in such a way that the 'developing' countries would eventually grow to produce economies that mirrored those of the classic industrial economies of the first world. International aid, support and investment were all predicated on this basic assumption and the monetary and political culture of Latin America was ordered to produce the maximum amount of penetration by the multinational companies and financial institutions of the first world to achieve this end. Dependency theory agrees that the Latin

American economy has been constructed politically and socially to achieve the maximum penetration of its economies by Western finance and business, but argues that this does not have the effect, nor the intention, of producing strong independent economies, but rather economies that will exist perpetually in dependence upon, and in service to, the economies of the first world. Latin American countries are on the periphery of an economic system that encourages riches at the centre but produces poverty on the periphery. In Gutiérrez's words: 'The Latin American countries are from "the beginning and constitutively dependent" '.[i]

In recognising that there are traditionally rich and powerful groups in Latin American countries who foster and benefit from the structural inequality that exists there and by arguing that this is not an accidental but necessary feature of the modern capitalist system, and in recognising the need for the poor to be 'conscientisized' (made aware) as to the facts of their true situation, Gutiérrez shows the influence of Marxist theory upon his thought.

In the face of the sheer scale of the structural and endemic poverty in Latin America (Gutiérrez has continued to live and work in one of the poorest areas of Lima), and as a response to the conflicts, alienations and tragedies that poverty produces, Gutiérrez called for a new way of doing theology. It was to be a theology that expressed and activated 'God's preferential option for the poor'. This theology, which reflects on the praxis of liberative action in the world, cannot simply stop at reflecting on the world or its situation (a common critique made of European political theologies), but rather tries to be 'part of that process through which the world is to be transformed'.[ii] This theological reflection cannot be done on behalf of the poor by an academic elite but must be done by the poor themselves. For the 'process of liberation requires the *active participation of the oppressed* ... it is the poor who must be the protagonists of their own liberation'.[iii] For this reason Gutiérrez has always felt that the emergence of 'base communities' where Christians live, work, reflect and carry on the struggle for liberation through imaginative acts of charity, grace, love and resistance to the oppressive forces of the world in the name of God are vitally important factors of the liberation movement. Such views, allied to Gutiérrez's clear approval of a form of democratic socialism as the best model of government for Latin American countries and combined with a clear preference for social ownership of the means of production, brought the accusation (from within his own church and elsewhere) that he had sacrificed the gospel to Marxist theory. Gutiérrez, however, is quite clear that commitment to the path of liberation requires that one be prepared to face such charges (and more), and he is also acutely aware that the spectre of communism has been a charge used by the ruling elites of Latin America to crush movements that call for recognition of even the most basic rights for the poor and working classes.

Liberation for Gutiérrez is a concept that has a threefold dimension to it. On the first level it involves liberation from the oppressive conditions and conflicts of the socio-economic world and its injustices – this is external liberation. The second level is the liberation of the internal life of human beings through the overcoming of the internalised conflicts, guilt, fears and repression that our unjust societies produce with us. On this level a new human being with a wider, broader, deeper understanding of the possibilities of human existence social and individual is realised. Finally, on the third level we reach that most complete and fundamental level of liberation – liberation from sin through Christ. This liberation makes human beings free to live in communion with their neighbours and with God.

Although Gutiérrez clearly affirms that the deepest and most fundamental level of liberation is that achieved by Christ, he has been criticised by many for focusing too much on the social and economic aspects of liberation and of failing to truly integrate these processes with the redemption that Christ brings. Often the Marxist analysis seems to render liberation as a necessary and inevitable feature of the historical process itself. There is some truth in this criticism, and Gutiérrez has some work to do here. However, perhaps he feels that tightly integrating the conceptual basis of his work is slightly less urgent than the overwhelming plight of the poor and broken of Latin America. This would be in line with his conviction that theology primarily has to be a truth done and not only affirmed. For in Gutiérrez's view authentic theology will lead to a subversive liberating practice that enables the transformation of the non-human beings of history into the new human beings.

Gutiérrez's work has been both fêted and rejected, too Marxist for some and not sufficiently Marxist for others. He came under the severe scrutiny of the Roman Curia and spent considerable time defending his position to them. In *The Truth Shall Make You Free* (1986), Gutiérez clarified his position in relation to Marxist philosophy – a cautious acceptance without agreeing with its atheistic or determinist conclusions. It is to his considerable credit that what once were scandalous political slogans in the eyes of many – for example, 'God's preferential option for the poor' – have become common Christian parlance in Latin America and beyond.

Gutiérrez's most recent work has tended to focus upon the faithful living in response to the gratuitous love of God. Rebecca Chopp has argued that the stress here is upon the presence of God in the midst of the suffering of the poor rather than the poor as the bearers of an inevitable historical process.[iv] This may be true but it is a change of emphasis rather than a significant movement of stance, for even in *A Theology of Liberation* Gutiérrez spoke of the need for a spirituality of liberation that expressed a faithful and prayerful gratuitousness in response to the gracious presence of God. Both themes – the prophetic role of the Church as a sign to the world and the contemplative role of prayer in response to God – come together in Gutiérrez's insightful commentary *On Job*.

> Vision of God ... and defence of the poor are thus combined in the experience of Job as a man of justice. They are two aspects of a single gift from the Lord and of the single road that leads to the Lord.
>
> For the same reason, emphasis on the practice of justice and on solidarity with the poor must never become an obsession and prevent our seeing that commitment reveals its value and ultimate meaning only within the vast and mysterious horizon of God's gratuitous love ... The world of unmerited love is not a place dominated by the arbitrary or the superfluous. Without the prophetic dimension the language of contemplation is in danger of having no grip on the history in which God acts and in which we meet God. Without the mystical dimension the language of prophecy can narrow its vision and weaken its perception of the God who makes all things new (Rev 21:5).[v]

Gutierrez has latterly produced a scholarly and monumental study of the figure of Bartolomé de las Casas, the Dominican friar who defended the rights and needs of the indigenous Indians at the time of the conquest of Latin America. The study is not simply a piece of inspirational history – although it is that – but is a challenge to us all to decide if we will 'join Las Casas' in attempting 'to transform this time of dissipation and death into a time of calling and grace'.

Gutiérrez's work has been timely, prophetic and deeply influential. His views on theological method as a reflection on liberating praxis and the concomitant commitment to the contextualisation of theology which that demands has been widely taken up, not least in the field of practical theology. There have been critiques of his use of Marxist categories and the general collapse of Marxism as an ideology has not served the liberation theologians well. As has already been mentioned there is a great need for a closer integration of political and social liberation with that liberation that Christ alone can bring. It is also true that events in Latin America have not fulfilled the promise that the late sixties and early seventies promised – if anything there has been a greater penetration of market forces and the poor continue to swarm in great numbers to the shanty towns surrounding the cities. Gutiérrez's work therefore remains critically relevant to the current situation both in addressing and describing what is in fact going on, and for its utilisation of the deep biblical themes of exodus and redemption in offering a vision of what can be if God's purposes are fulfilled.

Notes

i *A Theology of Liberation*, p.84
ii *Ibid.*, p.13
iii *Ibid.*, p.113
iv R. Chopp, 'Latin American Liberation Theology' in D.F. Ford (ed.), *The Modern Theologians*, Oxford: Blackwell, 1997, p.183
v *On Job*

Major writings

A Theology of Liberation, London: SCM, 1974
The Power of the Poor in History, Maryknoll, NY: Orbis, 1983
We Drink from Our Own Wells, London: SCM, 1984
On Job, Maryknoll, NY: Orbis, 1987
The God of Life, London: SCM, 1991
Las Casas: In Search of the Poor of Jesus Christ, Maryknoll, NY: Orbis, 1993

Further reading

C. Cadorette, *From the Heart of the People*, Oak Park, IL: Meyer Stone Press, 1988
M.H. Ellis & O. Maduro, *The Future of Liberation Theology: essays in honour of Gustavo Gutiérrez*, Maryknoll, NY: Orbis, 1989
J.B. Nickoloff, *Gustavo Gutiérrez – Essential Writings*, London: SCM, 1996

HARNACK, ADOLF VON (1851–1930)

Adolf von Harnack was one of the greatest Church historians of all time. He came from an accomplished academic family and he himself had a brilliant undergraduate career. He published an early outstanding study of *Marcion* and became a professor in Berlin at an early age. Although never fully trusted by Church authorities because of the radical and critical nature of his views on the development of doctrine he was eventually to become recognised as the leading humanities scholar of his generation. He was made director of the Berlin Academy of Sciences and played a highly constructive role in the enhancement of German academic life until his death in 1930.

Throughout his life Harnack continued to produce an endless flow of monographs and new editions of texts, from commentaries on the New Testament to works on early Church figures as well as pieces on Church law, on contemporary theology and even on the *social gospel*. At the same time he was an inspiring and admired teacher. Membership of his famous seminar on early Church history was prized by generations of students who flocked from all over the world, including Karl **Barth**, with whom he had a series of much publicised debates, and **Bonhoeffer**, whose moving tribute at his funeral spoke for the huge esteem in which he was held, as a scholar and also as a teacher – warm, unassuming and immensely stimulating.

Harnack was part of that school of theologians who were attempting to develop a contemporary theology which responded to the insights of **Kant**. The most notable figure in that development was Albrecht **Ritschl**, and his thinking led in three main directions, characterised by the work of three of his most famous pupils, **Troeltsch**, Herrmann and Harnack. Harnack, in faithfulness to Ritschl, wanted to develop a theology that was firmly grounded and rooted in the results of historical research. He was perhaps one of the two most learned theologians who ever lived (**Origen** being the other).

In the winter semester of 1899/1900 Harnack delivered in Berlin his famous lectures on 'the essence of Christianity' (published in English as *What is Christianity*, 1900). This essence is defined as 'trust in the message, which Jesus delivered, of eternal life in the midst of time, by the strength and under the power of God'. Harnack's account of Jesus' message was that Jesus taught: (i) 'the kingdom of God and its coming'; (ii) of God the Father and the infinite value of the human soul; and (iii) the higher righteousness and the commandment of love'.[i] The coming of the kingdom of God was interpreted by Harnack as meaning 'the rule of the holy God in the hearts of individuals'.[ii] Harnack believed also that Jesus taught a message about the Fatherhood of God and his providential care of every individual human being, rather than a message which was about himself: 'In the combination of these ideas – God the Father, Providence, the position of men as God's children, the infinite value of the human soul – the whole Gospel is expressed'.[iii] By referring to the 'higher righteousness and the commandment of love' Harnack interpreted Jesus to be rejecting external forms of religious practice in favour of a combination of religion and morality based around the intention or disposition of the believer: 'It was in this sense that Jesus combined religion and morality, and in this sense religion may be called the soul of morality, and morality the body of religion'.[iv]

This original message of Jesus always has to be freed from the fetters of doctrine and ecclesiastical institutions that have developed over time. One of the more controversial implications of Harnack's approach was that the early development of doctrinal statements about Jesus cast in metaphysical and philosophical terms (i.e. the 'two natures in one person' theory of Christ of the Council of **Chalcedon**) were regarded as unhelpful 'Hellenisations' of the original gospel message. The task was to strip away these unhelpful developments in favour of a return to the original and primitive message of Jesus. As such, Harnack retained a confidence in our ability to gain access to the historical Jesus which his contemporary Ernst Troeltsch no longer found to be a well-based supposition. The precise relationship between faith and the results of historical study were the basis of a famous disagreement between Harnack and Karl Barth, with Barth rejecting the notion that faith depended in any way upon the findings of the historian.

The standard theological characterisation of Harnack as much masks as reveals the scale of his achievement. Although most of his judgements, especially in his famous multi-volume *History of Dogma*, have been much questioned, this in itself is a tribute to his achievement in raising critical issues and suggesting constructive and imaginative solutions. His comments in the section on the history of Marcion, echoing his earlier monograph, demonstrate well his penetrating capacity for theological judgement.

> The innovations of Marcion are unmistakable. The way in which he attempted to sever Christianity from the Old Testament was a bold stroke which demanded the sacrifice of the dearest possession of Christianity as a religion, viz., the belief that the God of creation is also the God of redemption. . . . The bold Anti-Judaist was the disciple of a Jewish thinker, Paul, and the origin of Marcion's antinomian-ism may ultimately be found in the prophets . . . In basing his own position and that of his church on Paulinism, as he conceived and remodelled it, Marcion reconnected himself

with that part of the earliest tradition of Christianity which is best known to us, and has enabled us to understand his undertaking historically as we do no other.[v]

Harnack saw Marcion and his 'Gnostic' followers (i.e. those with 'knowledge' of the true mystery of God – see **Tertullian**) as the first systematic theologians, who sought to 'Hellenise' Christianity by combining it with Greek thought, and in turn provoked a 'Catholic' response which gave more weight to the Old Testament. Both sides added something of value to the tradition, and both were one-sided reflections of the true essence of Christianity, which Harnack sought to locate in a purified form of Protestantism. In the true essence, the dogmatic complexity and intolerance of doctrinal orthodoxy would be avoided, the Old Testament would play a very limited role, and the rituals of Catholicism would be reduced.

Immensely erudite, it would be hard to exaggerate the stimulus Harnack provided Church history and the study of Christian doctrine. Involved in educational foundations and in academic politics, he supported the German government's conduct of the First World War, much to the dismay of Karl Barth. His son Ernst was involved in the socialist opposition to the Nazis and like Bonhoeffer was murdered by them.

Notes

i   *What is Christianity?* p.51
ii   *Ibid.*, p.56
iii *Ibid.*, p.67
iv *Ibid.*, p.73
v   *The History of Dogma.* Vol. 1., pp.282–3

See also: **Barth; Bonhoeffer; Paul; Ritschl; Tertullian; Troeltsch**

Glossary: **Chalcedon; social gospel**

Major writings

History of Dogma, New York: Dover Publications, 1961 (1886; trans. 1894)
What is Christianity?, New York: Harper & Brothers, 1957 (1900; trans. 1901)
Marcion, trans. John E. Steely & Lyle D. Bierma, Durham, NC: Labyrinth Press, 1990 (1921)

Further reading

G.W. Glick, *The Reality of Christianity – a Study of Adolf von Harnack as Historian and Theologian*, New York: Harper & Row, 1967

W. Pauck, *Harnack and Troeltsch: two historical theologians*, New York and Oxford: OUP, 1968

M. Rumscheidt (ed.), *Adolf von Harnack: liberal theology at its height*, London: Collins, 1989

HEGEL, GEORG WILHELM FRIEDRICH (1770–1831)

German philosopher in the idealist tradition who exercised a huge influence over theology during the nineteenth and twentieth centuries. Born in Stuttgart, Hegel entered the theological school of the University of Tübingen in 1788 intending to train for the Lutheran ministry. However, dissatisfaction with his studies and the rather rigid form of confessional orthodoxy that he was taught meant that he became disinterested with his theological studies and concentrated instead upon philosophy. After graduating Hegel taught as a private tutor to families in Berne (1793–96) and Frankfurt (1796–1800). He went on to lecture at the University of Jena in 1801 where he collaborated with Schelling in editing a philosophical journal, and published his first book on the differences between Fichte and Schelling's systems of philosophy.

The disruption surrounding Napoleon's victory over the Prussians at the Battle of Jena in 1806 (Hegel tells us that he finished the *Phenomenology of Spirit* the day before the battle) caused Hegel to retire from teaching for a period, but in 1808 he became Rector of the Aegidien Gymnasium in Nuremberg. In 1818, after a brief period as Professor of Philosophy at Heidelberg, Hegel was appointed to the chair of Philosophy at the University of Berlin. There Hegel reached the height of his powers and achieved great fame, ranking alongside his equally famous colleague Friedrich **Schleiermacher**, with whom he differed substantially on almost every major point. In 1831 Hegel contracted cholera and died as an epidemic of the disease swept through Berlin.

Hegel's philosophical system was (as was so much else in the nineteenth century) an attempt to respond to the legacy of Immanuel **Kant**. Kant had famously described the boundaries and limitations of pure reason by asserting that we cannot know things as they are in themselves but only as they appear to us through the modes of perception that we impose upon them. Although agreeing with much of what Kant had taught, Hegel completely rejected the Kantian account of unknowable 'things in themselves', arguing that 'the rational is the real and the real is the rational'. What this meant for Hegel was the conviction that the real world is one holistic unity that is accessible to the processes of reason.

As heir to the Romantic movement Hegel was convinced that behind the seeming separateness, differences and paradoxes of life surrounding us, the world was nevertheless one unified reality. Unlike the Romantics, however, Hegel did not think that recognition of this ultimate unity was achieved through mystical intuition, an exercise of the imagination or (contra Schleiermacher), by a feeling for the wholeness of things. For Hegel the unity behind all things is a rational unity and is discernible to reason.

Thus, for Hegel, reality was an organic complex reality which he termed Absolute Mind or Spirit (Geist). However, he conceived of Absolute Mind or Spirit as being essentially a subject and as subject it is the nature of Absolute Mind or Spirit to embody itself in its polar opposite – the concrete forms and particularities of the natural world. However, this passing over of Spirit into nature is only the first part of a necessary phase that is followed by Spirit's return to itself in a new and dynamic synthesis that overcomes the diverse, the particular, the individual concrete expressions of Spirit. If we ask why Hegel arrived at this conception we have to remember that he was attempting to overcome the sharp Kantian contrast between nature, or the world of objective fact, and Spirit, or the world of free conscious agents, which were essentially separate and opposed in the Kantian schema. Hegel attempts to show that this absolute separation of mind and nature is ultimately mistaken by demonstrating that it is impossible to conceive of consciousness in absolute isolation. Hegel argues from this that consciousness is always consciousness of some object in the world. Similarly, one cannot conceive of a pure object without already implicitly imposing the notion of a thinking conscious subject to whom the object is an object of thought. Therefore, nature and mind (or Spirit, and the ambiguity is important here) exist in a relationship of polar interdependence.

As conscious agents we are ourselves finite and particular expressions of Absolute Spirit and so there can be no question of a hidden Kantian reality existing '*noumenally*' forever beyond the capacity of minds to describe it. Instead, for Hegel, the processes and structure of rationality themselves exhibit and reflect the deep structures of reality. Therefore to understand what reason is and its exemplification in history is to understand reality itself. In the process of the movement of idea through nature to Spirit, a superficial understanding (*Verstand*) can only detect the contradictions and oppositions of the historical process. Reason (*Vernunft*), however, penetrates to the depths and perceives the underlying unity behind apparent difference.

Hegel's famous triadic and dialectical pattern of logic – thesis, antithesis, synthesis – is thus an attempt to devise a new form of logic that will enable the philosopher to deal adequately with the necessary contradictions, oppositions and negations of this historical process. Indeed, it is itself the key to understanding this rational process developing throughout history. In this movement identity is mediated through difference in a process that reconciles the seeming contradictions contained in the polar opposites of the thesis and antithesis in a higher synthetic statement that retains and carries forward in a new expression what was true in the original statements. This universal process is a feature of both thought (the basic manner of acquiring knowledge) and reality (the historical, social and cultural processes of the world), for these are but expressions of the one Absolute reality in which all difference is ultimately overcome. Hegel did not invent the dialectical method, nor was he always faithful to strictly triadic patterns, but it remains central to his system of thought. This developmental and evolutionary movement is fundamental to the nature of reality as it moves ever forward to ever more complete expressions of the absolute unity of all things.

For Hegel it is the Absolute *Geist* (Mind or Spirit) that discloses itself in the historical process. The whole of reality is the self-development of Absolute subjective Spirit as it passes over into its contradiction in the finite processes of nature. If we ask why Absolute Spirit passes over into its opposite then we are reminded of the structure previously described. To think of pure undifferentiated Absolute Spirit in isolation from any relation to the world is unimaginable and so Absolute Spirit goes forth into that which is its polar opposite – objective and finite Spirit. It is part of Hegel's genius that he relates this movement of Absolute Spirit to the classical Christian doctrine of the creation of the world.

In this process Absolute spirit comes to self-consciousness through its diremption into finite forms of expression, and we perceive the underlying unity of these finite forms of expression in differing ways through art, literature, science and religion, etc. But this diremption into finite and particular manifestations of the Spirit is a form of separateness and alienation from its true being as Absolute Spirit, and Hegel believes this to be the central truth of the Christian doctrine of the fall. However, Hegel attempts to teach us, through an analysis of the historical, social, cultural and religious life of the world, that the progress of history and culture is nothing other than the self-realisation of Absolute Spirit. This is why in his *Phenomenology of Spirit* Hegel takes so much time to describe the development of reason, culture, religion and society through history – for in so doing he is describing the gradual self-realisation of Absolute Spirit as it overcomes its self-alienation in the finite world. It is a corollary of this that Absolute Spirit finally overcomes its self-alienation and achieves self-realisation in Hegel's mature system – not a bad day's work for any philosopher.

Although he clearly used religious imagery in his philosophical system, the precise nature of Hegel's true attitude to religion has been the subject of much controversy. Undoubtedly, many of his writings have a strongly religious and spiritual feel to them and Hegel himself remained a faithful member of the Lutheran church. However, his views were certainly not orthodox, and he could be viewed as a pantheist rather than a theist in the classical sense. But there are some who would say that the religious tone of his work was simply an accommodation to the age. Certainly, his followers were later to take divergent paths and to split into what is known as 'left- and right-wing' Hegelians. Left-wing Hegelians moved in various directions, some all the way into secular atheism (**Feuerbach** and Marx), others into radical heterodox expressions of Christian faith (D.F. **Strauss**). 'Right-wing' Hegelians tended to remain more or less faithful to the Christian tradition as a pictorial representation of the truth, but felt that the ultimate expression of the truth that Christianity attempted to portray was found in philosophy. The most responsible view might be to take Hegel at face value and accept his account that Christianity was the absolute or highest form of religion, although religious symbolism itself was inferior to the philosophical and conceptual expression of the truth it contained.

The youthful Hegel had not always thought that Christianity was the highest religion. His earliest sketches tended to praise the freedom and imagination of Greek folk religion over the formal, institutional and positivistic nature of Christianity. However, in early unpublished works such as the 'Life of Jesus' and 'The Positivity of the Christian Religion' Hegel begins to present a 'Kantianised' account of Christ who preaches the virtues of duty and obedience to the moral law over against the Jewish authorities who demand observance of external rules and ceremonies. However, the Church in its forms and institutions has reintroduced a positivistic element into the Christian faith despite Jesus' intentions, and this is the tragic nature of the origin of the Christian church.

In a slightly later piece, 'The Spirit of Christianity', Hegel, although still regarding Judaism as a religion of external authority, begins to break with the Kantian concept of obedience to an absolute moral law and to see that this is as external and positivistic as he believed Judaism to be. Instead, Hegel argues that Jesus did not make external demands on his followers but exerted a higher demand, the demand of love. Love no longer acts as an external compulsion over the believer and as such it annuls the law while at the same time making higher demands than that law. This inner demand of love negates and overcomes the dichotomy of obedience to an absolute revealed law or an external moral law that always stands over the free spirit of the individual. Here the demand of love is already the inner demand of finite spirit and it coincides and is at one with divine authority. Therefore, the contradiction between the demand of revealed law and the freedom of the individual is overcome in a new synthesis of love.

These early sketches are of interest in themselves, but their fundamental importance is to show how indebted Hegel was to the Christian faith for the development of the structure of his whole system. For here, in embryonic fashion, we already see the notion that seemingly polar opposites and contradictions are overcome in a higher synthesis that somehow unites both.

The concern with positivistic and external forms of religion would never leave Hegel. Later he would regard the Roman Catholic church as yet one further example of external, institutional and formal religion and would contrast it unfavourably with the free, internal faith of the Reformation, and particularly the Lutheran church. The mature Hegel would argue that religion is a necessary feature of the self-realisation of Absolute Spirit as it expresses in representational and symbolic form the truth that philosophy expresses conceptually. In this way it progresses beyond art which can only offer a sensuous and imaginative grasping after universal truth. Religion, however, expresses reality in symbolic and mythical fashion (although Hegel did not utilise the category of myth). For Hegel then, the necessary truth of Absolute Spirit's going forth from itself is conveyed religiously by the idea of the eternal generation of the Son in the Godhead. This going forth of the Son from the Father is united in the activity of the Spirit, and Hegel is one of the few people of his time to treat the doctrine of the **Trinity** as an essential truth of Christianity rather than an exercise in abstruse metaphysics. The nature of God is an eternal going forth from himself in a begetting of the Son and a returning to himself in the Spirit, although this returning to himself is something that is actualised in history. The incarnation is the symbol of the unity between Absolute Spirit and finite spirit in the God-man Jesus of Nazareth. But this unity has to be rent asunder and therefore Christ's death is necessary. So also is his resurrection and ascension to the Father as it makes possible the gift of the Spirit which makes immediate the fact of the incarnation to believers here and now. The goal is the overcoming of the separation of finite and absolute Spirit which is what Christian doctrine hopes for in the coming of the kingdom of God.

All this Christianity testifies to in symbolic and pictorial form and it is a true and necessary phase in human existence. It is this that makes Christianity the revelatory or 'absolute' form of religion according to Hegel. Nevertheless, everything that Christianity says can be better said conceptually or abstractly by philosophy, and Hegel's philosophy is the first to truly say it. From this it is clear why certain followers took Hegel at his word and interpreted his work in a purely philosophical and material sense and dispensed with the notion of Absolute Spirit. However, it is not clear that Hegel would ever have taken his system in that direction.

Although there are few today who are 'Hegelians' in the sense of adhering to the totality of his system, Hegel continues to exert a profound influence on contemporary theology. His recognition of the importance of the Trinity and its essentially relational nature can be seen to be a source for much contemporary Trinitarian theology, and particularly in the work of Jürgen **Moltmann** who most vigorously argues for some sense of the Trinitarian God's completion of Godself in the processes of history. The rediscovery of history as a theological category, and the idea that knowledge is historically and culturally shaped and determined, so stressed in contemporary philosophy, is clearly enunciated by Hegel. The notion of becoming as a central category for what it means to be – so prevalent in Process and related theologies – is the key to all of Hegel's thought. As such it is likely that this powerful and complex thinker, although certainly not straightforwardly orthodox in any normal sense, will continue to be a resource for Christian theology for some time to come.

See also: **Kant; Moltmann; Schleiermacher**

Glossary: ***Noumenal; Trinity***

Major writings

Early Theological Writings, trans. T.M. Knox, Chicago: University of Chicago Press, 1948
Hegel's Philosophy of Right, trans. T.M. Knox. London: OUP, 1967 (1977 printing)
Lectures on the Philosophy of World History: introduction, reason in history, trans. H.B. Nisbet with intro. by Duncan Forbes, Cambridge and New York: CUP, 1975
Phenomenology of Spirit, trans. A.V. Miller, Oxford: Clarendon Press, 1977
Lectures on the Philosophy of Religion, ed. P.C. Hodgson, Berkeley: University of California Press, 1984–85

Further reading

Michael Inwood (ed.), *Hegel*, Oxford: OUP, 1985
Terry Pinkard, *Hegel: a biography*, Cambridge and New York: CUP, 2000
Peter Singer, *Hegel: a very short introduction*, Oxford: OUP, 2001
Charles Taylor, *Hegel*, Cambridge and New York: CUP, 1975

HICK, JOHN HARWOOD (1922–)

One of the leading philosophers of religion in the English-speaking world during the second half of the twentieth century, John Hick has had a varied and interesting career teaching at Birmingham, Cambridge and Cornell universities as well as Claremont Graduate school in California. He has made significant contributions in a number of separate areas of discussion, virtually all of which have provoked intense discussion among his peers. Educated at Edinburgh and Oxford universities, Hick trained for the ministry of the then Presbyterian church in England at Westminster College, Cambridge. At Westminster he came under the influence of the Professor of Systematic Theology, H.H. Farmer. Farmer's thought was to provide a rich inspiration for Hick throughout much of his career and through him Hick was to be introduced to the theology of Farmer's teacher and predecessor, John Oman. Oman was the translator of Schleiermacher's *Speeches on Religion* (see **Schleiermacher**) and a major conduit for the promulgation of Schleiermacher's thought in Britain. Through his teachers, then, Hick was heir to that school of liberal Protestant theology that was dominant in Britain in the pre-Barthian era. Its charitable style, willingness to question received orthodoxy and strong sense of the importance of a free, personal response to divine grace were to be hallmarks of Hick's subsequent work too.

A significant portion of Hick's published output has centred around the concept of Christ's incarnation, analysing the ways in which it might be appropriate to say that Jesus is divine or the Son of God. Decisions taken in relation to these matters have had profound effects in relation to virtually every other area of Hick's thought. Thus we find that in 1958 in an article in the *Scottish Journal of Theology* Hick offered a critique of D.M. Baillie's Christology as outlined in his classic work *God was in Christ* (see **Baillie**).[i] Hick accused Baillie of developing an inadequate Christology as it was essentially adjectival in its affirmation of Christ's divinity. Hick argued that the litmus test for any valid Christology is that it should construe the deity of Christ in substantival, rather than merely adjectival, terms. However, in his most recent treatment of the topic of the incarnation, Hick acknowledges that it now seems ironic that one of his first forays into print was to critique Baillie for being insufficiently faithful to Chalcedonian orthodoxy when he wishes now to cite Baillie's approach as an example of the way ahead for 'inspiration/grace' models of Christology. Hick reads Baillie's approach to Christology as a way of so construing the divine/human relation that in principle it is possible that other examples of 'incarnation' could have occurred (and still could occur?) in other religious traditions.[ii] It is questionable whether either reading of Baillie is essentially accurate, but the example serves to show the range of movement in Hick's thought from the more or less broadly orthodox approach of his first work *Faith and Knowledge* (1957) to the later more questioning and heterodox work on religious pluralism.

Hick's early article on Baillie and his most recent work on Christology are punctuated rather neatly by his contribution in the mid-1970s to the celebrated volume of essays entitled *The Myth of God Incarnate* (1977) which Hick also edited. In his contribution to that volume, 'Jesus and the World Religions', Hick gave notice of the future direction that his work would take. His position in relation to the Christological claims of classical Christianity was crystallised in the famous statement: 'For to say, without explanation, that the historical Jesus of Nazareth was also God is as devoid of meaning as to say that this circle drawn with a pencil on paper is also a square'.[iii] Hick's point, of course, is to argue that although this claim has in fact been made it has no assignable content to it. Hick's view is that the New Testament affirmations of Jesus' divinity (if that is in fact what they are) are, strictly speaking, metaphorical statements rather than literal statements of fact.

It is interesting to note how consistent Hick's latest work on the incarnation is with his contribution to the original Myth of God collection of essays. For he continues to trade on the literal/

metaphorical distinction and the logical incoherence of traditional **Chalcedonian** Christology, but to this he adds the following arguments: (i) contemporary New Testament research shows that Jesus did not think he was God, nor did he make any such claim about himself; (ii) such claims made about Jesus by the Christian tradition have encouraged a domineering, superior and brutalising approach to other faiths and cultures and this attitude has served to legitimise many evils; and (iii) such an approach to Jesus is incompatible with our experience of a religiously plural world where we can acknowledge that genuine and equally valid experiences of the divine reality are made known and experienced in other faiths.

Serious engagement with such claims is beyond the scope of an essay of this sort but it is sufficient to point out that the simple distinction which Hick makes between literal, and therefore fact asserting language, as opposed to metaphorical, and therefore essentially figurative language, is one that would be challenged by many recent contributions in the field of religious language and hermeneutics. This is something of a surprising omission in Hick's case as he has been sensitive to the claims and nature of religious language ever since the publication of his first book *Faith and Knowledge*.

In that work Hick developed his celebrated theory of '*eschatological* (by which he meant postmortem rather than the end of all times) verification' as a response to the charge of the logical positivists that religious statements were neither true nor false but were strictly meaningless. The logical positivists held that such statements were meaningless because they were neither statements of necessary logical relationships, nor were they capable of empirical verification through the direct experience of our senses. Hick's response was to argue that in principle religious statements (but only those that were true) are capable of postmortem or eschatological verification, in that if beyond death one found oneself confronted by a loving God then Christian claims concerning God would thereby be shown to be true.

This theory was set within a larger framework that understood the nature of faith as an act of interpretation which 'sees' the world as providentially ordered. Hick concedes that the world is an essentially ambiguous place and the believer and non-believer are like two people on a journey. One construes the journey as a pathway to the Celestial City and interprets the entirety of the events and encounters of the journey in that light. The other sees the journey as essentially a meaningless ramble and interprets every experience from that perspective. Only at the end of the journey will one have been shown to have been correct and the other mistaken. However, they will not have been mistaken as to the 'factuality' of the things they experienced or the details of the journey. The difference between the two will be the understanding of these events and experiences within a totality of meaning. As Hick puts it:

> The theist and naturalist do not, qua theist and naturalist, necessarily expect different events to occur in the temporal process. They do not make characteristically differing historical predictions. But the theist does and the non-theist does not expect that when history is completed it will be seen to have led to a particular end-state and to have fulfilled a specific purpose, namely, that of creating 'children of God'. And this expectation assures for Christian theism the indubitable status of an assertion.[iv]

Hick's novel utilisation of postmortem existence as a means of verifying religious assertions and his stress upon the ambiguous nature of human living in the world were themes that were to be taken up again in what is perhaps his most celebrated work, *Evil and the God of Love* (1958). Here Hick contrasts the majority response of the Christian tradition to the problem of evil, which he traces to St **Augustine**, with another approach that Hick attributes to St **Irenaeus**.

According to Hick the Augustinian paradigm argues that an originally perfect creature (i.e. Adam and Eve), through the misuse of its God-given free will, chose to disobey God and thereby to introduce sin, suffering and death into the world. The origin of this free choice is ultimately lost in the mystery of human freedom and is inexplicable, but the effects are real and disastrous. Human beings have lost their original perfection and are now fundamentally flawed and prone to sin, and moreover their falling has had catastrophic effects on the natural order (perhaps due to the wrong choices of free spiritual beings – e.g. Satan and the fallen angels). Hick argues that this paradigm is no longer acceptable as an explanation for natural evil or suffering that is the result of the processes of the normal operations of the physical world. Furthermore, scientific theories about the evolution of the human species do not present us with an originally righteous and perfect creature who subsequently falls, but with the slow and painful emergence of human beings as rational and moral agents from the animal world.

In contrast to the Augustinian approach Hick retrieves and develops a distinction first made by Irenaeus. Irenaeus thought that there was a significant difference between the meaning of the terms made in the 'image' and made in the 'likeness' of God that we find in the Genesis accounts of the creation of human beings. He argued that we are made in the image of God and that the task of life is to grow into his likeness. Hick takes this suggestion as being potentially very fruitful for developing a contemporary response to the problem of evil and he argues that, instead of imagining an originally perfect creature who subsequently falls, we have to posit an amoral, immature creature with the propensity to grow and develop. This is in accord with what we know of human origins from science and it allows us to stop speaking of a fall from perfection but instead, using Hick's terminology, to speak of a 'fall up' to responsibility.

In order not to be overwhelmed by God's presence and in order to make a genuinely free response to God's loving presence it is necessary that this amoral creature is placed at an 'epistemic distance' from God. That is to say that our knowledge of God's presence is not so close as to overwhelm our free will. In order that the choices which the creature makes, and the virtues that are won as a result of those choices, are truly the creature's own it is further necessary that the creature is placed in a challenging and ambiguous environment. This environment then functions as a 'vale of soul-making' in which the creature develops virtues such as faith, generosity, courage, altruism, love, etc., through the free exercise of his or her will in the face of adversity. It is axiomatic for Hick that virtues freely developed as the result of the choices and actions of free creatures are intrinsically more valuable than would be the case if God had simply created creatures with those virtues intact. This much Hick concedes to the classical free-will defence, and it may be argued at this point that his whole position collapses to a defence of the intrinsic importance of human free will.

Hick is profoundly aware, of course, that on an individual level it is simply not the case that all human beings progress to higher levels of moral and spiritual behaviour through the experience of hardship and suffering. Realising this Hick is careful to argue that his position, if it applies at all, has to apply to humanity as a whole progressing through time. However, Hick is prepared to consider that human beings might live a series of lives whereby, on an individual level, they do gradually develop in their moral and spiritual response to God and neighbour. This might be seen as a Protestant and philosophically acute concession to the traditional Catholic concept of purgatory.

Generally speaking Hick's response to the problem of evil has been welcomed and some version of it may now even be the standard Christian response. However, many critics feel that it is an altogether too cosy view of evil and suffering the experience of which all too often seems crushing and destructive rather than edifying and constructive. The question is often posed: couldn't God have achieved the same result with a whole lot less evil in the world than there actually is? The scale of evil and suffering does seem wholly disproportionate to the putative gains that human beings make. Moreover, what image of God lies behind such an account?

Hick's solution to the problem of evil also had profound implications for his Christology, and it is no surprise that his next major area of discussion after *Evil and the God of Love* was the Myth debate discussed above. In modifying the classical perfection–fall– redemption account Hick had to devise a new place and rationale for the coming of Christ. For on his account human beings had no longer fallen and therefore could not require a redeemer in the traditional sense. Christ, therefore, becomes the exemplar of the divine/human relationship in that he embodies a paradigmatic human response to the divine presence and activity in the world. As we have seen, however, this response is simply one response mediated through a specific religious tradition and it can be matched and paralleled by other inspirational figures in the other great religious traditions of the world.

Hick's commitments to postmortem existence as part of his response to the problem of evil compelled him to deal with the substantial philosophical objections to any such existence in his next major book *Death and Eternal Life* (1976). Here Hick defended a 'replica' account of human immortality by arguing that beyond this life the conscious personality of the individual continues to exist in a dream–like form of mental existence. In order to justify this position Hick had to rebut the many arguments that deny the logical possibility of disembodied existence and he does this by utilising H.H. Price's account of a possible dream–like mental world where individuals exist in an environment that is mentally projected and characterised by wish fulfilment. However, Price's world will not do as a place of person formation as it would not provide the conditions for personal growth by constituting a challenging physical environment; and so, for Hick, this period must be an essentially transitional phase involving some form of self–evaluation, self–revelation and self–judgement.

The consistency of the related strands in Hick's thought is revealed once again by his assertion that beyond this dream–like transitional phase there will be another period (perhaps many others) of embodied existence (although not in the same physical universe that we now inhabit), and this corresponds to what the Christian tradition calls resurrection. These resurrected persons will have sufficient continuity in terms of memory and experience to satisfy the conditions of personal identity so that it is reasonable to make the claim that it is John Smith (in the case of John Smith) and not someone else who has been resurrected. This further stage of existence will also be a time of personal and spiritual growth through challenge until eventually the individual passes beyond embodiment into heaven, the presence of God or nirvana – in any event, beyond personal and separate egoity in space and time; this is what it means to be 'saved'. For Hick it is part of the conviction that God is love that this *'salvation'* is the eventual future of every person who has ever lived, although it will be the result of the free response of every creature to the gracious and luring love of God.

It will be clear from this that Hick has absorbed key themes and features from other religious traditions in developing his account of eternal life and what it might mean to be saved. This is fully in accord with another major movement in his thought which has been to acknowledge the validity and plurality of the various religious traditions of the world. Consideration as to the ways in which these separate and diverse movements might be said to be 'true' has led Hick to ever greater degrees of abstraction. He has tended to assert that the great world religions are paths to salvation and to speak of a universal salvific process. Although he is aware that salvation is a specifically Christian term, Hick believes that the term has functional analogues in the other great religious traditions of the world. This is by no means conceded and many would argue that Hick has a tendency to outline abstract concepts and principles that are held to apply across religions in such a way that they are divorced from the lived reality of a particular tradition and consequently lose their specificity and rich texture to a vapid and shallow assertion of sameness.

Nevertheless, Hick argues powerfully that we are in a time when a 'Copernican revolution' is taking place and consequently the Christian tradition has to move from a Christ-centred to a God-centred understanding of faith. Christianity can no longer see itself as the sole pathway to salvation, the Sun at the centre of the religious universe, but must now understand that it is but a particular mediation of the pathway to salvation that utilises the religious and cultural symbols of a particular religious tradition. In order to develop this approach Hick has explicitly adopted Kant's schema of an unknown **noumenal** reality and the **phenomenal** perception of that reality as it is mediated through space, history and culture (see **Kant**). On this model the Real (Hick's now preferred term for the divine reality in preference to God) in itself is unknown and unknowable, and the various religious traditions of the world are culturally specific interpretations of the Real which are always partial, limited and open to further development.

Given the scale and variety of the contributions that Hick has made (and may continue to make), it is hard to offer an assessment of his achievements. Certainly he has been one of the most significant figures in the philosophy of religion for most of the latter part of the past century, recognised by his invitation to be Gifford lecturer at the University of Edinburgh in 1986–87 (lectures published as *An Interpretation of Religion*, 1989). However, in a postmodern age there is a sense in which Hick's rationalist approach to faith is slowly moving out of favour. His response to the problem of evil, although suggestive, is often thought to be too neat, too academic and too tidy and not sufficiently sensitive to the tragic and disruptive extent of evil in the world. Sometimes he seems to be trying too hard to excuse the inexcusable. Similarly, his account of the ways in which the various religious traditions of the world may be said to be true, although laudable, has the air of academic and theoretical abstraction about it.

This may be a harsh assessment and it may be that the current predilection for the value of the particular, the local, the embodied tradition may be a passing phase and that once again the claims of universal and rational truth shall exert their fascination upon us. What cannot be denied is that Hick has constantly sought to wrestle with the central questions of religious faith and has done so with considerable intellectual vigour and honesty. Never content to be satisfied with the received certainties of tradition, Hick has probed and extended the boundaries of what is perceived to be religiously possible in ways that are suggestive if also profoundly challenging. No one knows what shape the future direction of theology will take but it is certain that the questions which Hick deals with will continue to fascinate the minds of subsequent generations of theologians.

Notes

i   J. Hick 'The Christology of D.M. Baillie', *The Scottish Journal of Theology*, Vol. 11. No.1, 1958
ii   *The Metaphor of God Incarnate*, pp.106–10
iii 'Jesus and the World Religions' in *The Myth of God Incarnate*, p. 178
iv   *Faith and Knowledge*, p.152

See also: **Augustine; Baillie; Irenaeus; Kant; Schleiermacher**

Glossary: Chalcedon; eschatological; noumenal; phenomenal; salvation

Major writings

Faith and Knowledge, New York: Cornell University Press, 1957
Evil and the God of Love, London: Fontana, 1958
Death and Eternal Life, New York: Harper & Row, 1976
The Myth of God Incarnate, ed. J. Hick, London: SCM Press, 1977
Problems of Religious Pluralism, London: Macmillan, 1985
An Interpretation of Religion, London: Macmillan, 1989
The Metaphor of God Incarnate, London: SCM Press, 1993

Further reading

P. Badham, *A John Hick Reader*, London: Macmillan, 1990
J. Hick, *John Hick: an autobiography*, Oxford: Oneworld Publications, 2002
T.R. Mathis, *Against John Hick: an examination of his philosophy of religion*, Lanham, MD: University Press of America, 1985
A. Sharma (ed.), *God, Truth and Reality: essays in honour of John Hick*, Basingstoke: Macmillan, 1992

IRENAEUS (c.130–c.200)

The most pre-eminent Christian theologian of the second century. Born in Asia Minor, Irenaeus is said to have known Polycarp, Bishop of Smyrna, who was a living link with the apostolic testimony of the early Church having heard the apostolic preaching first hand. This link with the apostolic witness to the faith was to provide Irenaeus with a ready-made strategy for dealing with the claims of his contemporary opponents – the Valentinian gnostics (see below). Irenaeus became Bishop of Lyons in Gaul around 177 after his predecessor had been martyred during a period of exacting persecution of the Church in those parts. It is important to realise that at this time Christian thought was extremely fluid and that a wide range of views existed within the Church. What we now know as orthodoxy had yet to establish itself as the definitive version of Christianity and Irenaeus was a key figure in the development of what was to become orthodox Christianity.

Irenaeus' complete works have not come down to us in an extant form and we only have late translations of two of them: *Against the Heresies* and *Proof of the Apostolic Preaching*. In *Against the Heresies*, which is the more considerable of the two works by far, Irenaeus attempts to refute the teaching of the Valentinian gnostics who claimed to possess a secret and special *revelation* of Jesus Christ to his apostles and who argued that knowledge of this spiritual truth (known only to an elite) was vital to salvation. In response to this Irenaeus argued that if the apostles had wished to vouchsafe a revelation of Jesus Christ they would have entrusted it to their successors the bishops. Irenaeus then proceeded to show the integrity of this succession of bishops by tracing the historical succession of bishops of the church in Rome back to the apostolic foundation of that church by Peter and by **Paul**. Irenaeus was wrong in assuming that Peter and Paul had founded the church in Rome and he also had to be creatively speculative in relation to the succession of bishops before Sextus (the sixth bishop of Rome). Rome had a position of prime importance for Irenaeus due to his belief in its doubly apostolic foundation, but also as the capital city of the Empire it had an especial significance for Christians everywhere. However, the point was made and it was to become increasingly influential that in contrast to the Gnostic stress upon secret revelations the Church stressed the public deposit of its faith in the persons of the bishops. It is, of course, important to note that Irenaeus was not slow to proffer the example of Polycarp, Bishop of Smyrna, who had known the apostles John and Philip, and who Irenaeus had personally heard, thus putting himself and his teaching at only one remove from the apostolic witness.

To further bolster his attack upon the Gnostics Irenaeus made use of the concept of a 'rule or canon of truth'. This was a brief and fairly flexible distillation of what the Church everywhere believed to be the essential scriptural witness to Christ. In essence it is very similar to his African contemporary Tertullian's 'rule of faith' (see **Tertullian**) and contains much that is similar to many early creeds. This 'rule' stresses the oneness and unity of God, stating that this God is the creator of heaven and earth, advocating a belief in one Christ Jesus who is the Son of God born for our salvation, the Holy Spirit, the Church and the future judgement. The question has been posed whether Irenaeus places this 'rule of truth' and the apostolic teaching of the bishops – what Irenaeus termed the 'tradition' of the Church – over the teaching of scripture. But this would be to misconstrue his intent. In an age when 'orthodoxy' had yet to be defined and where various 'canons of scripture' were favoured by differing churches and groupings within the Church, producing widely varying readings of the texts, then some regulative principle offering the essential and central understanding of the scriptures was necessary. The identity of this 'rule of truth' with the original apostolic message is safeguarded by the succession of bishops, but also, ultimately, by the Holy Spirit who inhabits the Church.

Irenaeus also stressed the validity of all four gospels as his Gnostic opponents tended to stress one or the other, or utilised only mutilated versions of the gospel texts. (There was as yet no 'official' canon of scripture agreed by all churches.) It is for this stress upon the scriptural message and his advocacy of the Old Testament as prefiguring the fuller and complete revelation of Christ given in the New Testament, allied to his conviction that scripture taken as a whole was self-explanatory as to its essential content, that Irenaeus is often described as a biblical theologian. Apostolic authorship was a key criterion for Irenaeus in deciding whether or not a specific text could be considered as a candidate for inclusion in the canon of scripture. Irenaeus then is a pivotal figure in the development of institutional Christianity in terms of an apostolic canon, an apostolic creed and an apostolic succession of bishops.

In addition to his development of the notion of a 'rule of truth' Irenaeus also made significant contributions to the doctrine of God, Christology and theological anthropology, some of which have proved influential even to this day. In opposition to the Gnostics who denied that the natural world was the work of God, Irenaeus stressed that the world and the heavens were the creation of the one true God and that God created them out of nothing rather than simply fashioning them from some pre-existent matter. This was to deny the Gnostic affirmation that creation was the work of a lesser God or even an angelic figure and that the material world was therefore inescapably evil and that salvation consisted of an escape from the constraints of our physical condition into a spiritual realm. This strongly physical character of Irenaeus' thought was to pervade his entire theology. In contrast to Gnostic speculation Irenaeus refused to allow any concept of a second God beyond the God who is the creator of everything, the only God and Father of all things.[i]

In agreement with his forebears in the faith Irenaeus argued that this God was one and unknowable in himself but contained within himself his Word and his Wisdom (which he identifies with the Spirit). This Word and Spirit Irenaeus termed the 'two hands of God' and it is through these 'hands' that God creates and inhabits the universe. In using this image of the Word (**Logos**) as the inherent rationality of God Irenaeus picks up and develops a theme developed by the Apologists. Unlike them, however, he refuses to speculate as to the origin of the Word and explicitly rejects the idea that the Logos is the immanent rationality of God expressed in creation in the same way as human speech is the expression of human thought, arguing that God is identical with his Word and always therefore complete in self expression.[ii] It is these two 'hands' of God active in creation that are the principal agents of God's revelation. Thus it is the Word who appeared to the Old Testament patriarchs and it is the Spirit who inspired prophecy in the Old Testament. The Word (or Son) is divine as whatever is begotten of God is God.[iii]

In relation to Christology Irenaeus forcefully asserted the unity of the person of Christ. This was against the Gnostic tendency to separate the human earthly Jesus of Nazareth from the heavenly Christ. Irenaeus' insistence upon the unity of God and man in Christ is directly related to his understanding of salvation. For only God himself (in the figure of the divine Word) could accomplish our redemption. Irenaeus' soteriology can be summed up in the famous phrase: ' . . . because of his measureless love he became what we are in order to enable us to become what he is'. Thus it is vital for Irenaeus that the Word assumed a real and true and entire human nature in order that human beings could be wholly and truly saved.

Underlying this concern is an anthropology which states that human beings were created in the image and likeness of God. Utilising this biblical imagery Irenaeus draws a distinction between the 'image', which refers to our rational and free natures, and the 'likeness', which refers to our possession of the Spirit. In the fall of Adam and through his act of disobedience human beings have lost the Spirit and the image has become incomplete. According to Irenaeus Adam was not the morally perfect super creature of some Christian speculation but was instead a morally neutral and child-like creature with the capacity for growth. However, all human beings share in some sense in his original act of disobedience and all are affected by the distortion of the image of God in us.

In the incarnation of the Word, which is the express image of the invisible God, the true image of God is revealed in human flesh. Just as human beings were included in Adam's original act of disobedience so now they are included in Christ's saving act through faith. A key concept for Irenaeus here is the notion of 'recapitulation' which asserts that the incarnate Christ 'recapitulates' in his life and death everything that Adam lost. It is important then that Christ should live a fully human life, being subject to the temptations of the devil (and overcoming such temptations through obedience) and eventually undergoing death itself to save humanity fully from sin. The concept of 'recapitulation' enables Irenaeus to marry the sacrificial imagery of the New Testament with the 'physical' account of salvation that seems uppermost in his thought. In relation to this some commentators have suggested that it is the incarnation itself rather than the death of Christ on the cross which accomplishes salvation in Irenaeus' scheme. However, by stressing the importance of Christ's obedience – an obedience even unto death on the cross – and its pivotal place in Christ's recapitulation of Adam's disobedience, Irenaeus is able to bring together what might initially seem to be two disjunctive themes. Thus he writes '. . . in obliterating the disobedience of man originally enacted on the tree, He became obedient unto death, even the death on the cross, healing the disobedience enacted on a tree by obedience on a tree'.[iv]

Irenaeus' strong commitment to the physical and fleshly nature of salvation and his complete rejection of Gnostic attempts to spiritualise the matter, allied to an inherent faithfulness to biblical imagery as opposed to philosophical speculation, led him to argue vociferously for a bodily resurrection, the coming of the new Jerusalem and the earthly reign of the saints.

It would be hard to overemphasise the importance of Irenaeus in the development of Christian theology at the time during which he lived. Faced with a powerful and attractive call to 'spiritualise' the message of salvation into secret Gnostic myths Irenaeus boldly contested both for the public nature of Christian truth and for its firm attachment to physical reality. The created order was not an evil to be escaped from but was instead a gracious gift of God which was to be the theatre of God's glory as he carried out the work of our salvation within it. The strong affirmation of a Christian commitment to a creator God and the goodness of creation were to become keynote themes in the Christian rejection of Gnosticism. Similarly, his realisation that the incarnation necessarily involved the assumption of a fully human nature in Christ was an insight that proved crucial in the development of later Christological theory – although some of Irenaeus' successors were almost to lose sight of its fundamental importance at times. Contemporary thinkers have also found his thought congenial, most notably the philosopher John **Hick**, who has utilised Irenaeus' distinction between the 'image' and 'likeness' of God as well as the related idea that Adam was not created perfect but was in fact morally neutral as the basis for his own response to the problem of evil.

Notes

i   *Against the Heresies*, 2.1.1
ii   *Ibid.*, 2.30.9

iii *Proof of the Apostolic Preaching*, p.47
iv *Against The Heresies*, 5.16.3

See also: **Hick; Paul; Tertullian**

Glossary: **Logos; revelation**

Major writings

Proof of the Apostolic Preaching / St. Irenaeus, trans. & annotated Joseph P. Smith, New York: Newman Press, 1978
Against the Heresies / St. Irenaeus of Lyons, trans. & annotated Dominic J. Unger, with further revisions by John J. Dillon, New York: Paulist Press, 1992

Further reading

Grant, Robert M. (Robert McQueen), *Irenaeus of Lyons*, London: Routledge, 1997
Minns, Denis, *Irenaeus*, London: Geoffrey Chapman, 1994

JOHN OF DAMASCUS (c.675–749)

Often regarded as the greatest theologian of the Eastern Church in the period between Maximus the Confessor and Gregory Palamas, John of Damascus wrote one of the first and greatest comprehensive summaries of the Christian faith in his *The Fount of Knowledge*. John Damascene, as he is often known, was born into a prominent Christian family named Mansour (victory) that served in the court of Omayyad Caliph Abdul-Malek in Damascus. John thus grew up and understood the world as one who viewed matters from the perspective of the fringes of the Christian world and in an Islamic context. His father Sergius had held high political office and after his death John succeeded him as a high official of the Caliph.

During the iconoclastic controversy instigated by Emperor Leo III's ban on the use of images and icons in Christian churches – a ban which John vigorously opposed – it is said that the emperor had documents forged that implicated John in a plot to attack Damascus. Called to account for his actions by the Caliph, John asked leave to retire from his post to the St Sabas Monastery near Jerusalem. There, after a period of some testing in which the monks expected the brilliant Mansour to desist from writing and study, he was eventually allowed to devote himself to a life of writing, preaching and teaching. He was ordained a priest around 735.

In the monastery John of Damascus devoted himself to writing commentaries upon biblical texts, treatises supporting the veneration of images and icons, works on Christology as well as the already mentioned summa on The *Fount of Knowledge*. In addition he was a prolific hymn writer and composer and creator of many liturgical canons for the Eastern Church. After his death around 749, he was anathematised as an image worshipper by his iconoclastic opponents at the pseudo Great Council of Constantinople in 752.

The iconoclastic controversy began in 726 when Emperor Leo III ordered the destruction of all paintings, statues and mosaics representing Christ. John Damascene defended the veneration of images in three significant treatises entitled 'Orations on the Holy Images' (c.727–33). John argued for the appropriateness of the use of images in churches on many counts. He pointed out that as cherubim and seraphim had once adorned the Ark of the Covenant and as Solomon had adorned the walls of the Temple in Jerusalem with images then Christians should also be permitted to adorn their churches. More positively, he argued that icons act as aids to devotion in that that they make Christ and the saints more real to the believer. He also insisted that the prohibition against images which is expressly found in the ten commandments no longer applied since Christ came in the flesh. Citing Basil of Caesarea (see **Cappodocian Fathers**) as an authority who said that 'The honour and veneration of the image is transferred to its prototype', John argued that it is not the visible object that is worshipped but that which it represents. Furthermore, John made a distinction between true worship (*latreia*) which is reserved for God alone, and that form of lesser worship or reverence (*proskynēsis*) which is afforded to visible things. Finally, as a *coup de grâce*, John argued that to fail to venerate things because they are material is to treat matter as evil and thus to fall into an unwanted dualism: 'I do not worship matter, but I worship the Creator of matter, who for my sake became material and accepted to dwell in matter, who through matter effected my salvation. I will not cease from reverencing matter, through which my salvation came to pass ... Do not insult matter: for it is not without honour. Nothing is to be despised that God has made. That is a Manichaean error.' In relation to the whole manner of the attempt by the emperor to impose his will upon the Church in this matter John argued for the freedom of the Church over against the emperor's attempts to force his will upon it.

John's major contribution is of course *The Fount of Knowledge*, sometimes referred to as the *Source of Gnosis* and variously dated between 728 and 743. It is divided into three parts: the first dealing with matters philosophical, the second dealing with heresies and the third offering an orthodox exposition of the Christian faith. The first section is entitled 'Dialectica' and opens with the words 'Nothing is more excellent than knowledge'. John proceeds thereafter to offer an analysis of various concepts such as being, substance, accident, species and genus in terms which are characteristically patristic and Aristotelian. The second section deals with heresies and closely follows in form and content a previous work on heresy by Epiphanius, save that Epiphanius did not consider the case of Islam whilst John adds a significant and lengthy comment on the nature of Islam in his discussion. In a manner later to be followed by Adolf **Harnack**, John controversially viewed Islam as a Christian heresy. John, of course, had lived among Muslims and experienced Islam as the dominant culture and this may account for his fiercely polemical approach to it. He saw in the advent of Islam a forerunner of the Anti-Christ, and he considered Muhammad to be a false prophet who had a very confused and superficial knowledge of the Bible and who was influenced by an Arian monk (see **Arius**).

The third section is John's 'Exposition of the Orthodox Faith', which offers a systematic presentation of the faith of the Eastern Church. It is heavily influenced by the three Cappadocian Fathers whose thought is followed most closely, although **Athanasius** is also referred to frequently. In common with prevailing practice **Origen** is regarded as an heretic and is cited only when John wishes to differ from him and thereby to condemn his opinion.

The work is divided into 100 chapters and the first fourteen deal with the being of God. Following the Cappadocians, John presents God as incomprehensible and ineffable – which is to say unknowable. God is above and beyond all existing things and exists in a perfect form of existence that is unique to God alone. Since knowledge has to do with what is and God is above all being, so God is above all knowledge. In a phrase that was to become influential throughout the Christian tradition and to influence the later work of Thomas **Aquinas**, 'it is beyond our capacity to say anything about God or even to think of him, beyond the things which have been divinely revealed to us . . .'

Yet God has implanted in our minds certain convictions about himself and the creation and preservation of the world show us that he exists and reveal his power and majesty. Moreover, through the law and the prophets, and most especially in Jesus Christ, God has told us all that is possible and needful to know. Beyond this we must not go and John is especially strong on warning against the desire to know more than has been revealed.

Despite God's incomprehensibility we can know that he is eternal, uncreated, unchangeable, incorporeal, infinite, etc., as well as the fact that he is the creator of all things. Similarly, revelation in the form of the scriptural injunction to baptise in the name of the Father, Son and the Holy Spirit teaches us that God is *trinitarian*, existing in one substance and three hypostases. John's account of the Trinity is couched in fairly standard terms which would have been familiar to anyone versed in the traditional Eastern approach. He points out in passing that the Eastern Church does not confess the double procession of the Holy Spirit from God the Father and God the Son because the Father alone is the true source of the Godhead, but this does not seem to be a major point of conflict for him.

In relation to creation John argues that God created the world by thinking it into existence, the Logos carrying out his thought and the Spirit perfecting it. God created the angelic realm – spirits of immaterial fire – intelligent essences with the power of free will whose function was to minister to God. Angels are not immortal by virtue of their natures but by grace, for God alone is eternal. Evil is a result of the fall of the devil who was an angel who used his free will to rebel against God. Evil, according to John, is thus the absence of good as darkness is the absence of light. Fallen angels have no possibility of repentance. In relation to human free will and the providence of God all things are foreknown but are not predetermined by God. Thus God does not cause evil but permits it.

In a lengthy series of chapters on the person of Christ John defends the orthodox view that Christ had two natures – human and divine, and two wills – human and divine – in opposition to the counter positions which asserted that Christ had one hybrid nature and one divine will. John thus gave formal and rigorous expression – utilising a host of previous thinkers – to the orthodox and received account of the Christian faith. He marshalled his forces into a coherent and powerful, if not very creative, synthesis that served as a basis for Christian orthodoxy for many years to come and which, as we have already seen, was known and used by that great systematiser of the medieval period, Thomas Aquinas.

John was an important figure not least for his many hymns and liturgical writings which are still in use in the worship of the Orthodox Church today. He also wrote a sort of thesaurus of scriptural and patristic passages dealing with ethical issues entitled *Sacra Parallela* as well as rewriting a Buddhist tale which he titled *Barlaam and Josaphat*.

John's position with regard to the use of icons was to be vindicated at the seventh ecumenical Council of Nicaea in 787 which provided a theological rationale for the use of icons in worship which broadly followed the principles set down by John. John has always been an authoritative source for the Orthodox Church and in 1890 he was also declared a doctor of the Roman Catholic church.

See also: **Aquinas; Arius; Athanasius; Augustine; Cappadocian Fathers; Harnack**

Glossary: **Revelation; Trinitarian**

Major writings

Saint John of Damascus: Writings, trans. F.H. Chase, Washington: Catholic University of America Press, 1999 (1958)
On the Divine Images: the apologies against those who attack the divine images, trans. David Anderson, New York: St. Vladimir's Seminary Press, 1980
A Select Library of the Nicene and Post-Nicene Fathers of the Christian Church, Second Series, 14 vols, ed. H. Wace & P. Schaff, New York, Vol. 9, *Hilary of Poitiers, John of Damascus*, Peabody, MA.: Hendrickson, 1999

Further reading

D.J. Sahas, *John of Damascus on Islam. The 'Heresy of the Ishmaelites'*, Leiden, Brill, 1972

JUSTIN MARTYR (c.100–65)

Justin is the first 'Father' of the Greek Church. Just as the Christian literature of the New Testament in its developed form, and the little treatises of the so-called Apostolic Fathers which followed it, were written in Greek, so Justin remains within the Greek tradition of language and culture which was to be a central factor in the history of the early Church. Of course Greeks thought in many different ways, and their culture was permeated by Semitic influence in all sorts of ways, but still this Hellenistic (Greek) legacy was to be extremely potent.

The Greek Fathers lived at a time when the canon of the New Testament scriptures was becoming firmly fixed. They could no longer see themselves as direct witnesses to Christ in the way that certain writers of the New Testament were believed to have been direct witnesses. For them the direct witness is contained in the literature of the New Testament, and they rest on this foundation for the whole of their work. As Von Campenhausen said: 'They did not write gospels, apocalypses and apostolic letters but interpretations and treatises, polemical and apologetic tracts of a devotional, systematic and occasionally historical nature, keeping to their own background of knowledge and method'. It is the beginning of the first forms of systematic reflection on the nature of Christian faith and of the attempts to relate that faith to the culture at large. Justin is important in making that transition as he offers an apology (a defence) of the Christian faith to the cultured men and women of his day.

Justin was born near Sichem (Schechem) in Palestine. He was reasonably well off, did not have to earn his living and so could devote himself to philosophy, to the pursuit of knowledge and truth, as he thought of it. It was as a budding philosopher that he first came into contact with Christians, and himself became a Christian, describing the faith as 'the only reliable and useful philosophy that I have found'. His early work, *Dialogue with the Jew Trypho*, described how after a long search through all the philosophies then available Justin came to accept Christian truth. Around 155, when more than 50 years old, he published in Rome his *Apology* – a defence of his faith addressed to the emperor and his counsellors, and to the heathen – and it was there in Rome that Justin was martyred fairly soon afterwards.

In the *Apology*, typical of many such works, Justin described his search for truth in Stoic philosophy, and criticised the Stoics for having no real interest in God. The Peripatetic (another sort of wandering philosopher) always expects to be paid for his scraps of so-called wisdom. And there was (in his opinion) no real point in looking for help from the Pythagoreans (another ancient school of philosophers) because they presuppose a mass of musical, astronomical and geographical learning which Justin neither possessed nor had the time to acquire. For him philosophy is merely a shadow of the ultimate truth embodied in Christianity. Justin is attempting to create a bridge between the wisdom found in the biblical writings and the wisdom of classical antiquity. Thus Plato is not to be discarded, but is seen now as someone who reiterates the true meaning of another group of ancient philosophers, namely the Old Testament prophets, Ultimately, Plato is viewed as prefiguring the teaching of Christ and so is a sort of Christian before Christ.

Justin was attempting to make Christianity intelligible to the intellectual culture of his day and he tried to show that platonism had been allied to Christianity from the beginning. Hence his stress that Plato is a fore-runner pointing to the prophets. It is made to seem more or less an historical accident that Plato did not live to see the fullness of God's revelation in Christ. For Justin, inasmuch as Plato lived his life in accordance with reason, he was practically a Christian.

Thus for Justin God has acted at all times among all people everywhere, before finally revealing himself in Jesus Christ. A key concept for Justin is the development of the term Logos – by which he meant the expressive rational activity of God throughout the world. It is through the Logos that God is present everywhere in the universe. Jesus Christ is identified with the eternal Logos or reason, i.e. the divine reason itself, and is thus the perfect embodiment and unique incarnation of God's universal presence in the world. Therefore, all who have lived according to reason (*kata logon*), all who have responded to God's universal prompting and enlightening through the Logos, have shared in some sense in God's purpose and activity. Thus the wise men of the world have had some apprehension of the truth that is fully known only in Jesus Christ. Although it is true that Christ suffered and died, that is the fate of all true philosophers.

It might be thought that God's involvement and crucifixion and resurrection flies in the face of reason. But for Justin these events are irrefutable certainties based on the witness of the Bible, itself a book full of proofs of the truth of Christianity.

As far as the Bible is concerned, Justin stresses that the mere mechanical repetition of texts is of no value. He seeks scriptural proofs by applying allegorical interpretation of the kind current in the rabbinical and Hellenistic Judaism of the time. This involves assembling hidden clues in scripture to prove that the Old Testament is the prefiguration of Christ, e.g. that the tree of life in paradise, the stone pillar of Bethel, the staffs of Aaron and Moses, the rod and staff of the twenty-third psalm are 'types' of the cross of Christ and prophecies of Christ himself. The truth of Christianity is thus plain for all to see, on the unquestionable authority of the prophets who point to Christ. Proof is also to be found in the miracles. In his *Apology* Justin pleads for a fair hearing, commends the faith and life of Christians, stresses the superiority of Christianity to paganism, emphasises the argument from prophecy, notes that paganism is an imitation of Christian worship and invites his detractors to Christian worship.

The truth in Christ is essentially universal, and can take in other forms of truth. But whereas philosophy requires education and few can have access to truth in this way, no one is excluded from the truth manifest in Christ the Logos. In terms of later orthodoxy Justin's thought is embryonic and incomplete. He referred to the 'Son' as a second or lesser God for example. He had little to say about the Spirit's relation to the Father and the Son and so rarely offers a genuinely **Trinitarian** account of the nature of God. Indeed, insofar as he seems to regard the Logos as being the immanent principle of reason within God the Father that is not fully expressed until the moment of creation when God says 'Let there be light', then it could be argued that Justin does not regard the distinction of the person within the Trinity as being eternal. Nevertheless, we have to remember that much was still fluid and uncertain about the development of Christian doctrine during this period and that Justin was attempting as best he could to state the faith in terms that were meaningful to his age.

Glossary: **Logos; Trinity/Trinitarian**

Major writings

Apology and Dialogue with Trypho, in *The Ante-Nicene Fathers: the writings of the Fathers down to A.D. 325*, ed. Alexander Roberts & James Donaldson; rev. A. Cleveland Coxe; Vol. 1, *Apostolic Fathers, Justin Martyr, Irenaeus*, Peabody, MA: Hendrickson, 1995

Further reading

L.W. Barnard, *Justin Martyr: his life and thought*, Cambridge: CUP, 1967
E.F. Osborn, *Justin Martyr*, Tübingen: Mohr (Siebeck), 1973

KANT, IMMANUEL (1724–1804)

German philosopher born in Königberg in East Prussia in 1724. Kant was to live, teach, write and die in this city. He was a man whose outward life was relatively uneventful and it is said that he was so regular and punctual in his habits that the housewives of the town set their clocks by the timing of his afternoon walk (except for a famous occasion when Kant was profoundly shaken from his routine by reading Rousseau's *Emile*). Kant eventually became Professor of Logic and Metaphysics at Königberg University in 1770. He wrote and published many works and his earliest writings touched upon scientific as well as religious and mystical issues, but for the sake of brevity we must here focus on his principal writings on religion.

Kant is often regarded as the greatest philosopher of the modern age and he both epitomised the spirit of the **Enlightenment** in its veneration of the powers of reason while at the same time demonstrating the proper limits and boundaries of that reason. Kant, who seems himself to have been of Scottish descent on his father's side, claimed to have been awoken from his dogmatic slumbers by the Scottish empiricist philosopher David Hume.

Hume, in common with other empiricist philosophers such as Locke and Berkeley, had famously argued that there was no knowledge beyond that which could be acquired by sense-experience. On this model the mind simply receives sensory impressions and forms judgements concerning them and consequently the only objects of knowledge as such are the objects of sensation. Beginning from this basic premise Hume argued that scepticism concerning our knowledge of the external world was the logical outcome as we could only be said to have perceptions derived from sensory experience. For Hume this caused great difficulty with such everyday concepts as causation, and even the idea that there are underlying substances to which our everyday experience of colour, taste and touch apply. According to Hume, although it may be the case that we universally observe a number of conjunctions in which one event always follows another, nevertheless, it is true to say that as we never actually possess a 'sensory experience' of the cause itself we have no rational or logical basis for inferring that one event is in fact the cause of another We may, and do, infer it, but this is merely a psychological disposition on our part rather than a certain feature of the external world. Similarly, we may taste, touch, see and feel the properties of a putative substance, but as we have no direct experience of substances themselves apart from the properties that we experience, we therefore have no basis for inferring a substance beyond the properties. This approach had serious implications for claims to knowledge about suprasensible realities and Hume was not slow to point out the implications for theism (particularly in relation to arguments focusing upon God as First Cause), but also, it must be said, he pointed out the negative implications of his arguments for the practice of science too.

Kant initially inclined towards a different view of the matter and he followed the continental rationalist school of philosophy exemplified by Wolff and Leibniz which, in contradistinction to Hume's empirical leanings, believed that not all ideas were derived from sensory experience but that some were innate to reason itself. Kant's first critique (*Critique of Pure Reason*, 1781) is best understood as a synthesis that attempts to bridge these two positions. Kant sought to argue that the mind does not simply receive ideas but actually imposes order and structure upon the sensory experiences that it receives. The mind utilises formal concepts, which Kant termed *a priori* concepts, to make sense of the raw data of experience. Among these *a priori* concepts are categories such as space and time which do not belong to things in themselves but are imposed upon them by the mind. Space and time therefore are innate concepts that act as a schema through which the mind actively imposes order and structure upon the manifold diversity of sensory experience.

Important as this move was as a response to Hume it did have the implication of effectively conceding at least something to Hume's sceptical position in that it meant that we do not know things as they truly are in themselves, but only as they appear to us via the structuring concepts which we must inevitably impose upon them if we are to 'know' at all. Kant's famous distinction for this is that we can only know the '*phenomenal*' reality of things, that is things as they appear to us, but we cannot know the '*noumenal*' reality of things as they are in themselves. On first sight this may seem a strange concept, and Kant suggested that his views constituted a 'Copernican revolution' in philosophy in that he denied we had access to a world which is 'out there' independent of our experience of it. However, if we concede that space, time and causation are structuring categories of the mind then we see at once that we cannot know things as they are in themselves. For in Kant's view objects in the world do not exist in space and time and this is a form of existence which is completely alien and unintelligible to us given our innate predisposition to understand and interpret everything via these categories. Knowledge is thus an interaction between that which we perceive via sensory input and the innate concepts in our minds by which we order and interpret our perceptions – in Kant's famous phrase, 'Percepts without concepts are blind; concepts without percepts are empty.'

Obviously, such a view imposes great difficulty in assuming any form of knowledge of a suprasensible reality such as God. Kant did not shrink from such a conclusion and he maintained that speculative reason could not demonstrate the existence of God, nor could God be regarded as an *a priori* concept of pure reason. Kant dealt with the problematic nature of the knowledge of God in a section of the *Critique of Pure Reason* entitled the 'Transcendental Dialectic'. In this section Kant attempts to deal with the contradictions or antimonies that reason necessarily enters into when it strays into areas that are beyond the boundaries of what is possible for it.

Although Hume had already effectively dismantled many of the traditional arguments for the existence of God, Kant subjects three of the arguments to further penetrating and devastating criticism. Kant considers and rejects the ontological argument for the existence of God (see **Anselm** for more detail), famously arguing that existence is not an attribute or predicate. The argument, if it is to work, depends upon existence being a property or attribute such that a perfect being would necessarily possess as an implication of being perfect. But existence is not an attribute and to say that some thing 'exists' is not to add anything to the concept of the thing itself but is rather to say that there is an instantiation of such an entity in the world of things. In Kant's own example, to assume the existence of a triangle and at the same time deny that it has three angles is contradictory, but there is no contradiction in denying both the triangle and its three angles. Similarly, there is no inconsistency in rejecting the existence of an absolutely perfect being.

Kant rejects the cosmological argument (an argument from the sheer fact of the world to the inference of a necessary cause of the world) because it depends upon the notion of causation which is applicable only to the world of sensory experience and thus cannot demonstrate the existence of something outwith the sensory world. It also contains within it an implicit appeal to the ontological argument with its utilisation of the concept of an absolutely necessary being which is again to make the same mistake as the ontological argument by making a logical transition from concept to reality. The third argument that Kant considers is what he termed the physico-theological argument which is better known as the design argument. This argument appeals to the order, design and purpose that is found in the world and argues that there must be a 'designer' to explain these features. This argument too is fallacious, although Kant does allow it some psychological appeal. Nevertheless, upon examination it appears to perpetrate most of the failings of the other two arguments, but also it fails because even if it were successful it at most proves the existence of an architect of the world whose powers, although impressive, would not be those of God.

Kant thus concludes that there can be no transcendental theology based on reason, but he was not himself an atheist and he famously argued: 'I have found it necessary to deny *knowledge*, in order to make room for *faith*'.[1] As we have seen, God, for Kant, is not an object known through the exercise of speculative reason, but is rather an undeniable postulate of practical or moral reason. Kant turned specifically to consider the arena of practical reason in his second great critique – *The Critique of Practical Reason* (1788). Here Kant turned his attention to that aspect of existence which was fundamental to his whole philosophy – the field of moral action. It is vital to an understanding of Kant to understand that for him the central and most important truth about human beings is not that they are observers of the world, but that they are agents in the world. The world as the arena of moral action was of central importance to Kant. He regarded the moral duty that all human beings recognise as an obligation upon them to be a fundamental feature of human existence. But morality is also rational and is governed by rational laws or maxims: Kant termed these maxims the 'categorical imperative'. Kant described the categorical imperative in various ways, but two of the most common forms of description are that human beings should act in such a way that the maxim behind their actions could be generalised as a universal law for everyone, and that we should always treat people as ends in themselves, never as merely means.

Moral action consists in following one's duty for duty's sake and not on the basis of the consequences of our moral choices. On the basis of the unconditional demand exerted upon us by our moral nature, Kant argued for his famous three postulates of practical reason: God, freedom and immortality. His moral argument for the existence of an absolute being is linked to his notion of the highest good which will obtain when virtue and happiness are dispensed appropriately. It is self evidently the case in this life that virtue does not always coincide with happiness in that the just may live squalid, short and unhappy lives whilst the evil and vicious may enjoy all manners of pleasures throughout a long and carefree existence. Consequently, we have to postulate those conditions whereby virtue, justice and happiness will coincide. This involves an absolute being who has the power and the insight to punish and reward appropriately and, since such conditions do not pertain in this life, and must therefore be satisfied beyond this life, we must also presuppose the condition of immortality. From the basis of the fact that true morality has to be an autonomous act of our rational will then we have to postulate freedom. It is important to recognise that these postulates are not rationally demonstrable truths but function in the moral sphere as *a priori* conditions which underpin our moral action in the world and without which our moral acts would be meaningless.

Kant turned to a treatment of religion specifically in *Religion within the Limits of Reason Alone* published in 1793. Most of Kant's references to formal religion *per se* are negative in that he was against creeds, confessions and rituals as essentially contradicting the rational and moral autonomy of the individual. The only religion that he truly considers is the Christian religion and within that only its Protestant form. This form of the Christian religion is the 'moral' religion *par excellence*. But is there a place for religion at all given what Kant has said of the autonomous basis of morality? Religion in a sense fulfils morality rather than replacing it in that it images a 'lawgiver whose will ought to be man's final end'.

Kant begins the book with a discussion of the presence of evil in human beings and the world and he recognises that we have both a universal propensity for evil acts which we seem powerless to control (which need not be formally proved due to the multitude of crying examples),[ii] but nevertheless because we are free agents it is the case that it is possible for us to overcome this basic inclination. Here, in a manner which shocked many of his admirers, Kant treats of the traditional Christian doctrine of original sin, that great *bête noir* of Enlightenment thinkers. Kant agrees that the notion of an original fall from grace in the person of Adam is a most unhelpful explanation of the matter. However, unlike many of his Enlightenment predecessors, he is not convinced of the innate goodness of human beings either. For experience teaches that there is no denying our propensity for evil acts that deny the moral law. And as the moral law is denied as a divine command it is therefore sin. However, human beings are not stuck fast in subjection to this propensity for evil for as 'the moral law commands that we *ought* now to be better men, it follows inevitably that we must *be able* to be better men'.[iii]

For Kant the purpose of religion is to bring into being a community of morally perfect human beings. Christ on this model is the historic exemplar of the perfect moral life, although strictly speaking we do not need an historical example of this. The radical nature of Kant's thought in relation to the traditional Christian dogma of the incarnation can be clearly seen in the following quotation:

> Now if it were indeed a fact that such a truly godly-minded man at some particular time had descended, as it were, from heaven to earth and had given men in his own person, through his teachings, his conduct, and his sufferings, as perfect an example of a man well-pleasing to God as one can expect to find in external experience (for be it remembered that the *archetype* of such a person is to be sought nowhere but in our own reason), and if he had, through all this, produced immeasurably great moral good upon earth by effecting a revolution in the human race – even then we should have no cause for supposing him other than a man naturally begotten .... But to suppose the latter can in no way benefit us practically, inasmuch as the archetype which we find embodied in this manifestation must, after all, be sought in ourselves (even though we are but natural men).[iv]

It is no surprise that after the publication of this volume Kant was required to promise to his king that he would thereafter refrain from publishing on such matters. It will also come as no surprise to learn that Kant had little place for the doctrine of the *Trinity* in his account of religion. Kant's ethical commonwealth of free moral agents is distinguished by the fact that its members freely obey the moral law without coercion. The goal of what Kant terms ecclesiastical faith (scriptural and revealed faith under the social and historical forms of existence) is to make the gradual transition from 'ecclesiastical faith to the universal religion of reason and so to a (divine) ethical state on earth ... ' – and this for Kant would constitute the kingdom of God on earth.

There is no gainsaying Kant's immense influence upon all subsequent Christian theology – either positively or negatively. **Hegel** would attempt to overcome Kant's bifurcation of reality into the noumenal and the phenomenal by a grand unifying theory of Absolute Spirit. **Schleiermacher** sought to deny that religion was primarily a Kantian 'doing' by re-describing religion as a 'feeling' or sense of the infinite wholeness of things. Nineteenth-century theology in the form of the neo-Kantian school of **Ritschl**, Hermann and **Harnack** would explore the outer limits of his moral conception of religion, along with his portrayal of Christ as our moral exemplar. Whatever one makes of his philosophical system as a whole – and it has many critics – there is no doubt that Kant's critical philosophy acts as a pivotal fulcrum in the history of theology. The development of modern Christian theology can almost be wholly read as an attempt to respond to the challenges that Kant laid down. His restriction of the role of reason to the world of sensory experience and his related destruction of the proofs for the existence of God continues to influence debates on the rationality and possibility of belief in God today – even when the proponents do not always recognise that they are drawing upon Kantian themes. However, Kant's moral grounding for religion has fared less well. His basic premise that there is a universally experienced moral obligation is not everywhere accepted, and even where it is accepted it is argued that Kant was not sufficiently aware of the social, cultural and historical conditionings of that sense of obligation. Neither is it generally accepted that the notions of God, freedom and immortality are uncontested postulates that form the necessary and basic conditions of moral experience in the world.

Notes

i   *Critique of Pure Reason*, p.29

ii   *Religion within the Limits of Reason Alone,* p.28
iii   *Ibid.,* p.46
iv   *Ibid.,* p.57

See also: **Harnack; Hegel; Ritschl; Schleiermacher**

Glossary: Enlightenment; noumenal; phenomenal; Trinity

Major writings

Critique of Pure Reason, trans. N. Kemp Smith, London: Macmillan, 1929 (1781); corrected 1933
Prolegomena to any future Metaphysics that can qualify as a science, New York: Bobbs-Merrill, 1950 (1783)
Groundwork of the Metaphysics of Morals, trans. H.J. Paton, New York: Harper & Row, 1964 (1785)
Critique of Practical Reason, trans. L. Beck, Chicago: University of Chicago Press, 1949 (1788)
Critique of Judgement, trans. J.C. Meredith, Oxford: Clarendon Press, 1952 (1790)
Religion within the Limits of Reason Alone, trans. T.M. Greene & Hoyt H. Hudson, New York: Harper & Brothers, 1960 (1793)

Further reading

G. Di Giovanni, *Religion and Rational Theology,* trans. A.W. Wood, Cambridge: CUP, 1996
G.E. Michalson, Jr, *Kant and the Problem of God,* Oxford: Blackwell, 1999

KIERKEGAARD, SØREN (1813–55)

Søren Kierkegaard was a highly influential nineteenth-century thinker, although his importance for theology was to emerge only in the early twentieth century through his impact on **Barth**, **Bultmann** and the *existential* movement in philosophy and theology. Born in Copenhagen in 1813 Kierkegaard's childhood was dominated by his father, whose mournful disposition was based on a mysterious moral lapse that haunted him all his life. Kierkegaard grew up lonely and introverted but highly intelligent and well educated. Most of his siblings died at an early age. He studied philosophy and theology at the University of Copenhagen from 1830, passing his final theological exam ten years later. He was much influenced by the thought of **Hegel** whose philosophical system much of his own work is attempting to overthrow. He became engaged to Regine Olsen, with whom he was deeply in love, but he broke off the engagement in 1841 for reasons which remain a mystery, and instead devoted his life to writing. It is clearly a decision which haunted Kierkegaard and many of his later writings seem to have been prompted by his reflecting upon his mysterious inability to follow through on his love for Regine. Practically all of his life was spent in Copenhagen, with the exception of three visits to Berlin in 1841–42.

In a series of books, of which the best known perhaps are *Fear and Trembling* (1843), *Either/Or* (1843), *Philosophical Fragments* (1844) and *Concluding Unscientific Postscript* (1846), Kierkegaard produced a highly original critique and reaffirmation of Christian faith. The problem of how to be a Christian in a Christendom (state-sponsored and supported Christianity in which members of a nation are presumed to be Christian by virtue of their birth and infant baptism) which was largely, in his view, a contradiction of the gospel was central to virtually all of his work.

In *Either/Or* Kierkegaard describes human existence under two forms of existence – the aesthetic and the ethical. The aesthetic form of existence consists simply in a fairly hedonistic form of life in which the individual is concerned with the satisfaction of his or her own urges. The ethical form of existence is presented as a higher and more fulfilling form of existence in that it provides a sort of *telos* for the merely aesthetic form of existence. For example, the aesthetic concern and interest in purely romantic love finds its higher fulfilment in the ethical sphere of marriage. Later works, however, point to the transcendence of the ethical sphere of existence in the religious sphere of human existence. This might be regarded as a critique of those forms of post-Kantian Christianity (see **Kant**) which had identified the ethical and moral with Christianity. The intellectual path of the believer according to Kierkegaard involved a progression from the aesthetic to the ethical, and then to the religious.

But this progression to the religious sphere of existence is not natural or rational. It is not – as it seems it is in Hegel – the result of an inevitable and natural process working itself out through history. In *Fear and Trembling* Kierkegaard considers the example of Abraham as the paradigmatic expression of religious faith. He considers Abraham's willingness to sacrifice his son Isaac in obedience to God's command as revealing of the true nature of religious existence. God here is not reasonable, indeed the demand violates all logic, denies God's own promise to Abraham and is shatteringly inexplicable on the ethical sphere which can only declare Abraham mad or a murderer. Yet Abraham is commended for his faith and trust in God even though he cannot explain his actions rationally to another living soul. He is beyond words, his reasons are inexpressible – he is 'beyond mediation'.

Ethically Abraham's actions are unjustifiable yet in obedience to God there is a higher demand which 'teleologically suspends the ethical'. Thus for Kierkegaard obedience to God in the religious sphere of existence transcends the demands of ethics.

The unreasonableness of Christian faith is a continuing theme in *Philosophical Fragments* and the *Concluding Unscientific Postscript*. Here Kierkegaard considers the paradoxical nature of the Christian faith in that it asserts that God and man – two polar opposites – are incarnated in the figure of Christ. This is not a truth that we can come to know via a Socratic process of reflection on that which we intuitively know to be the case. The understanding that God and human beings share an affinity is not – again as in Hegel – a natural and reasonable affirmation. It is instead an offence – a paradoxical assertion – the 'Absolute paradox' in relation to human reason. For Kierkegaard is quite clear that the 'infinite qualitative difference' between God and man remains even in God's incarnation in Jesus Christ. Jesus, unlike Socrates, does not offer us a series of truths that are separable from himself, but presents himself to us as the one who is the truth. This fact can only be recognised in faith, in obedience to Christ who encounters us now in the present. It is not a matter of making a judgement based on the historical evidence about Jesus – it is a personal encounter with Christ here and now. Kierkegaard famously argued that 'the believer at second hand' (i.e. people at an historical distance from the life of Christ) is not at any disadvantage in relation to the original disciples when it comes to making a response to Jesus. Both the original disciples and all those who come after them must make the same leap of faith in God.

Kierkegaard's style is intended to bring out the nature of this offence to reason. He writes dramatically, ironically, passionately and existentially in order to bring about a change in his readers' attitudes towards the issues that he is raising. He does not want to 'convince' his readers simply on an intellectual level, but to present them with a form of life which the reader can actualise in his or her own existence. Kierkegaard had written *On the Concept of Irony* with constant reference to Socrates and his own style is also allusive and indirect (often employing pseudonymous authors to make it difficult to know exactly which point of view reflects Kierkegaard's own opinion), seeking to bring about an existential change in the hearts and minds of his readers. His later life was overshadowed by a quarrel with the Danish literary magazine *Corsair* which he had attacked and which attacked him in turn, exposing him to considerable ridicule on the public stage. For a man as sensitive as Kierkegaard this was a huge blow. But he continued to write prolifically until his tragically early death.

Human beings, according to Kierkegaard, have to make important decisions. They have to decide between living an aesthetic life, viewing the world without commitments, or living an ethical life. But beyond the ethical there is a further stage, that of the religious sphere or the sphere of grace, based solely on Jesus Christ. We have to choose – Either/Or. In *The Concept of Dread* (1844) and in *Sickness Unto Death* (1849) Kierkegaard diagnoses the human condition and by way of a penetrating psychological and philosophical study presents the human condition as one which lives under the shadow of despair. Although despair or guilt are categories which are discoverable by human beings, only God can disclose the fact of sin and this is an offence to human self-understanding. The offensive nature of Christianity is not therefore confined to the intellect, but to the very core sense of our self-understanding which is offended by God's estimation of it as sinful.

For Kierkegaard, as for Hegel, the dialectic method was central. But he sought to turn Hegel's dialectic on its head, and he protested passionately against what he saw as a too-close identification of the Creator and creature in Hegel's thought. God, as we saw above, is wholly other, and there is an 'infinite qualitative difference between God and man'. Hegel's philosophical system encompassed God (or Absolute Spirit) in an overarching rational system which Kierkegaard felt was destructive to true Christian faith. Christian faith is thus always paradoxical, always against reason. True faith involves a leap, a leap beyond that which reason can strictly prove. It is thus a leap in trust, but also in a measure of uncertainty, because of the paradox of sin, which estranges us from God.

There are two main strands in Kierkegaard's thought. One is his contrast between genuine Christian faith and 'official Christianity' in Christendom. (His prime target is the established Lutheran church of his native Denmark which in his time had thoroughly absorbed Hegel's system into its presentation of the Christian faith.) The other is his stress on the sin of human beings: human beings are totally incapable of achieving their own salvation. This can only come through grace, the paradox of grace, received from the God who is wholly other than man. Only by faith can we know God.

Truth is subjectivity – a key phrase (although not all subjectivity is truth). To be appropriated the truth must be acted upon and lived out in genuine rather than in official Christianity, which may appear to take the form of the opposite of faith. This corresponds to the offence of the cross. Such an understanding is not intended to be a rational interpretation of the world, as in Hegel. Rather, it is a commitment to transform the world through the power of individual changed lives; lives lived on the basis of a renewed leap of faith from moment to moment. This subjective appropriation of truth is instantly translated into existential commitment, inducing both despair and triumph over despair through trust in God alone, whatever the appearance of things.

It is clear from this why Kierkegaard is regarded as the main father of twentieth-century existentialism. But it would be wrong to mention Kierkegaard simply as a theologian, for he stressed that doctrine could be a snare and a delusion. As he put it in *Training in Christianity* (1850), 'Christianity is not a doctrine. All talk about offence in relation to Christianity as a doctrine is a misunderstanding. It is a device to mitigate the shock of offence at the scandal – as for example when one speaks about the offence of the doctrine of God, and of the atonement. No, the offence is related either to Christ or to the fact of oneself being a Christian'. It was Kierkegaard, inevitably, who said that a professor of theology is someone whose subject is someone else being crucified.

Kierkegaard is often depicted as an irrationalist *par excellence*. But that is far from accurate. He had a carefully worked out theory of the role of logic in philosophy and theology, This included a critique of Hegel's logic, which appeared to him to confuse good and evil, God and Man, time and eternity, through the introduction of movement into logic. In a number of ways, with his stress on the cross, on sin, despair, and the humanity of Christ the God-man, Kierkegaard echoes **Luther** more than any other of his contemporaries. Like Luther, he was not afraid to follow truth, as he saw it, wherever it might lead him.

In his later writings, *Training in Christianity, For Self-Examination* and *The Attack upon Christianity*, his style is more direct. After the death of his father's friend Bishop Mynster he attacked directly his successor, Bishop Martensen. Kierkegaard argued that official Christianity was a sham which in fact immunised people against truth faith. Doctrine was a device under which people sheltered from the true offence of the cross. As before, truth is subjectivity and it means personal, existential involvement, staking one's complete existence on faith in God. Yet Kierkegaard did not mean by this that all depended on human effort. On the contrary, the paradox is that everything is dependent on the prevenient grace of God. This is a dynamic form of faith in which there are no permanent states, but always the call to be faithful from moment to moment.

Kierkegaard saw himself as a religious poet. His vision is that of the individual who is called upon to take profound decisions which will shape his life, rather than that of a vast integrated system of philosophy or theology in which the individual is lost sight of. Life depends on paradox, often on the absurd. Once we realise that we are always in sin, then faith becomes possible.

Kierkegaard had very little influence in his lifetime, but his work was to be greatly influential during the twentieth century when he was recognised as the father of the existentialist movement that was to be developed by Heidegger and others. His main impact on theology, however, was through the work of Karl Barth, whose *Commentary on the Epistle to the Romans* was deeply influenced by Kierkegaard, as a protest against the historicising and idealist forms of theology which Barth believed had led to the First World War. There have been few more eloquent exponents of the unconditional grace of God, especially as a contrast to all ecclesiastical formalism, than Søren Kierkegaard.

See also: **Barth; Bultmann; Hegel; Kant; Luther**

Glossary: **Existential**

Major writings

Philosophical Fragments, trans. H.V. Hong, Princeton: PUP, 1967
The Concept of Dread, ed. R. Thomte, Princeton: PUP, 1980
Fear and Trembling; Repetition, ed. & trans. with notes & intro. by H.V. & E.H. Hong, Princeton: PUP, 1983
Sickness unto Death, trans. H.V. Hong & E.H. Hong, Princeton: PUP, 1985
Either/Or, trans. H.V. Hong & E.H. Hong, Princeton: PUP, 1987
Practice (Training) in Christianity, trans. H.V. Hong & E.H. Hong, Princeton: PUP, 1991
Concluding Unscientific Postscript, trans. H.V. Hong & E.H. Hong, Princeton: PUP, 1992

Further reading

A. Hannay, *Kierkegaard*, London: Routledge & Kegan Paul, 1982
D.R. Law, *Kierkegaard as Negative Theologian*, Oxford: OUP, 1993
G. Pattison, *Kierkegaard and the Crisis of Faith*, London: SPCK, 1997
G. Pattison, *Kierkegaard, the Aesthetic and the Religious*, London: SCM, 1999
G. Pattison, *Kierkegaard, Religion and the Nineteenth-Century Crisis of Culture*, Cambridge: CUP, 2002
M. Sinnett, *Restoring the Conversation: Socratic dialectic in the authorship of Søren*

Kierkegaard, Fife: Theology in Scotland for St Mary's College, University of St Andrews, 2000

KÜNG, HANS (1928–)

Controversial Roman Catholic theologian and prolific author who was born in Sursee in Switzerland on 19 March 1928. Küng was educated at the Gregorian University in Rome and then at Paris where he came into contact with such notable Catholic thinkers as Hans Urs von Balthasar and Yves Congar. In 1957 Küng completed his doctoral thesis on Karl Barth's doctrine of *justification* (see **Barth**). Its central argument was that there was a fundamental agreement between Barth's presentation of the Reformed theory of justification and Roman Catholic teaching on the matter as presented in the Council of Trent. Küng's thesis, both in its choice of subject matter and in its conclusions, showed Küng to be a Catholic scholar much interested in Protestant theology and much influenced by Protestant methodology. Such a bold thesis, effectively attempting to heal the great fault line between Roman Catholicism and Protestantism, brought Küng early fame and attention. However, it also brought him to the attention of the Sacred Congregation for the Doctrine of the Faith who opened a file on Küng at this point.

Despite this Küng's star was very much in the ascendant as evidenced by his appointment in 1960, when he was still only 32, to the Chair of Fundamental Theology at the Catholic faculty in Tübingen. The young professor turned his theological attention to matters of ecclesiology and began to write a series of works devoted to the subject of Church reform. Preparations were being made for the Second Vatican Council and Küng was one of many young Catholic theologians who were similarly turning their attention to Church matters. Küng was invited to act as an adviser to the German Bishops at the Second Vatican Council and he was much heartened by the proceedings there. His own book on the subject (published just prior to the opening of the Council), *Council, Reform and Reunion* (1961), anticipated many of the concerns of Vatican Two, but was to go even further than the Council itself did in calling for radical reforms in the Church.

After the Council Küng was to call for major reform in the Catholic church in a series of works devoted to ecclesiological concerns such as *Structures of the Church* (1962), *The Church* (1967) and *Infallible?* (1970). In these works Küng shows a deep concern to root the life and practice of the Church in the teaching of scripture and he was prepared to be quite critical of the traditions and offices of the Church when he felt that they departed from scripture. *The Church* analyses and critiques the then current structures and practices of the Catholic church from a biblical and historical perspective. In almost Protestant fashion, Küng sharply contrasts the Church with the kingdom of God, outlines the concept of the priesthood of all believers and argues that it is the Church as a whole and not a few appointed individuals who continue in the apostolic succession. The concluding section also questions the biblical and historical basis of the Petrine office. In *Infallible?*, Küng denied the traditional doctrine of papal infallibility in place of a theory which argued that God alone is infallible and that the Church should be spoken of in terms of 'a fundamental remaining in the truth in spite of all possible errors'.[i]

Küng's commitment to the methods and findings of modern historical and biblical criticism were to have even more dramatic implications for his work on Christology. In his phenomenally popular book *On Being a Christian* (1974), Küng articulated a Christology from below that would have been very familiar to anyone versed in the discussions and proposals of Protestant writers such as Dietrich **Bonhoeffer**, J.A.T. Robinson and Wolfhart **Pannenberg**. Küng did not deny the traditional dogmas concerning Christ, but his suggestion that the early dogmatic accounts of the person of Christ, although an understandable Hellenisation of what Jesus meant in the concepts and thought forms of Greek culture, are not particularly helpful or insightful models for today raised suspicions in the minds of many believers. His own more positive proposal was to understand Jesus within the context of his time and to try and see what questions he poses for faith today.

> As a concrete task this means that, from the history of this Jesus, from his words, from his conduct and his fate, the undiluted claim and the true meaning of his person can and should be made intelligible. It should be recognised from history how he then set and still sets ultimate questions before the individual and society in a way quite unparalleled in its criticism and promise, how in person he is invitation, challenge, encouragement to faith...
>
> Hence I do not simply believe various facts, truths, theories, dogmas: I do not believe this or that. Nor do I believe merely in a person's trustworthiness: I do not believe this man or that. But I venture quite confidently to commit

myself to a message, a truth, a way of life, a hope, ultimately quite personally to someone: I believe 'in' God and in him whom God sent.[ii]

Küng was writing before the current third quest for the historical Jesus got fully underway, but many of his findings, indeed his whole approach to the question, is congenial to many of the results of that quest. Küng effectively presents a 'functional' Christology in that Jesus is God's 'representative, delegate, deputy and pointer to God the Father'. Jesus is the true man who is for faith the 'real revelation of the one true God and who shows us what it is to be truly human'. Küng had already canvassed some of these views in a technical treatment of Hegel's thought as a prolegomena to any future Christology, entitled *The Incarnation of God*. Hegel's system is the spur for understanding Jesus' person in terms of its true historicity, and Küng concludes:

> In Jesus faith therefore has good cause and evidence for acknowledging that in him, his life, teaching, death and new life, we have to do with God *himself*, that the *vere homo* and the *vere deus* meet in his person, that the humanity of our God is revealed in him, and that in him precisely as the *Word* of God God truly became man so that man might become human.[iii]

Although Küng might have intended his statements on Christology to be a faithful contemporary presentation of the biblical understanding of Christ it immediately aroused opposition within the Catholic church. Already under suspicion because of his views on ecclesiology and Church hierarchy, and described by his former friend Karl **Rahner** (to whom *Structures of the Church* was dedicated) as a 'liberal Protestant', Küng's licence to teach as a Catholic theologian was withdrawn in 1979. This meant that he could no longer teach officially in the Catholic faculty of the University of Tübingen, but the university found him a new post as Professor and Director of the Research Centre for Ecumenical Theology.

Being deprived of his official licence to teach Catholic theology did not in any way inhibit Küng's output. If anything it increased. In his next major work, *Does God Exist* (1978), he sought to offer a rational and compelling response to secular modernity. In so doing Küng acknowledges that the development of what he termed 'critical rationality' was a good thing and even has its place in theology. Its proper results in their proper spheres cannot be ignored. Küng, however, opposes extreme claims to rational knowledge about the world which attempt to rule out all other forms of knowledge as knowledge. Atheism, for example, is often thought to be the logical end result of secular reason, but Küng is anxious to point out that neither atheism nor theism can be proven on strictly rational grounds. The decision for atheism or theism are 'basic decisions' on which everything else depends.

Küng's account of critical rationality draws upon developments in the philosophy of science, particularly in relation to the works of Karl Popper and Thomas Kuhn, to show that reality is a complex phenomenon which is only ever susceptible to a partial and diffuse apprehension through the use of reason. Our grasp upon the 'real' world is tentative and uncertain, ever open to the possibility of a new description. In relation to reality then, we are forever engaging in acts of trust that commit us to a belief in the ultimate rationality of the universe. Strictly speaking this cannot be absolutely proven but it is the hypothesis which best accords with human experience of the world.

In Küng's terms human beings cannot escape the situation of having to make a decision in relation to the nature of reality. This decision is free and uncoerced. Either reality is ultimately trustworthy and dependable or it is untrustworthy and unreliable. Either it is a place of meaning and value or it is an absurdly meaningless and contingent event. There is, strictly speaking, no compelling rational argument that will convince one way or the other. Nevertheless, most people opt for a fundamental trust in reality (in so far as they are not Nihilists) and find that the universe is a place of meaning, value and hope. Küng attempts to argue from this phenomenon of fundamental trust that only belief in a transcendent God can provide a basis and support for this fundamental conviction about the nature of reality in that certain questions about the nature of human existence in the world are thereby answered. Alternatively, if God does not exist then the phenomenon of fundamental trust is ungrounded and illusory.

It is important to recognise that Küng does not believe that this argument functions as a deductive proof of the existence of God. He has already conceded that the criticisms of the traditional proofs for God's existence are valid. Neither theism nor atheism can be proved by reason. However, it is an indirect proof in that it suggests that to postulate the existence of God provides a more comprehensive and explanatory hypothesis of the nature of human existence in the world than its alternatives.

Needless to say this has proved a controversial suggestion and it is by no means the case that everyone has been convinced by Küng's arguments. However, his suggestion does have certain structural similarities with related suggestions of Rahner and Pannenberg and it may be that it is simply the case that further work needs to be done in this area.

The encounter with the philosophy of Thomas Kuhn, and in particular his notion of paradigm shifts, was to prove decisive for Küng's later work. Increasingly, his interests were to be set against the larger canvas of the world religions. *Ecumenical* dialogue could no longer simply mean dialogue between Christian denominations but had to embrace dialogue with the great religious traditions of the world and involve a recognition by Christianity that they too are pathways to salvation. Küng's diligence in engaging with the other major religions of the world is to be commended. In *Christianity and the World Religions* (1985) he engages with Islam, Hinduism and Buddhism directly. He has also produced a massive volume on Judaism and is producing one on Islam.

For Küng we are on the brink of a paradigm shift from modernity to postmodernity. Critical rationality will continue to have a place in this new paradigm (Küng is no postmodern despiser of the Enlightenment claim to reason) but it will be reason that knows the limitations of its methods. The role of critical rationality in relation to theology will be to free it from the accretions of past and outmoded paradigms (such as the paradigm which governed Hellenistic and classical Christianity) in order that the new paradigm might be born. The prevailing emphasis in Küng's most recent work has been strongly ethical. In *Global Responsibility* (1990) Küng argues that the world requires a global ethic in order to survive the crises it faces, but it cannot arrive at peace without first achieving religious peace.

It is always hard to evaluate the work of a living scholar and this is a task which is made even more difficult when their work is as wide ranging and voluminous as is that of Küng. He remains one of the most widely read theologians of the day, but it is not clear that his proposals are gathering a wide following in the theological community. The decision to withdraw his licence to teach as a Catholic theologian may have both encouraged and fostered the broader and wider range of interests that Küng has developed, but it also seems to have meant that he is no longer as widely discussed or criticised by his contemporaries in the Catholic theological world. The popular audience that he once commanded has not borne well the increasing size and complexity of his books. Although, in one sense Rahner's charge that he is simply a liberal Protestant is patently false (Küng steadfastly regards himself as a Catholic theologian), yet there is no doubt that in his methodological approach and in certain of his findings Küng's trajectory clearly shows a deep engagement with, and sympathy for, the path of post-Enlightenment Protestant theology. For it could be argued that his theology of the Church owes much to Karl Barth, his conception of the 'Hellenisation' of dogma to Adolf Von **Harnack**, his understanding of biblical criticism is broadly drawn from Ernst Käsemann, his Christology mirrors the approaches of Bonhoeffer, Donald **Baillie** and Robinson, and his views on world religions follow a similar path to that proposed by John **Hick**. This may be a harsh assessment, and Küng has certainly not simply slavishly followed these thinkers for he too has clearly taken his own route. Nevertheless, from his early call for reform in the institutional Church to his eventual call for a paradigm shift in Christianity's self-understanding, it is fair to describe him as showing that a liberal and engaged Catholic theology is capable of making a creative and insightful response to the challenges of the modern and postmodern world.

Notes

i   *Infallible?*, p.153
ii   *On Being a Christian*, p.162
iii *The Incarnation of God*, p.508

See also: **Baillie; Barth; Bonhoeffer; Harnack; Hick; Pannenberg; Rahner**

Glossary: **Ecumenical; Enlightenment; justification**

Major writings

The Church, London: Search Press, 1968
Infallible?, London: Collins, 1971
On Being a Christian, London: Collins, 1977
Does God Exist?, London: Collins Fount, 1980
Christianity and the World Religions, London: Collins Fount, 1986
The Incarnation of God, Edinburgh: T & T Clark, 1987
Paradigm Change in Theology, ed. H. Küng & D. Tracy, Edinburgh: T & T Clark, 1989
Global Responsibility, London: SCM, 1991
Theology for the Third Millennium, London: Collins, 1991

Further reading

W. Jeanrond, 'Hans Küng' in D.F. Ford (ed.), *The Modern Theologians*, 2nd edn, Oxford, Blackwell, 1997

K.J. Kuschel & H. Häring (eds), *Hans Küng. New Horizons for Faith and Thought*, trans. John Bowden, London: SCM, 1993

C. Mowry LaCugna, *The Theological Methodology of Hans Küng*, New York: Scholars Press, 1982

LUTHER, MARTIN (1483–1546)

German theologian of the sixteenth century whose protest against what he saw as the abuses of the Roman Catholic church led to the Reformation and the beginnings of Protestant churches separated from Rome. Luther brought about a revolution in the Church and cultural life of Western Europe and is one of that small band of people who might rightfully claim that the impact of their thought has changed world history. Martin Luther was not a scholar whose life was spent in a study but someone at the heart of turbulent and world-changing events and the course of his highly eventful life was of great importance for his theology. His works are not systematic and reflective but polemic, occasional betraying the strong feelings associated with the heat of battle.

Luther was born into a poor family in Einsiedeln, Germany, in 1483, and although his father originally intended him for a career in law Luther decided to become a monk after a frightening experience during a thunderstorm in which he feared he would die without receiving the sacraments. The monastery that he chose to enter, and in which he was theologically trained, was the Augustinian monastery at Erfurt, at that time the leading centre of the ascetic ideal among the Augustinians. The greatest single theological inspiration of this institution, as of its most notorious student, was **Augustine**. The fundamental stress of this order was the fact of sin and the impotence of human will. Human beings are sinners and are in need of *salvation* which is effected by the intervention of grace in Jesus Christ.

According to medieval Catholic teaching grace was received through the act of penance on the part of the believer followed by the reception of the sacraments of the Church. The model here is that human beings are contrite and sorrowful over acts of sin and as they confess and make penance for their faults God rewards them with justifying grace. The practical mechanism for receiving the grace of God was through the sacraments of the Church – baptism and the eucharist. Baptism healed the effects of original sin and the eucharist provided justifying grace. The process however is cyclical as people once again fall prey to sinful acts and fall once more into a state of sin for which they must perform a further act of penance before again receiving the grace of God. This process continues throughout life and beyond in purgatory (although here it is the prayers and contrition of others that are effective on the individual's behalf) until the human soul is finally made righteous and enters into the presence of God.

As a pious and faithful monk Luther followed the penitential process but felt that his sins were still with him. It did not seem to matter how rigorous he was in observing the rule of his order, he could not find a gracious God, nor achieve any certainty with respect to salvation. He was always aware that he was not contrite enough, that he had omitted something from his act of confession. In short he seems to have suffered from a particularly acute religious conscience and could not understand how he, a sinner, could make an act of sufficient contrition or penance that would satisfy a righteous and just God. The righteousness of God was a fearsome concept that hung over Luther like a cloud, for he believed that he could do nothing that could please such a God. If God was truly righteous and just and judged everyone impartially then surely God could only condemn the sinner that Luther knew himself to be.

Luther became a teaching member of his order and from 1513 until 1515 was lecturing to other monks on biblical exegesis, especially on the Psalms (his 'little bible'), and he slowly began to work out a new theology through trial and error which freed him from his worries and which was to change the religious map of Western Europe. He came to see his temptations and suffering in the light of a new theology of the cross of Christ. Rather than a distant righteous and judgemental God, God, Luther now believed, was intimately involved in his suffering.

Luther began to see that the penitent monk or Christian could not put their trust in the value of their own penance. Rather, he began to see that the righteousness which the Bible speaks about is the righteousness of Christ which is promised to all who put their trust in him. It is the act of faith which is the channel for the reception of the grace of God into the believer's life. The whole of salvation was an act of grace on the part of God – Christ himself was the gift of grace – it was all of grace – *sola gratia*.

Prior to this breakthrough Luther had understood the justice or righteousness of God as the demand to obey the law. And how could that be good news? For who could say that they obeyed the entirety of the law? Now he understood that the righteousness of God and the righteousness of Christ were one and the same thing and were granted to the believer as a gift.

Traditional Catholic theology had regarded the righteousness of Christ as a gift mediated through the sacraments of baptism, penance and the eucharist whose purpose was to deal with sin. Then, however, the believer had to measure up to the demand of God's righteous law on the basis of the help they received from the righteousness of Christ in the sacraments. Who could possibly do this, thought Luther? His breakthrough was to realise that the righteousness which God confers is a real forgiveness, not simply an imputed acknowledgement of earned merit. This leads to a view of God centred on the doctrine of *justification*. God is gracious towards human beings who must be made good before God, by an act of God, before they can do good. Luther explained his breakthrough in the following terms:

> I had indeed been captivated with an extraordinary ardour for understanding Paul in the Epistle to the Romans. But up till then it was not the cold blood about the heart, but a single word in Chapter 1[:17], 'In it the righteousness of God is revealed,' that stood in my way. For I hated that word, 'righteousness of God', which ... had been taught to understand philosophically regarding the formal or active righteousness as they called it, with which God is righteous, and punishes the unrighteous sinners ... At last by the mercy of God, meditating day and night, I gave heed to the context of the words, namely, 'In it the righteousness of God is revealed, as it is written, "He who through faith is righteous shall live".' There I began to understand that the righteousness of God is that by which the righteous lives by a gift of God, namely by faith ... as it is written, 'He who through faith is righteous shall live'. Here I felt that I was altogether born again and had entered paradise itself through open gates.[i]

Luther was not afraid to pursue truth, as he saw it, wherever it might lead him. He is sometimes seen as an opponent of reason but his condemnation of reason was much more qualified than is often assumed. Reason has its own realm – all matters relating to this world, and to the assessment of theological arguments. But reason could not itself be a means of acquiring knowledge of God or of salvation. That was the sphere of grace alone.

At some stage in his theological journey Luther had a conversion experience – the famous 'tower experience' – which has been dated at various times to between 1509 and 1515. In the context of reading the

Psalms he gradually came to this new understanding of 'justification by faith' – which as we have seen was a radicalising of the Augustinian tradition. Traditional Catholic teaching on the matter couldn't be true because it underestimated the force and power of sin. Human beings were turned in upon themselves – curved and distorted – in various forms of self-idolatry. In this state of sin there was little or no hope of them being sufficiently contrite or performing pure enough acts of penance to merit God's grace. Human beings were sinners and all their acts were conceived in sin, and as such the good works of the individual were a hopelessly inadequate basis for salvation. Now Luther understood that it was God himself who gifted the righteousness that the individual required but could never hope to obtain through grace by faith in Christ.

The clear implications of Luther's insights brought confrontation with his superiors. As various scholars and representatives of the Church were sent to talk with him it gradually became clear that the whole ecclesiastical system, and especially the penitential system, would eventually come under attack. For if God gives his grace and regards as righteous all those who freely put their trust in him, what then is the rationale of the Church's sacramental system? Moreover, that system was believed to actually bring about the gradual inward transformation of the individual over time through the infusion of grace which was an active substance in the life of the believer. Luther's view seemed to change grace into the mere attitude of God towards the believer and as such the righteousness achieved was a false righteousness as it involved no actual change in the individual, but merely in God's view of him or her. Indeed Luther's views seemed to cut away the foundation of existing views of morality – God regarded the sinner as righteous. Such views were bound to be contested by the Church authorities and they duly were: Luther was to be drawn into a dispute which created an ever widening gulf between him and the Church.

The occasion of Luther's protest was the famous indulgence controversy of 1517. The Pope, who was in need of revenue for the building of St Peter's in Rome, had declared an indulgence whereby faithful Christians could receive remission from the torments and pains of purgatory by buying an indulgence from the Church. The practice was widespread and subtle reasons could be given by theologians for denying the clear implication that the poor were being encouraged to buy their way into heaven, but the sale in Luther's German province seems to have been particularly direct and crude and it offended his acute sensibilities on the matter.

On 31 October 1517 (as popular legend has it although we don't know if he actually did this) Luther nailed his famous *95 Theses* to the door of the church in Wittenberg hoping to encourage academic and scholarly discussion of the points he was making – one of which was a protest against the sale of these indulgences. The Theses were characteristic of his direct and challenging style and set out the range and scope of his differences with the practices of the Church. We gain something of the flavour of his challenge from the following:

1   When our Lord and master Jesus Christ said, 'Repent' (Mt 4.17), he willed the entire life of believers to be one of repentance.
2   This word cannot be understood as referring to the sacrament of penance, that is, confession and satisfaction, as administered by the clergy.
3   Yet it does not mean solely inner repentance; such inner repentance is worthless unless it produces various outward mortifications of the flesh.
4   The penalty of sin remains as long as the hatred of self (that is, true, inner repentance), namely until our entrance into the kingdom of heaven.
5   The pope neither desires nor is able to remit any penalties except those imposed by his own authority or that of the canons.

And so on. Luther outlined his arguments with determination and courage – the fifth obviously directly calling into question the authority of the Pope and challenging an extremely lucrative practice of the Church.

These points were to be expanded and developed in a series of debates that Luther was drawn into and which included the Heidelberg Disputation of 1518, the subsequent debate with John Eck at the Leipzig Disputation of 1519, and also later his published debate with Erasmus on *The Freedom of the Will* (*De Servo Arbitrio*, 1524). At the Leipzig Disputation, Luther was drawn into making the profoundly controversial statement that the Pope was not infallible. Worse was to come for he also said that general councils of the Church had on occasion been mistaken also. The infallibility of the Pope and/or of the general councils of the Church were the two staples of the authoritative interpretation of scripture and the faith of the Church. If Luther denied these two where then did final authority lie? The scale and scope of the controversy was growing wider and more bitter.

Luther's views were unsurprisingly condemned in a papal pronouncement of 1520 which directly controverted forty-one specific points that he had made and ordered the burning of Luther's books. In an act of public defiance Luther burnt a copy of the pronouncement as well as various books of canon law. The die was cast. Luther was resisting papal power. He argued that the Pope was subject to a general council of the Church and that both were subject to the authority of scripture. The appeal to the authority of scripture alone (*sola scriptura*) was to become the clarion call of all those who took up the cause of reforming the Church. The issue is one of authority. Catholicism had never denied the authority of scripture, but it was acutely aware that scripture required to be interpreted and it held that the final authority in contested matters was that of the Pope and/or a general council of the Church. Prior to Luther there had been – and still was – an acknowledged debate within the Catholic church as to whether the Pope or a general council was finally authoritative. Luther, however, was stepping well outside the parameters of that legitimate debate for he was setting up his 'own' interpretation of scripture against that of the Pope. The Catholic response to Luther (and later reformers) on this matter was that this setting of private judgement against the authority of the Church effectively made each individual their own Pope. Whatever the various merits of the case Luther's refusal to submit to the teaching of the institutional Church over the dictates of his own conscientious reading of scripture was heroic, and is often regarded as one of the landmark events that was eventually to lead to the modern conception of the freedom of the individual.

Three of Luther's most famous and most controversial tracts were written in the year that the papal pronouncement against him was issued: *On the Babylonian Captivity of the Church*, *To the Christian Nobility of the German Nation* and *On Christian Freedom* (1520). *Babylonian Captivity* criticised the entire medieval sacramental system and reduced the number of sacraments from seven to three – baptism, communion and penance (Luther later was to omit penance). The basis of this reduction was that a sacrament had to have been specifically sanctioned by the Word of God (in practice, to have been clearly instituted by Jesus and to have an identifiable material element and sign associated with the Word – water in the case of baptism and bread and wine in the case of the eucharist). Luther also protested against the medieval habit of giving only the bread to the people while retaining the wine solely for the priest.

In his address to the German nobility he called upon them to reform the Church in their lands because the clergy were unable or unwilling reform it for themselves. They were to correct its various abuses which now included (according to Luther) matters such as enforced clerical celibacy, masses for the dead and a profusion of extravagant processions and festivals. The power of the Pope to intervene in secular matters was to be curtailed and bishops were to attend to preaching the faith rather than exercising civil authority.

In his work *On Christian Freedom*, written in the dialectical style which characterised so much of his thought, Luther outlined the implications of his doctrine of justification for the life of the believer. Set free in Christ from worrying over his or her own salvation the Christian is free to love his or her neighbour as Christ: 'A Christian is a free man over all things and subject to no one: a Christian is a servant of all and subject to all.' Luther was formally excommunicated in 1521.

One of the reasons for Luther's success – and one of the reasons why he stayed alive when earlier figures with similar views had been burned by the Church – was due to the political situation in the German states at that time. Local princes and rulers had great powers of protection within their respective territories and often had their own reasons – not always religious – for resisting the incursion of papal power in their lands. As it was, different German princes sided with or against Luther and the country was eventually to become 'balkanised' between Lutheran, Catholic and Reformed territories. The matter in short became politicised. In 1521 Luther's teachings were formally condemned by the Emperor Charles V at the Diet of Worms. Charles was Emperor of Spain and the German remnants of the Holy Roman Empire and he had no wish to see his empire divided on religious grounds. However, his own conflicts with the Pope and with France, as well as the ever present threat of the Turkish-Islamic presence in neighbouring Hungary, meant that there was often little that he could do directly. As and when he could Charles tried to suppress the movement for reform until at the Diet of Speyer in 1529 the German princes favourable to Luther issued their protest against the actions of the emperor and the Catholic princes (this is the true origin of the word Protestantism). The result of the protest was to establish the right of German princes to choose the religion of their own state. What had begun as a matter of religion for Luther had ignited a political conflagration which was to lead in the next century to the Thirty Years War. As Luther had put it in the introduction to his *Open Letter to the Christian Nobility* of 1520, against the 'Romanists':

First, when pressed by the temporal power, they have made decrees and said that the temporal power has no jurisdiction over them, but, on the other hand, that the spiritual is above the temporal power. Second, when the attempt is made to reprove them out of the Scriptures, they raise the objection that the interpretation of the Scriptures belongs to no one except the pope. Third, if threatened with a council, they answer with the fable that no one can call a council except the pope.

Luther's social and political teaching reflected his inherently conservative views. He had been shocked when the impact of his views on religious freedom and the consequent loosening of the bonds of civil authority were interpreted much more radically by others during the Peasants' Revolt of 1524/25. Religious freedom was interpreted as a cry for social and political freedom and a series of peasant uprisings swept through southern Germany. Luther was horrified by the threat of anarchy and civil disorder and he thundered forth with an ill-tempered tract *Against the Murdering Thieving Hordes of Peasants* (1524), urging the princes and magistrates to strike the wicked – 'to stab, smite and slay all you can'.

Later Luther developed his famous theory of the two inter-related kingdoms of Church and State. Luther attempted to distinguish between two forms of human existence – human existence 'before God' and human existence 'before the world'. He argued that with respect to the law the Christian was bound to obey the State authorities as they had been appointed by God. With respect to the gospel the Christian was free from the law and led a life led by the Spirit in grace. Luther was aware that not every person in the State – even though they might be baptised – was a faithful Christian and therefore could not be expected to exist by the principles of the 'sermon on the mount' or Christ's injunction to love. Only true believers guided by the Spirit could live without the need for external regulation. However, in a mixed society the role of the State authorities – princes and magistrates – was to wield the power of the sword to restrain the forces of sin and anarchy and to punish evildoers. Luther does not seem to have developed a third more positive view of the law – as **Calvin** did for example, when he asserted that the law was a 'trainer in righteousness'. Luther's views of the power of the State and law were essentially negative. The law revealed sin and human failing and State power restrained its anarchic and disruptive tendencies.

The result of Luther's understanding of the two kingdoms was to create two totally different spheres: the sphere of the private Christian ethic in which the believer lives by grace, and the public sphere of social life which is governed by force and coercion. His insistence, especially in later life, on the need for obedience in civil matters to the powers that be, following Paul in Romans 13, was to cast a long shadow over German life in that it gave a divine mandate for civil authority. The eventual (if perhaps unintended) effect of Luther's private/public account of the life of the individual meant that the State had a right to expect absolute obedience from the individual in the public and social sphere. This divinely mandated obedience to State authority was to be utilised by the Nazi authorities to justify their attempts to claim an absolute obedience to the State. However, in defence of Luther this view was consistent with his understanding of the Christian life as *simul justus et peccator*, at once both justified and a sinner, and with his understanding of the realm of reason as applicable in temporal matters, although not in the realm of faith.

With respect to Church reform Luther was more conservative than many who followed him. He was satisfied to leave alone those practices and rituals that were not specifically prohibited by scripture or contradictory to its spirit. Luther's innate conservatism is best exemplified by his disagreement with **Zwingli**, the Swiss Reformer of Zurich, over the manner of Christ's presence in the eucharist. Luther believed that the body and blood of Christ were truly present in the eucharist and truly received by the believer 'in, with and through' the bread and wine. Zwingli had outlined a position which seemed to say that the eucharist was simply a memorial of Christ's death which strengthened faith by recalling Christ's sacrifice. The difference threatened the cohesion of the emerging Protestant movement and they met at the Marburg Colloquy of 1529 to resolve the matter. Unfortunately no agreement could be reached. For Luther, Christ's statement 'This is my body' as recounted in gospel accounts of the Last Supper was sufficient. If Christ said 'This is my body' then that was enough for Luther and he truly believed that he received the body of Christ for salvation – although he rejected the Catholic theory of transubstantiation. Zwingli argued that the meaning of the 'is' here was metaphorical, pointing out that Christ also made statements such as 'I am the bread of life', but that no one took that to mean that Christ literally was a loaf of bread. Again no agreement was reached, and the Protestant movement was to drift apart into the differing groupings of Reformed and Lutheran churches that remain to this day. Later attempts at a Lutheran mediation with Catholicism, such as the

Diet of Regensburg, failed, not so much out of theological disagreement as from lack of political will. By the time of Luther's death Europe was divided for and against reformation and much blood was to be shed over the ensuing centuries.

As Luther grew older he became ever more alarmed at the prospect of anarchy. We have already seen something of this in his notorious advice to the princes to kill the peasants and prevent a proletarian revolution. His writing on *The Jews and Their Lies* of 1543 is another of his massive failures of Christian discernment, advising the destruction of the synagogues, houses and books of the Jews. It no doubt reflected current sentiment, but that in no way excuses it and it was to serve the aims of Nazi propaganda in a later and even more cruel age.

Luther was not infallible, but his achievements were great. There is no doubt that his ideas represented profound developments in the theology of the European tradition. Even among his opponents they were to provoke new and more penetrating theologies. His contribution stretches beyond theology, to the cementing of a German language, largely through his translation of the Bible into German. Without Luther other reformers (Calvin, Zwingli) would have been unable to act as they did, and even the Anglican reformation would not have happened. Luther's prolific works, notably his biblical commentaries, have remained deeply influential for Christian thought. He also produced a huge number of occasional pieces, often of a polemical nature, and hundreds of sermons. The warmth and power of his personality is directly conveyed to us in his 'Table-talk' – a collection of statements and observations made in the company of friends which was gathered together and published after Luther's death.

It should also be noted that he was fond of music, and personally composed a number of hymns which had great influence and which are still sung in many Christian churches – notably 'A Mighty Fortress is our God' and 'Now Thank We All Our God'. Modern theologians, for example **Tillich**, have continued to look to Luther as the source of the Protestant principle of faith alone. Like all theologians he had blind spots – in the case of his anti-Semitism with tragic consequences for the future. But Luther remains one of the greatest of all Christian theologians.

Notes

i Luther, 'Preface to the Complete Edition of Luther's Latin Writings', in *Luther's Works*, Vol. 34, ed. L.W. Spitz, Philadelphia: Muhlenberg Press, 1960, pp.336–7

See also: **Augustine; Calvin; Tillich; Zwingli**

Glossary: **Justification; salvation**

Major writings

Works, Missouri: Concordia House Publishing, 1960. See especially *95 Theses, On the Babylonian Captivity of the Church, On Christian Freedom* and *On the Bondage of the Will*

Further reading

R.H. Bainton, *Here I Stand, a Life of Martin Luther*, London: Hodder & Stoughton, 1951

H. Bornkamm, *Martin Luther in Mid Career 1521–1530*, ed. with foreword by Karin Bornkamm, trans. E. Theodore Bachmann, London: Darton, Longman & Todd, 1983

G. Ebeling, *Luther*, London: Collins, 1970

B. Lohse, *Martin Luther's Theology: its historical and systematic development*, Edinburgh: T & T Clark, 1999

H.A. Obermann, *Luther: man between God and the Devil*, London: Fontana, 1993

MOLTMANN, JÜRGEN (1926–)

Jürgen Moltmann was born in 1926 in Hamburg. Placed in the army as a schoolboy, he was captured and spent three years in internment camps, first in Scotland and then near Nottingham (the University of Nottingham later conferred on him an honorary D.D.). After the war the returning soldier, deeply affected by the realisation of the horrors of the Nazi regime, began to study theology in the Reformed tradition in Göttingen, writing a doctoral thesis on Christoph Pezel, a sixteenth-century Reformed theologian. Because of his own wartime experiences, but more importantly because of the cataclysmic events of the Holocaust and Hiroshima, Moltmann came to concentrate on the *eschatological* significance of the cross, and the Christian concept of hope. After the Holocaust the only God that could be spoken about was the God of the cross – the God who suffered.

In his thinking Moltmann was to be much influenced by the three-volume work written by the Marxist Tübingen philosopher Ernst Bloch, *The Principle of Hope*. Moltmann's first book, entitled *A Theology of Hope*, appeared in 1964. This work found an instant resonance among the then current theological student generation in Germany. That generation was caught in an impasse between the differing approaches to theology represented by **Barth** and **Bultmann**, and

Moltmann's approach seemed to provide a way forward. Moltmann suggested that the centre of the gospel was promise. God was a God 'with future as his essential nature, who moved out in exodus to liberate the captives'. This work was to have parallels, although worked out in different ways, in the eschatological emphases of Gerhard Sauter and Wolfhart **Pannenberg**. It was also to strike chords outside Germany, lending focus to the development of 'liberation theology' (see **Gutiérrez**) in various parts of the world. Like the liberation theologians, Moltmann harnessed the basically Marxist political hope, so prevalent during the 1960s, to a solid core of biblical imagery, providing a theology which was Christologically based, yet which spoke to concrete social situations of need, poverty and the requirements of justice.

This basic theme of hope was to be developed in further studies. The theological basis was deepened by Moltmann's study of the crucifixion, *The Crucified God* (1974). This book took up another current and prevalent theme – that of the death of God – and related it to the centre of Christian faith. For Moltmann God is the crucified God or he is not God at all. All proper Christian language about God must begin with the cross of Christ. The crucified God who is made known in the cross of Christ stands in solidarity with all who are oppressed through the ages, especially with the suffering of the Holocaust and with those who were murdered in Auschwitz. In contra-distinction to classical approaches to Christian theology which asserted that God was incapable of suffering, Moltmann argued that God is a suffering God. Indeed, after Auschwitz the only God worth speaking about – the only God that makes any sense – is a God who suffers with and in the name of the unnumbered and unnamed sufferers throughout history.

In the crucifixion/resurrection event, God does not die as such, but participates in death. That is, in the experience of the death of the Son of God in the cross God takes death into the heart of the divine life and overcomes it via the resurrection. Understanding the death of Christ as an event in God requires a *Trinitarian* understanding of the cross.

> [I]n that case one will understand the deadly aspect of the event between the Father who forsakes and the Son who is forsaken, and conversely the living aspect of the event between the Father who loves and the Son who loves. The Son suffers in his love being forsaken by the Father as he dies. The Father suffers in his love the grief of the death of the Son.

In that case, whatever proceeds from the event between the Father and the Son must be understood as the spirit of the surrender of the Father and the Son, as the spirit which creates love for forsaken men, as the spirit which brings the dead alive ... Here we have interpreted the event of the cross in trinitarian terms as an event concerned with a relationship between persons in which these persons constitute themselves in relationship with each other.[1]

This theme of God's participation in death was to be taken up around this time by others, notably **Rahner**, von Balthasar and Jüngel, who also spoke of the perishability of God. For Moltmann the necessity arises for a new doctrine of God, in solidarity, as he says, with protest atheism which protested against God in the name of the suffering of the world; but also against the non-suffering God of traditional metaphysics and natural theology, who is seen as the echo of the Constantinian monarchy rather than the serving, self-limiting and humbling God revealed in Christ.

Moltmann developed the Trinitarian implications of his basic approach in *The Trinity and the Kingdom of God*. This work was to be a springboard for the major rethinking of the understanding of the Trinity that has been such a marked feature of Western theology since the 1970s. Moltmann rejects the monarchical understanding of the God of classical monotheism which he believes has legitimated authoritarian forms of power in the world and hindered the full expression of human freedom. In contrast to the unitary conception of God, Moltmann develops a 'social' account of the Trinity in which the individuality of the three persons existing in an eternal community of mutual self-giving and receiving love is stressed. The relationship between the three persons is not hierarchical and there is no intrinsic ordering to the Trinity (classical accounts tended to stress the Father as the fount of divinity). This community of divine persons is open to the world and is affected by the history of the world which it is carrying forward in the Spirit to history's consummation in the kingdom. The Trinitarian persons then are (in a Hegelian fashion) affected by the events of the world and we can speak of God completing Godself through the processes of history. This community of self-giving and receiving love is offered as a model for human forms of communal living. Authoritarian forms of power are rejected in the name of a God who rules solely through the rule of love.

Moltmann also offered a profound reintepretation of the under-standing of the Church in his equally influential *The Church in the Power of the Spirit*. In faithfulness to Barth and **Calvin**, the Church remains a creature of the Word, a messianic fellowship constituted and called together out of the world by the Spirit. Thus the Church, as the messianic community of the new age, 'anticipates' and lives out the promise of the coming kingdom: 'Christianity is not yet the new humankind but it is its vanguard. In an anticipatory and fragmentary fashion and naturally imperfect form the Church represents the future of the whole of reality and so mediates this eschatological future to the world'.[ii] The Church does this as it exists in the power of the Spirit who carries history on the way to the future realisation of the kingdom of God. But the Church is not the whole content of the gospel of the kingdom and never will be.

Moltmann, in Reformed fashion, interprets the classical marks of the Church – 'One, Holy, Catholic and Apostolic' – in terms of the categories of *'kerygma'* (gospel), *'koinonia'* (fellowship) and *'diakonia'* (service). For Moltmann 'the true church is found where Christ is present'. In a moving and insightful reinterpretation of the classical theory of the two states of Christ's person – his exaltation and his humiliation – Moltmann speaks of Christ's presence in the following terms. The exalted Christ is present in the gospel (*kerygma*), the sacraments and fellowship (*koinonia*) which anticipate the kingdom. But the humiliated Christ is also present in identification with the poor. The Church exists in the presence of Christ only when it links the two forms of Christ's presence by missionary presence among the poor – 'the church with its mission would be present where Christ awaits it, amid the downtrodden, the sick and the captives' (*diakonia*).[iii]

Moltmann's conception of the Church is best summed up by saying that the Church is a preliminary and fragmentary part of the coming whole which is the universal kingdom of God. As such it represents and anticipates the kingdom for the sake of the rest of the world whose future the whole is. It is important for Moltmann – and this has become an increasingly prominent theme – that Judaism is not replaced by the Church. God's promises to the people of Israel are not void and the Church and Israel during this interim period both point to God's coming kingdom.

Like Barth, Moltmann rejected any easy association between Church and society and the concept of a Christian society is one that worries him deeply. He has offered powerful arguments against the practice of infant baptism (again like Barth) because he views it as the last vestige of a Christian society whereby one enters the

Christian church simply by virtue of being born. His vision of the Church is that of a committed messianic fellowship of believers and he finds the English non-conformist free church tradition particularly attractive.

Moltmann's subsequent work has dealt with the doctrine of creation and Christology. *God In Creation* outlines an account of the traditional doctrine of creation which is focused in relation to the ecological crisis that is facing the world. *The Way of Jesus Christ* (1989) attempts to develop a Christology in faithfulness to the biblical pattern of Christ's life: his messianic mission, his apocalyptic passion on the cross, his resurrection from the dead, his reconciliation of the cosmos as ascended Lord, his return as judge to bring in the kingdom. The focus is upon a Christology that walks in the 'way of Christ' and as such it is a Christology that is on the way – it is not the final word but is open to development. It is a Christology that is about practising the way of Christ as much as it is about believing certain things about Christ, and as such Moltmann takes time to reflect upon certain martyrs who have shared in the fellowship of Christ's sufferings: Paul Schneider, Dietrich **Bonhoeffer** and Arnulfo Romero.

In 1995 Moltmann again returned to the theme of eschatology or the Christian hope. If *Theology of Hope* had resurrected the category of eschatology for theology then *The Coming of God* (1995) attempts to fill out that category with substantial content. Moltmann brilliantly skewers various forms of secular and political forms of messianic hope – including the 'manifest destiny' doctrine of modern America – before turning to a description of authentic Christian and biblical hope. Traditional categories of last judgement, *predestination*, universal salvation and new creation are given a new twist before Moltmann describes the goal of creation as the fullness of God joyfully indwelling in his creation.

It may be that Moltmann does not display the philosophical subtlety of Jüngel or the theological finesse of Pannenberg. But there is no doubt that his work offers a profoundly moving and benign vision. Moreover his constant engagement with the political and social dimensions of theology, including his appreciation of the concerns of feminist theology (he has written collaboratively with his wife, Elizabeth Moltmann-Wendel, a feminist theologian in her own right) and his growing concern with ecological matters, succeed in demonstrating at an important time that theology can be written with direct application to social and political issues in society.

Notes

i   *The Crucified God*, p.245
ii   *The Church in the Power of the Spirit*, p.196
iii *Ibid.*, p.129

Glossary: **Eschatological; predestination; Trinity/Trinitarian**

Major writings

Theology of Hope, London: SCM, 1967
The Crucified God, London: SCM, 1974
The Church in the Power of the Spirit, London: SCM, 1977
The Trinity and the Kingdom of God, London: SCM, 1981
God in Creation, London: SCM, 1985
The Way of Jesus Christ, London: SCM, 1990
The Spirit of Life, London: SCM, 1992
The Coming of God, London: SCM, 1996

Further reading

R.J. Bauckham, *The Theology of Jürgen Moltmann*, Edinburgh: T & T Clark, 1995
C. Morse, *The Logic of Promise in Moltmann's Theology*, Philadelphia: Fortress Press, 1979

NEWMAN, JOHN HENRY (1801–90)

John Henry Newman was born in Old Bond Street in the City of London on 21 February 1801. His childhood was happy and he was especially devoted to his mother. 'I was brought up as a child to take great delight in reading the Bible: but I formed no religious convictions until I was fifteen. Of course I had perfect knowledge of my Catechism.' Thomas Paine's *Tracts on the Old Testament* prompted religious doubts at the age of 14 and a very decisive, although 'not violent', religious experience at 15. Under the influence of his headmaster at Ealing he absorbed a Calvinist doctrine of **predestination**, believing himself to be of the elect. From Thomas Scott's writings he gained an unshakeable belief in the doctrine of the **Trinity** and imbibed Scott's resolute opposition to Antinomianism: 'For years I held almost as proverbs what I considered to be the scope and issue of his doctrine ... Holiness before peace and Growth is the only evidence of life'. William Law's *Serious Call to a Devout and Holy Life*, Newman says, brought him the doctrine of eternal punishment, Milner's *History* a first attraction for the early Fathers of the Church, and Isaac Newton's work on biblical prophecies the belief 'that the

Pope was the Antichrist predicted by Daniel'. The autumn of 1816 brought 'a quite unexplained conviction ... that it was the will of God that I should lead a single life'. It would be interesting to know how this conviction arose.

Newman went straight from Ealing to university, attending Trinity College, Oxford, and always regretted that he did not go to a public school. The famous *Apologia pro Vita Sua* has a gap between 1816 and 1822, when 'I came under very different influences from those to which I had hitherto been subjected', i.e. not White or Hawkins. He says nothing of his spectacular failure in his university Finals, probably caused by over-anxiety and over-work. Retaking the exams he was elected a Fellow of Oriel College in April 1822. Here he met Hawkins, who taught him the value of tradition: 'If we would learn doctrine, we must have recourse to the formularies of the church'. He lists as an influence at this time Butler on the unreality of the material world and the doctrine of probability. Still, even in 1826, 'The truth is, I was beginning to prefer intellectual excellence to moral, and I was drifting in the direction of Liberalism'. From 1823 he came under the influence of Pusey, and by 1828 of Keble (whose *The Christian Year* came out in 1827), brought together by Hurrell Froude, who was also to be a profound influence. Froude was a highly eccentric character, a Fellow of Oriel by 1826. 'He made me look with admiration towards the Church of Rome, and in the same degree to dislike the Reformation.' Although we may laugh at the confession about 'contrite reminiscences of a desire for roasted geese, and of an undue indulgence in buttered toast', Froude was undoubtedly influential upon Newman

The year 1827 brought Newman to the verge of a nervous breakdown, and in 1828 his sister Mary died. In 1828 he also became Vicar of St Mary's in Oxford, still retaining his college post. between 1830 and 1832 he wrote his first book, *The Arians of the Fourth Century* (see **Arius**), published on his return from a visit to the Mediterranean with Froude. It was at this point that Keble was to preach his famous Assize Sermon, and Newman sat down to write *A Tract for the Times*: choose your side, the Oxford Movement was about to be launched. Newman always felt the need of close companions in his enterprise – after 1845 he was conscious of being alone, and he did not enjoy it. In 1832 he was forced to resign his fellowship after a dispute with the Master of Oriel College, but he remained in Oxford as Vicar of St Mary's until 1843. His sermons were brilliantly crafted and exercised considerable influence. He wrote hymns and poetry including in 1833 the famous 'Lead, Kindly Light'.

The Oxford Movement, of which Newman was the central figure, was a movement, first and foremost a religious movement, within the Church of England, especially between 1833 and 1845. Centred in Oxford, it aimed at the restoration of 'High Church' ideals of the seventeenth century and the period of the early Church in the Church of England. It sought to recall the Church of England to a true expression of Catholicity which would constitute a mediating position between Roman Catholicism and Protestantism. It was thus not the product of a philosophical programme. Developed in Newman's *Tracts for the Times*, from 1833 to 1841, it sprang from a concern at the progressive decline of Church life and the spread of liberalism in all fields of thought including theology. It had roots too in the impetus of the Romantic movement, which inspired a new interest in primitive and medieval Christianity. It sought to defend the Church of England as a divine institution, the doctrine of the apostolic succession and the Book of Common Prayer. The Church is the apostolic norm of authority, and also the community of living piety and the quest for holiness.

The opposition of many Anglican bishops, guardians of the apostolic succession, to the movement was to create an intolerable tension which in the end was to help Newman on his way to leaving the Church of England and joining the Roman Catholic church. For the movement the ancient Church was looked on as the undivided norm of Christian truth, and the true interpreter of the scriptures. In 1841 the famous *Tract 90*, which could be read as being compatible with Catholicism, was condemned by the Anglican authorities in Oxford. Newman withdrew to a semi-monastic life at Littlemore outside Oxford. In October 1845 Newman was received into the Roman Catholic church, and published his *Essay on the Development of Doctrine* as a theological justification for the move. Later he was to establish the Oratory of St Philip Neri in Birmingham and to act as rector of the Catholic University of Ireland, from 1854 until 1858. He was not used by the Catholic church as much as he might have been, although he was made a Cardinal in 1879.

Newman published *Parochial and Plain Sermons*, an edited version of his Anglican discourses, in 1843. In *The Idea of a University* (1852) he set out a classical account of the Christian ideal of the university. His famous *Apologia pro Vita Sua* (his spiritual biography) came out in 1864, and *An Essay in Aid of a Grammar of Assent* in 1870. Newman was a religious thinker of profound sensitivity and imagination, and has come to be increasingly appreciated as such in recent decades.

Glossary: **Predestination; Trinity**

Major writings

Tracts for the Times, London, 1840–42.
Parochial and Plain Sermons, New York, 1843
A Grammar of Assent, London, 1870
The Idea of a University, London, 1873
The Arians of the Fourth Century, London, 1919
Essay on the Development of Doctrine, Harmondsworth and Baltimore: Penguin Books, 1974
Apologia pro Vita Sua, London: Sheed & Ward, 1987

Further reading

W.O. Chadwick, *From Bossuet to Newman*, Cambridge: CUP, 1957
W.O. Chadwick, *Newman*, Oxford and New York: OUP, 1983
S. Gilley, *Newman and his Age*, London: Darton, Longman & Todd, 2003
I. Kerr, *John Henry Newman, a Biography*, Oxford, OUP, 1988
D. Nicholls and Fergus Kerr, *John Henry Newman: reason, rhetoric and romanticism*, Bristol: Bristol Press, 1991

NIEBUHR, REINHOLD (1892–1971)

Reinhold Niebuhr, born in Wright City, Missouri, the son of a German immigrant Lutheran pastor, was to become one of the great Christian social thinkers of the twentieth century. He attended the local high school and then studied at Eden seminary before attending Yale University (BD 1914, MA 1915). He served as the pastor of Bethel Church, Detroit, for 13 years and while there became acutely aware of the exploitation of the workforce in the expanding Ford car factory, waging verbal and legal battles on behalf of the workers. This experience was to be crucial for Niebuhr's development as he began to understand the profound extent to which modern industrial society exerted crushing pressures on individual men and women.

> We went through one of the big automobile factories today. So artificial is life that these factories are like a strange world to me though I have lived close to them for many years. The foundry interested me particularly. The heat was terrific. The men seemed weary. Here manual labor is drudgery and toil is slavery. The men cannot possibly find any satisfaction in their work. They simply work to make a living. Their sweat and dull pain are part of the price paid for the fine cars we all run.

And most of us run the cars without knowing what price is being paid for them.[i]

The communal and social distortions of modern life were to be a constant theme of his later work and caused Niebuhr to break with the optimistic and liberal theology that he was trained in at seminary. It also marked his break with the *social gospel* tradition of American church life and a turn towards political socialism.

Niebur was called as a Professor of Preaching to Union Theological Seminary, New York, in 1928 and there he exercised a hugely influential teaching and preaching ministry for more than 30 years. He wrote prolifically – books, articles, newspaper columns – and became a well-known national figure. Through his German contacts he was strongly and early on opposed to the Nazis, befriended a young Dietrich **Bonhoeffer** and encouraged America to enter the war against Hitler. After a stroke in 1952 he was unable to continue his teaching programme at the same pace as before but he continued to write for another 20 years and was everywhere consulted, retaining a powerful influence in American public life. His work owed much to the support of his wife Ursula Niebuhr (*née* Keppel-Compton), herself a considerable theologian in her own right.

Niebuhr is most famously associated with the turn in theology to 'Christian Realism' (see below) which took place in the 1930s, and also with a deepening of the Christian critique of society through the social gospel. He was perhaps the greatest American theologian since Jonathan **Edwards**. Along with a group of friends – Henry Van Dusen, Henry Sloane Coffin, John **Baillie**, John Bennett and his brother H.R. Niebuhr – he was hugely influential in persuading America to take a renewed interest in international statesmanship in the period 1930 to 1950, and in leading the *ecumenical* movement worldwide on that basis.

His early book *Does Civilisation Need Religion?* (1927) was already critical of much conventional middle-class religious practice. In *Moral Man and Immoral Society* (1932) Niebuhr suggested a difference in the moral behaviour of individuals and groups.

It also reinforces the break with his earlier more liberal optimism in favour of the position that was to become known as 'Christian Realism'. Niebuhr rejected the suggestion that society can be improved by the moral and rational intentions of individuals. Groups, notably illustrated by factory employers, acted in their own interests and were rarely unselfish. Here he stressed the powerful corporate nature of sin. A measure of coercion becomes necessary in forming, maintaining and, if necessary, in opposing groups.

The Selfishness of human communities must be regarded as an inevitability. Where it is inordinate, it can be checked only by competing assertions of interest; and these can be effective only if coercive methods are added to moral and rational persuasion. Moral factors may qualify, but they will not eliminate, the resulting social contest and conflict.[ii]

Here Niebuhr drew on his pastoral experience in Detroit, where he opposed the poor working conditions of Ford factory workers. His recognition of the need for coercion upon occasion in group dynamics led him to be a firm supporter of armed opposition to the Nazis.

Perhaps best known for his Gifford Lecture volumes, in *The Nature and Destiny of Man* (1941 and 1943) which is a powerful examination of human existence in the world, Niebuhr attempted to reinterpret the traditional Christian doctrine of sin, arguing that that particular doctrine is the only empirically verifiable doctrine of the Christian faith. He argued that the Christian doctrine of sin is far more true to actual human experience than the various forms of optimistic accounts of human existence that characterise the modern world. Sin arises from the fundamental tension inherent in the fact of freedom. Human beings are free and therefore the misuse of freedom is a real possibility although human beings remain responsible for their sin and thus feel guilt. The primary characteristic of sin is pride – the desire to be completely autonomous and self-sufficient. (This account of sin has been much criticised by feminist theologians as failing to express the primary female form of sin or failing to sufficiently assert a self rather than the over-assertion of self-hood).

Niebuhr expanded his account of individual sin to incorporate and account for collective and social forms of sin and he thus mounted a powerful and prophetic critique of collective human oppression, championing the cause of the under-privileged and helping to create the conditions for later developments such as the civil rights movement in America. Here we have his fully developed under-standing of 'Christian Realism' – the attempt to come as close as possible to the realisation of the impossible ideal set by the gospel within the real world of actual political and economic conditions. Controversially Niebuhr argues that Jesus' practice of selfless sacrificial love (*agape* love) cannot be the normative ethic for Christian living – it is an 'impossible possibility' in the current sinful conditions that pertain. *Agape* love in history always ends in suffering and a cross. *Agape* love can inspire the individual and can reveal the extent of human fallenness, but for social regulation justice is the primary ethical category. Justice recognises the competing range of self-interests that exist in society, but the resolution of them will involve a measure of coercion. Justice itself is measured 'realistically' in that it is not some absolute timeless virtue. What is actually the 'just' action at any given time depends upon the historic, cultural and social conditions that pertain at that particular time.

His realist perspective sought to combine the best of the American liberal tradition with a concern for Christology. For Niebuhr Christ is the Son of God and the Second Adam, and the cross of Christ is central to his understanding of faith as it reveals the true nature of the human condition: '[T]he same Cross which symbolises the love of God and reveals the divine perfection to be not incompatible with a suffering involvement in historical tragedy, also indicates that the perfection is not attainable in history'. The biblical proclamation of Christ and his cross opens us up to the possibility of self-transcendence through an encounter with the grace of God. Thus we can know of ourselves as being made in the image of God while at the same time understanding the true extent of our sinfulness. The cross reveals the profound crisis of humanity while at the same time revealing that the solution to that crisis is not to be found within the processes of history or human self-achievement.

Niebuhr wrote many other books, notably *An Interpretation of Christian Ethics* (1933). There he sums up the Christian ethic as follows:

> The crown of Christian ethics is the doctrine of forgiveness.
> In it the whole genius of prophetic religion is expressed.
> Love as forgiveness is the most difficult and impossible of
> moral achievements. Yet it is a possibility if the impossibility
> of love is recognised and the sin in the self is acknowl-
> edged.[iii]

This was to be followed in the war years with the equally successful *The Children of Light and the Children of Darkness* (1945):

> The preservation of a democratic civilization requires the
> wisdom of the serpent and the harmlessness of the dove. The

children of light must be armed with the wisdom of the children of darkness but remain free of their malice.

Niebuhr also wrote widely on the Christian understanding of history, politics and society. These works continued his powerful critique of religious individualism and naïve liberal optimism. His developed Christian Realism bore certain resemblances to the thought of Karl **Barth**, from whom however he (and even more so Ursula) differed in many respects. Niebuhr famously said that Barth's theology was 'in danger of offering a crown without a cross, a triumph without a battle, and a faith which ignores the confusion of human existential life without transforming it'.

In 1941 he founded the periodical *Christianity and Crisis*, which served to focus his opposition to the Nazis, and to encourage American action against them. After a debilitating stroke, he continued to work and to write, especially on the complex relationship between love and justice and its consequences for world politics. Retiring finally from Union Seminary in 1960, he died on 1 June 1971. The Niebuhrian legacy was later to be invoked to support armed intervention in Vietnam as the lesser of two evils. In reaction, support for Christian Realism was to decline, as theologians began to turn to the more radical forms political theology.

Notes

i   *Leaves from the Notebook of a Tamed Cynic*, 1925, p.65.
ii   *Moral Man and Immoral Society*, p.272.
iii   *An Interpretation of Christian Ethics*, p.233

See also: **Baillie; Barth; Bonhoeffer**

Glossary: **Ecumenical; social gospel**

Major writings

Does Civilisation Need Religion?, New York: The Macmillan Company, 1927
Leaves from the Notebook of a Tamed Cynic, New York: Willet, Clark & Colby, 1929
Moral Man and Immoral Society, New York: Charles Scribner's Sons, 1932
An Interpretation of Christian Ethics, New York: Harper & Brothers, 1935
The Nature and Destiny of Man, 2 vols, New York: Charles Scribner's Sons, 1941 – 1943
Christian Realism and Political Problems, New York: Charles Scribner's Sons, 1953

Further reading

Charles Brown, *Niebuhr and his Age*, Philadelphia: Trinity Press, 1992
R.W. Fox, *Reinhold Niebuhr*, New York: Pantheon, 1985
R. Harries (ed.), *Reinhold Niebuhr and the Issues of our Time*, London: Mowbray, 1986
R.W. Lovin, *Reinhold Niebuhr and Christian Realism*, Cambridge: CUP, 1995

ORIGEN (c.185–254)

Origen, perhaps the most learned theologian until Adolf von **Harnack**, was born in 185, probably in Alexandria. He is one of the pivotal thinkers of the early history of the Church and his thought was to have a massive influence – both positive and negative – on the development of Christian doctrine in the third and fourth centuries – particularly in relation to the influence of Greek philosophy on Christian faith. Most of the information we have on Origen comes from the 6th book of Eusebius' *Church History*. He studied the Bible from an early age with the aid it is said of his father Leonides, who was martyred in 202, and Origen could scarcely be restrained from joining him in martyrdom. After a short interval he returned to study with a new intensity, living a life of strict asceticism, around what was soon to become the catechetical school for Alexandria. Critically aware from early days of the dangers of Gnosticism (see **Irenaeus** and **Tertullian** for more details) he decided to study philosophy, and in particular the Gnostic systems, more deeply, in order to refute them. He was quite probably a pupil of Ammonius Saccas, and possibly later became acquainted with Plotinus.

Origen's studies took up most of the decade between 212 and 222. At this time he probably began work on the *Hexapla*, his magnificent edition of the Old Testament, and laid the foundation for the vast number of biblical studies which poured from his (or his secretary's) pen for the rest of his life. The *Stromata*, a collection of papers on theological topics, another work on the resurrection and the first-ever Christian systematic theology *On First Principles*, were all written before he left Alexandria.

Origen perfected a method of allegorical interpretation of scripture which he took over in part from the Old Testament interpretation of Philo of Alexandria and which was to be the model for Christian biblical interpretation for centuries to come. Biblical statements that have no obvious literal meaning must be interpreted allegorically or spiritually to get at their real sense. In his great commentary on

St John's Gospel, of which large pieces remain, he engaged in debate with the exegesis of the Valentinian Gnostic heretic Heracleon, who was perhaps the true author of the biblical commentary as we know it. He also produced homilies on most of the books of the Bible.

Origen's *On First Principles* is a kind of summary of his basic theological system. The questions he raises are: What is God? What is the Son? What is the Holy Spirit? What is the devil? To what end is the universe created? Its title follows the style of secular philosophical treatises in the famous philosophical tradition of Alexandria. The whole work is extant only in the Latin translation of Rufinus, who attempted to cut out all the heresies he felt it contained, and therefore it is difficult to know how much of it is Origen's original work. However, we can compare it with other original individual sections of the work existing in Greek as well as a Latin collection of controversial passages in the work of Jerome in order to try and get some sense of Origen's views.

Although it deals with the being of God, the preface begins with reference to Christ as the truth. It speaks of God as Father, Son and Spirit although the relationship is hierarchical and God the Father is God alone in the strictest sense. Only the Father is 'ingenerate' – having no explanation or origin for his existence save himself. Origen appeals to Christ's words that the Father is the 'only true God' in support of this claim and immediately we see the importance of the scriptures to him. The Father has his Son who is his express image and who mediates on behalf of the Father with the whole plurality of beings that comprise the created order. The Son is generated eternally by the Father outside of time. Father, Son and Spirit are three persons (hypostases) existing from all eternity, but the relationship does seem to be hierarchical, with the Son and Spirit subordinate to the Father. The role of the Spirit is an underdeveloped aspect of Origen's theology as it tends somewhat to be subsumed under the activities of the Word. Origen believed that the whole world of spiritual beings (angels and eternal souls) existed alongside God for all eternity. The rationale for this conviction seems to stem from the fact that Origen believed that the Father must always have had a created reality over which he exercised his power.

Stress is laid on the incorporeality of God, and Book One re-emphasises that God does not have a body. God's nature is beyond human understanding. Christ is the Word and the Wisdom of God. Christian life comes through Father, Son and Holy Spirit and human beings have fallen away from God into sin but are destined to participate in a final consummation of all things.

Jesus Christ is the Word of God incarnate: 'We believe that the very Logos of the Father, the Wisdom of God himself, was enclosed with the limits of that man who appeared in Judea.' Origen believed in the eternal pre-existence of all human souls and that through misusing their free wills these souls have fallen away from union with God. Embodied existence in the world as human being is in fact the soul's punishment for the fall. Only one soul did not turn away from God but remained in faithful contemplation of, and union with, the Word. This soul was the soul destined to be the soul of Jesus Christ, and when this soul was eventually born in Bethlehem the union between Word and soul was thus incarnated in a human life.

Through the incarnation the Word illuminates fallen human minds and restores our true rationality to us. The Word is the pattern of the perfect life and human beings are being transformed into his likeness. This is a mystical process but Origen seems to envisage that human beings participate in the divine nature through the incarnate Word: 'discoursing in bodily form and giving Himself out as flesh, He summons to Himself those who are flesh, in order that He may first of all transform them into the likeness of the Word Who has been made flesh, and after that may exalt them so as to behold Him as he was before he became flesh'. The thought here is that incarnation of the Word in Jesus Christ has united divine and human nature so that human nature is being transformed and saved from its mortal weakness through union with the divine.

Christ's death and resurrection is also victory over the powers of the fallen angels and demons who currently hold sway in the world. The devil believed that he had defeated Christ on the cross but is himself defeated through Christ's resurrection from the dead. However, Origen seemed to believe in the universal restoration of every creature that God has created – including the devil – in the consummation of the kingdom when the original perfection of God's good creation is restored. God created the world in time, and will bring it to an end, in a consummation of all things.

For Origen the scriptures are divinely inspired, but their interpretation requires a differentiation between the literal and the spiritual senses. Origen, by 222, now famous, went off for visits abroad, as modern academics tend to do, and immediately fell into disfavour with his local bishop and ecclesiastical superior Demetrius because he delivered public lectures on the scriptures which as a layman he should not have done. In 215 Origen had been allowed to preach at a service in Caesarea – against the rules, for he was not a priest. In 231 or thereabouts, he was ordained priest by the Bishop of

Caesarea. That same year he was banished from Alexandria and his ordination declared null and void (probably on the ground that a eunuch could not be a priest – he was said to have had himself castrated as a youth in an excess of evangelical zeal).

In 231–32 Origen moved to Caesarea, where he soon attracted huge numbers of admiring students. He taught them just about everything – logic, dialectics, physics, mathematics, astronomy and of course biblical exegesis. From here he travelled to engage in disputation with heretics. Here too the main part of his writings was composed – on prayer, on martyrdom, the magnificent *Apologia Contra Celsum*. In *Contra Celsum* Origen was able in a remarkable way to play off the arguments of the various pagan schools of philosophy against each other, in the cause of Christianity. From this period too date a large number of his biblical commentaries and sermons. Origen may also have written lost works of 'straight' philosophy.

During the Decian persecution Origen was imprisoned and severely tortured, but he refused to renounce his faith. A year or two later he died, probably around 254. The further implications of his thought and in particular its development in relation to the Trinity were to be played out in the Arian controversy. (see **Arius**; **Athanasius**).

See also: **Arius; Athanasius; Justin; Irenaeus; Tertullian**

Major writings

Some of Origen's writings can be found in *The Ante-Nicene Fathers: the writings of the Fathers down to A.D. 325*, ed. Alexander Roberts & James Donaldson, rev. & chronologically arranged with brief prefaces & occasional notes by A. Cleveland Coxe; Vol. 4, *Tertullian, part fourth; Minucius Felix; Commodian; Origen, parts first and second*, Peabody, MA: Hendrickson, 1995.

Apologia Contra Celsum, trans. with intro. & notes by H. Chadwick, Cambridge: CUP, 1953

An exhortation to martyrdom; [and] Prayer; [and] First principles, book IV; [and] Prologue to the commentary on 'The song of songs'; [and] Homily XXVII on 'Numbers' / Origen, trans. & intro. by Rowan A. Greer, London: SPCK, 1979

Commentary on the Gospel according to John, books 13–32, *Origen*, trans. Ronald E. Heine, Washington: Catholic University of America Press, 1993

Further reading

Henri Crouzel, *Origen*, Edinburgh: T & T Clark, 1989
R.P.C. Hanson, *Origen's Doctrine of Tradition*, London: SPCK, 1954
N.R.M de Lange, *Origen and the Jews*, Cambridge: CUP, 1976
A. Scott, *Origen and the Life of the Stars: a history of an idea*, Oxford: Clarendon Press, 1991
Joseph Trigg, *Origen*, London: Routledge, 1998

PANNENBERG, WOLFHART (1928–)

Wolfhart Pannenberg was born in 1928 and like his contemporary **Moltmann** studied theology in Germany after the war, when the **Barth–Bultmann** debate was at its height. Pannenberg is rightly celebrated for attempting to overcome the impasse between Barth and Bultmann on the question of how history relates to the gospel. Historical and social criticism of the Bible had seemed to make history a problematic areas for theologians. How could one base the absolute certainties of faith on the provisional and revisable findings of the historian? Barth had responded to this problem by detaching his theology from historical study. If he spoke of history at all it was to speak of a supra-history which was God's history above human history and not discernible in human history apart from God's *revelation* in Christ. Bultmann, as a New Testament scholar, was more sympathetic to the aims and practices of historical study; nevertheless in relation to faith he tended to retreat from the larger questions of history into the existential impact and meaning of history as *Geschichte* – which is to say history as it transforms and challenges individual human existence in the world. Pannenberg's whole programme is in one sense aimed at recovering the arena of history for theology.

Pannenberg studied at Heidelberg under a very orthodox Lutheran theologian, Edmund Schlink, but a powerful stimulus of another kind at Heidelberg was the famous Old Testament theologian Gerhard von Rad. Von Rad emphasised that the history of Israel was not just an abstract concept but a matter of real concrete events in the everyday world of Israel; were decisive for an understanding of the God revealed in the Old Testament. Israel's God was the God of exodus – the God who brought the slaves out of Egypt – and those acts and others were determinative for Israel's understanding of God's character.

Pannenberg and a group of friends reflected on Von Rad's Old Testament theology and published a collection of essays under the title *Revelation as History* (1957). The theme of the Pannenberg circle was that, as they put it, the *kerygma* (the proclaimed gospel) without history is a meaningless noise. The preaching of the word of God is an empty assertion if it is severed from what really happened in history. Faith cannot live from a *kerygma* which is detached from its historical basis and content. For after all the *kerygma* is itself nothing but the declaration of what God has actually done in the course of the events of ordinary human history. The standard history of salvation theology has always foundered on a dualism between revelation and history. It fled, as in Barth, from the historical floodtide into the harbour of a supra-history and in Bultmann the theology of existence withdrew from objective history to the 'historicality' of the individual.

But Pannenberg was to argue that *revelation* comes not merely in or through history but as history. He outlines his position in the following manner:

1   The self-revelation of God has occurred indirectly through his historical acts.

2   Revelation in its fullest sense happens not at the beginning but at the end of history, because we can only know the true and definitive meaning of things from the perspective of their fulfilment in the end.

3   Historical revelation is there for anyone who has eyes to see and not only (again as in Barth) for those with the eyes of faith. It is thus universal in character.

4   The universal revelation of the Godhead of God was not yet realised in the history of Israel, but first in the destiny of Jesus of Nazareth, in so far as the end of history occurs beforehand in him.

5   The Christ-event (the whole totality of Christ's life, preaching and impact) does not reveal the Godhead of the God of Israel as an isolated event, but only in so far as it is part of God's history with Israel.

6   The universality of the *eschatological* self-disclosure of God in the destiny of Jesus was expressed using non-Jewish ideas of instruction in Gentile Christian churches.

7   The revelation of the Word to the world is in terms of prophecy, instruction and report.

The accent on the universal historical scope of revelation is a break from Barth and Bultmann. The totality of reality as history is not just the world, but God's world, which he created and through which he reveals himself. Pannenberg would agree that he borrows much from **Hegel** – but Hegel was wrong in identifying his own philosophy with that end standpoint from which one could view the whole. The final revelation of God's future plans for his creation has taken place in the resurrection of Jesus from the dead. But what has happened to him still remains outstanding, unaccomplished, for us, and so history goes on and promises have yet to be fulfilled.

Pannenberg is an acute and complex thinker and he has developed a distinctive approach to many classical theological issues. If we consider the relationship between faith and reason then Pannenberg allows that faith is a gift of the Holy Spirit and is not simply a product of reason. Nevertheless, reason, in its essential structure, is sufficient to grasp God's revelation in history. The *kerygma* is not to be absolutised, but the *kerygma* or gospel message and the Spirit are factually necessary to drive reason to seek God's revelation in history and establish the life of faith.

In relation to Christology and the importance of the historical life of Jesus of Nazareth, Pannenberg is famously associated with a 'theology from below'; that is, with an approach to Christology that begins with the historical life, death and resurrection of Jesus of Nazareth and which attempts to found the claims of faith on those events. This is contrasted with a 'theology from above' which begins with the Church's proclamation of the exalted and ascended Christ as Lord. (This is again *contra* to Barth who famously refused to regard the historical events of Jesus' life and teaching as the basis of faith, preferring to make his foundation the proclamation of the Church. In a real sense for Barth the historical events of Jesus' life veil God as much as they reveal him, and he was even prepared to concede that there was nothing which was that remarkable about the life of Jesus, historically considered.) For Pannenberg, however, it is not possible to base the gospel on the Christ of faith. The Jesus of history himself must be the actual starting point of Christology. A theology of the resurrection must establish itself squarely upon the earthly Jesus.

Because of his commitment to basing his theology on history Pannenberg has to offer an historical account of the resurrection of Jesus. It is important for him that the resurrection did not happen in a vacuum. Judaism already expected a resurrection from the dead. But that resurrection of the dead was to take place at the end of the world when God would be fully and finally revealed. In this context the Christian proclamation that God has raised Christ from the dead could only be understood as an anticipation – a foretaste of the end of the world. But as God would be fully and finally revealed at the end of the world he must be revealed in the life, death and resurrection of Jesus. If this is a complete revelation of God in Christ then there must be an identity between that which reveals (Christ) and that which is revealed (God) or we would not have a full and final revelation but some other imperfect mediation. Christ therefore is one with God.

Thus for those who already had faith in God, the resurrection would be a sign of the coming of the end of the world and a corroboration by God of Jesus' claim to authority. It would facilitate the identification of Jesus with the coming Son of Man, and would show that God's final self-revelation had occurred in Jesus of Nazareth. The resurrection also provides a motive for mission to the Gentiles in that the nations of the world were to be included in Israel's hope at the end of the world. This is all contrary to the claim of Bultmann that the resurrection has no intrinsic meaning apart from the mere summons to faith. For Pannenberg, 'Why the man Jesus can be the ultimate revelation of God ... remains incomprehensible apart from the horizon of apocalyptic expectation'.[1]

But how is primitive Christianity as a whole to be related to the present, if not through the Word? Pannenberg's answer is framed in terms of a theology of universal history, which deals with what he calls the horizon of the historical process. The gap between past and present is bridged by the continuing history of God's unfolding plan for the world. The Church and its tradition have a structural significance in a hermeneutic of universal history.

What then of the Protestant tradition of *sola scriptura* and the relation of scripture and tradition? Here too Pannenberg has a searching analysis and an illuminating answer. In a seminal early essay on 'The Crisis of the Scripture Principle' Pannenberg detected the collapse of the Reformation doctrine of scripture in the Enlightenment. This creates a basic crisis for modern theology. The central position of scripture had not been questioned in the Church until the late Middle Ages when the authority of the Church was asserted to be higher than that of scripture. Luther's teaching was a contradiction of this (see **Luther**). But the principle of *sola scriptura* – the Bible alone as a source of authority – meant that all later work had to be grounded in historico-critical exegesis, and this led to the modern crisis. The subject matter of scripture, the person and history of Jesus Christ, can no longer be found in the external clarity of the text. We have to find a new understanding of the relation between past events and present faith by creating a new hermeneutic bridge. We cannot simply call for obedience to the authority of the Word of God. The problem would appear to be that the 'totality of history' to which Pannenberg calls us may prove to be at least as elusive as the Word mythology which he rightly questions.

For Pannenberg, Israel came to understand itself in terms of its own history, and understood its God as a God who is active within that history. This understanding was reinforced by God's revelation in Jesus, in whom the end of history has broken in anticipation such that the ultimate meaning and end of history is revealed in the life of Christ.

Pannenberg's constructive theology was developed in numerous books and articles on Christology, on anthropology, on theology and science, on ethics, and in a systematic theology. Such an impressive and ambitious programme naturally attracts argument and debate on all fronts. Some examples will help to illuminate Pannenberg's main emphases.

Panneberg sets much store by hermeneutics and the search for meaning. Some critics have echoed the Marxist point that the theological must be concerned not only to interpret but to transform the world and human history.

Some have criticised his emphasis on apocalyptic imagery. Perhaps apocalypse was not as central to the biblical narratives as is often thought. Furthermore, the apocalyptic horizon may not be as closely connected to the coming Son of Man as Pannenberg thinks. Jesus' authority may be seen to be based on direct persuasion in the present rather than on an eschatological basis. Pannenberg draws connections between contingency in physics and contingency in history. There is no direct link between a statistically indeterminate future and the eschatological future of God, and so Pannenberg's 'fusion of horizons', which should create universal meaning, does not quite take place.

Pannenberg is thought to underplay the importance of the Word in the New Testament, which produces and influences history and does not simply report it. Nevertheless, Pannenberg's criticism of the verbalisation of the gospel in much of the tradition, especially the Protestant tradition, may still be important. There may be problems with his treatment of scripture. But his ability to draw on the whole range of human history, on the natural and the human sciences, creates fresh and imaginative theology – this is particularly seen in his theological anthropology. Here Pannenberg argues that human beings are by nature historical creatures. The combination of events in a person's life gives them their individuality and drives them forward to seek a meaningful future. By looking at human beings in their historical environment we can see who they really are. We may come to see that this existence can only be fully realised in the light of Christ, who is the key to true humanity. All human reflection on humanity may help us in this search. Again there is the counter-argument that God's prophetic Word may cut across the development of human history. But Pannenberg would say that the fact of sin and alienation does not detract from the basic effectiveness of the paradigm of historicality.

Pannenberg has produced what is perhaps the most comprehensive modern Christology after Barth. Looking at his treatment of this doctrine will illustrate many common characteristics of Pannenberg's approach. He is radical in deciding that the incarnation is not the correct starting point, and stresses the need to study Christology from below, or at least from before. Yet he takes a fairly traditional view of the resurrection and of many other aspects of the tradition.

For Pannenberg we cannot simply unfold the *Chalcedonian* formulae. We are concerned with rational grounds, with historical and logical grounds for the assertions of faith. We cannot begin with experience of God in the present, e.g. through the self-revelation of the Word, for experience is notoriously deceptive. We have to look at Jesus in the past, and ask about his own self-understanding. Christology is not to be swallowed up in soteriology (the saving work of Christ), in his meaning for us today. His own claim to authority was only confirmed with his resurrection. Apocalyptic expectation provides the essential background to understanding Jesus' life and claims. Jesus' resurrection is not a meaningless event but has several strands of specific meaning. The resurrection brought God's self-revelation by anticipating the end of world history. Through the resurrection we can understand history in its totality. Jesus reveals God and is identified with God's being. This was the case before his earthly existence. We cannot use the *Logos* Christology, of which pre-existence was an important component, any more. We must work from below, moving back from the resurrection to the man Jesus. Although he knew himself to be one with God, yet his self-consciousness, like all human self-consciousness, was centred on the future. This status was confirmed by the resurrection. Through his personal communion, Jesus received from his father his self-consciousness, which was the personality of the son.

We may think it somewhat paradoxical to be reminded on the one hand that we must seek solid rational grounds for theological argument, and yet be invited to regard the strange, eminently culture-related imagery of The apocalyptic as normative for theology for all time. However, there is no doubt that, within his chosen framework, Pannenberg builds up a powerful and coherent case.

For Pannenberg, Israel came to understand itself in terms of history and historical existence, and to understand God as the key to history. This understanding was reinforced by God's revelation in Jesus, in which the end of history has broken in anticipation such that the ultimate meaning and end of history is revealed in the life of Christ. This new understanding of God's historicality in turn opens up a deeper explanation of the historical basis of all reality. How do we know that this interpretation of God, Jesus and the world is correct? Because correlation with all the disciplines shows that reality is best understood as historical. As we see that reality is historical, we find the

God who is the source of historicality and we put our trust in him. It might be said in criticism that the crucified God does not necessarily 'make sense' of the world, but reveals himself in hiddenness, in fragments, in solidarity with suffering. Nevertheless, we must seek such rationality as we can find, and Pannenberg provides an intelligent and critically alert guide.

Other significant issues are involved. Pannenberg holds that revelation in its deepest sense means salvation. But it may be that salvation includes more than knowledge. It involves commitment, and an element of faith in things unseen. Pannenberg's stress on historical acts seems to rule out the Old Testament examples of God's personal self-communication, in which God directly communicates his purpose. In his vision the axis of history becomes all-comprehending, and may obscure other themes. Pannenberg rightly stresses the value of tradition, yet tradition itself may not be able to say which traditions are correct. How do we know that the way a tradition was first shaped is correct? The role of the grace of God in inviting response in faith perhaps needs some greater emphasis than Pannenberg allows for here. Nevertheless, his programme is ambitious, all-embracing and intellectually sophisticated and thus offers a powerful alternative to those Christians who are dissatisfied with alternatives which remain wholly locked within the circle of faith.

Note

i   *Jesus, God and Man*, p.83

See also: **Barth; Bultmann; Hegel; Luther; Moltmann**

Glossary: **Chalcedonian; eschatological; Logos; revelation**

Major writings

Revelation as History, London: Sheed & Ward, 1961
Jesus, God and Man, London: SCM, 1968
Basic Questions in Theology, London: SCM, 1970–73
Theology and the Philosophy of Science, London: Darton, Longman & Todd, 1976 (1973)
Systematic Theology, 3 vols, Edinburgh: T & T Clark, 1991f.
Anthropology in Theological Perspective, Edinburgh: T & T Clark, 1999

Further reading

A. Galloway, *Wolfhart Pannenberg*, London: Allen & Unwin, 1973
S.J. Grenz, *Reason for Hope: the systematic theology of Wolfhart Pannenberg*, Oxford: OUP, 1990

F. LeRon Shults, *The Postfoundationalist Task of Theology: Wolfhart Pannenberg and the new theological rationality,* Grand Rapids, MI: W.B. Eerdmans, 1999

E.F. Tupper, *The Theology of Wolfhart Pannenberg,* London: SCM, 1974

PAUL (?–c.64)

First-generation Christian and the most profound thinker of the apostolic era, Paul was not a systematic theologian but a preacher and missionary who was responding off the cuff to situations and crises as they presented themselves to him. Nevertheless, in his wrestling with some of the most intractable and difficult issues that faced the first generation of Christian believers, he was able to articulate a theology of the crucified and risen Christ that was to prove seminal for all subsequent Christian thought.

Paul was a Jew from Tarsus in Cilicia, an important town in Asia Minor. We don't know precisely when he was born but his birth date must be roughly contemporaneous with that of Christ himself, suggesting a birth date just before or after the beginning of what is now known as the Christian era. Little is known of his early life apart from what can be gleaned from some occasional hints in his letters. The biblical book of Acts (22:3) tells us that he studied under the great Gamaliel in Jerusalem, but this is not certain. Paul, or Saul as he was originally known, seems to have been born into a relatively comfortable, albeit not wealthy, family of Hellenistic Jews. We can glean from his letters that he was an educated man, although his Greek is not of the highest quality. Similarly, his letters show an awareness of the broad outlines of Greek philosophy and some understanding of the principles of rhetorical argument, but they do not suggest a mind that has studied these issues in depth. This is hardly surprising as Paul's inclination was to pursue the faith of his ancestors and we are told that prior to his conversion to the Christian faith he was a zealous Pharisee. Both the book of Acts (7:58) and Paul's own letters (1 Cor. 15:9, Gal. 1:13, 14) – not always in close agreement on the details of Paul's life – agree that Paul was a Pharisee and was someone who zealously persecuted the early Christian movement. This early persecutor of Christians was to encounter the risen Lord Jesus Christ either on the way to Damascus or in Damascus and was thereafter a faithful follower of the Christ he had once reviled, and a tireless servant of the community he had once persecuted.

The nature of Paul's encounter with the risen Christ is not clear. Acts tells us that he saw a blinding light while Paul says that he saw the risen Lord (Acts 9:3; 1 Cor. 9:1). However, although the precise details of the actual event may be forever lost to us there is no doubting its lasting impact on Paul. From this point on he was to understand the risen Christ as the *eschatological* fulfilment of Israel's hope and the coming Lord who was to return in judgement upon the world. This understanding of Christ caused him to believe that Gentiles were now included in God's plan and he directed himself to proclaiming the message of Christ to them in order that there might be an ingathering of the nations of the world before God brought history to a close.

The radical nature of Paul's understanding of the significance of the risen Christ should not be underestimated. The early Church had not yet come to a clear assessment of its own role and position *vis-à-vis* the Jewish faith at this point. Some seemed to understand Christ simply as the fulfilment of the Jewish faith and therefore wished to continue living and worshipping as Jews, save for the fact that in addition to Temple sacrifice, circumcision and observance of the law they added a commitment to Christ as Lord. No real thought (or at least no further thought than was already current in Palestinian Judaism) was given to the question as to what this meant for Gentiles. Other Christians (perhaps largely drawn from Hellenistic Jews) did understand that the significance of Christ's death and resurrection had profound implications for the Gentile world. The question then arose between these two groups as to what the conditions of entry were for Gentiles who embraced the Christian faith. Were they to become Jews by being circumcised, observing dietary and cultic regulations and obeying the law (the traditional approach of Judaism itself)? Or did the eschatological finality of Christ's death mean that Gentiles no longer had to become Jews to become part of God's chosen people? Paul was not the first to ask these questions, nor was he the first person to take the gospel to Gentiles, but he was the one who was to provide the most radical answer to such questions. The working out of the implications of the answer he provided is the substance of much of his letters and became the anvil on which his theology was beaten out.

After his conversion, usually dated around 33, Paul was to go into Arabia for a period and then return to Damascus, and we know very little about his time there. By his own account he did not gain his gospel nor his knowledge of the faith from any of the apostles, although he went up to Jerusalem to meet with Peter three years after his conversion (Gal. 1:18). Paul was certain that he too was an apostle, even though he had never met Jesus and had not therefore been part of the original group of twelve disciples (Gal. 1:1). He eventually became associated with the church at Antioch, where Gentiles were first admitted into the Christian faith, and he seems to have been an emissary from Antioch to the Jerusalem Council which was the first attempt to solve the problem that the admittance of Gentiles into the Christian faith had raised (Acts 15:2ff). The time between his first visit to Peter in Jerusalem and his second visit to the council seems to have been the time when he embarked upon what is known as his first missionary journey with Barnabas, as recounted in Acts 15:37. This may also have been the time when he made the later journeys that were made without Barnabas, but of this we can't be certain as it is difficult to reconcile Paul's account of his life and movements with that presented in Acts. For this reason Acts has to be treated as a secondary and subsidiary source to Paul's own letters when considering details of his life.

Thus from Antioch, initially in association with Barnabas, but subsequently on his own with a group of younger associates, Paul embarked upon a series of missionary journeys to Asia Minor and Greece, focusing upon cities such as Ephesus, Philippi, Thessalonica and Corinth. From these and other bases Paul was successful in establishing a network of small Christian churches both in the cities themselves and in the surrounding hinterland. It is clear from Paul's letters, and from other parts of the New Testament, that Paul was not the only one involved in the mission to the Gentiles, but the book of Acts clearly represents him as the major figure in the expansion of the early Church and this seems to indicate the centrality of his role.

It is as he moved to and fro between these various bases that Paul wrote the correspondence that we now have in the epistles of the New Testament. Thirteen letters bear his name but scholars today would generally regard only seven as indisputably belonging to Paul. These are 1 Thessalonians, 1–2 Corinthians, Galatians, Philippians, Philemon and Romans. These letters provide rich insights into the life and thought of Paul as well as the early Church as it comes into view in history for the first time. The letter to the Galatians is of particular significance as it provides a clear picture of Paul's response to the pressure from Judaising Christians to enforce strict observance of the law upon non-Jewish Christians. Remembering a prior occasion in Antioch, Paul describes how he rebuked no less a figure than the great apostle Peter himself for compromising upon what Paul understood to be a fundamental aspect of the faith (Gal. 2:11f). Of course we only have the rebuke presented in hindsight as Paul recollects the event, and we don't know how Peter responded to the charges made against him. The clear implication from Paul's account is that his version of events carried the day, but there may be some significance in the fact that after this argument Paul, who has hitherto always been an emissary of the church of Antioch, is never associated with that church again. The precise chronological relation between the affair in Antioch and the Council held in Jerusalem in Acts 15 is not known exactly. However, it is sufficient to note that by Paul's own account his position was accepted by the other apostles in Jerusalem in that they agreed he could continue to win Gentile converts without imposing upon them the requirement of circumcision. It was also agreed that he would take up a collection from his churches for the church in Jerusalem (Gal. 2:6–10). Much of the rest of Paul's endeavours were devoted to the gathering of this collection.

The collection is of interest in that the precise reason for its gathering is not fully known. The obvious assumption is that it was to alleviate conditions of poverty in the church at Jerusalem. But the reference to the collection being for the poor may just mean that it was for the Jerusalem church itself without implying that they were experiencing any significant poverty – the term 'the poor' was a Jewish term often adopted as a self-description by the pious in Judaism. Rather then than being a collection to alleviate poverty the collection may have been consciously modelled on the Temple tax levied on Jews of the Diaspora for the upkeep and maintenance of the building. On this understanding the collection (if accepted) would have meant the recognition by the Jerusalem church of the legitimacy of the Pauline churches, as well as a recognition by the Pauline churches of the prior position of the mother church in Jerusalem. Whether the Temple tax was the model for the collection or whether it was simply a collection for the relief of poverty among the Christians in Jerusalem, there is no doubting its importance to Paul (Romans 15:25–28). Indeed Paul's eschatological outlook opens up a third option in that he could have viewed the collection as a fulfilment of the vision of Isaiah 60:5 in which the wealth of the nations is pictured as coming to Jerusalem as part of the fulfilment of Israel's hope.

In bringing the collection to Jerusalem Paul was opening himself to great danger as he was a hated figure to many observant Jews. Acts seems to have little interest in the collection but the implication is that it is accepted (Acts 21:17–26). The note of tension in the visit is maintained by the fact that Paul has to partake in (and pay for) a rite of purification for himself and four others so that his credentials as a faithful and practising Jew may be established. In the process of this purificatory act Paul is accused by his opponents of taking a Gentile into the Temple and is arrested. He was never to be a free man again. After spending some time as a prisoner in Caesarea Paul was sent to

Rome for trial. He spent a further two years as a prisoner in Rome before suffering death as a martyr there, probably under the persecution begun by Nero, sometime between 62 and 64. This last statement is conjectural as we do not know precisely how and when Paul died but it remains the most likely outcome of the final stages of his life. The tradition that he was released, at least for a period, and managed to travel to Spain as he had long hoped, is intriguing, but without any real basis in historical record.

Paul's theology continues to present many problems even to the skilled interpreter and so what follows can only be understood as the distilled findings from what continues to be an energetic and ongoing debate. There are several key themes in Paul's basic message, all of which are the subject of considerable scholarly disputation. Suffice it to say that the broad outlines of Paul's thought can be said to be that God has begun the eschatological consummation of all things in the death and resurrection of his Son Jesus Christ. This death, which Paul presents in a variety of terms, is understood as a sacrifice which restores the rightful relationship between human beings and God. In some passages (Romans 3:23–25) Paul stresses the sacrificial aspect of Christ's death in terms of the blood that is shed, and in others he is capable of focusing upon the whole life of obedience which Christ lived as somehow restoring and repairing the original disobedience of Adam. Christ as the new Adam who restores and recapitulates all that the original Adam lost is a powerful theme in Paul's theology (Romans 5:12–21). Through participation in the death and resurrection of Christ, Christians are saved from this age, which is the age of sin, wrath and judgement in which they are subject to the powers and principalities of the age. Participation in Christ's death and resurrection is gained through faith and baptism in which the believer is united with Christ and receives the gift of the Holy Spirit. This reception of the Holy Spirit is a sign and foretaste of the age which is to come, but which has begun to manifest itself now through the presence of the Spirit. The presence of the Spirit in the life of the believer manifests itself in lives that are marked by peace, love and joy and which shun the practices of the old age such as fornication, dissension and malicious and slanderous gossip. Ecstatic utterances, prophecies and visions are also signs and gifts of the Spirit and were a commonplace feature in Pauline churches. Those who have died with Christ will be raised with him to a new and transformed life in the Spirit in which they will have spiritual bodies (Romans 8:23 and 1 Cor. 15). The coming of Christ as Messiah had radically altered the status of Gentiles in that they no longer had to fulfil the requirements of the law to be part of God's chosen people, but are included in God's covenant through faith in Christ. In Romans and Galatians Paul spent considerable time analysing the figure of Abraham, who believed in God prior to the law, to show that being made right with God has always been a matter of faith. The function and role of the law is negative in that it enslaves us, works death in our bodies and reveals sin. At best the law functions as a sort of schoolteacher that trains believers in conduct that is appropriate for God's covenant people. However, Paul wishes to argue that being made right with God is not a function of the law, but that membership of God's covenant people and consequently salvation, for both Jew and Gentile alike, is and always has been a matter of faith. The people of Israel continue to have a place in God's plan and their seeming rejection has simply been for the sake of the inclusion of the Gentiles (Romans 9–11).

Paul appeared to believe that Christ would return in judgement very soon and the delay in this happening caused some concern in his churches as to what was the fate of those who had died before the Lord returned (1 Thess. 4:13–17). Paul assured his followers that they too would be included in the Lord's promise of salvation. The strong eschatological note in Paul's theology gave something of a sense of urgency to his moral teaching – he taught that it was better for Christians not to marry unless absolutely necessary given the crisis that was about to unfold (1 Cor. 7:28–31). Similarly, he seems to have been understandably unconcerned about setting down regulations for the long-term governance and order of his churches (save that women should keep quiet and cover their heads). Paul's churches seem to have been characterised by a complete dependence upon the Spirit to bring forth a plenitude of gifts such as prophecy, administration, preaching, healing, evangelism, etc. from the gathered believers in Christ to enable them to function effectively as a church. The later pastoral epistles (which are not from Paul's hand) show how once the initial apocalyptic fervour had passed the Church had to contend with issues such as the structure and legitimacy of an ordered settled ministry.

Paul's rich and insightful imagery continues to prompt new and exciting theological reflection. Paul's Christ-centred theology, which claims to know nothing but Christ crucified, is seen to be a powerful reflection on the meaning of the death and resurrection of Christ and its significance for the world. Although he has been accused of showing little interest in Jesus' life and teaching (and there is remarkably little about this in his letters), nevertheless we can assume that he existed in a milieu in which Jesus' story was fairly well known and recited. He can hardly have had a meeting with Peter little more than a very few years after the death of Christ and not gleaned some information about the life of Jesus. However, it is clear that for Paul the central most significant feature of Jesus' life was his death on the cross and subsequent resurrection. This fact had changed everything and was now the exclusive focus and content of the Christian message. It was God's act of raising Jesus from the dead that established Jesus as the new Adam, that made him the Son and which inaugurated the kingdom of God (Romans 1: 4) Understandably Jesus' death and resurrection could not have been the content of his own preaching and Paul is one of the central figures of the apostolic age who fuses Jesus' teaching of a coming kingdom with the proclamation of the cross and resurrection. In a phrase of **Bultmann**, 'the proclaimer became the proclaimed', and Paul is one of the great developers of that proclamation. Consequently, we must deny the nineteenth-century picture of Paul as someone who distorted the original simpler and more profound message of Jesus by fusing it with categories drawn from Graeco-Roman mystery religions. There are deep continuities between Paul and Jesus and the necessary difference of perspective should not blind us to that fact.

One of the great issues in Pauline interpretation is how far Paul is prepared to go in attributing divine status to the risen Lord. It is quite clear that the Lord Christ occupies an exalted position in Paul's system and is someone who acts with the authority of God himself in the inauguration of the new age. However, in the final analysis Paul probably does not break the bounds of his inherited commitment to monotheism – although it is remarkable how close he comes to so doing. In the words of James Dunn: 'Jesus as Lord does not infringe on God as one, and even the highest accolade given to the exalted Christ is "to the glory of God the Father" '.[i]

Note

i   J.D.G. Dunn, *The Theology of Paul the Apostle*, p.265

Further reading

C.K. Barrett, *Paul: an introduction to his thought*, London: Geoffrey Chapman, 1994

J.D.G. Dunn, *The Theology of Paul the Apostle*, Edinburgh: T & T Clark, 1998

E.P. Sanders, *Paul and Palestinian Judaism*, London: SCM, 1997

D. Wenham, *Paul, Follower of Jesus or Founder of Christianity*, Grand Rapids, MI: W.B. Eerdmans, 1995

RAHNER, KARL (1904–84)

If Karl **Barth** is the most significant Protestant theologian of the twentieth century, then perhaps Karl Rahner must be deemed the most significant Catholic theologian of that century. Listening to what others are saying and asking questions are characteristic of Rahner: he describes dogmatics as 'the understanding and appropriating science of listening'. Rahner himself attempted to practise theology by listening to the living faith of the Church and by listening to the questions of people outside the Church. He laments the 'graveyard calm of weariness and boredom' which characterises much doctrinal statement. Doctrinal statements are not just ends but beginnings. They are means to goals, pointers, incomplete. Even the *Chalcedonian* formula is incomplete – it 'does not resolve but in fact preserves'.

Born in Freiburg, Baden, Rahner became a Jesuit in 1922 and was ordained in 1932. He was much influenced by the *existentialist* philosophy of Martin Heidegger, with whom he studied in Freiburg in 1934–36. This largely determined his anthropological approach to theology. Human beings are a mystery which cannot be completely defined. They are aware of being questioned by existence. Grace can be understood properly only when it is personally experienced at the point of one's own need. Rahner's theology was not only existentialist but also essentialist. There are basic structures in reality which can to some extent at least be known and described. It is possible to make true statements about the real God whose grace man encounters in salvation, and even in life after death.

There is a close correlation between anthropology and Christology. Human beings exist because God externalises himself in that which is other than himself. Human beings are made in the image of God, and there is a close correlation between nature and grace. Grace is the action by which God communicates with human beings and enables them to participate freely in God's own life. Human life as we know it is thus already 'graced'. Grace acts not only within the Church but outside it. However, although grace is operative everywhere, only in the Church can it be experienced in the fullness that makes salvation a present reality. The Church is empowered to proclaim the Word of God in preaching and sacrament. The Word as sacrament is salvation actually achieved. The eucharist is in all truth the sacrament of the Word absolutely, the absolute instance of the Word in general. Even the justified sinner must die, since death is the wage of sin. But through Christ's death a permanent destiny for man is achieved. The

Christian dies with Christ and shares in his victory. This is the meaning of the resurrection of the body.[i]

Few modern theologians have been able to handle the classical tradition with as much freedom and sophistication as Karl Rahner. He was able to criticise ancient formulas, reinterpret them radically, and still affirm their role in illuminating the centre of Christology. For example, he looks at the Chalcedonian 'one person in two natures' understanding of the incarnation and argues that this suggests a profound reflection on the relation of God as person to human persons. 'This is precisely an attribute of his divinity as such and his creative activity, to be able, by himself and through his own act, as such, to constitute in being something which by the very act of its being radically dependent, also acquires its own autonomy, independent reality and truth. So God's grace makes possible not only a dependence but a radical independence for the created order.'

Later, in his *magnum opus Theological Investigations*, Rahner returns to the reality of the incarnation. 'The incarnation of God is the unique supreme case of the total actualisation of human reality, which consists of the fact that man in so far as he gives himself up to God can become something. He who is unchangeable in himself can become subject to change in something else.'[ii] The basic element is the **kenōsis** and genesis of God himself, who can come to be by becoming another being. Jesus' consciousness includes a direct presence to God which is both there from the first and develops further through his life and this has soteriological significance for all humanity.[iii] In Christ, God's self-communication takes place basically for all humanity and there is a 'hypostatic union' precisely in so far as this unsurpassable self-communication of God 'is there' irrevocably in an historically tangible and self-conscious manner.

Human nature then for Rahner is ultimately mysterious, and open to the mystery of transcendence. It fulfils its nature most perfectly when it loses itself in God, who has given himself away in creating in the first place independent persons. In the act of *kenōsis*, or giving himself away, God posits the other as his own reality. Humanity is the medium of God's presence in the world: the Word become flesh.

It would be difficult to state firmly that this is a Christology either 'from above' or 'from below'. It does begin with concepts of incarnation and the Chalcedonian model, with the grace of God the Creator. But it is also to be understood as a transcendental Christology, as the fulfilment of humanity in the ultimate mystery of its own being. Jesus of Nazareth as a human being in all integrity is central to this project.

This remarkable Christological balance can readily be illustrated using *Theological Investigations*. In a discussion of 'current Problems in Christology' Rahner says of Chalcedon: 'This formula is – a formula'. Thus we have not only the right but the duty to look at it as end and as beginning. The old speculation about the ***Logos***, which ascribed to him an activity and history in creation, 'before Christ but Christ-like, distinct from the invisible Father, could be well worth rethinking, after being purified of its subordinationist elements'.[iv] Thinking of the humanity and divinity he can say that 'The only way in which Christ's common humanity may be conceived of in itself as diverse from the logos is by thinking of it in so far as it is united with the logos. The unity of the logos must constitute it in its diversity from him, that is precisely as a human nature: this unity must itself be the ground of the diversity.'[v]

Rahner explores the humanity of Jesus further in the eternal significance of the humanity of Jesus for our relationship with God. Again there is the characteristic meditation on independence through dependence. He says of God: 'The nearer one comes to him, the more real one becomes; the more he grows in and before one, the more independent one becomes oneself. Jesus the man is now and for all eternity the permanent openness of our finite being to the living God of infinite, eternal life'.[vi] In his discussion of dogmatic questions on Easter Rahner develops the meaning of the Word of God becoming man. God can become something. He who is unchangeable in himself can himself become subject to change in something else. The understanding of Easter begins from a true theology of death: 'The risen and exalted Lord must be the permanent and ever active access to God.'

The universal significance of Christ is developed further in an essay on 'Christology within an evolutionary world view'. Christ is light in darkness, 'for every fall into the abyss and the incomprehensible in spirit and life means falling into the hands of the one whom the Son addressed as his Father, when in death he commended his soul into his hands'.[vii] The abyss into which human beings may easily fall includes the abyss of atheism.

Rahner has much to say concerning the Spirit, and experience of the Spirit. He notes that 'The essential nature of genuine experience of the Spirit does not consist in particular objects of experience found in human awareness but occurs rather when a man experiences the radical re-ordering of his transcendent nature in knowledge and freedom towards the immediate reality of God through God's self-communication in grace'.[viii] Such commitments may be infrequent but are decisive for our lives. How is such experience related to charismatic experience, glossolalia (speaking in tongues) and the like? The strangest variety of experiences may be the channel of authentic encounter with God. Such encounter gives rise to faith, which may be anonymous or explicit.

This raises the issue famously connected with Rahner of anonymous Christianity. How can a person be an anonymous Christian? 'Without reflection he accepts God when he freely accepts himself within his own unlimited transcendence'.[ix] He may then come later to understand the transcendent self-communication of God through Jesus Christ in history. Faith follows a median path between rationality and emotion, and is characterised by Christian freedom, free action in decisive self-determination.

In an atmosphere of secularisation Rahner stressed the continuing importance of the spiritual, in continuity with the tradition. In an historical study of the spiritual senses, he notes in **Origen** five spiritual senses, all of which may help a man on his journey through life towards the mystical knowledge of God. This development continued through **Augustine** and flourished in the Middle Ages. In Bonaventure spiritual vision is not to be confused with the final beatific vision, and takes account of the dark night of the soul. This vision may be recovered in modern piety and in the experience of retreats. The Ignatian exercises, for example, may lead to a radical self-discovery before God, and in turn to a reconstruction in Christian community. Through Jesus we may find 'indifference', freedom from the pressures of the world in the mystery of God.

As man seeks understanding, he may be able to experience God precisely in his incomprehensibility. Mysticism may be a focus for renewal.

The Christian community, the Church, has a constant need of criticism, and this applies not least to statements from the Congregation for the Doctrine of the Faith. Transforming itself, the Church may be able to transform secular society. Even infallibility is capable of further interpretation, especially in the 'third church' of modern society. Piety is the experience of God, inside or outside the Church, and its abuse does not take away its proper use.

Reconstruction is required in fundamental theology. Characteristic of Rahner's genius, and perhaps of his limitation, is this infinite capacity for hermeneutical retrieval. This may often be a profound source of renewal – but on occasion it may be best to start where we are at in the modern world, as was more characteristic of his distinguished Catholic contemporary Edward Schillebeeckx.

There are some potential difficulties in Rahner's thought which may be mentioned here. It may be wondered whether Rahner's explanation of the relation between creator and creature preserves the identities of God and man. God is able to give himself away, so positing the other as his own finite reality. Creation is the loving self-differentiation of God's perfection, and incarnation brings this self-emptying to fulfilment. The one is self-differentiated in the many which ultimately become one again. Perhaps there is a problem with human freedom here.

This is related to the role of grace. For Rahner, God's promise of grace is effective and irrevocable. It seems almost inevitable that faith should respond to sacramental grace. What then of authentic human freedom? There has been some criticism too of Rahner's account of sin. It may be thought that human death is simply part of the created order as such. It is related to sin in the sense that life without God is for us a kind of death, and is restored in new life through faith.

Rahner served as an official expert before and during the Second Vatican Council, and had considerable influence on its deliberations. He is a theologian of rescue rather than of repetition or demolition. He respected the tradition and official doctrine, but this leaves enormous scope for interpretation and exploration. From his existential philosophy he insisted on faith and doctrine being grounded in personal experience, echoing the Enlightenment, **Kant** and **Schleiermacher**. But this faith is also built on God's objective action through grace in history. In other words, Schleiermacher's 'religious man' is now understood as man inspired by the Holy Spirit. Grace is stronger than sin. The life of the Spirit is a reality for human beings. Life now is lived with God and it continues forever in the communion of saints. There is no doubt that Rahner was one of the great theologians of modern times.

Notes

i   *Theological Investigations*, Vol. 2., p.203
ii   *Ibid.*, Vol. 4., p.107
iii   *Ibid.*, Vol. 5., p.199f.
iv   *Ibid.*, Vol. 5., p.149f.
v   *Ibid.*, Vol. 5., p.181
vi   *Ibid.*, Vol. 3, p.35
vii   *Ibid.*, Vol. 3, pp.35, 49
viii   *Ibid.*, Vol. 5., p.192
ix   *Ibid.*, Vol. 16, p.27

See also: **Augustine; Aquinas; Barth; Kant; Schleiermacher**

Glossary: **Chalcedonian; existentialist; kenōsis; Logos**

Major writings

Theological Investigations, 23 vols, London: Darton, Longman & Todd, 1961–92
Studies in Modern Theology, London: Burns & Oats, 1965
Spirit in the World, London: Sheed & Ward, 1989 (1968)
Foundations of Christian Faith, London: Sheed & Ward, 1978

Further reading

W. Dych, *Karl Rahner*, London: Chapman, 1992
H.D. Egan, *Karl Rahner: the mystic of everyday life*, New York: Crossroad Pub. Co., 1998
G.A. McCool, *A Rahner Reader*, London: Darton, Longman & Todd, 1975
H. Vorgrimler, *Karl Rahner*, London: SCM, 1986
K.H. Weger, *Karl Rahner. An Introduction to his Theology*, trans. David Smith, London: Burns & Oates, 1980

REIMARUS, HERMANN SAMUEL (1694–1768)

Hermann Samuel Reimarus was born in Hamburg, studied theology and philosophy in Jena and Wittenberg, and then became Professor of Hebrew and Oriental languages at the Akademisches Gymnasium in Hamburg, where he worked for forty years, turning down various positions including a professorship at Göttingen. He produced various works including a book on logic, a commentary on *Job* and an edition of the Greek historian *Dio Cassius*. Between 1744 and 1767 he wrote a critique of Christianity after being much influenced by English Deism. He laid great stress on the power of natural reason.

Reimarus published in 1755 a collection of papers on the central truths of natural religion. Five years later he published again on issues in natural religion, in the context of a study of the behaviour of animals. He thought that their patterns of inherited behaviour might be the basis for human morality But his main impact was to come through the posthumous publication of his work on natural and revealed religion, the *Apology*.

Reimarus was one of the fathers of modern biblical criticism, which was to have such an enormous influence on the development of theology. His most controversial work, in which he reflected on a range of philosophical and theological issues, was published only after his death by Lessing between 1774 and 1778, in the famous seven *Wolfenbuettel Fragments*. Publication during his lifetime would no doubt have had disastrous consequences for Reimarus' position in Hamburg. In the *Fragments* he suggested that there could be no revelation binding on all men for all time – this much he shares with the spirit of the English Deists and Voltaire. The truths of natural religion are the existence of the wise creator God and the immortality of the soul. These truths are discoverable by reason, and natural religion is much superior to revealed religion. It is also superior to atheism, which is an equally irrational position.

What then are we to make of the Bible and especially the Christian religion? Jesus had preached a practical, non-miraculous gospel. The centre of his significance was, and is, an ethical teaching and a moral way of life. Jesus should be understood as an historical person rather than as a divine being. After his death Jesus' disciples were much disappointed. They then consoled themselves by creating the classical Christian system of salvation and redemption, and justified this by appeals to alleged communications from the risen Christ. The resurrection was not an historical event. The disciples took the body of Jesus and concealed it. Reimarus, echoing Deist and classical **Enlightenment** position, argued that what we need to do is to get away from preoccupation with the risen Christ and get back to the real Jesus who is the historical Jesus. Whatever the disadvantages of this call, it had the good practical effect of stimulating scholars to look much more closely at the whole question of the historical Jesus, and not simply regard it as inconsequential because of the manifold certainties associated with the Christ of faith. Christology after Reimarus was to be rather different from Christology before.

In the last of the fragments, 'On the aims of Jesus and his disciples', Reimarus suggested that it was important to distinguish clearly between what the apostles wrote in their accounts and what Jesus really said and taught. Jesus was completely Jewish, and had no wish to produce new expressions of faith nor to found something called Christianity. He called for repentance and preached the coming of the Messianic kingdom on earth in a Jewish context. It was only when this hope was dashed through Jesus' death that the apostles 'created the system of a spiritual suffering saviour of the whole human race'. They produced this new system in order to maintain their own claims on privilege in the world, and by stealing the body of Jesus they made possible the preaching of the resurrection. It was possible only to find a few traces of Jesus' teaching in the gospel narratives because the apostles had introduced their new framework.

A glance at the text of the *Apology* reveals Reimarus' trenchant critical style.

Thus the goal of Jesus' sermons and teachings was a proper, active character, a changing of the mind, a sincere love of God and of one's neighbour ... These are not great mysteries or tenets of the faith that he explains, proves and preaches; they are nothing other than moral teachings and duties intended to improve man inwardly and with all his heart.[i]

The new system of a suffering spiritual saviour, which no one had ever known or thought of before, was invented after the death of Jesus, and invented only because the first hopes had failed.[ii]

It is always a sign that a doctrine or history possesses no depth or authenticity when one is obliged to resort to miracles in order to prove its truth. Miracles do not possess in and by themselves any principle containing a single article of faith or conclusive fact.[iii]

Lessing was much criticised for publishing this material, whose true authorship was finally made known only in 1814. Although much of the detail was mistaken, Reimarus is often regarded as the founder of research into the Jesus of history. He borrowed much from the Deists, and invented the idea of the disciples' betrayal of Jesus for material reward. Nevertheless he raised the central historical issues, and not least the relation of the earliest Christian community to Judaism. It was to be a long time before these issues were taken up again in such a decisive manner. Reimarus' stress on the *eschatological* nature of the preaching of Jesus anticipated the work of Albert Schweitzer more than a century later. Like David Friedrich **Strauss** after him, Reimarus was vulnerable to scholarly critique of the details of his arguments. Where he found errors in the Bible, others found errors in his judgements. His critique of the doctrine of eternal punishment was especially offensive to the orthodox. But these details do not detract from the magnitude of his intellectual achievements and the innovative nature of his scholarship.

Notes

i   *Fragments*, p.69
ii   *Ibid.*, p.151
iii *Ibid.*, p.234

See also: **Strauss**

Glossary: **Enlightenment; eschatological**

Major writings

Fragments/Reimarus, ed. Charles H. Talbert, London: SCM, 1971

Further reading

W.G. Kummel, *History of the Study of the New Testament*, London: SCM, 1973

RITSCHL, ALBRECHT (1822–89)

Albrecht Ritschl was one of the most important influences on modern theology, but is often much underrated, in part due to the views of Karl **Barth**. Beginning to teach systematic theology when Hegel's influence was at its height, he quickly tired of the delights of metaphysical speculation, as he saw them. For Ritschl it was possible albeit fruitless to speculate as you may speculate on anything you like and establish nothing. This basic conviction meant that he distrusted traditional approaches to metaphysics, rejected idealism and turned back to **Kant** and the moral law as the basis for authentic religion.

God for Ritschl is a loving will. His purpose for humanity is the kingdom of God as the supreme good. Jesus was the founder of the kingdom of God. Human beings were to follow him and share in his attitude to the world. Our separation from God is removed when we learn through Jesus that God is our Father. In being reconciled with God through this realisation we may join together in organised moral action to bring in the final realisation of God's kingdom. Ritschl was to be a most influential theologian, whose pupils may be divided into a right- and a left-wing group, the schools of **Troeltsch** and Herrmann respectively.

Albrecht Ritschl was born in 1822 in Berlin. Like **Schleiermacher** he came from a clerical family, his father soon becoming general superintendent. Like most German students he studied for a term or two at a number of universities, touring the lectures of the great men, in this case at Bonn, Halle, Heidelberg and Tübingen. In Tübingen he studied under the great Ferdinand Christian Baur. Ritschl himself began lecturing in New Testament studies in Bonn in 1846, moving into the history of doctrine and then from 1852 into Dogmatics or 'systematic theology'. He became a full professor in Bonn in 1859, then moved to Göttingen in 1864, where he taught to an ever-growing and international audience from Britain, America and other countries until his death in 1889. He began in New Testament and historical studies, and this concern for historical and exegetical issues characterised all his work. A pupil of Baur, the second edition of his book *The Early Catholic Church*, on the Church during the first two centuries, destroyed some of Baur's central theses, although it was still faithful to the critical spirit which Baur instilled into his pupils. His main work after 1852 was to be in systematic theology.

Like Schleiermacher Ritschl was interested in the notion of the essence of Christianity, in what he calls 'the complete and correct idea of the Christian religion'. This echoes and modifies Schleiermacher's famous definition, and is stated as follows: 'Christianity is the monotheistic, completely spiritual and ethical religion, which, based on the life of its author as Redeemer and Founder of the Kingdom of God, consists in the freedom of the children of God, involves the impulse to conduct from the motive of love, which aims at the moral organisation of mankind, and grounds blessedness on the relation of sonship to God, as well as on the kingdom of God.' Immediately notable is the stress on the life of Jesus as the author of the faith, the Redeemer and the Founder of the kingdom of God. Thus speaks the ex-New Testament scholar and church historian.

When Ritschl talks about God he does not begin as Schleiermacher had done with the feeling of absolute dependence. He begins with God as a person, a person whose will it is to love. This will is to be fulfilled in the creation of the kingdom of God as the supreme good. Concern for the will of God, and for the supreme good, led him to take over a highly distinctive theory of the basis of religious knowledge, not in feeling or dependence but in so-called value judgements. 'Religious knowledge moves in independent value judgements, which relate to man's attitude to the world, and call for feelings of pleasure and pain in which man either enjoys the dominion over the world vouchsafed to him by God, or feels grievously the lack of God's help to that end.'[i]

It is through a value judgement that we recognise the spiritual significance of Jesus. Jesus was the historic founder of Christianity, the one who follows the perfect **revelation** of God: 'If Christ by what he has done and suffered for my salvation is my Lord, and if, by trusting for my salvation to the power of what he has done for me, I honour him as my God, then, that is a value judgement of a direct kind'.[ii] On the basis of our experience of God's loving will through him, we call Christ divine. As Ritschl puts it: 'The twofold significance we are compelled to ascribe to Christ as being at once the perfect revealer of God as the manifest type of spiritual lordship over the world, finds expression in the single predicate of his Godhead'.[iii]

What is the nature of the salvation which Christ brings? Through him we come to realise that God is the Father, and that he forgives sinners. Through him we realise the meaning of trust in God, taking up, as Herrmann was to do in following him, Luther's emphasis on trust as the centre of faith (see **Luther**). Through Christ's endurance of suffering he achieved a unique freedom from the pressures of the world and lordship over the world. By reflecting on his life and fate we too can have this freedom, this spiritual and moral lordship. To exercise this freedom and lordship is to enter into the kingdom of God.

The concept of the kingdom is very important to Ritschl. As reconciled in Christ we are called to discipleship, to a life of moral action in love. The life of Jesus suggests to us not just piety but activity, concrete moral action. So he can say of the kingdom: 'In Christianity the Kingdom is represented as the common end of God and of the elect community in such a way that it rises above the natural limits of nationality and becomes the moral society of nations'. This is an international vision. For Jesus the kingdom meant 'not the common exercise of worship but the organisation of humanity through action inspired by love'. This concept of the kingdom has been much criticised and can easily be turned into the worst sort of religious do-gooding exercise, of the feeblest sort. But this need not happen, and perhaps the abuse of the concept need not take away its proper use and value.

It has been noted that Ritschl attempted carefully to avoid specifically metaphysical concepts. That smacked of Hegel and was, he thought, the weakness of Schleiermacher. But if Jesus is indeed the way, the truth and the life, Christian faith does raise just metaphysical issues and it may be thought that by abandoning these issues or by implicitly importing them in weakened form, Ritschl left his own system so weak that it was instantly vulnerable to all sorts of distortion and trivialisation. Yet his stress on 'the gospel' given in Jesus Christ as the starting point, rather than the Christian consciousness, was perhaps an improvement on Schleiermacher, and was indeed to be taken up, although quite without acknowledgement, by Barth, despite the fact that the latter never had much time for Ritschl.

Ritschl laid stress on the practical rather than the speculative side of religion. It is essentially a matter of our conduct in living in this world. We cannot know God in himself (a very Kantian viewpoint) either by mysticism or metaphysical speculation. We come to know more of redemption by participation in the work of the kingdom. 'He that doeth the will shall know of the doctrine' was one of Ritschl's favourite texts. We must take action. This corresponds, in a sense, to the stress on value judgements. Christian faith is not a matter of accepting doctrines which are self-evidently true. What matters is that we believe through personal conviction, and that is what a value judgement is. This is the response of faith. But at the same time, Ritschl stresses with Luther that justification does not involve human effort, but is solely of grace. Moral effort is the result of justification, not the precondition of it.

In keeping with his distaste for pietism, Ritschl stressed, with Schleiermacher, the corporate nature of Christian faith. Discipleship is worked out together with others, and is expressed in terms of vocation (as with Luther) in working towards the ideal of Christian perfection.

We have stressed the importance of historical study in Ritschl's development. Despite the stress on decision through judgement, it sometimes seems that he expects too much of history as such. History may simply not be able to do all the jobs which, in the theology he criticised, were left to metaphysics. As certain critics have said, it sometimes appears that in Ritschl the facts simply *qua* history are revelation. To say of Jesus that he is the historical founder of Christianity is for all practical purposes like saying that he is the revelation of God. But history does not automatically provide a divine disclosure. Indeed, it may be said that there may be as many possible interpretations of a particular history as there are historians. But it belongs to the nature of theology that none of its practitioners solve all of its problems The assured results of one generation become the data from which the next generation carries forward the investigation.

Notes

i   *Justification and Reconciliation*, p.205
ii   *Ibid.*, p.398
iii *Ibid.*, p.389

Major writings

Theology and Metaphysics in *Three Essays*, trans. Philip Hefner, Philadelphia: Fortress Press, 1972 (1881)

The Christian Doctrine of Justification and Reconciliation; The Positive Development of the Doctrine, ed. H.R. Mackintosh & A.B. Macaulay, Edinburgh: T & T Clark, 1900

History of Pietism, trans. of intro. ed. P. Hefner, Minneapolis: Fortress Press, 1972

Further reading

D.L. Mueller, *An Introduction to the Theology of Albrecht Ritschl*, Philadelphia: Westminster Press, 1969

J. Richmond, *Ritschl, A Reappraisal. A Study in Systematic Theology*, London: Collins, 1978

Rolf Schaefer, *Ritschl*, Beiträge zur historischen Theologie, no. 41, Tübingen, 1968

RUETHER, ROSEMARY RADFORD (1936–)

Rosemary Radford Ruether, who teaches at Garrett-Evanston College in Illinois, is well known as one of the outstanding and distinctive feminist theologians of the twentieth century. Feminist theology is a far from monolithic enterprise, and a number of writers have developed very original perspectives. They have also much in common, in recognition of the virtual suppression of women's talents, and their place in the Christian understanding of society, throughout most of the history of the Church.

Ruether, a distinguished theologian in her own right, may stand as representative of the growing dimension of feminist theology in the contemporary Church. Born in 1936 into a Catholic family she studied humanities, especially classics and Roman history, at Scripps College, Claremont, California from 1954. Her PhD thesis was on the work of Gregory of Nazianzus (see **Cappadocian Fathers**). She married and became associated with a Benedictine community at Valyermo in California, also making friends with Thomas Merton and Gregory Baum. She became deeply interested in feminist and other forms of liberation theology, and in Jewish–Christian relations, making several visits to the Middle East. These issues are explored in relation to her own background, in her book ***Disputed Questions: on being a Christian*** (1989).

Ruether has always been concerned with the understanding of the Church as community. In *The Church Against Itself* (1967) she took up the theme of constant renewal and argued that the Church is called to reconsider its life in relation to matters such as poverty, oppression, anti-Semitism and the emerging environmental crisis.

According to Ruether, humanity is alienated from God in brokenness and estrangement. This is largely the product of a pervasive yet destructive mind–body dualism that has been dominant for so long in Western culture. This has profoundly disruptive effects as the tendency is for us to identify ourselves solely with our mental selves in a form of denial of our embodied nature in the world. Thus alienated from our bodies we are alienated from ourselves and this fosters discriminatory practice in relation to others.

Ruether argues that human beings have no essential or fixed nature and thus we can be transformed. The nature of this transformation is worked out in *The Radical Kingdom* (1970). God's grace may provide transformation for the individual but the stress is overwhelmingly social and communal. As such the messianic hope of the Hebrew prophets remains a historical and social hope for us too. As she puts it in *To Change the World: Christology and cultural criticism* (1981), the centre of theology is not an idea but a person – Jesus of Nazareth. The theme of identifying and opposing anti-Semitism is a pervasive feature of Ruether's work. Christians are called upon to embrace a genuine human pluralism that recognises and respects the integrity of the other – that which is different. The Church's role in this is not to be overly concerned for its own life as an institution but to mediate the reality of God to the world. The Church must constantly repent of its own sin, its own failure, to a transforming community that is open to the other. As such it must seek to embody and practice those forms of openness in which it invites all of society to participate.

A major part of this agenda involves the liberation of women, not least in the Church. Ruether's early exploration of feminist themes is expounded in her *Sexism and God-talk*. Much more radical is the movement into eco-feminism, typically set out in *Gaia & God: an ecofeminist theology of earth healing* (1989). Here Ruether explores myths of a matricentric society which preceded the domination of patriarchy. Patriarchy is inevitably linked with violence and oppression, not only of women but also towards the natural environment. An eco-feminist theology would restore appropriate environmental concerns, as well as contribute to a more sane society.

It is interesting that Ruether writes as a Roman Catholic, and she is radical in calling her own denomination to reform itself in relation to its communal life. In *A Democratic Catholic Church* (1992), jointly edited with Eugene Bianchi, she brings together a number of authors on the subject of Catholic reform. Democratic Church reform is to be based on two premises: First, 'the recognition that all forms of social structure are human creations, partial, historical, and open to revision, is a view truer to historical reality than the belief that social and Church order should reflect an unchanging hierarchical cosmos'.

Second, 'democratic, participatory forms of government are more appropriate for the expression of respect for persons and safeguarding against abusive relationships than hierarchical and monarchical systems of government that treat the governed as rightless dependents'. Her own chapter in the volume, entitled 'Spirituality and Justice – popular church groups in the United States', underlines these values: 'In relation to the Roman Catholic Church as an institution, they have discovered a remarkable way to be faithful to this Church as a historical community, while being entirely free from its hierarchical control'. Key principles include participation, conciliarity, pluralism, accountability and dialogue. Ruether argues that 'It was hope, not fear, that inspired the Pope of Vatican II. For him, a truly renewed church could be a catalyst for other great reforms towards social justice and peace amid an ecologically enlightened humanity. May this vision prevail'.

See also: **Cappadocian Fathers**

Major writings

The Church against Itself: an inquiry into the conditions of historical existence for the eschatological community, London: Sheed & Ward, 1967

The Radical Kingdom: the Western experience of Messianic hope, New York: Harper & Row, 1970

Mary, the Feminine Face of the Church, Philadelphia: Westminster Press, 1977

To Change the World: Christology and cultural criticism, New York: Crossroad Pub. Co., 1981

Sexism and God-talk: toward a feminist theology, London: SCM, 1983

Disputed Questions: on being a Christian, Maryknoll, NY: Orbis, 1989

The Wrath of Jonah: the crisis of religious nationalism in the Israeli–Palestinian conflict, New York: Harper & Row, 1989

Gaia & God: an ecofeminist theology of earth healing, London: SCM, 1993

Women Healing Earth: Third world women on ecology, feminism, and religion, ed. Rosemary Radford Ruether, London: SCM, 1996

Introducing Redemption in Christian Feminism, Sheffield: Sheffield Academic Press, 1998

Further reading

B. Penn, *On Being the Church in the United States: contemporary theological critiques of liberalism,* New York: P. Lang, 1994

W.M. Ramsay, *Four Modern Prophets: Walter Rauschenbusch, Martin Luther King, Jr., Gustavo Gutiérrez, Rosemary Radford Ruether,* Atlanta, GA: John Knox Press, 1986

K.M. Sands, *Escape from Paradise: evil and tragedy in feminist theology,* Minneapolis: Fortress Press, 1994

J. Vaughan, *Sociality, Ethics, and Social Change: a critical appraisal of Reinhold Niebuhr's ethics in the light of Rosemary Ruether's works,* Lanham, MD and London: University Press of America, 1983

SCHLEIERMACHER, FRIEDRICH DANIEL ERNST
(1768–1834)

The end of the summer of 1799 saw the publication of a small volume entitled *On Religion, Speeches to its Cultured Despisers*. It was written by a young man who was to have more influence on nineteenth-century theology than any other, and perhaps on twentieth-century theology too – meriting him the oft-repeated title of 'Father of Modern Theology'. His name was Friedrich Schleiermacher and it is virtually impossible to imagine the development of theology in the twentieth century without his magnificent contribution.

The major themes of all Schleiermacher's later works are already present in *Speeches*. In his second speech on the nature of religion, he understands religion in terms of piety. What is piety? 'In itself, it is an affection, a revelation of the infinite in the finite, God being seen in it and it in God. Piety appears as a surrender, a submission to be moved by the whole that stands over against human beings. It resigns, at once, any claims in anything that belongs to either science or morality.' Speaking to an age where educated and cultured men and women have an interest in everything but religion, Schleiermacher presents religion as a 'sense of the infinite which every soul that looks within can find'. Only in the final speech does Schleiermacher attempt to move from a discussion of religion in general to one of Christianity in particular. If religious apprehension can be defined as an awareness of surrender to the infinite, what can be special about the man Jesus of Nazareth? Answer: 'The truly divine element in him is the glorious clearness to which the great idea he came to exhibit attained in his soul'.[i]

All of this would be further developed in Schleiermacher's *magnum opus The Christian Faith* (1821–22). In this groundbreaking work there is nothing of the exact science of God of older dogmatic theologies. There is nothing of the biblical fundamentalism of seventeenth-century orthodoxy, nor is there the less literal, but still purely biblical, imagery of pietism. But at the same time there is nothing of the cold logic and confident scepticism of the eighteenth-century rationalists. For Schleiermacher, the fundamental human experience, which is the fundamental experience of religion, is the awareness of absolute dependence on the divine, and awareness of surrender to one who cannot in himself be known. There is in other words a general and identifiable sense of being posited in the world and having one's origin and explanation in another. All religions share this experience as it is part of being human in the world. Schleiermacher's attempt to ground theological discourse in the universal structures of human consciousness is often termed as a pivotal 'turn to the subject' in modern theology.

However, *The Christian Faith* is distinguished from the earlier *Speeches* by its focus on the person of Christ. Although he begins with a general account of religion the special place of Christ as the Redeemer is retained. However, Schleiermacher was critical of the logical confusions of the traditional credal formulations of Christ's person such as the **Chalcedonian** 'one person in two natures' formula. This could be accepted if we understood it to mean the existence of God in Christ and our brotherly communion with Christ but simply as it stands it leads to confusion and logical inconsistency. According to Schleiermacher Christ as Redeemer is distinguished from all other people through the clarity and intensity of his consciousness of God, which was a real presence of God in him. Furthermore, the God-consciousness of Christ was communicated to his disciples and continues in a powerful way in the life of the Christian community. Christ's God-consciousness then is active and dynamic and the believer can encounter the potency of that God-consciousness in the preaching, teaching and fellowship of the contemporary Christian community. As such Christ works his redemption by taking up the faithful into the power of his consciousness of God.

All of Schleiermacher's theology is outlined in terms of the basic overarching theme of 'absolute dependence' and anything which cannot usefully be explained by or contribute to a deeper understanding of this phenomenon is to be discarded. Famously, Schleiermacher argued that the doctrine of the **Trinity** was not an immediate utterance concerning Christian self-consciousness but only a combination of such utterances. In other words the basic thrust of the Trinity is that the divine reality was present in Christ and persists today in the Church through the presence of the Spirit and that is the value of expressing the doctrine. However, Schleiermacher was clear that although these assertions were legitimate inferences from the Christian consciousness of God this did not – and could not – necessitate the assumption of eternal distinctions in God. Schleiermacher thus called for a reinterpretation of the traditional doctrine of the Trinity and expressed some approval for a qualified form of modalism. This feeling of absolute dependence, which is the Christian consciousness of God, is localised not simply in individuals but within the Christian community. Therefore, 'Dogmatic theology is the science that systematises the doctrine prevalent in a Christian Church at a given time'.[ii]

Such a theology, written with brilliance and elegance, relating Church, community and the human spirit in general with a constantly refreshed awareness of absolute dependence on the divine, was exactly the recipe to excite the enthusiasm of a generation which saw the rise of the early Romantic movement. It became a best-seller at once, and thousands who perhaps came to differ on the details owed their first serious involvement with theology to Schleiermacher. If **Kant** had put away knowledge to make room for faith, it was Schleiermacher who transformed the Kantian moral approach to religion into a warm affection for Christ the Redeemer, the supreme example of a man totally engulfed in the consciousness of God.

Schleiermacher was born in 1768. His father and grandfather were clergymen and he was sent at an early age to a school run by the Moravian Brethren at Barb, and then to the Moravian theological seminary. Although he was to rebel there against the moralism and restricted lifestyle of the place, yet he was deeply affected by the life of Christ-centred piety which the Brethren taught, and always regarded himself as 'a Moravian of a higher order'. Eventually he persuaded his father to allow him to study theology at the University of Halle. There he was exposed to the most modern versions of critical theology. He spent some time in the Berlin area as a tutor to an aristocratic family, took his second (practical) theological exam, and worked for a short time as an assistant pastor. During this period he wrote a long critical essay on Kant and the freedom of the will, which was to be influential for his development. He also published sermons and became chaplain to the Charity hospital in Berlin. Here in Berlin he developed a literary circle which intensified his concern with theology and culture. In 1799 he published the *Speeches*, an apologetic for a modern Christian faith. He also produced *Soliloquies*, and began what was to become a famous translation of Plato.

Finally, aged almost 40, he was appointed to more significant posts – as pastor at the Trinity church in Berlin and then Professor of Theology in Halle. Finally, he was appointed Professor of Theology at the new University of Berlin in 1808. Schleiermacher drew up the theological curriculum for this new university thereby creating the modern structure of theological studies in most Continental universities that persists to this day. Indeed he was crucial in arguing for the legitimacy of having a theological faculty in this new modern research university. It was here he also married and had a son, who died tragically early.

All of this took place against the background of the invasion of Prussia by Napoleon. Schleiermacher became a convinced Prussian patriot. He was often to be consulted by the government on education in universities – he had a rather stormy relationship with the ministry of education. Meanwhile the first, and then a second, edition of his *The Christian Faith* appeared. The number of students of theology increased dramatically during his tenure of office until his death in 1834. He delivered lecture courses, not only in systematic theology but in New Testament studies, producing commentaries and writing an influential work on hermeneutics (the science governing the interpretation of texts). Schleiermacher is thus not only the father of modern theology but also of modern hermeneutics.

In his early lectures Schleiermacher was concerned to relate particular texts to the nature of language, to find their basic meaning in the context of a universal language. In his later lectures he strives to relate texts to the intention of their particular author, and so to seek 'to understand the author better than he could have understood himself'. This became a classic aim of traditional hermeneutics, developed notably by Dilthey. Hans George Gadamer was to take this tradition further during the twentieth century, seeking to find the meaning of expressions in relation to the tradition of language in which they arose. For Schleiermacher hermeneutics is intimately related to the Word by which all things were made, centred on the Word made flesh.

Schleiermacher has been endlessly criticised, first by his colleague **Hegel**, and in modern theology especially by **Barth**, as being too subjective and anthropomorphic in his approach to theology. Barth said of Schleiermacher's approach that 'one cannot speak of God by speaking of man in a loud voice'. Yet Barth was also quick to recognise Schleiermacher's stature as the person whose framework had to be challenged. As theology has sought to move beyond the Barth/Schleiermacher impasse, and to appropriate new dimensions, e.g. in Catholic and liberation theologies, it will remain indebted to Schleiermacher for his threefold emphasis on experience, Christology and community, and for his concern with hermeneutics.

Notes

i   *On Religion*, p.246
ii   *The Christian Faith*, p.88

See also: **Barth; Hegel; Kant**

Glossary: ***Chalcedonian; revelation; Trinity***

Major writings

The Christian Faith, ed. H.R. Mackintosh & J.S. Stewart, Edinburgh: T & T Clark, 1928 (1821–22; reprinted 1999)
On Religion, Speeches to its Cultured Despisers, trans. J. Oman, New York, 1893; London: Harper & Row, 1958
Brief Outline of Theology as a Field of Study, translation of the 1811 and 1830 editions, with essays and notes, Terrence N. Tice, Lewiston, NY: Edwin Mellen Press, 1990
Lectures on Hermeneutics, Criticism and Other Writings, trans. Andrew Bowie, Cambridge: CUP, 1998

Further reading

T.H. Curran, *Doctrine and Speculation in Schleiermacher's Glaubenslehre*, Berlin and New York: W. de Gruyter, 1994
B.A. Gerrish, *A Prince of the Church: Schleiermacher and the beginnings of modern theology*, London: SCM, 1984
G. Nicol (ed.), *Schleiermacher and Feminism: sources, evaluations, and responses*, Lewiston, NY and Lampeter: Edwin Mellen, 1992
M. Redeker, *Friedrich Schleiermacher*, Philadelphia: Fortress Press, 1973
T.N. Tice, *Schleiermacher's Sermons: a chronological listing and account*, Lewiston, NY and Lampeter: Edwin Mellen, 1997
R.R. Williams, *Schleiermacher the Theologian: the construction of the doctrine of God*, Philadelphia: Fortress Press, 1978

SCHÜSSLER-FIORENZA, ELISABETH (1938–)

Elisabeth Schüssler-Fiorenza was born to German parents in Tschanad, Romania, in 1938. She studied theology at the University of Würtzburg (MDiv, Lic Theol) and Münster (Dr Theol). In 1970 she and her husband Francis (also a theologian) emigrated to the United States. She taught New Testament studies at the University of Notre Dame from 1970 to 1984, at the Episcopal Divinity School in Cambridge, Massachusetts, from 1984 to 1988, and since then has been Krister Stendahl Professor of Divinity at Harvard. She is a Member of the American Academy of Sciences, a past president of the Society for Biblical Literature, and was a founding co-editor of the *Journal of Feminist Studies in Religion*.

Schüssler-Fiorenza is an international authority on New Testament studies, and especially on biblical interpretation and feminist theology. Her best-known book is perhaps *In Memory of her – A Feminist Theological Reconstruction of Christian Origins* (1983). She has also published many other books, including *Bread not Stone – The Challenge of Feminist Biblical Interpretation* (1984), *The Book of Revelation* (1985),

Discipleship of Equals (1993), *Jesus, Miriam's Child* (1995), *Jesus and the Politics of Interpretation* (2001) and *Wisdom Ways* (2001).

In *Memory of Her* brings out her characteristic theological concerns and is perhaps the best introduction to Schüssler-Fiorenza's work. The introduction underlines the importance of historical context for the interpretation of the Bible today.

The book is divided into three parts. The first, 'Seeing – Naming – Reconstituting', explores a feminist critical hermeneutics. She considers models of biblical interpretation, paying special attention to **liberation theology**, notably the pioneering examples of Elizabeth Cady Stanton and Letty Russell.

> The basic insight of all liberation theologies, including feminist theology, is the recognition that all theology, willingly or not, is by definition always engaged for or against the oppressed. Intellectual neutrality is not possible in a world of exploitation and oppression.[i]

Schüssler-Fiorenza develops a feminist critical method, and immediately portrays the problem of androcentrism. Androcentric language mentions women only when women's behaviour presents a problem, or when women are exceptional individuals. This is a particular problem with biblical translations which have mainly been done by men. Jesus, however, never seemed to have demanded the submission of women; indeed he has notable encounters with women and women are among his closest followers. On the other hand the early Church Fathers, especially **Tertullian** and Jerome, consistently attacked the leadership of women in the Church.

In the face of such patriarchalism, how is a feminist model of historical reconstruction possible? Schüssler-Fiorenza argues that the early Christian situation was not monolithic but multi-faceted. She demonstrates how for 200 years Christianity was essentially a movement among the disprivileged and in that regard the status of women was more privileged than it was later to become. But what the German New Testament scholar Gerd Theissen has called 'love-patriarchalism' eventually prevailed and women were increasingly submerged in structures that privileged the male. Oppression of working-class men may in turn have generated more oppression of women in their culture.

The second and central part of the book is entitled 'In Memory of Her: Women's History as the History of the Discipleship of Equals'.

Here Schüssler-Fiorenza examines the Jesus movement as a renewal movement within Judaism. Viewed from this perspective Jesus' movement can be seen as an alternative to the dominant patriarchal structures that then existed within Judaism.

> The power of God's *basileia* (realm/rule) is realised in Jesus' table community with the poor, the sinners, the tax collectors and prostitutes.[ii]

Women were decisive for the continuation of the movement after Jesus' arrest and execution. 'Without question the discipleship of Jesus does not respect patriarchal family bonds.'[iii]

Schüssler-Fiorenza then examines the Early Christian Missionary Movement as 'Equality in the Power of the Spirit'. She demonstrates, using the Pauline literature and the book of Acts, that women were among the most prominent missionaries and leaders in the early Christian movement.[iv] This is the clear impact of such New Testament texts such as Galatians 3.28 where it says 'There is neither male nor female in Christ'. Furthermore, in light of the priority of God's coming realm, 'Patriarchal marriage – and sexual relationships between male and female – is no longer constitutive of the new community in Christ'.[v] It is still the case though that in Paul's stricter injunctions about the role of women he is concerned to preserve order and propriety (see **Paul**).

The third section of Schüssler-Fiorenza's *magnum opus* is entitled 'Tracing the Struggles: Patriarchy and Ministry'. She argues that this vision of a discipleship of equals created tensions in the prevailing patriarchal culture. Christians were suspected of political subversion and of threatening the social fabric of society. This led to tensions between the patriarchal household of God and the *ekklesia* (called out assembly) of women, notably in the struggle against Montanism (an early heretical sect of spiritual enthusiasts). However, Mark's Gospel insists on the necessity of suffering and the call to suffering discipleship and this is exemplified by the women disciples. Mary Magdalene is 'the primary apostolic witness to the resurrection'[vi] – a challenge to the tradition that Peter was the first apostle to see the risen Christ. The gospels of Mark and John both 'accord women apostolic and ministerial leadership'.[vii]

Schüssler-Fiorenza's concluding epilogue turns on 'Towards a Feminist Biblical Spirituality: The Ekklesia of Women' and argues that conventional images of women must be revised.

Rather than defining women's relationship to God by their sexual relationship to men and through the patriarchal structures of family and church, a feminist Christian spirituality defines women's relationship to God in and through the experience of being called into a discipleship of equals, the assembly of free citizens who decide their own spiritual welfare.[viii]

She concludes:

In breaking the bread and sharing the cup we proclaim not only the passion and resurrection of Christ but also celebrate that of women in biblical religion.[ix]

This is a powerful and deeply erudite example of a critical liberation theology which may serve as an eloquent paradigm for other theologies within the range of emancipatory concerns, and brilliantly illustrates the innovative developments in contemporary theology. It shows among other things how a theology can be liberal but within an inclusive Catholic tradition, without the need to embrace the anti-modernism of some other developments in recent Christian thought.

Notes

i   *In Memory of Her,* p.6
ii   *Ibid.,* p.121
iii *Ibid.,* p.146
iv   *Ibid.,* p.184
v   *Ibid.,* p.210
vi   *Ibid.,* p.332
vii *Ibid.,* p.334
viii *Ibid.,* p.349
ix   *Ibid.,* p.351

See also: **Paul; Tertullian**

Major writings

In Memory of Her – A Feminist Theological Reconstruction of Christian Origin, New York: Crossroad Pub. Co., 1983
Bread not Stone – The Challenge of Feminist Biblical Interpretation, Edinburgh: T & T Clark, 1984
The Book of Revelation – Justice and Judgement, Philadelphia: Fortress Press, 1985
Discipleship of Equals: a critical feminist ekklesia-logy of London, London: SCM, 1993
Jesus, Miriam's Child, Sophia's Prophet, London: SCM, 1995

Rhetoric and Ethic: the politics of biblical studies, Minneapolis: Fortress Press, 1999
Jesus and the Politics of Interpretation, New York and London: Continuum, 2001

Further reading

A. Loades (ed.), *Feminist Theology: a reader*, London: SPCK, 1990

STRAUSS, DAVID FRIEDRICH (1808–74)

German theologian of the nineteenth century famous for writing a
critical life of Jesus. This work, entitled *The Life of Jesus Critically
Examined (Das Leben Jesu, kritische bearbeit)*, published in 1835, caused
an uproar in theological and Church circles throughout Europe. In it
Strauss revealed for the first time the full implications for understanding the life of Jesus if one applies the historico-critical method to
the study of the gospels. The ensuing furore cost Strauss his job and
any future prospect of academic preferment in Germany and
elsewhere at that time.

Strauss was born in Ludwigsburg in Würtemberg in 1808. He
studied at Tübingen under F.C. Baur, who introduced Strauss to the
work of **Hegel**. Strauss was later to serve as an assistant pastor in a
small village church where he struggled to accommodate his Hegelian
account of the faith with the more traditional sensitivities of his
parishioners. After serving for a period as a teacher in a seminary in
Maulbronn he was appointed to a lectureship at his former seminary in
Tübingen in 1832.

Strauss may have been surprised at the strength of the reaction to his
famous work. For he could reasonably have claimed only to be making
explicit what was in fact implicit in the writings of Hegel and
Schleiermacher, both of whom were still regarded as the theological
giants of the age. While this is almost certainly true, it is the case that
Strauss's analytic and precise style made clear, in a way that had not
been done before, the devastating impact of such views on dearly held
notions of the faith. This, allied to Strauss's somewhat detached tone in
relation to the founder of the faith, and the complete lack of any sense
of reverence in his handling of material which was of fundamental
importance to Christian believers throughout the world, marked the
book out as being substantially different from all previous treatments of
the topic.

Strauss examined the life of Jesus from the perspective of the natural
science of his day. As a result he began by excluding any possibility of
the miraculous or supernatural events recounted in the gospels as

being factual or historically true. However, Strauss also refused to accept the approach of the extreme rationalists to such accounts either. These accounts tended to explain away the supernatural elements of the gospel story in a completely naturalistic fashion, which, in an important sense, distorted the meaning of the text as much as an overtly supernatural reading had done. In place of a rationalistic and naturalistic reading of certain events in the gospels Strauss proposed that the category of 'myth' was a better tool for revealing the true meaning of the gospel account.

By using the category of 'myth' Strauss did not mean to suggest that the gospel texts were simply legendary and untrue. The poetic and mythical form of expression, according to Strauss, was a vehicle of truth. However, the truth that it seeks to represent is not simply historical or factual truth, but is instead the truth of the 'Idea' in historical form. In adopting and developing the category of myth Strauss was attempting to solve a problem implicit in Hegel's philosophy. It was not clear in Hegel's account whether the 'Idea' of the reconciliation of the infinite and the finite, as exemplified in the incarnation of Jesus Christ, had only one instance in history, or if the incarnation of God in Jesus Christ was merely a representation of a larger more universal process.

Some sense of what this means for Strauss can be gleaned from the following quotation:

This is the key to the whole of Christology, that as the subject of the predicates which the church applies to Christ, we place instead of an individual an idea, but an idea that exists in reality ... Conceived in respect of an individual, a God-man, the attributes and functions that the church's doctrine ascribes to Christ are contradictory; in the idea of the species they concur. Humanity is the union of the two natures, the incarnate God: [i.e.] the infinite spirit divested to finitude and the finite spirit recalling its infinitude.... By faith in this Christ, especially in his death and resurrection, man is justified before God; that is by the kindling within him of the idea of Humanity, the individual man participates in the divinely human life of the species ... Our age demands to be led in Christology to the idea in the fact, to the race in the individual: a theology which, in its doctrines on the Christ, stops short at him as an individual, is not properly a theology, but a homily.[i]

Strauss offered the following criteria for identifying mythical elements in the gospel narratives. First, in keeping with his commitment to a closed nexus of cause and effect, we recognise that we are dealing with the mythical when events are presented which could not possibly have taken place because they contravene the known laws of nature. Second, inconsistencies and contradictions within the narratives themselves, or between the various gospel accounts, suggest once again the presence of the mythical. More positively overt poetical forms of expression, and language which seems to be beyond the education and capacity of the speaker, are also strongly indicative of myth.

Strauss did not suggest that the gospel writers simply invented the myths concerning Jesus. As an historically minded scholar he was probably well aware that the period of time when stories concerning Jesus circulated as oral tradition, before the gospels took written form, was altogether too short for completely original myths to gather around the person of Jesus. For Strauss the origin of the myths concerning Jesus was to be found in the Jewish expectation of the Messiah. These myths, which existed prior to Jesus and independently of him, were nevertheless applied to him as a result of the fact that his followers believed him to be the Messiah. Therefore, for example, the genealogies and birth narratives concerning Jesus have no basis in history but arise out of the concern to portray Jesus as a descendant of King David in line with Jewish messianic expectation.

In this fashion some myths gathered around the person of Jesus purely as a result of the application of prior themes and motifs of Jewish messianic expectation to him. Others, however, had their source in the impact of the life and teaching of Jesus himself, such as the account of the rending of the curtain in the Temple at the moment of Jesus' death. This mythical event has its origin in the hostile attitude of Jesus and his followers to the Temple itself.

As a result of the hostility to which he was subjected, losing not only his job at the seminary in Tübingen, but also the professorship in theology at Zurich in 1839 for which he had been recommended, Strauss understandably moderated his views in a later edition of the work. He conceded the fact that Jesus must have been a person of considerable, and possibly unique, spiritual power and personality to account for the reaction of his followers to him. Moreover, and more importantly, Strauss accepted that Jesus may have been conscious of his own Messiahship and that this consciousness developed throughout his ministry. Strauss, in this the third edition of *The Life of Jesus*, also commented favourably upon the authenticity of the fourth gospel, much loved by conservative Christians and disciples of Schleiermacher alike.

However, Strauss's period of recantation as a repentant scholar was to be short-lived. It was probably the denial of the chair in Zurich which finally convinced him that he was not going to be forgiven for his earlier views, and so, in the fourth edition of the *Life of Jesus* Strauss withdrew all his previous concessions and attributed the fourth gospel to a forger who merely passed himself off as the apostle John. In the preface to this edition Strauss declared that 'My recent work has consisted in sharpening my good sword which I had myself blunted'.

It would be easy to dismiss Strauss as an iconoclast predisposed to tilting at windmills for the sake of causing controversy. However, his work was painstaking and scholarly and he was well versed in the developments in biblical criticism that preceded his own work. However, it is now generally conceded that his definition of myth is too general and imprecise to be a useful tool. Moreover, the current predilection for treating the gospel narratives as 'history-like' and 'reality depicting' has made Strauss's approach seem dated and passé. But there can be no gainsaying the fact that he was the first person to apply this important category to the figure of Christ and therefore to begin a process of discussion which was to continue into the twentieth century, most notably in the work of Rudolf **Bultmann**.

Nor can we simply ignore Strauss's picture of the historical figure of Christ and its enduring influence. If we compare the broad results of his portrayal with some of the portrayals given in the current 'third' quest of the historical Jesus we find that it looks remarkably contemporary. For example, he considered Jesus to be a disciple and successor of John the Baptist who continued the Baptist's message about the coming of the kingdom of heaven and the need for repentance. For a brief period we know that Strauss regarded it as possible that Jesus believed himself to be Messiah, although he wavered periodically on this. He maintained that Jesus taught that his kingdom was not to be brought about by force but by the supernatural intervention of God. According to Strauss Jesus did not perform miracles but could heal people who were purportedly possessed by demons. Albert Schweitzer, in a not uncritical assessment of Strauss, considered it likely that he thought that Jesus eventually came to believe his kingdom would be brought about only after his death, subsequent to which he would return in glory. Strauss could also say of Jesus' sense of mission ' . . . it was the national, theocratic hope, spiritualised and ennobled by his own moral and religious views'. That this account of the historical figure of Jesus continues to be very close to certain noted contemporary accounts of the historical life and mission of Jesus of Nazareth is surely ample testimony to the power and clarity of Strauss's vision at that time.

In his *Christian Dogmatics*, published in 1840, Strauss devoted himself to tracing the origin of every major doctrine from the Bible, through their development in ecclesiastical history, to their eventual sublimation and consummation in philosophy. Strauss traces the historical process of the formation of doctrine from often inchoate and confused beginnings to their full expression in the flowering of Christianity. But he goes on to reveal the inevitable contradictions and negations that such doctrines are susceptible to once the full power of modern scientific thought and philosophy is brought to bear on them.

However, it was with the publication of *The Old Faith and the New* in 1872 that Strauss announced his definitive break with Christianity. This work, heavily influenced by the thought of Darwin, considers the question: Are we still Christians? In an attempt to answer this question Strauss engages in an examination of the major articles of the Apostle's creed and shows how faith in these original affirmations has gradually been diluted and lost as a result of the interpretative efforts of modern theologians. He concludes that the traditional account of the faith is without any historical foundation. In a prophetic announcement of the coming age of 'man', Strauss argues that children should no longer be marked by the sign of the cross at baptism. For the cross no longer reflects the religious consciousness of humanity as it is the symbol of a humanity which is broken and helpless. We should instead help our children to be what they in fact are – autonomous individuals. The answer to the question 'Are we still Christians?' is a resounding no.

Strauss died in 1874. Outside the field of professional scholarship he is often sadly neglected today. In his own time he was infamous as the 'anti-Christian' before being overtaken for that title by his close contemporary Ludwig **Feuerbach**. Nevertheless, the judgement of history cannot be completely negative, for as we have seen his findings in Christology were to point to the way ahead for future historical scholarship on the life of Christ. No less a figure than Albert Schweitzer, in his famous *Quest for the Historical Jesus*, was to note that Strauss's positive achievement was to portray an historic personality emerging from the mist of myth who was recognisably a 'Jewish claimant of the Messiahship, whose world of thought is purely eschatological'.

Note

i   *The Life of Jesus Critically Examined*, par. 151, pp.780–1

See also: **Bultmann; Feuerbach; Hegel; Schleiermacher**

Major writings

Other than *The Life of Jesus* Strauss has not been well served in the area of English translations of his major works
The Old Faith and the New, trans. M. Blind, London: 1874.
D.F. Strauss, *The Life of Jesus Critically Examined*, ed. Peter C. Hodgson, London: SCM Press, 1972

Further reading

H. Frei, 'David Friedrich Strauss' in N. Smart *et al.* (eds), *Nineteenth Century Religious Thought in the West*, Vol. 1, Cambridge: CUP, 1985
Harris, Horton, *David Friedrich Strauss and his Theology,* Cambridge: CUP, 1973

TERTULLIAN, QUINTUS SEPTIMIUS FLORENS
(c.160–c.225)

The Latin Fathers, such as Tertullian and Cyprian, and later Jerome and **Augustine**, were the younger pupils of the Greek Fathers. Until the rise of Latin Christianity the intellectual stream had always flowed from East to West. Naturally the Latin Church began to develop a vigorous and independent form of Church life and theology – and this stream of Latin thought proved in the long run to have a greater effect on the history of Christianity than the Greek stream. Christianity takes on as it were a new intellectual mould. Church organisations are developed in new ways and there is a theological movement away from the philosophical and the speculative tendencies of the Greeks towards a more biblical approach combined with the rediscovery of **Paul** (law and grace) and of the historical significance of the Old Testament. It is often said, probably with a measure of truth, that the Roman interest in government and in law in part explains their restraint in regard to philosophy. The down-to-earth attitudes of the Old Testament are in some ways more in line with Latin thought than the rarefied world of the New Testament. Certainly Tertullian was to find Old Testament legalism particularly congenial to his own frame of mind.

Tertullian was born in Carthage about 160. He was thoroughly educated in rhetoric and law and, aged about 35, he went to Rome and may have begun to practise there as a lawyer. It was about that time too that he became a Christian. Shortly afterwards he returned to Carthage and henceforth devoted his time entirely to the service of the Church.

Tertullian was a man of keen and penetrating intellect, but one not at all fitted for the contemplative life in the Greek style. He was impetuous and reckless, often complaining that he could never learn the precious virtue of patience. A man who had strong convictions and whose arguments carried the whole weight of his intellectual and moral stature in many ways – uncompromising and rigid too – this was a limitation which finally overcame him.

Some of his early writings are pastoral in intention, for example those on prayer, baptism and repentance. But most of his work is quite different. The larger part of it is polemical, directed against the enemies of the Church, persecutors and heretics. He was eager to defend Christianity against suspicion and defamation – against such charges as that Christians were lawless citizens, or that they were atheists or even cannibals. His intention is fairly similar to that of **Justin Martyr**, but his method of attack is quite different. Justin and the others had directed their apologies to the emperors. Emperors, however, seldom if ever read them. Instead they were read and studied mainly by the Christians themselves rather than by the pagans for whom they were intended.

Tertullian thought that his predecessors had tried to accomplish too much while lacking the necessary intellectual capacity. He wrote not for emperors, but for governors and lesser government officials, and in doing so decided typically that the best method of defence is attack. He argued that it was madness for the authorities to persecute Christians as they were trustworthy citizens, adding also the phrase, 'Your iniquity is the proof of our innocence'. He further pointed out that 'the blood of Christians is the seed of the martyrs. For when we are condemned by you, we are acquitted by God.' Tertullian's main purpose is not simply to catalogue the virtues of Christians in a defensive manner, but to bring the false charges of his opponents into the light and to treat them for what they are worth.

We may look at the position Tertullian takes in his *Prescriptions against Heretics*. Most of the heresies which Tertullian cites come under the heading of **Gnosticism**. Gnosticism is derived from the Greek *gnosis* which means knowledge. The emphasis on knowledge as the means for attainment of salvation, or even as the form of salvation itself, and the claim to possession of this knowledge in one's own doctrine, are common features of the numerous sects in which the

Gnostic movement historically expressed itself. There are two main theories about the roots of Gnosticism. One, followed by the Church Fathers and by many scholars, is that it was a Christian heresy growing within Christianity itself. The other, held particularly in Germany, is that it is independent of Christianity, is in fact pre-Christian, a religion on its own. For our purpose we may note that Tertullian regarded it as a Christian heresy.

The origin of Gnosticism is somewhat confused. Some hold that it is a form of Greek philosophy misunderstood and misinterpreted. Others have tended to favour the idea that it is really a syncretism, a mixture of all sorts of religious beliefs, some of which are Hellenic, some Babylonian, some Iranian. The nature of Gnostic knowledge is knowledge of God and of everything that belongs to the divine realm of being. To know God is to partake of the divine life – thus knowing is salvation, not only a means to perfection but the actual goal of salvation. Sources of Gnostic teachings are found in the Fathers themselves – direct sources include the sacred books of the Maddens, a sect which still survives in the region of the lower Euphrates, the Coptic Gnostic writings, Manichaean (see **Augustine**) literature, probably from Syria, the Greek 'Poimandres' and also the Gnostic material of the New Testament Apocrypha such as the Acts of Thomas.

The cardinal feature of Gnostic theology is the radical dualism between God and the world. God is absolutely transcendent. He didn't create the world and he is hidden from all creatures – knowledge of him requires supernatural *revelation* and illumination. In Gnostic cosmology, the world, the universe, was created by a being called the Demiurge. The world is often understood as a vast prison whose innermost dungeon is the earth. Around and above it the cosmic spheres are arranged like concentric enclosing shells, separating man from God and ruled by demonic powers. Human beings are composed of flesh and spirit and are captive in a world which is their prison. Soul and spirit belong to the world which was created by lesser evil powers. The body is evil, and is in turn the prison of the spirit. The spirit in a person is asleep and ignorant – its awakening and liberation is effected through knowledge.

Eschatological salvation comes when the bearer of salvation descends from the realm of light into the realm of darkness to reveal the knowledge of God, of the Way, or of the Spirit's way out of the world. This messenger gives knowledge of magical and sacramental preparations, secret names, formulae and words which enable the spirit to find its way through each sphere. Equipped with this knowledge the spirit travels upwards, and thus set free becomes enriched with the divine substance. When the whole drama is complete, light in the cosmos will be extinguished and the cosmos will come to an end.

The morality of Gnosticism is two-sided. If the body is evil, some would say that it doesn't matter what you do with it – and so on the one side there is libertarianism. On the other side there is often an extreme asceticism, which seeks to avoid all contact with the world.

For Tertullian, Gnosticism in all its forms is a destructive syncretism which invites human beings to overestimate their spiritual nature by obliterating the distinction between creature and creator. At the same time it expresses a hostility to the true God who created the universe and who has revealed himself in the incarnation of the Word.

Tertullian traces the whole problem of heresy to its roots in philosophy. According to him the essential problem is that heretics rely only on their own opinions and not on God's word. The basic reason for their error is their insatiable curiosity and conceit. Tertullian chides them on their use of their favourite biblical text, 'Seek and you shall find', and says that they refer to this only to spread their 'endless fables and genealogies', their unproductive questions, and their talk which crawls at a crab-like pace to confuse innocent listeners. Tertullian argues that the heretic never seems to grasp the fact that a search is only sensible when one does not yet know the truth. But with Christ and his gospel we have reached the end of our teaching.

The heretic does not know what it really means to believe and would rather follow human teachers than be satisfied with God's final truth in Christ. He wants to know instead of letting himself be taught by God. Tertullian points out that the Gnostics deny the very centre of revelation when they deny the incarnation. As such the Gnostics can only point to a God who changes nothing and saves nothing but remains distant and aloof in his transcendence. The Gnostic takes positive offence at the ugly, inglorious, humiliated figure of Christ the Saviour. For Gnostics such a figure is beneath contempt.

Tertullian goes on to argue that the Church possesses God's Word. Its traditions are reliable and binding, and any deviation from its 'rule of faith' is heresy. This of course is the main thesis of the 'Prescriptions', and the text has had considerable influence on the development of Christian thought. Tertullian shows how the Catholic church received its teaching as well as its scriptures directly from the apostles at a time when all the present heresies had not yet arisen. The Church has thus preserved the original truth concerning Christ and his salvation faithfully and it stands in undisturbed communion with the ancient churches founded by the apostles. The proper and responsible attitude of the believer is to remain faithful to the teaching of the Church and to understand the Bible in the sense which corresponds to the creed (the phrase 'rule of faith' occurs here for the first time). According to Tertullian heretics have no place whatsoever in the Church and have no right to appeal to scripture. Indeed they have no right even to possess scripture. For scripture belongs to the Church alone and can be rightly interpreted by the Church alone.

All of this has clear implications for Tertullian's attitude to philosophy in general. He finds nothing positive in philosophy and tends to dismiss it as mere speculation. Hence the famous phrase which is associated with him – 'What has Athens to do with Jerusalem?' Philosophers are regarded as mere sophists and as people who are not genuinely seeking the truth but who are simply seeking their own glory and success. Their dialectical tricks are vain, their knowledge deceitful, their way of life questionable. Even the most sacred symbol of philosophical freedom, Socrates, does not arouse any admiration. For Socrates' wisdom was artificial, and there can never be any common ground between 'a philosopher and a Christian, between a disciple of Hellas and a disciple of heaven, or between Athens and Jerusalem, between the Academy and the Church'.

Tertullian did not deny that there were similarities between certain ideas of classical philosophy and some Christian convictions. But he explained these in terms of the old theory that the Greeks had actually stolen the idea of the wisdom from the Old Testament. Consequently, wisdom is denied to all outside the Church, since for Tertullian all truth belongs by right to God and to the Church.

Despite this radical denial of the claims of philosophy, Tertullian still makes use, as we have already mentioned, of his own philosophical education – in his references to radon and to nature, to substance and accidents. His arguments involve recognisable philosophical presuppositions. Nevertheless for him philosophy and theology belong to two different spheres. Above all he is concerned to demand a limitation of man's intellectual pride, his hubris, a limitation which is required in obedience to the word of God as interpreted by the rule of faith.

To understand his views we must I suppose remember that Tertullian was a Westerner (in fact North African) living in a world in which philosophy never had quite the same position of prestige that it had enjoyed in the Greek world. Like many Romans he was more active, practical and less given to speculative questioning. At the same time we have to imagine that some of his adversaries at least were no doubt equally self-assured and self-satisfied – hence the character of his polemic.

Most of Tertullian's work is concerned with the fight against heresies. It is perhaps ironic that he finally became a heretic himself – a Montanist. The movement begun by Montanus sprang up during the second century in Asia Minor, traditional home of unusual cults. Its adherents believed themselves to be instruments of a new outpouring of the Holy Spirit, preaching that the kingdom of God would come soon. When the movement reached Africa, Tertullian joined it. It seems that he finally broke with the Montanists and founded a sect of his own in Carthage. Yet despite this deviation from the Catholic tradition his heritage has come down through the ages and has had a considerable influence on the development of Latin theology and Church practice.

Positively speaking his theological influence consists in the fact that he was the first to introduce the term **Trinity** (*trinitas*) in relation to the Godhead. Tertullian is clear that God is one, but also that God has a Son who is generated out of Godself (in the act of creation; and perhaps prior to this point it was not true, according to Tertullian, to say that God had a Son), and this Son has then sent the Holy Spirit. Tertullian attempts to safeguard the unity of God by arguing that the three, although distinguishable, are nevertheless one substance. In relation to Christology Tertullian anticipated some of the later terminology that came to be used in describing Christ's person when he spoke of Christ being composed of two conjoined substances (Word and flesh), with both substances retaining their particular, distinct and individual characteristics in the union and not amalgamating into a third hybrid combination of the two. This was to form the basis of the Latin (Western) Church's approach to the Christological problem from then on and meant that this terminology was able to be drawn on when churches in the East appealed to Pope Leo over the correct understanding of Christ's person at the Council of Chalcedon in 451.

See also: **Augustine; Justin Martyr; Paul**

Glossary: **Eschatological; Gnostic/ism; revelation; Trinity**

Major writings

On the Soul, Against Praxeas and *On the Prescription of Heretics* can be found in *The Ante-Nicene Fathers: the writings of the Fathers down to A.D. 325*, ed. Alexander Roberts & James Donaldson; rev. & chronologically arranged with brief prefaces

& occasional notes by A. Cleveland Coxe; Vols 3 –4, *Tertullian – Fathers of the Third Century*, Peabody, MA: Hendrickson, 1995

Further reading

T.D. Barnes, *Tertullian*, Oxford: Clarendon Press, 1985
E. Osborn, *Tertullian, First Theologian of the West*, Cambridge: CUP, 1997
D. Rankin, *Tertullian and the Church*, Cambridge and New York: CUP, 1995

TILLICH, PAUL (1886–1965)

German-born theologian who was forced to flee Germany during the Nazi period, subsequently settling in America where he lived, taught and wrote, achieving great fame both within and without Church circles. During his lifetime Tillich was equal in stature and fame to the great German theologian Karl **Barth**, although his theological system could not have been based on more different presuppositions. However, since his death, and with the general demise of *existentialist* philosophy as a dialogue partner for theology, Tillich's theology has suffered something of an eclipse. There are few theologians writing today who are thoroughgoing disciples of Tillich, although Langdon Gilkey, the Catholic theologian David **Tracy** and the pastoral theologian Don Browning all show traces of his influence in their respective approaches to the topic.

Tillich was born in 1886 in Starzeddel, near Guben in Brandenburg, the son of a Lutheran clergyman. He was educated at the Universities of Tübingen, Berlin Breslau and Halle. In 1912 he was ordained into the ministry of the Evangelical Lutheran church but served only for a brief period before volunteering himself as a chaplain in the army on the outbreak of the First World War in 1914. The gruesome nature of that war had a profound effect upon the young Tillich and he suffered a nervous breakdown and the virtual collapse of his faith. But it was not only his faith that collapsed, it was his confidence in nineteenth-century culture and society that also disappeared. Tillich can even fix an exact date to the time when his commitment to idealism faltered; it was the night before the battle of Verdun and the young chaplain wandered around during a bombardment comforting the dying before finally falling asleep among the dead. 'When I awoke, I said to myself, This is the end of the idealistic side of my thought! In that hour I realised that idealism had been destroyed.'[i]

For all the differences that exist between Tillich, Barth and **Bultmann**, the one thing that they share in common is the awareness that the horrific events of 1914–18 marked the endpoint of the symbiotic accommodation between liberal Protestant theology and European culture. Not only was it at an end, they each separately understood that the whole enterprise was fatally flawed from the beginning and had been wholly damaging to the gospel of Christ in the process. For all his attempts to create a 'theology of culture' it should not be forgotten that Tillich too made his own break with the liberalism of the past era.

A further development in Tillich's thought that he attributes to his wartime experiences was his commitment to socialism, and he was to be thereafter an ardent promoter of the religious socialist movement. In 1932 Tillich produced a small work on socialism entitled *The Socialist Decision* in which he attacked the then emerging philosophy of National Socialism. After the war Tillich had taken up various posts as a teacher of philosophy in the Universities of Dresden, Leipzig and Frankfurt, but he was to be dismissed from his chair in Frankfurt in 1933 due to his outspoken condemnation of National Socialism.

Tillich was now under severe threat from the Nazis and he went into exile in America at the invitation of the Niebuhr brothers (see **Niebuhr**). In 1933 he was appointed visiting Professor of Philosophical Theology at Union Theological Seminary and was to spend the rest of his life living and working in America. Tillich achieved great fame and was the first (and only) 'pop' theologian of the twentieth century. His volume of collected sermons, **The Shaking of the Foundations** (1948), became a best-seller and inspired a generation of theological students and churchgoers. **The Courage to Be**, published in 1952, was to prove equally as popular to a wide non-theological readership. In this famous book, which combines existential philosophy with in-depth psychology, Tillich analyses the basic angst-ridden condition of human beings in the world. Contemporary human beings suffer from an existential anxiety which is due to the threat of non-being and this anxiety must be faced and accepted. To do this human beings need 'the courage to be' in the face of non-being, the courage to be upheld by the creative power of being itself. This book and the appearance of Tillich's first volume of his three-volume **Systematic Theology** in 1951 established him as a major thinker on the contemporary cultural scene. He was lionised by the media and fellow academics alike, even achieving a place on the cover of **Time** magazine as the most influential Protestant thinker of the age. Tillich was to retire from Union Seminary in 1955, but only to take up the post of university professor at Harvard University, perhaps the most prestigious academic post in America. Tillich remained there until 1962 when he moved to Chicago to take up the post of Nuveen Professor of Theology at the Divinity school there. He died of a heart attack on 22 October 1965.

Part of Tillich's early similarity with the dialectical theologians of the *Zwischen den Zeiten* journal (Barth, Bultmann, Gogarten) can be seen in his insistence that theology can only be conducted from within the circle of faith. For to begin theology is to make an existential decision, a decision to make the content of the theological enterprise a matter of ultimate concern.[ii] This links to Tillich's two formal criteria for theology. First, 'the object of theology is what concerns us ultimately. Only those propositions are theological which deal with their object in so far as it can become a matter of ultimate concern for us'.[iii] With this formulation Tillich means to offer an abstraction of the first commandment that you should love the Lord your God with all your heart, your mind and your soul. In this commandment the religious concern is ultimate and it excludes all other concerns from having ultimate significance.

However, Tillich is insistent that this first criterion is only formal and general and that the content of our ultimate concern is not a special object, not even God himself. If we wish to say more about the nature of our ultimate concern then it must arise from an analysis of the concept of ultimate concern itself. It is at this point that Tillich introduces his second formal criterion of theology: 'Our ultimate concern is that which determines our being or not being. Only those statements are theological which deal with their object in so far as it can become a matter of being or not-being for us'.[iv] Again, this second criterion is only formal and general as it does not point to any special content, symbol or doctrine which must be included. It does, however, have a negative role in that it excludes from the object of theology any concept which does not have the power of threatening or saving our being. Even a God who is thought of as the highest being is excluded unless he is that which is able to determine our being or non-being. Thus Tillich's famous definition of God:

> God is the answer to the question implied in man's finitude; he is the name for that which concerns man ultimately. This does not mean that first there is a being called God and then the demand that man should be ultimately concerned about him. It means that whatever concerns a man ultimately becomes God for him, and conversely, it means that a man can be concerned ultimately only about that which is God for him.[v]

In keeping with his ontological and metaphysical concerns Tillich's preferred terminology for God is 'Being – itself', or the 'ground of being' or even the 'power of being'. By utilising such terminology he is seeking to preserve the wholly otherness of God in that God is not just another being, not even the highest being, among others. God is the infinite source and power of being and as such is beyond the polarities of essence and existence as he cannot contradict himself by succumbing to non-being. This is the reason why Tillich made his famous statement that 'It is as atheistic to affirm the existence of God as it is to deny it. God is being itself, not a being'.[vi] As the 'ground of being' all finite reality participates in this ground and is sustained in being by its power.

A key element in understanding Tillich's theology is his method of correlation. This method reveals that Tillich's theology is an apologetic theology in that it attempts to stand at the boundaries of religion and culture and to engage in a process of mutual clarification. The method of correlation attempts to explain the contents of the Christian faith through existential questions that arise from the polarities and tensions of human existence in the world and which are answered by reference to the deep symbolic structures of the Christian message. The questions that human existence poses cannot be answered from experience but only by a speaking to existence from beyond it, from the final revelation in Jesus as the Christ.[vii]

A full understanding as to how the method of correlation operates in Tillich's theology requires an understanding of other key themes. Theology has an apologetic function which is to state the truth of the Christian message to each new generation. The unique and distinctive claim that theology makes is that the **Logos** became flesh, that the principle of divine self-revelation became manifest in the event Jesus as the Christ.[viii] If this claim is true then by virtue of its universal scope it provides theology with a foundation that transcends any other claim or system, a foundation which cannot in principle be transcended itself.

Although theology is thus a special discipline and a special realm of knowledge, dealing with its own special object, it must nevertheless relate itself to other forms of knowledge such as science and philosophy (*contra* Barth). In so doing, however, the primary source for theology remains the Bible which is the original document in which the events on which Christianity is based are recounted. The Bible is not itself revelation but is a source of revelation and an indirect witness to **revelation**. In a similar way Church History is also a source of theology as its 2.000-year practice of reading and reflecting upon the biblical witness exerts an enormous influence upon our own practice of reflection today. Similarly, the history of religion and culture can be a source of revelation and a resource for theology as it provides the theologian with the language concepts and symbols that he must understand and use if his message is to be meaningful to his generation. This reinforces Tillich's assertion (against Barth) that revelation cannot simply drop in unannounced from the heavens, but must have some preparation in the life and culture of society if it is ever to be understood. Even the Bible itself could not have been understood or appreciated had there been no preparation for it in human religion and culture.[ix]

For Tillich revelation has both an objective 'giving' element and a subjective 'receiving' element. In relation to the biblical revelation, although the words on the page are not in themselves revelation, it nevertheless contains the original witness of those who participated in the revealing events. And this participation is crucial, for it is the individual's response to revealing events that bestows upon such events their revealing nature. Human reason, according to Tillich, is subject to the polarities and tensions of finite existence, e.g. autonomy versus heteronomy, relativism versus absolutism and formalism versus emotionalism. These antimonies require reconciliation and pose questions arising out of the nature of human existence that reason itself cannot resolve but only revelation can answer. The dichotomy that finite reason finds itself in is that it seeks a knowledge that is not simply relative and subjective. But nor can it be satisfied with a certain knowledge that is simply based on some external norm or law that is alien to it and imposed upon it. However, it is in the nature of finite reason to seek certainty. The answer to this dichotomy, according to Tillich, is the revelatory activity of the Logos. In the giving and receiving nature of the revelatory act the Logos overcomes the tension between heteronomy and autonomy, relativism and absolutism. Revelation, then, is not words but a sign event which communicates the power of being itself and it does so through history, nature and social groups. The final revelation is the New Being in Jesus Christ which overcomes estrangement and disruption and offers reconciliation, reunion and creativity. In Jesus Christ this New Being is manifested and brings in the new eon, the reality that overcomes the threat of non-being. And it is important for Tillich that it is the man Jesus who brings the new reality, for without him the new being would remain at the level of the ideal and not be a reality.

Tillich's Christology focuses upon the Christ as the bearer of a new age – the kingdom of God. For Tillich, what was important about Jesus was not the historical fact of his life and teaching but the power of being that he conveyed and mediated. In this regard he was very close to Schleiermacher's understanding of the person of Christ (see **Schleiermacher**). Jesus as the Christ answers humanity's need to be reunited with its essential being. For human beings as they exist are no longer what they essentially are but are instead estranged from the ground of being. This estrangement from the ground of being is what the symbol of the 'Fall' points to in the Christian tradition. For Tillich, estrangement is a universal and fundamental, although not necessary, fact of finite human existence in that as soon as human beings exercise free will they 'fall' from their essential union with being itself and enter into estranged finite existence. This 'fall' from a state of 'dreaming innocence' into the state of estrangement is part of the transition from essence to existence and is an inescapable fact of existence. The only alternative would be to remain forever in a state of unactualised existence, and thus there is a tragic element to human existence in that if human beings are to 'be' at all then it seems that they can only come into being in a fallen existence and are thus incapable of 'authentic being' which is to remain in essential union with the 'ground of being' itself. This fall is due to the exercise of their free will, which they must exercise as a necessary feature of existence, but which as an exercise of finite freedom cannot overcome the ensuing estrangement, but can indeed only serve to make them feel responsible for every exercise of free will which further actualises their estrangement. Tillich strove to show that this understanding of sin did not in fact ontologise sinful existence by making sin identical with finite existence in the world, and thus a necessary feature of the created order, but it is not clear that he was successful in his attempts to refute this. His understanding of our essential nature as being the potential for existence and of existence as to be literally a 'standing out' from our essence does seem to imply that simply to exist is to enter a state of estrangement from ourselves, others and the power of being.

Tillich's Christology has proved controversial in many respects. His willingness to concede at least the possibility that Jesus of Nazareth never lived dismayed many who might otherwise have been attracted to his position. However, Tillich's position at this point is more subtle than is often realised, as although he is able to countenance the fact that biblical criticism might be able to dispense with every supposed fact in the New Testament they cannot dispense with the 'reality of New Being' that is demonstrated within the portrait of Jesus' life. In the New Testament Jesus is portrayed as the Christ, the Son of God, the Logos, and this portrait has the power to transform lives as it is received by the individual. Here Tillich anticipates many of the moves made by contemporary 'textual' theologians and philosophers such as Ricoeur and Frei by arguing that there is no way 'behind' the biblical portrait of Christ to some historical fact that can be demonstrated. All that faith can say is that the portrait of the power of 'New Being' in this concrete personal life has the power to mediate 'New Being' in the 'immediate awareness' of the individual. Faith in Christ therefore becomes the recognition and reception of the power of 'New Being' that is mediated by him. The parallels with Schleiermacher's account of the potency of Christ's God-consciousness and its transmission through the community of the Church are obvious. The radical nature of Tillich's position is obvious when he asserts that 'Participation not historical argument guarantees the reality of the event upon which Christianity is based – It guarantees a personal life in which the New Being has conquered the old being. But it does not guarantee his name to be Jesus of Nazareth'.[x] The radical nature of this assertion should not blind us to the fact that Tillich believed that in Jesus Christ the power of New Being has appeared in a personal life, that is to say the universal Logos became concrete in an individual life.

Tillich accepted liberal theology's critique of the classic doctrine of the two natures of Christ but he sought to reinterpret it by saying that Jesus participates in estranged existence as a fully human person without succumbing to its threat. To say that Jesus is divine is to say that his life existed at all points in union with God and did not therefore succumb to the existential estrangement that is the lot of human existence in the world. The power of 'New Being' was so potent in him that he overcame the disruption between essence and existence and as the symbol of New Being that appears under the condition of existence we too are able to participate in that reality which Jesus as the Christ disclosed.

This participation is achieved by way of the power of symbolic language in that the symbol of New Being, in Christ, like all symbolic language, participates in the reality to which it points. The nature of symbolic language is that it opens up to us levels of reality that are otherwise closed to us and they draw us into a participation in that reality. Once again we can see how Tillich's basic insights into the revelatory nature of symbolic language flow into contemporary hermeneutical concerns that focus upon the ability of texts to open up and disclose, through an act of creative re-description, a world in front of us that we can inhabit and in which new forms of existence are made possible to us. Tillich's caveat that all religious language is symbolic save the statement that 'God is being – itself' must be remembered at this point.

As stated earlier Tillich's theology has not resulted in a continuing school that continues to advance and develop his approach to the subject. Part of this is surely due to the general and widespread demise of existential philosophy as a suitable dialogue partner for theology. Also, his proposals seem to have been too radical and heterodox for them to have gained widespread acceptance in the Christian community, although this may be due to a lack of knowledge about how 'orthodox' some of his seemingly radical viewpoints were. It is also true that the modern temperament of theological and philosophical discussion is running in quite the opposite direction from Tillich's ontological and universalising concerns. The tendency to see the Christian 'story' as one self-contained textual description of reality that refuses to be interpreted by way of broader and more universal philosophical categories of human nature is not congenial to Tillich's method of correlation. Furthermore, it is generally felt that Tillich's method of correlation tended to place too much emphasis upon the questions arising from existence and to allow them to overly shape and influence the supposed answers that were coming from Christian revelation, in spite of Tillich's claims to the contrary.

Similarly, his Christology does seem to posit a Jesus (if there was in fact a Jesus) who manifested a union with God that is in principle possible for every human being, and this has never been acceptable to the mainstream Christian tradition, despite the best endeavours of a number of theologians from Schleiermacher onwards who have attempted to argue just this point. However, here and there, in the writings of a number of disparate theologians and philosophers – Tracy, Gilkey, Ricoeur and perhaps even Newlands – one continues to find echoes of Tillich's approach and concerns. Whether these echoes will grow in volume to become full-blown Tillichian voices it is too early to say.

Notes

i   'On the Boundary', in *The Interpretation of History*, New York; London: Scribner's, 1936, p.52

ii   *Systematic Theology*, Vol. 1, London: SCM, 1951, p.10

iii   *Ibid.*, p.12

iv   *Ibid.*

v   *Ibid.*, p.211

vi   *Ibid.*, p.237

vii   *Ibid.*, p.64

viii   *Ibid.*, p.16

ix   *Ibid.*, p.34f.

x   *Ibid.*, p.114

See also: **Barth; Bultmann; Niebuhr; Schleiermacher; Tracy**

Glossary: **Eschatological; existentialist; Logos; revelation**

Major writings

The Protestant Era, trans. with concluding essay by James Luther Adams, Chicago: University of Chicago Press, 1948

The Shaking of the Foundations, London: Nisbet: 1950

Systematic Theology, Vols 1–3, London: SCM, 1951, 1957, 1963

The Courage to Be, New Haven: Yale University Press, 1952

Theology of Culture, ed. Robert C. Kimball, New York: OUP, 1959

Further reading

L. Gilkey, Gilkey on Tillich, New York: Crossroad Pub. Co., 1990

C.W. Kegley & R.W. Brettal, The Theology of Paul Tillich, New York: Macmillan, 1956

D. Kelsey, 'Paul Tillich' in D. Ford (ed.), The Modern Theologians, Oxford: Blackwell, 1997

M. Kline Taylor, Paul Tillich, Theologian of the Boundaries, London: Collins, 1987

A.J. Mackelway, The Systematic Theology of Paul Tillich. A Review and Analysis, London: Lutterworth, 1964

W. & M. Pauck, Paul Tillich, His Life and Thought, London: Collins, 1967

TRACY, DAVID (1939–)

David Tracy is undoubtedly one of the leading Christian theologians of our time. He has combined a profound appreciation of traditional theology with an acute perception of the issues raised for theology in the modern and postmodern worlds. He has become an inspiration to many scholars within and beyond the Catholic tradition in which he stands.

Born in New York in 1939 Tracy studied theology in the United States and completed a doctorate in Rome during the Second Vatican Council. This time of ferment and exploration was seminal for his future development. Although his doctoral thesis (in Latin) was on the Trinity, his first book, The Achievement of Bernard Lonergan (1970), was a comprehensive exposition of Lonergan's thought which showed how formal theological method could become plastic in the hands of an imaginative and innovative thinker. His next major work was the much acclaimed Blessed Rage for Order (1975). This volume, reflecting his involvement in the theological curriculum at the University of Chicago Divinity School, explored the legacy of **Kant**, **Schleierma-cher** and the **Enlightenment**, taking the hermeneutical enterprise of

Schleiermacher into the centre of Catholic theology. But it was also careful to affirm the mainstream of Catholic tradition, not in opposition to, but in complementarity with, Enlightenment thought.

This imaginative employment of different streams of tradition in interaction with one another was then taken a stage further in *The Analogical Imagination* (1981), which examined the idea of a 'classic' in theology. A classic is a work of art or an event in which persons express themselves in a manner which has universal significance. The classic provokes new insights and leads to decisions. The Christian classic is God's self-manifestation in Jesus Christ. Through reflection on the pluralism of approaches to the events concerning Jesus we may reach a new understanding of the divine presence in the world.

At this time Tracy was identified as one of the chief figures in the Chicago school of theology, which sought to develop a theology of correlation with contemporary culture, in contrast with the Yale school, which concentrated on the exposition of the biblical narrative within its own framework – associated especially with Professors Lindbeck, Frei and Childs. But Tracy was careful to stress tradition, especially the medieval legacy, as well as the modern. An excellent initiation into the issues of modernism/postmodernism for theology was provided in his *Plurality and Ambiguity* (1987).

Whether or not we agree with his programme, his description of the fluidity of historical perspective and the variety of textual hermeneutics is brilliant and highly persuasive. Tracy is acutely aware of the ambiguities of the Enlightenment inheritance. Yet there is still hope: 'We can continue to give ourselves over to the great hope of Western reason. But that hope is now a more modest one as a result of the plurality of both language and knowledge and the ambiguity of all histories, including the history of reason itself. And yet that hope of reason – a hope expressed, for Westerners, in the models of conversation and argument created by the Greeks – still lives through any honest fidelity to the classic Socratic imperative, "The unreflective life is not worth living".'[i]

In a 1991 contribution to a Christian Century essay collection on 'How My Mind Has Changed' Tracy searches for a way to speak of God which is both mystical and prophetic, a new form of spirituality. From this methodological basis, which already incorporated a great range of systematic reflection, especially on Christology, Tracy has begun to develop a large-scale project on the doctrine of God. Hints of the shape of this perspective appear in the collection of essays entitled *On Naming the Present* (1994) originally published by Concilium, for which he has been an editor since 1976. Here he analyses premodern, anti-modern, modern and postmodern concepts of God. He stresses the importance of memory in the Christian apprehension of presence:

> For the memory of the Christian is, above all, the memory of the passion and resurrection of Jesus Christ. It is that dangerous memory (Metz) which is most dangerous for all who presume to make his memory their own. And that memory releases the theological knowledge that there is no innocent tradition, no innocent classic, no innocent reading. That memory releases the moral insistence that the memory of the suffering of the oppressed – oppressed often by the Church which now claims them as its own – is the great Christian counter-memory to all tales of triumph: both the socio-evolutionary complacent narrative of modernity and the all too pure reading of 'tradition' by the neo-conservatives.[ii]

The tradition of course includes the biblical narratives: 'Christianity is a religion of a revelatory event to which certain texts bear an authoritative witness'.

A more detailed version was delivered in his Edinburgh Gifford Lectures in 2000, and will appear as the first volume of his *Lectures* on God. In these lectures Tracy stressed the importance of the apophatic in theology, especially in the work of Nicholas of Cusa. He identified triumphalism as the major sin of the Church, and called for a genuine humility in theology. Our theological treatises are essentially to be seen as fragments. In the end God in Christ will gather up all the fragments to himself.

Tracy has always been concerned to offer a public theology. He is concerned with the relationship between theology, politics and society. How are the relationships between theology and culture to be related to the relationships between theology and society? Typical of his insights are these comments from the 1992 essay *Critical Social Theory and the Public Realm*:

> Without a critical social theory, the link between the debates about rationality and the debates on modernity (and postmodernity) are difficult if not impossible to clarify. That methodological failure has important substantive conse-quences: first. The correlational category 'situation' (as with **Tillich** in the systematics or most of my own work) has the

strength of allowing for good cultural analysis. Yet most 'situationalist' analysis is in danger of being trapped in purely 'culturalist' or even 'idealist' categories unless the correlational theologian can show the links between the cultural resources of our situation and the materialist (economic, social, political) conditions of our society.

Tracy goes on to stress the importance of both dialogue and solidarity in action. It is important not to see culture as something which floats mysteriously above society, but rather as something constantly present within society.

David Tracy must be considered to be one of the most profoundly imaginative as well as one of the most erudite theologians of our time.

Notes

i   *Pluralism and Ambiguity*, p.113
ii   *On Naming the Present*, pp.14/15

See also: **Kant; Schleiermacher; Tillich**

Glossary: **Enlightenment**

Major writings

The Achievement of Bernard Lonergan, New York: Herder & Herder, 1970
Blessed Rage for Order, New York: Seabury Press, 1975
The Analogical Imagination, London: SCM, 1981
Plurality and Ambiguity: hermeneutics, religion, hope, San Francisco: Harper & Row, 1987
On Naming the Present, Maryknoll, NY: Orbis and London: SCM, 1994

TROELTSCH, ERNST (1865–1923)

Typical and most brilliant of the left wing of the school of Albrecht **Ritschl** was Ernst Troeltsch, who combined Ritschl's concern for the ethical and the historical with the conviction that Christianity could not be considered apart from the culture in which it developed – in other words, it might be at the moment the highest and most suitable religion for us Western Europeans, but it need not be for others, or at a future date. As a European, he himself wished to speak of being 'conscious of the Father of Jesus Christ as a living presence in our daily conflicts, labours, hopes and sufferings, but at the same time he saw –

rightly – that there is no method of objective or historical demonstration of the special place of the Christian religion among other world religions. The result was that he died in a kind of despair, feeling himself to be at the beginning of an immense task, the solutions for which he hardly saw. It was no accident, and yet it gave some of his students a shock, when in 1914 he moved from the divinity to the arts faculty in Berlin.

Troeltsch was born near Augsburg in 1865. He studied in Erlangen, Berlin and Göttingen, and became a Professor of Theology in Bonn in 1892 and in Heidelberg in 1894. In 1914 he moved to a chair of philosophy in Berlin. In 1919 he became a secretary of state in the Ministry of Culture, and died on 1 February 1923.

Troeltsch was particularly concerned about the relationship of theology to history, and the consequences of the application of the historico-critical method to the investigation of faith. He based his understanding of the issue on three critical principles. First came the principle of criticism. Our judgements about past events cannot be seen as absolutely true or false, but can claim only a greater or lesser degree of probability. They must therefore always be open to revision. Second was the principle of analogy. We can only make judgements if we presuppose that our own experience is not totally unlike that of people in the past. Finally there is a principle of correlation. Events can only be understood in relation to what came before and after them. No event can be isolated from its cultural background in time and space.

Orthodox belief, speaking of Jesus as divine in the context of performing miracles and being raised from the dead, operates outside these criteria and therefore cannot be discussed within a framework of proper critical rationality. The difficulty with Troeltsch's position is that there may be, and indeed are, genuinely unique events and discoveries for which no existing analogies can prepare us, e.g. in the field of quantum theory. (The danger on the other side is that we then extrapolate from these to find miracles everywhere – a course against which Troelsch gives suitable warning!)

It may be that as a matter of fact we have only probability as a guide when discussing for example the words of Jesus. But we cannot rule out *a priori* the possibility that precise historical records could in theory appear. Troeltsch was clear that history could not in itself create faith. Equally, faith could not be divorced from history, without turning into **fideism**. He himself saw faith in the God of Jesus Christ as part of his European tradition, which could not be demonstrated to have absolute truth, but which could still responsibly be adhered to as the best available perspective on God. Troeltsch in his own time was broaching the problems of cultural relativity and pluralism which could then be ignored by the majority of Christian thinkers, but which would ultimately return to challenge Christian theology a century or so later and which still challenge it today.

If Søren **Kierkegaard** was a theologian of separation and drastic prunings, Troeltsch was a theologian of synthesis. For Troeltsch it was vital, if theology was to survive as a respectable discipline, to relate the principles and presuppositions of theology to those of philosophy and history, indeed to all human culture in general. Above all, and as we have seen, he was concerned with the relation between theology and historical method. Historical method for Troeltsch had in essence three components. There is a critical component, which tells us that all historical judgements are only probable. There is an analogical moment, by which we move in historical judgement from the more to the less familiar, and there is the principle of correlation, the mutual interaction of all the phenomena of the spiritual historical life.

Christianity must be evaluated and understood within the historical study of the world religions. We cannot single out isolated events in a history of salvation. But Christianity is its own history and development. We can find no historical grounds for asserting the special significance of Christianity. Still, for European history at least it has been a transforming power, and so its main claim to validity is the fact that it has been experienced historically in Europe as 'a mighty spiritual power and truth'. In other religions, or in the future, God may reveal himself in a quite different manner. We cannot then speak of an historical essence of Christianity, to which we can objectively attribute an absolute validity. In speaking of an essence we can only speak of elements which we personally have found valuable. We accept our own cultural relativity without qualification. This was the basis of the dogmatic positions of the so-called History of Religions school (*Religionsgeschichtliche Schule*), which was critical of the modern theology of Ritschl and **Harnack** as being, for all its stress on history, both historically and methodologically naïve. If there is a solution to be had to the problems raised by Troeltsch, it will probably be reached not by softening his rigorous approach to the problems of history, but by seeing these historical problems as themselves enmeshed in a wider metaphysical framework, in which not only the individual in history but also the individual in relation to God, who is the creator of the physical universe, comes to expression.

In his famous *The Social Teaching of the Christian Churches* Troeltsch applied sociological method to theology, and in his work on the absolute nature of Christianity he considered seriously the truth claims of other religions beside Christianity. Much of this new impetus was the fruit of his intellectual partnership with Max Mueller.

See also: **Harnack; Kierkegaard; Ritschl**

Glossary: Fideism

Major writings

The Absoluteness of Christianity, London: John Knox Press, 1972 (1902)
The Social Teaching of the Christian Churches, 2 vols, Chicago: Chicago University Press, 1981 (1912)
Protestantism and Progress, Philadelphia: Fortress Press, 1986 (1912)
Religion in History, trans. J.L. Adams & W.F. Bense, Edinburgh: T & T Clark, 1991

Further reading

J.P. Clayton (ed.), *Ernst Troeltsch and the Future of Theology,* Cambridge and New York: CUP, 1976
S. Coakley, *Christ without Absolutes, a Study of the Christology of Ernst Troeltsch,* Oxford: Clarendon Press, 1988
H. Drescher, *Ernst Troeltsch: his life and work,* London: SCM, 1992

ZWINGLI, HULDRYCH (1484–1531)

Swiss reformer and almost exact contemporary of Martin **Luther**, who carried out a parallel and independent programme of reform in Zurich that mirrored Luther's efforts in Wittenberg. Indeed it was to be the programme of reform initiated by Zwingli, supplemented and modified later by the efforts of **Calvin** in Geneva, that was to prove the more influential in the Protestant Swiss cantons and much of Northern Europe.

Zwingli was born in Wildhaus in 1484, the son of a local civic leader. He was educated at the universities of Basle and Vienna where he was introduced to both the traditional scholastic approach to learning and the newly emerging humanist approach to faith and learning. In 1506 Zwingli was ordained and became a priest at Glarus where he was to serve for ten years. During this period Zwingli further developed his interest in humanist studies by learning Greek in order to read the New Testament in its original language (and also the early Eastern Fathers of the Church). The reading of the scriptures and the early Fathers of the Church in their original languages were key humanist themes.

Zwingli served as a chaplain to the Swiss mercenary forces that fought at the battles of Novaro (1513) and Marignano (1515). Originally supportive and patriotic, the carnage that he witnessed in these places led Zwingli to be bitterly critical of the Swiss practice of using mercenary soldiers to fight foreign wars, even in the name of the Pope. The young priest's progress towards becoming an eventual reformer was further advanced when he met Erasmus in 1515. Erasmus was the pre-eminent scholar in Europe at this point in time and the leading figure of humanism. The famous scholar was very critical of war in general and the overtly military nature of Pope Julius' reign drew particularly sharp criticism from the man of letters. Erasmus was also very critical of the manifold abuses existing in the life of the Church. His humanistic agenda for reforming the abuses in the Church focused upon the production of the scriptures in their original languages, producing a much praised edition of the Greek New Testament. The production of the scriptures in their original languages meant that preachers could read the New Testament in a direct fashion free from the glosses and accretions of medieval religious life. The intended effect was that the primitive and supposedly purer life of the early Christian communities could be held as a mirror against the current practices of the Church. Erasmus also advocated the moral regeneration of the individual through the development of inner piety by imitating Christ, but also by reforming the structures of society. During this period we see Zwingli, under the influence of Erasmus, acting as a young humanistically inclined priest copying out the letters of Paul from the Greek originals and using the early Fathers (as opposed to the scholastic tradition) to interpret Paul's meaning.

In this period we have to think of Zwingli as part of that group of young priests and thoughtful lay people, fully faithful to the Church, who nevertheless were committed to its renewal through a programme of reform construed along broadly humanist lines. It was thus possible to engage in reasoned debated with Church authorities and even criticise such practices as the trade in indulgences while still being thought of as a faithful Christian. Unlike Luther, Zwingli does not seem to have had a particularly intense religious crisis concerning salvation prior to becoming a reformer and this helps to explain the marked differences in emphasis and tone between the reformation programmes in Zurich and Wittenberg.

Even Zwingli's celebrated sexual lapses as a young priest, brought to light as an accusation against him when he was called to be preacher at the Great Minster in Zurich in 1518, did not overly trouble his conscience. To be sure he regretted his failure to fulfil his vow of celibacy, but he did not seem to doubt his salvation because of these lapses. His famous defence was that, although guilty of sexual immorality, he had never defiled a 'virgin, nun or married woman'. Clerical unchastity was a widespread problem at the time as evidenced by the fact that Zwingli's main competitor for the post at Zurich was found to have fathered six children.

Thus it was on 1 January 1519 that Zwingli entered the pulpit of the Great Minster of Zurich for the first time. He purposed to preach systematically through the gospel of Matthew, simply and straightforwardly, as the early Fathers had done, without the adornment of appeals to the lives of the saints that dominated so much preaching at this time. This was very much in line with Zwingli's prior practice for he claimed that 'In the year 1516 I began to preach in such wise that I never mounted the pulpit without personally taking to heart the Gospel for the day and explaining it with reference to Scripture alone'.[i] The year 1519 was to be pivotal for Zwingli, because it was in that year that he first came into contact with the writings of Luther. Although Zwingli would always zealously claim to have embarked upon a programme that was independent of Luther's (and there is some considerable truth in this), there is no doubting that contact with Luther's writings – and awareness of the crisis that Luther provoked within the Church – sharpened and intensified many of the issues for Zwingli at this time.

In the same year, however, a crisis of a different sort engulfed Zwingli. Zurich experienced a terrible epidemic of the plague and in his work as chaplain to the sick and dying Zwingli succumbed to the disease. For some time Zwingli lay ill and close to death and it was feared that he would not survive, but he managed to pull through. Zwingli's feelings at this time are recounted in the famous 'Plague Hymn' he wrote upon recovery.

> Help, Lord God, help
> In this need.
> So let it be;
> Do what thou wilt
> I nothing lack.
> Thy vessel am I; To make or break altogether.
> My tongue is dumb,
> It cannot speak a word.
> My senses are all numbed

Therefore is it time
That thou my fight
Conductest hereafter[ii]

This 'hymn' is marked by a strong sense of submission to God's will and the divine ordination of all things. This stress upon divine sovereignty and **predestination** were to be key features of Zwingli's thought from this time onwards. The near death experience seems to have left Zwingli believing himself to be completely at the disposal of the purposes of God, even to the extent that he could say – when his own brother fell victim to the plague – 'I am far from nourishing resentment against God, for I have learnt to submit myself utterly to his divine will'.[iii] Notably, neither the hymn itself, nor Zwingli's thoughts on the death of his brother, make any reference or appeal to the saints or the intercessory role of the Church. It would appear then that some sort of shift seems to have taken place in the mind of Zwingli, although it is a matter of great debate in Zwinglian scholarship as to precisely when Zwingli can be said to have moved from being a humanistically inclined proponent of change to becoming an evangelical reformer proper.

A series of important events mark the relevant crucial points. In 1520 the city council decided that preaching should be in accord with scripture – undoubtedly a victory for Zwingli. In 1522 the 'affair of the sausages' took place. A group of printers broke the lenten fast by eating sausages. Zwingli was present but refused to eat the forbidden meat. The authorities moved to punish this flagrant breaking of lenten rules and Zwingli responded by preaching on the freedom of the Christian to observe or not observe the fast according to the dictates of conscience. He made the point that scripture nowhere commands a lenten fast and argued that scripture should take priority over the tradition and practices of the Church. In tandem with his support for the printers, Zwingli petitioned the bishop and the Swiss authorities, arguing for the free preaching of the gospel, an end to clerical celibacy and began to question such matters as the intercession of the saints. At the same time Zwingli secretly married Anna Reinhart Meyer, a widow, although the marriage did not become public until 1524.

To settle these disputed matters a public disputation was called for in 1523 where representatives from both sides could debate these issues. It is significant that the civic authorities called the meeting, and that they requested that debate on the Bible take place in the German language rather than Latin. They also asserted that the Holy Scriptures were to be the sole basis of forming a judgement in these matters. A vivid example of this *sola scriptura* principle was to be provided by the sight of Zwingli and his colleagues sitting facing their opponents with open Bibles on their laps.

In preparation for this disputation Zwingli prepared his famous *67 Theses* which provide the programme for reform in Zurich and form the basis of all his subsequent theology. The first 23 of the articles are all related to Christ and his work, including the definitive Article 20 – 'God will give us everything in his (Christ's) name, whence it follows that for our part after this life we need no mediator except him'.[iv] Article 28 anticipates Zwingli's later views on the sacrament of the Lord's Supper: 'Christ having sacrificed himself once and for all, is for all eternity a perpetual and acceptable offering for the sins of all believers, from which it follows that the mass is not a sacrifice, but is a commemoration of the sacrifice and assurance which Christ has given us'.[v] Zwingli further asserted in Articles 51 and 52 that God alone remits sin through Jesus Christ and that the practice of confession does not remit sin but should be regarded simply as seeking advice. Moreover, he claimed that scripture teaches nothing concerning purgatory and the fate of the dead is known to God alone. The practice of enforcing celibacy upon the clergy was also repudiated. The most radical article of all is perhaps the first, which asserts that 'All who say that the gospel is invalid without the confirmation of the Church err and slander God', for here the priority of the gospel is given precedence over the Church.

Zwingli and his supporters were victorious (something anticipated by the Bishop of Constance who did not attend the disputation in person but allowed a representative to attend) and the civil authorities ordered that the Zurich clergy were henceforth to confine their preaching to that which scripture taught. Later that year a second disputation was called to deal with questions relating to the mass and the use of images in churches. The result was that in June 1524 the council ordered the removal of all images from Zurich churches. In April 1525 the mass was abolished in Zurich and replaced by a new order for the administration of the Lord's Supper. At this point it is finally clear that the tentative and gradual steps taken towards reform had now resulted in a definitive break with the Roman Catholic church.

Zwingli's major works other than the *67 Theses* are his *Commentary on the Sixty Seven Theses* (1523), *On True and False Religion* (1525), *On the Providence of God* (1530), *'That these words of Christ: this is my body (etc.)'* (1527), *Baptism, Re-baptism and the Baptism of Infants* (1525) and *'Of the clarity and certainty of the Word of God'* (1522). In these and other pieces Zwingli's theology emerges in a consistent albeit less systematic and precise way than that of the later Calvin.

In *On True and False Religion* Zwingli stresses the mystery and the absoluteness of God. This God, who can be known from a distance via natural theology, shows sinful human beings the extent of their sin, the magnitude of Adam's betrayal and their complicity in his disobedience while at the same time revealing to them the extent of divine mercy. *On the Providence of God* continues the theme by once again affirming that there is a natural knowledge of God. However, in this work it is the sovereign purpose of God which is at the forefront of Zwingli's mind. The work is more philosophical than biblical and Zwingli is eager to show that belief in God's providential ordering of the affairs of the world leads not to despair but to a faithful submission to God's will. Providence is related to predestination in that the individual's election to **salvation** is entirely the work of God and not dependent upon human merit. The rationale behind such a strong emphasis upon divine election is the desire to locate the act of salvation solely in the plan and activity of God, thus forestalling and undercutting any attempts to speak of human cooperation or achievement in salvation. Good works and acts of love flow from election, they are not the basis of election, and they offer some (although not a guaranteed) assurance that we belong to the elect. It is a corollary of this that the evil works of the reprobate are a sign that they are reprobate, although this is confused by Zwingli's admission elsewhere that sin is a possibility for the elect. He is prepared to consider that good and virtuous pagans may belong to the elect and offers the pastorally sensitive view that the death of premature infants may be a sign of their election.

Zwingli took his stand on the clarity and simplicity of scripture interpreted on its own terms. He anticipated Calvin's later stress on the necessity of the Spirit for understanding scripture: 'Even if you hear the gospel of Jesus Christ from an apostle you will not follow it unless the heavenly Father teaches you and draws you by his Spirit'.[vi] Again, 'It [scripture] is certain and cannot fail us; it is clear and does not let us wander in darkness. It teaches itself, it explains itself and it brings the light of full salvation and grace to the human soul'.[vii] For Zwingli scripture is trustworthy and authoritative because God (the Spirit) is its ultimate author. As a humanist scholar he could note discrepancies and inconsistencies in the text but these were not held to affect fundamental matters of faith. Ultimately such discrepancies can only be apparent as the Spirit does not contradict himself.

Undoubtedly the views that Zwingli is most remembered for are his views on the Lord's Supper or eucharist. Zwingli rejected the mass and the theory of the *transubstantiation* of the elements that were at the centre of it. He also differentiated his views from Luther's theory of consubstantiation. Zwingli viewed the sacred meal as a 'eucharist', an act of thanksgiving for the sacrifice of Christ which achieved our salvation. Every Christian was to faithfully participate in it as a sign and pledge that they were members of Christ's church.

The differences between Zwingli and Luther on this matter were to be resolved at the Marburg Colloquy of 1529. The colloquy came very close to achieving an agreement between the Lutheran and Zwinglian movements. They came to an agreement on almost every issue that divided them save the presence of Christ in the eucharist. As a good humanist and literary scholar Zwingli could only believe that when Jesus said 'take, eat, this is my body', the 'is' in question was an 'is' of signification rather than identity.

The question remains: did Zwingli have any concept of a real presence of Christ in the Lord's Supper? The answer depends on what you mean by real presence. It is clear that for Zwingli Christ is not present in the elements, but he is however present in the hearts and minds of believers in the act of commemoration. His final statement on the issue reads:

> I believe that in the holy meal of the eucharist (that is, of giving thanks), the true body of Christ is present in the mind of the believer: … Thus everything done by Christ becomes as it were present to them in their believing minds. But that the body of Christ, that is his natural body in essence and reality, is either present in the supper or eaten with our mouths and teeth as the papists … assert, we not only deny but firmly maintain to be an error opposed to the word of God.[viii]

Zwingli's general view of the sacraments (a term he did not like) is that there were two: baptism and the Lord's Supper. Drawing upon the original meaning of the term sacrament he stressed that they are acts of allegiance or pledges of faithfulness made by the Christian community that serve to strengthen faith. In relation to infant baptism this understanding of the sacraments originally left Zwingli vulnerable to the attacks of the Anabaptists, a radical group of Christians who practised only believer's or adult baptism and argued that infant baptism was both unscriptural and meaningless if understood as the pledge of an infant. Initially, Zwingli confessed to having doubts about the propriety of infant baptism but developed his views to argue that although scripture has no overt example of a child being baptised it does not expressly forbid the practice. He further argued that the household baptisms described in the New Testament probably included children.

Zwingli accepted that baptism was not a means of grace nor essential for salvation, but it was a sign. However, Zwingli's view changed from understanding the sacraments as a sign or pledge of our faithfulness to God, to a more nuanced view which understood it as a sign of God's covenant promise to us. Baptism then becomes an initiatory sign of our inclusion in God's covenant and is the New Testament parallel to circumcision in the Old Testament. This view profoundly influenced Calvin and has become the classic expression of the Reformed understanding of baptism.

Zwingli's problems with the Anabaptists led him to place great stress on the divine ordination of the civil authorities, and of their right to wield the power of the sword 'outside the perfection of Christ'. In so doing he showed himself to be a man of his times. Zwingli's work of reform was, of course, wholly dependent upon the agreement of the civil authorities as Zwingli never held an official political position in Zurich. He was also remaining faithful to the early humanist programme inherited from Erasmus that stressed the reordering of society as a means to moral regeneration. However, he has been accused of over-identifying the political reality of the canton of Zurich with the spiritual reality of the kingdom of God. Certainly he lacks even the cautious note of critique, and possible basis for revolt, *vis-à-vis* civil authority that Calvin allows for in his account of the matter.

Zwingli's eventful life came to an end at the battle of Kappel on 11 October 1531. Zwingli, acting as chaplain to the Swiss Protestant forces that were engaged in a civil war with the forces of the Swiss Catholic cantons, was wounded and left on the battlefield. Recognised where he lay, the wounded Zwingli was unceremoniously killed, his body quartered and burned and his ashes scattered.

Zwingli's theology continues to have a widespread but diffuse influence in the Protestant world. This makes it hard to quantify the precise scale and scope of his legacy. Part of the reason for this is that Zwingli picked up and utilised many concepts and ideas that were common currency during his own time (as indeed we all must do), so that Erasmus famously asked what had Zwingli written that he himself had not previously written or said? (Zwingli did break with him over the question of free will however.) None the less, it is clear that there is more to Zwingli than the simple repetition of Erasmus, although it has been the more systematic and precise Calvin who has gained the major place in Reformed theology. Yet, many of Zwingli's views were adopted and developed by Calvin, particularly in relation to baptism. As to the manner of Christ's presence in the Lord's Supper there is good reason to believe that Zwingli's views have been the more influential on the common Protestant believer's understanding of what s/he is doing when s/he partakes of the bread and the wine than Calvin's more 'spiritual' understanding of the real presence.

Notes

i   Cited in Rilliet, *Zwingli: third man of the Reformation*, p.43
ii   'Zwingli's Plague Hymn' in Potter, *Huldrych Zwingli*, p.15
iii   Rilliet, *Zwingli*, p.54
iv   Potter, *Huldrych Zwingli*. Article 20 of Zwingli's 67 theses, p.23
v   Potter, *Huldrych Zwingli*, p.23
vi   *Ibid.*, p.30
vii *Ibid.*
viii *Ibid.*, p.108

See also: **Calvin; Luther**

Glossary: **Predestination; salvation; transubstantiation**

Major writings

Huldreich Zwinglis Samtliche Werke in C.G. Bretschneider (ed.), *Corpus Reformatorum*, Vol. 88, Zurich: 1905
Ulrich Zwingli (1484–1531): selected works, ed. Samuel Macauley Jackson; Philadelphia: University of Pennsylvania Press, 1972
Selected Writings of Huldrych Zwingli, ed. Edward J. Furcha, Allison Park, PA: Pickwick Publications, 1984

Further reading

U. Gabler, *Huldrych Zwingli: his life and work*, Edinburgh: T & T Clark, 1999
G.R. Potter, *Huldrych Zwingli*, London: Edward Arnold, 1978
J. Rilliet, *Zwingli: third man of the Reformation*, London: Lutterworth, 1964
W.P. Stephens, *Zwingli*, Oxford: Clarendon Press, 1992

GLOSSARY

Atonement Literally to make 'at-one'. Atonement theories are thus interpretations of Christ's death on the cross which explain how and why his sacrifice
makes humanity be at one or reconciled with God. Various options have been
canvassed at different points in the Church's history. An early view was that
Christ's death was a ransom paid to the devil who had effective ownership of
human beings due to the fall of Adam. Alternatively, Christ's death and
resurrection was also viewed as a victory over the powers of death and the devil
which therefore no longer have power over those who put their faith in Christ.
Anselm corrected the ransom theory by stressing that Christ's death was not a
payment to the devil (for God owes no obligation to the devil) but instead was a
satisfaction of God's offended honour. A later account often associated with John
Calvin argues that Christ's death was a penal substitutionary sacrifice whereby the
penalty for sin, i.e. death, that properly belonged to human beings is taken on our
behalf by Christ on the cross. Recent discussions of the matter have tended to
stress the usefulness of many of these theories and suggest that we need to use a
wide variety of models and constructs to explain the mystery of God's action in the
cross of Christ.

Chalcedon/Chalcedonian An ecumenical Council of the Church called
together in 451 to settle the disputed issue of the precise understanding of the
relationship between the divine and human natures in Christ. Chalcedon
determined that the incarnate figure of Christ was one person in two natures,
human and divine, though the natures are neither to be confused nor
commingled, neither separated nor teased apart. Each nature retains its own
distinctive qualities in the union and the union takes place in the person
(*hypostasis*) of the Son of God. This has been the orthodox statement of Christian
belief ever since, and a Chalcedonian Christology is therefore a Christology which
adheres to this formula.

Ecumenical/ecumenism The word is derived from the Greek *oikoumene*
which means the whole inhabited world. However, theologically it has come to
refer to the whole Church and the various relations between its individual
member churches. The modern ecumenical movement therefore is an attempt to
overcome divisions within the universal Church through the attempt to foster

greater understanding and unity, to share in mutual service to the world and by the creation of theological agreement on points of difference. The World Council of Churches (WCC), founded in 1948, is the leading ecumenical agency for such tasks.

Enlightenment (Ger. *Aufklärung*) A term applied to a particular period of European intellectual history including figures as diverse as John Locke (1632–1704) in England, David Hume (1711–76) in Scotland, Voltaire (1694–1778) and Rousseau (1712–78) in France, before culminating in the philosophy of Immanuel Kant (1724–1804) in Germany. Its key themes were: (1) everything should be placed before the bar of reason as the final arbiter in all matters; (2) a strong emphasis upon scientific and empirical methods and the importance of observation as forming the proper method of inquiry; (3) a rejection of the concept of received authority such as the teachings of the Church or the scriptures as being determinative in the making of sound judgements; (4) a reasonably firm commitment to human progress through education and the application of reason – although this was not so universally held to be as self-evident as the other principles. Kant's philosophy is pivotal in showing the precise limits of reason even as the themes of the Enlightenment period reach their greatest and clearest expression in his mature thought.

Epistemology/epistemological Theories of knowledge – from the Greek *epistēmē* meaning knowledge. In general the study of how we know what we know. Therefore, epistemological theories will concern themselves with questions such as: What is knowledge? What are its warrants and bases? What are the criteria by which we can judge that which is sound and certain knowledge?

Eschatology/eschatological The study of the 'last things' or the events that are to take place at the end of the world. In classical dogmatics, eschatology was concerned with such matters as the second coming of Christ, the resurrection from the dead, the last judgement and life eternal. There were great disagreements among theologians and New Testament scholars in the nineteenth and twentieth centuries as to the precise meaning of eschatology. Some argued that it related to wholly future events, others that it referred to a present reality that had begun in the life, teachings and ministry of Jesus and was continuing now. Yet others argued that the proclamation of the gospel brings an encounter with God in the response of faith that qualifies the whole of one's Christian existence in the present, thus enabling the believer to live in openness to the future. Generally speaking, the contemporary emphasis is to understand eschatology in terms of the present anticipation of God's future promise for this world and the hope that this promise will be concretely transformed in the consummation of all that is in God's coming kingdom.

Existentialism/Existentialist That approach to philosophy which stresses the dimension of human experience in the world as the primary datum for philosophy. In general it is distrustful of the classical philosophical tradition which attempted to philosophise from the standpoint of the disinterested, rational spectator. Existentialism tends to stress the fact that the human individual is already caught up in the world of being and has to make decisions about his or her own existence. Rather, then, than engaging in abstract discussion about the general categories of being, existentialism focuses upon the specificity of what it means to be human in the world. It tends to ask 'Who am I?' and, 'What is my situation?', rather than 'What are human beings?' Consequently there is a strong stress on subjectivity, that is, on the personal experience and appropriation of truth. A key point in existential philosophies and theologies is the notion that 'existence precedes essence'. This testifies to the existentialist conviction that human beings do not have their essential natures given to them but have to realise them and seize hold of them via the decisions they make.

Fideism From the Latin *Fides* meaning faith. Fideism is a word which is used to describe those approaches to faith which stress the independence of religious belief from reason. On this account Christian belief therefore makes no appeal to universal categories of reason for its justification but depends upon its own internal and self-consistent logic as revealed by God. Truth in all matters of theology is thus apprehended by faith.

Filioque The Western insertion into the Nicene creed statement on the Trinity which asserts that the Spirit proceeds from God the Father and God the Son rather than from the Father alone as was the customary teaching of the Eastern Church. This teaching was one of the reasons for the eventual split that took place in 1054 between the Roman Catholic and the Orthodox branches of the Christian Church. Although it is now widely recognised that the Western insertion of the clause into the creed itself was a mistake, there is still some sense that the Western stress upon a double procession of the Spirit is a more faithful rendition of the gospel narrative. However, the Orthodox Church has always stressed that God the Father is the sole source of divinity in the Godhead and fears that the Western teaching implies two generating principles in the divine life. A compromise solution which states that the Spirit proceeds from the Father through the Son is sporadically offered as a possible solution to the impasse but as yet to no avail.

Fundamentalist A term describing a movement in American evangelical theology during the early twentieth century. It takes its name from a series of short booklets entitled 'The Fundamentals' which were published between 1910 and 1915. These booklets constituted a vigorous reaffirmation of what their authors took to be the fundamentals of the Christian faith as opposed to what was perceived as the liberalising trend of modern culture. It is particularly marked by a stress on the authority, infallibility and inerrancy of the original biblical texts and a requirement that the text be interpreted literally wherever possible. Today the term is often applied more loosely (and perhaps inaccurately) to describe anyone who tends towards a more conservative expression of the Christian faith.

Gnostic/ism From the Greek word *gnosis* meaning knowledge. A religious movement paralleling the development of early Christianity (and perhaps at various times even part of early Christianity) which emphasised knowledge as the means for attainment of salvation, or even as the form of salvation itself. To know God is to partake of the divine life, and thus knowing is salvation, not only a means to perfection but the actual goal of salvation. The cardinal feature of Gnostic theology was the radical dualism between God and the world. God is absolutely transcendent and is hidden from all creatures – knowledge of Him requires supernatural revelation and illumination by the Spirit. Gnostic sects therefore often claimed to possess hidden words or teachings which would guide the initiate through the various levels of spiritual reality on their path back to God.

Homoousios Literally, of 'one substance' or more prosaically 'one stuff'. The term was used at the Council of Nicaea in 325 to describe the relationship between God the Son and God the Father. Nicaea declared that what the Father was, the Son was also. This was extremely worrying to a great many Christians of that period who would have wished to make a distinction in kind between God the Father and God the Son. A compromise term – *homoiousios* – of 'like substance', which suggested a form of divinity for the Son but not absolute equality with God the Father, was suggested at the Council but was rejected. The Church has never gone back on this basic Christian declaration.

Immutability A term which in classical Christian theology refers to God's inability to undergo change. The term has a defensive function in that it is meant to protect the otherness and perfection of God as opposed to God's creation. For if God is perfect existence then any change can only imply a diminution of that perfection. However, it is often queried how God can be actively and truly involved in His creation without undergoing change, and therefore contemporary accounts have tended to interpret immutability as referring to God's constancy of character and purpose.

Justification A term derived from the Greek *dikaiosynē* which means to be 'made righteous'. Justification by faith is the key term of Martin Luther and all subsequent Protestantism which asserts that human beings as sinners are 'made righteous' (or justified) by faith through the gracious action of God and not through any deed or merit of their own.

Kenōsis A Greek term meaning 'emptying' which refers to the self-emptying of God the Son of His divine attributes in the act of incarnation. It takes its inspiration from Philippians 2:5–11 which speaks of Christ Jesus emptying himself and taking the form of a slave not regarding being in the form of God. Although it has been argued that these verses do not mean to speak of Christ as a pre-existent divine being, nevertheless the concept of *kenōsis* has been widely accepted as a profound and attractive way of attempting to explain how a divine being can take on the constraints of human existence by divesting itself of those divine properties which are incompatible with finite existence. However, it is by no means clear that even a divine being is able to divest itself of those properties essential to being divine.

Liberation/ist theology A development in theology particularly associated with a group of theologians from Latin American countries of the 1960s and 1970s who argued that the gospel has profound liberating consequences economically and socially as well as spiritually. Influenced in the initial stages by Marxist critiques of society and religion they attacked the lack of interest in concrete matters of justice, peace and righteousness that was such a feature of classical European theologies. The themes and aims of the movement known as liberation theology have many points of contact with other contextual and emancipatory theologies such as feminist theology and black theology, as well as with the earlier social gospel movement in the United States and European political theologies.

Logos   From the Greek meaning 'Word' or 'reason'. In neo-platonic philosophy the second principle of the universe that gives order, coherence and form to all reality. The term is appropriated early in the Christian tradition in the gospel of John to say that the Word of God became incarnate in Jesus Christ. Early Christian writers such as Justin Martyr and Tertullian used this notion to explain the Christian faith to their contemporaries in terms they could understand. Thus the Logos/*Word* is God the Father's immanent reason expressed in the act of creation. This rational expressive outreach of God in creation is then pictured as achieving its unique and complete realisation in the incarnation of Jesus Christ. The Logos concept therefore gave the early Christian writers a means of showing how the unique events of Christ's incarnation were to be related to God's action in creation since the beginning of time.

Neo-platonism/neo-platonic   A term which refers to the development of the philosophy of Plato which began with the writing of Plotinus (205–70) and which continued through to the sixth century, exerting a huge influence on the development of early Christian theology. Its basic theme is that of the 'One' from whom all being derives through a series of emanations, although these do not involve change in the 'One', and to which all that is desires to return. In order to account for the manifest diversity of the universe, neo-platonism asserts that there is a descending chain of being beginning with the Word or Reason which is immediately below the One. The Word is followed by the World-Soul and so on down to the level of matter and human beings. Human beings are a duality of soul and body and the soul desires to return to the 'One' through a mystical ascent which begins with the purging and denial of sensory and bodily experiences, rising through the practice of contemplation of the divine until it reaches mystical union with the 'One'.

Nominalism   A view which denies that universal categories really exist and which positively states that only individual entities actually exist. Universal and abstract concepts are thus only constructs used by the mind to note similarities between individuals. In its strictest theological form nominalism tends to stress the omnipotence of God and denies the plurality of his attributes, these being defined in terms of God's absolute will. See also *universals* and *realism*.

Noumenal   A term that refers to things as they are in themselves apart from the categories and constructs that we apply to them. Immanuel Kant famously argued that we have no knowledge of 'noumenal' reality as it is in itself, but can only know its phenomenal appearance to us through the structuring categories of the mind which include the concepts of space, time and causation.

Phenomenal   Strictly speaking, a term which means 'appearance', but in philosophy it refers to that which is cognisable by the senses. It is opposed to the *noumenal*, and questions with regard to the phenomenal in theology relate to how and what human beings can be said to perceive of God and God's relation to the created world.

Plērōsis A Greek term meaning fullness or completeness.

Predestination The doctrine that God foreordains those who will be saved. It finds its basis in certain biblical passages such as Romans 8:29: 'Those whom he foreknew he also predestined to be conformed to the image of his Son'. It is especially associated with Augustine who stressed that salvation is wholly dependent upon the grace of God who saves whom he will. Augustine, however, stressed predestination to salvation; it was John Calvin who articulated a theory of double-predestination whereby God not only chooses those who will be saved but also actively chooses to send the unbelieving and reprobate to hell. Although it seems a harsh doctrine the issue which it tries to address is whether it is finally God or human beings who are the authors of their own salvation. Predestination stresses that human salvation is wholly and completely the work of God, whereas theories that stress the importance of a free human response in the matter tend to make God the spectator and not the author of salvation.

Realism The view that things actually exist independently of our knowledge of them. In relation to ***nominalism*** it embodies the claim that universal properties do actually exist apart from the individual entities which embody them. Many contemporary theological accounts of epistemology take a 'critically realistic' perspective – which is to say that they acknowledge that our terms, though socially constructed and always revisable, nevertheless do give some sort of approximate epistemic access to the world as it is. See also ***universals***.

Revelation The unveiling or disclosing of that which was previously unknown. In theological terms the disclosure of knowledge concerning God that is due to the action of God and is not as such directly accessible to reason. There is, however, also a form of general revelation which takes place through natural reflection on the world. Revelation can be regarded as taking place in the Bible through a direct encounter with God in faith or indirectly through God's action in the events of history.

Salvation The state or condition of being saved by being brought into a right relationship with God. Salvation thus implies that human nature is disordered in some way and that God has acted to heal that disorder in Christ. The biblical images of salvation are many and diffuse, but all serve to portray a sense of human wholeness, flourishing, completeness and blessedness that is found only in union with God. The biblical thrust concerning salvation is that it is wholly and completely a work of God and is His gracious gift to human beings. Although salvation is often presented in individualistic terms, and indeed is personally appropriated through faith, the biblical thrust is always to present the fullness of salvation in terms of a redeemed community.

Sanctification The process by which Christians are made holy through the indwelling and operation of the Holy Spirit in their lives. This process begins at baptism when the believer receives the Holy Spirit and is the corollary of being justified by faith (see *justification*). The Christian life therefore is a process of growing in love for God through the power of the Spirit's sanctifying grace which frees the Christian from the power and hold of sin.

Scholastic/ism   The method and type of theology associated with the medieval period which stressed the role of reason in matters of faith and which was marked by an intense concentration in the application of logic and the formal analysis of concepts and terms as part of the systematic presentation of the Christian faith. In the long term the movement was associated with the shift in medieval society whereby the centres of learning moved from the monasteries to the emerging universities. The method practised was that of the articulation of a specific question followed by an objection and a response before a thorough exposition of the problem was provided. This procedure of methodological doubt exemplifies the normative method of the scholastic period and is captured in Abelard's phrase, 'in order to understand one must first begin by questioning, for it is by doubting we come to questioning, and by questioning we perceive the truth'.

Social gospel   A movement in late nineteenth- and early twentieth-century American Church life which is particularly associated with Walter Rauschenbush (1861–1918). Rauschenbush had been a minister in New York's underprivileged Hell's Kitchen area and came to realise the plight of the urbanised poor in American life. He criticised the overly individualistic emphasis of normative Protestantism and called for the political and social redemption of the structures of society as well as individuals. A key concept used in critiquing the prevalent practices of society was the ethical requirements of the kingdom of God.

Theodicy   A term used to describe those theories which attempt to defend the righteousness of God in the light of evil in the world. A term first used by G.F.W. Leibniz in 1710 in his famous attempt to argue that this world was the best of all possible worlds.

Transubstantiation   The Roman Catholic theory concerning the changes that the bread and wine served in the celebration of the mass are said to undergo. In this rite it is stated that the bread and wine are substantially changed from bread and wine into the body and blood of Christ although the external appearance (accidents) of the bread and wine remain.

Trinity/Trinitarian   The distinctive and uniquely Christian doctrine of God that asserts that although God is one (in agreement with Jewish and Muslim accounts of the oneness of God), nevertheless this one God exists in three persons: Father, Son and Holy Spirit. The doctrine arose out of the early Church's conviction that in the figure of Jesus Christ God the Son was uniquely incarnate and that it was appropriate to offer worship to Him. The early Church also experienced the gift of God's presence in the form of the Holy Spirit and knew that this presence was not simply the presence of the Father or the Son but was a third unique and individual gift of God's presence. As such the primitive Church from its very earliest proclamation and in the setting down of its scriptures uses the formula Father, Son and Holy Spirit to express its distinctive understanding of God. Although the precise relationship between Father, Son and Holy Spirit is never formally expressed in scripture the classical doctrine arose as a result of controversy and confusion as the Church wrestled with competing ways of construing the divine relationships. The formal doctrine that emerged asserts that Father, Son and Spirit are one God in three persons, each equally divine, lacking none of the characteristics of divinity, and differing from each other only in terms of their inner relations. For example, the Son differs from the Father only with respect to the fact that He is the Son and not the Father and in all other respects He is equal in power, dignity and attributes to the Father. Ditto with the Spirit in relation to the Father and the Son. The technical language for the distinction of the Trinitarian persons is that God exists as one substance (*ousia*) in three persons (*hypostases*), although here the sense of person does not carry the modern sense of an individual subject of consciousness. *Hypostasis* (person) is a complex term which in this instance carries the sense of a concrete and individual presentation of a substance. This was the classic view, but more recently many contemporary accounts of the Trinity have argued for an understanding of the Trinity along the lines of a social community of individual persons – a community of being – and this entails that the three persons should be thought of as individual persons in the modern sense, albeit persons who exist in an eternal relationship of mutual self-giving and receiving love.

Universals   Those categories by which philosophy attempts to account for the commonality that pertains between discrete individual things that are regarded as forming a species or a genus. Universal categories are therefore utilised and appealed to in the attempt to comprise individual entities under some more overarching and general description. See also **nominalism** and **realism**.

INDEX

Abelard, Peter (1079–1142) 3–8, 284; and atonement 6–7; background 3; and doctrine of the Trinity 5–6; and Héloïse 5; *Historia Calamitum* 3; and incarnation 6; on morality 7; *Scito te ipsum* 7; *Sic et Non* 7; *Theologia Christiana* 6; *Theologia Scholarum* 6; *Theologia Summi Boni* 5; and universals 3, 4, 110

Abraham 169–70, 219

Absolute Spirit 136, 137–8, 139, 140, 167, 171

Abwehr 73

Adam 13, 46, 97, 114–15, 152, 153, 166, 218

Albert of Cologne 18

Albert the Great 16

Albinus 67

Alexander, Bishop 26

Ambrose of Milan, Bishop 39, 41

Anabaptists 275, 276

analogy: Aquinas and doctrine of 24

androcentrism 241

Anselm of Canterbury (1033–1109) 7, 9–15, 69; as Archbishop of Canterbury 15; and atonement theory 6, 13–14, 278; background 9–10; Barth's book on 60–1; *Cur Deus Homo* 13; and doctrine of Trinity 14–15; 'faith seeking to understand' phrase 9, 11; and God 11–13; *Monologion* 10; *On the procession of the Holy Spirit* 15; *Proslogion* 11, 12; stress on appropriate use of reason 9; teaching style 9–10; and universals 20, 110 Anselm of Laon 5

Anthony, St 34

anthropology: and Christology 221

Apollinarius 108

Apologists 151

apostles 227

Apostolic Fathers 158

Aquinas, Thomas (1225–74) 12, 16–24, 99, 156; background 16–17; as a biblically orientated theologian 17; and Christology 22, 23, 24, 63; and doctrine of analogy 24; and God 21–2; influence of 24; interpretation of Aristotle's philosophy 23–4; and origins of sin 23; and revelation 18–20; and sacraments 23; *Summa Theologiae* 18, 20; and Trinity 21, 22; and universals 20, 110

Arians/Arianism 32, 67

Aristotle 16, 17, 18, 20, 23–4, 68, 69

Arius (c.270–336) 25–31, 36, 104, 196; and Christology 25, 26, 27; refusal by Athanasius to accept back into communion 30, 32, 33; on relationship between God the Father and the Son and controversy over 25, 26–31, 32, 104, 206; *Thalia* (Banquet) 28, 31

Arsenius, Bishop of Hypsele 33

Athanasius (295–373) 32–7, 105, 156; *Against the Pagans* 34; banishment of 33; and Christology 36; defender of Nicene orthodoxy 29, 30, 32; *The Life of Anthony* 34; *On the Incarnation of the Word* 34, 35; opponents of 33; *Orations against the Arians* 34–5, 36;

refusal to accept Arius back into communion 30, 32, 33; *Tomus ad Antiochenos* 36

atheism 177, 227

atonement 98, 278; and Abelard 6–7; and Anselm 6, 13–14, 278; and Baillie 56; and Barth 64; and Calvin 278; and Forsyth 124, 125; 'moral influence'/subjectivist account of 6–7; and Paul 218; 'ransom' theory of 6, 13, 278

Augustine (354–430) 15, 17, 20–1, 38–47, 68, 99, 180, 224, 249; background and education 38–9, 40; and the Bible 38, 41, 43–4; and Christology 63; *The City of God* 38, 39, 43, 47; conception of Church as visible and invisible 45; *Confessions* 39–40, 43–4; conversion 39, 40, 41–2; and Donatists 38, 45; on evil 44; influence of classical culture on 40; influence of 45; linkage of sex with sin 44; and Manichees 39, 40–1; and neo-platonism 17–18, 21, 39; *On Christian Doctrine* 21; *On the Trinity* 43, 47; and original sin 46–7; and Pelagius 45–6, 110; and predestination 38, 46, 283; *Soliloquies* 42; and Trinity 5, 38, 43, 47, 108; understanding of the divine illumination of the human intellect 17, 18; use of Platonic imagery 42

Baillie, Donald (1887–1954) 48–57; background 48, 53; and Christology 53, 56–7, 142; criticism of by Hick 142; *Faith in God* 53; *God was in Christ* 53, 56–7, 142; *Theology of the Sacraments* 53–4

Baillie, John (1886–1960) 199; *And the Life Everlasting* 51; and atonement 56; background and career 48–9, 50–1, 52; *A Diary of Private Prayer* 51; and *God's Will for Church and Nation* report 52; *The Interpretation of Religion* 49, 50; *Invitation to Pilgrimage* 51; mediation of knowledge of God 51–2; and moral 50, 55; *Our Knowledge of God* 51; *The Roots of*

Religion in the Human Soul 49; *The Sense of the Presence of God* 54–6

baptism 46, 105, 180; and Barth 66; and Calvin 100; and Moltmann 193–4; and Zwingli 275–6

Bari, Council of (1098) 14

Barmen Declaration (1934) 72

Barnabas 216

Barth, Karl (1886–1968) 51, 58–66, 71, 80, 101, 126, 179, 190, 221, 231; and atonement 64; background 59; and Bible 61, 64–5, 87; and Bonhoeffer 72; and Brunner 83; and Christology 61–2, 63, 89–90, 209; *Church Dogmatics* 59, 61, 63, 64, 66; *Commentary on the Epistle to the Romans* 60, 173; and creation 63; criticism of First World War 60, 65, 173; doctrine of justification 174; education 60; and ethical issues 65; *Fides Quaerens Intellectum* 60–1; and God 21, 59–63, 64; and Harnack 132, 133; and history 207; and kerygmatic theology 59, 90; Niebuhr on 202; rejection of liberal theology 58–9, 60, 86; rejection of natural theology 82, 84; and revelation 61, 62, 64, 74, 75; and sacraments 65–6; sceptical about Church doctrines 65; on Schleiermacher 239; and scripture 96–7

Basil of Caesarea (330–79) 31, 102, 103–6, 108–9, 155; background and education 103–4; and distinction between *ousia* and *hypostasis* 105–6; and Holy Spirit 104–5; *On the Holy Spirit* 105

Baum, Gregory 233

Baur, Ferdinand Christian 229, 230, 241

Bec monastery 9

Bell, G.K.A., Bishop of Chichester 72

Bennett, John 199

Bernard of Clairvaux 8

Beveridge Reports 52

Bianchi, Eugene 234

Bible 23, 207, 227, 258; and Augustine 38, 41, 43–4; and Barth 61, 64–5, 87; and Brunner 82; and Bultmann 87; and Justin Martyr 160; and

Origen 204; and tradition of *sola scriptura* 210, 273
Biel, Gabriel 110
Bloch, Ernst 190
Boethius, Anicus Manlius Torquatus Severinus (c.480-c.525) 67–70; background 67–8; *On Catholic Faith* 68; *The Consolation of Philosophy* 67, 68, 69–70; definition of a person 68; and God 68–9; and universals 68, 69
Bonhoeffer, Dietrich (1906–45) 70–9, 175, 194, 199; arrest of and imprisonment 73–4; background 70–1; and *Bethel Confession* 72; and Bultmann 87, 90; and Christology 76, 78; and contrast between cheap and costly grace 77–8; *The Cost of Discipleship* 73, 77–8; *Ethics* 77, 78; and German Resistance 70, 71, 72–3; and God 75–6; hanged for high treason 70, 74; and Harnack 132; *Letters and Papers from Prison* 74–5, 77; *Life Together* 73, 77; and nature of Church 77; and 'world come of age' 75–6
Book of Common Prayer 197
Browning, Don 255
Brunner, Emil (1889–1966) 64, 80–5, 121; background 80; and bare point of contact 83, 84; and Barth 83; and Bible 82; commitment to eristic theology 84; critical of liberal theology 80; *Dogmatics* 63, 84; and God 81; *Man in Revolt* 83–4; *Nature and Grace* 82; and revelation 64, 80–1; and theory of knowledge 81, 82; *Truth as Encounter* 84
Buber, Martin 80
Bucer, Martin 93
Bultmann, Rudolf (1884–1976) 65, 75, 80, 85–90, 190, 220, 247; background 85; and Bible 87; and Christology 86, 88–9; *Commentary on the Fourth Gospel* 86; criticism of liberal theology 86; criticism of 87–8; existential theology 86–7; and faith 89; *The History of the Synoptic Tradition* 84–5; *Jesus* 86; as New Testament scholar 87, 89; and resurrection 88, 210

Buri, Fritz 90

Cairns, David 54
Calvin, John (1509–64) 46, 64, 91–101, 123, 187, 269, 274, 276, 277; *Articles on Ecclesiastical Organisation* 92–3; and atonement 278; background 91–2; banished from Geneva 93; Christology of 97–8; and Church 99–100, 101; *Commentary on the Psalms* 92; conversion to Protestantism 92; and doctrine of the internal illumination of the Spirit 96–7; and Farel 92; in Geneva 95; and humanist approach 91; influence of 101; *Institutes of the Christian Religion* 91, 92, 93, 94, 95–101; invitation to return to Geneva and reforms initiated 93–4; and justification of faith 98; knowledge of God 95–6; on law 187; and predestination 98–9, 283; and Reformed cause 94; on relationship between Church and civil magistrates 100–1; and sacraments 100; and scripture 96–7; and Servetus 94–5
Campbell, Mcleod 124
Campbell, R.J. 123
Canaris, Admiral 73
capitalism: and Calvinism 101
Cappadocian Fathers 31, 47, 102–9, 156; *see also* Basil of Caesarea; Gregory of Nyssa; Gregory of Nazianzus
Catholic Church 14, 234–5, 252
causation 162
Chalcedon, Council of (451) 62, 223, 254; 'one person in two natures' account of Christology 6, 13, 22, 37, 68, 133, 143, 221, 222, 237, 261, 278
Charles V, Emperor 186
Chicago school 264
Chopp, Rebecca 130
Christian Realism 199–201, 202
Christianity and Crisis (periodical) 202
Christology: and anthropology 221; and Aquinas 22, 23, 24, 63; and Arius 25, 26, 27; and Athanasius 36;

and Augustine 63; and Baillie 53, 56–7, 142; and Barth 61–2, 63, 89–90, 209; and Bonhoeffer 76, 78; and Bultmann 86, 88–9; and Calvin 97–8; Chalcedonian definition of 'one person in two natures' 6, 22, 37, 68, 133, 143, 221, 222, 237, 261, 278; and Forsyth 123–4; and Gregory of Nazianzus 108; and Hick 141–2, 143, 146; and Irenaeus 152; and John of Damascus 157; Kierkegaard 170; and Küng 175–6; and Moltmann 194; and Niebuhr 201; and Pannenberg 209, 211–12; and Rahner 222–3; and Reimarus 227; and Schleiermacher 237, 260; and Strauss 245, 246–8; and Tertullian 254; and Tillich 259–61, 262

Church: and Augustine 45; and Bonhoeffer 77; and Calvin 99–100, 101; and Erasmus 270; Küng and reform of 174–5, 179; Luther and reform of 188; and Moltmann 193; and Rahner 224; and Ruether 233

Church councils 19

Church Fathers 241

Church of Scotland 52

Cicero 41, 68; *Hortensius* 40

classic, a 264

Coffin, Henry Sloane 50, 57, 199

Confessing Church 72, 73, 85, 87, 89

confessional system 14

Congar, Yves 174

Constantine, Emperor 27, 30, 32, 34

Constantinople, Council of (381) 30, 108

Constantius, Emperor 30, 34

Cop, Nicholas 92

Copleston, F.C. 12

Corsair 170–1

Cox, Harvey: *The Secular City* 79

creation: and Augustine 41, 43; and Barth 63; and Brunner 82; and Edwards 115; and Gnostics 151; and Irenaeus 151; and John of Damascus 157; and Moltmann 194; and Rahner 225

critical rationality 178; Küng on 176–7

cross 124, 190, 191, 201

crucifixion 191; *see also* atonement

Cupitt, Don 120

Cyril of Alexandria 37

Deists 226, 227, 228

Demetrius 205

Denmark 171

dependency theory 127–8

Descartes 12

dialectical theology 60, 63, 80, 84

Diet of Speyer (1529) 186

Diocletian, Emperor 33, 45

discipleship 78

divine/divinity 26, 27, 42, 118

Donatists 38, 39, 45

Dunn, James 220

Duns Scotus, John (c.1265–1308) 109–11

Early Christian Missionary Movement 242

Easter 223

Ebner, Ferdinand 80

Eck, John 184

eco-feminism 234

ecumenical/ecumenism 50, 71, 72, 178, 199, 278–9

Edward VI, King 94

Edwards, Jonathan (1703–58) 112–16, 119; background 112–13; 'A Careful and Strict Enquiry into the Prevailing Notions of the Freedom of the Will' treatise 113–14; 'Concerning Religious Affections' treatise 113; and doctrine of original sin 114–15; 'The End for Which God Created the World'; 'The Nature of True Virtue' 115; neo-platonic influence on 115; sermons 112

Eliot, George 119

Eliot, T.S. 53

Enlightenment 58, 161, 210, 227, 263, 264, 279

Epipanius 156

epistemology/epistemological 64, 279; *see also* knowledge

Erasmus 92, 184, 270, 276

Erfurt, monastery at 180

eristic theology 84

eschatology/eschatological 143–4, 190, 194, 208, 215, 228, 251

eternal life: and Hick 146–7
eucharist 180, 188, 221, 274–5
Eusebius, Bishop of Nicomedia 26, 30, 33, 34
Eusebius of Caesarea, Bishop 26, 29, 103–4
evil: and Augustine 44; and Hick 144–6, 148; and John of Damascus 157; and Kant 166 existentialism/ existentialist 86–7, 168, 172, 173, 221, 255, 279–80
extra-calvinisticum 98
Ezekiel 4

faith 181; as an act of interpretation 143; and Baillie 54, 55; and Bultmann 89; and Hick 142, 143; justification by 98; and Rahner 224, 225; relationship between reason and 209; relationship between results of historical study and 133; and Troeltsch 267–8
Farel, Guillaume 92, 93
Farmer, H.H. 53, 141
feminist theology 233, 240, 241; and Schüssler-Fiorenza 242–3; *see also* Ruether, Rosemary Radford
Feuerbach, Ludwig (1804–72) 63, 116–20, 248; background and education 116–17; break with Hegel 116, 117–18; *Critique of Hegelian Philosophy* 117; critique of religion 119–20; *The Essence of Christianity* 117–18, 119; *The Essence of Religion* 119; and materialism 117; and notion of divine 118; *Preliminary Thesis for the Reform of Philosophy* 119; *Thoughts on Death and Immortality* 116, 117
fideism 89, 90, 267, 280; *see also* faith
Filioque 14, 280
First World War 60, 65, 255–6
Forsyth, Peter Taylor (1848–1921) 121–6; and atonement 124, 125; background 122; and Barth 126; and Christology 123–4; *The Cruciality of the Cross* 124; and God 121, 123; and *kenosis* and *plerosis* 123–4; *The Person and Place of Jesus Christ* 123; *Positive Preaching and the Modern*

Mind 123; rejection of liberal theology 121, 123, 125; *The Work of Christ* 124
Fourth Gospel: Bultmann's book on 86
Free Church of Scotland 48–9
free will 38, 44, 45–6, 68, 97, 145, 157
French Protestant church 94
Freud, Sigmund 120
Froude, Hurrell 196
Fundamentalism 54, 280

Gadamer, Hans George 239
Gaunilo 12
Genesis 42
Geneva 92, 93, 94
Genevan Academy 94
Gentiles 215–16, 218–19
Germany 49, 53, 186
Gilkey, Langdon 255
Gnosticism/Gnostics 15, 86, 203, 250–2, 280–1; and creation 151; feature of theology 251; Irenaeus and Valentinian 149, 150, 153; morality of 252; roots and origins 251; and Tertullian 252
God 24; and Anselm 11–13; and Aquinas 21–2; and Arius 25, 26–31, 32, 104, 206; and Baillie 51–2; and Barth 21, 59–63, 64; and Boethius 68–9; and Bonhoeffer 75–6; and Brunner 81; and Calvin 95–6; and doctrine of analogy 24; and Forsyth 121, 123; and Irenaeus 151–2; and John of Damascus 156–7; and Kant 163–4, 167; and Küng 177; and Moltmann 191–2; and Rahner 223; and Ritschl 229; and Tillich 257–8; and Tracy 264–5; and Zwingli 274
God's Will for Church and Nation 52–3
Gogarten, Friedrich 80, 90
gospels 244–5, 247, 273
grace 23, 38, 42, 46, 57, 62, 77–8, 171, 172, 173, 180, 183, 221, 222, 225
Greek Church 158
Greek Fathers 158
Greek philosophy 28, 203
Greeks 249

Gregory of Nazianzus (329–90) 31, 40, 102, 103, 104, 106, 107–8
Gregory of Nyssa (335–95) 31, 102, 104, 106–7, 109
Gutierrez, Gustavo (1928-) 127–31; background 127; *In the Truth Shall Make You Free* 129–30; and liberation concept 128–9, 130; and Marxism 129–30; *On Job* 130; *A Theology of Liberation* 127, 130

Harnack, Adolf von (1851–1930) 71, 131–4, 156, 167, 179, 268; background 131–2; and Barth 132, 133; and doctrine 132, 133, 134; *History of Dogma* 133–4; lectures on essence of Christianity 132–3, 134; and theology 132
Harnack, Ernst 134
Hartshorne, Charles 13
Hegel, Georg Wilhelm Friedrich (1770–1831) 12, 50, 120, 135–40, 168, 176, 208, 239, 244, 245; and Absolute Spirit 136, 137–8, 139, 140, 167, 171; attitude towards religion 138–9; background 135; centrality of dialectic method 171; criticism of by Feuerbach 116, 117; critique of logic of by Kierkegaard 60, 172; influence of 140; and Kant 135–6; and logic 137; *Phenomenology of Spirit* 138; and reason 136–7; and Trinity 139–40
Heidegger, Martin 86, 221
Heidelberg Disputation (1518) 184
Héloïse 5, 8
Henry I, King 15
Heracleon 204
heresy/heretics: and John of Damascus 156; and Tertullian 252–3
hermeneutics 239
Hick, John Harwood (1922-) 141–8, 153, 179; assessment of achievements 148; background and career 141; and Christology 141–2, 143, 146; *Death and Eternal Life* 146–7; and evil 144–6, 148; *Evil and the God of Love* 144–6; and faith as an act of interpretation 143; *Faith and Knowledge* 142, 143; and *The Myth of*

God Incarnate 142; and salvation 147; theory of eschatological verification 143–4; and world religions 147–8
Hilary of Poitiers: *De Trinitate* 31
history: and Barth 207; and Pannenberg 207–8, 209, 210, 213; and revelation 207–8; and Ritschl 232; and Troeltsch 267, 268
History of Religious school 268
Hitler, Adolf 70, 72, 73
Holocaust 190, 191
Holy Spirit 36, 63, 65, 104, 204; and Cappadocian Fathers 104–5, 107–8, 109; and Paul 218; and Rahner 223–4; *see also* Trinity
homoiousios 30, 68, 103, 281
homoousios 28–9, 30, 32, 36, 37, 103, 104, 281
hope 191, 194
Hume, David 162
hypostasis 105–6, 285

iconoclastic controversy (726) 154, 155
immutability 62, 281
incarnation 120, 245; and Abelard 6; and Aquinas 21, 22; and Arius 27, 30; and Athanasius 36, 37; and Baillie 57; and Hick 141–2; and Kant 166; and Origen 205; and Pannenberg 211–12; and Rahner 222
indulgence controversy (1517) 183–4
Irenaeus (c.130-c.200) 145, 149–53; *Against the Heresies* 149–50; as a biblical theologian 151; and Christology 152; and doctrine of God 151–2; and orthodox Christianity 149; and 'recapitulation' concept 152–3; and 'rule of truth' 150–1; and Valentinian Gnostics 149, 150, 153
Islam 17, 156
Isocrates 40
Israel 207, 210, 212

Jaspers, Karl 90
Jena, Battle of (1806) 135
Jerome 241, 249
Jesus Christ *see* Christology

Jesus movement 242
Jews 72, 73, 189, 215
John of Damascus (c.675–749) 154–8; approach to Islam 156; and Christology 157; and creation 157; *The Fount of Knowledge* 154, 155–7; and iconoclastic controversy 154, 155, 158; and Trinity 157
Judaism 139, 209, 228, 242
Julian, Emperor 34
Julius, Pope 270
justification 75, 232, 281; and Barth 174; Luther and doctrine of 182, 183, 186, 281
Justin, Emperor 2, 67, 68
Justin Martyr (c.100–165) 158–61, 250; *Apology* 159, 160; and Bible 160; *Dialogue with the Jew Trypho* 159; and Logos 160, 161, 282; and Plato 159–60

Kant, Immanuel (1724–1804) 12, 50, 89, 132, 147, 161–7, 229, 238, 279, 282; *The Critique of Practical Reason* 164–5; *Critique of Pure Reason* 162–3; and doctrine of original sin 166; and evil 166; and God 163–4, 167; and incarnation 166; influence of 167; on knowledge 163; and moral 165, 167; and reason 135–6, 161, 162–3, 164–7; *Religion within the Limits of Reason Alone* 165–7; and Trinity 167
Käsemann, Ernst 179
Keble 196
kenosis 123, 222
kerygmatic theology 59, 90
Kierkegaard, Søren (1813–55) 60, 125, 168–73, 268; background 168–9; centrality of dialectic method 171; and Christology 170; *The Concept of Dread* 171; *Concluding Unscientific Postscript* 170; contrast between genuine Christian faith and 'official Christianity' 171–2; *Either/Or* 169; *Fear and Trembling* 169–70; human existence as aesthetic and ethical 169, 171; influence of 173; and logic 172; *On the Concept of Irony* 170; *Philosophical Fragments* 170;

seen as father of existentialist movement 172, 173; *Sickness Unto Death* 171; stress on sin of human beings 171; *Training in Christianity* 172
knowledge 54, 81, 162, 163, 250
Kuhn, Thomas 177, 178
Küng, Hans (1928–) 66, 174–9; call for paradigm shift in Christianity's self-understanding 178, 179; calls for reform in Catholic church 174–5, 179; *Christianity and the World Religions* 178; and Christology 175–6; *The Church* 174, 175; *Council, Reform and Reunion* 174; on critical rationality 176–7; *Does God Exist* 176–7; *Global Responsibility* 178; *The Incarnation of God* 176; *Infallible?* 174, 175; *On Being a Christian* 175; opposition to within Catholic church 176; thesis on Barth's doctrine of justification 174

Las Casas, Bartolomé de 130
Latin America 127–8, 131; *see also* Gutiérrez, Gustavo
Latin Church 249, 254
Latin Fathers 249
Law, William: *Serious Call to a Devout and Holy Life* 195
Leibniz, G.F.W. 12, 162, 284
Leipzig Disputation (1519) 184
Leo III, Emperor 154, 155
Libanius 40
liberal-evangelicalism 48
liberal theology 58–9, 79, 80, 86, 121, 256
liberation theology 191, 241, 243, 281–2
Locke, John 112, 162
logic, and Kierkegaard 172
Logos 26, 27, 35–6, 42, 87, 95, 98, 151–2, 157, 160, 161, 204–5, 210, 211, 212, 221, 223, 258, 259, 282
Lombard, Peter 17, 110
Lonergan, Bernard 263
Lord's Supper 23, 100; and Zwingli 273, 274–5, 277
Löw, Bertha 117
Lucian of Antioch 26

Luther, Martin 39, 72, 78, 89, 97, 99, 180–9, 210, 231; achievements 189; alarm at prospect of anarchy 187, 189; background 180–1; and Church reform 188; conflict with papacy 185; contestation of views of by Church 183; conversion experience 182–3; and doctrine of justification 182, 183, 186, 281; excommunication 186; hymn composer 189; and indulgence controversy (1517) 183–4; *The Jews and Their Lies* 189; and *95 Theses* 184; *On the Babylonian Captivity of the Church* 185; *On Christian Freedom* 186; *Open Letter to the Christian Nobility* 186–7; and personal salvation 21; and righteousness of God and Christ 181–2, 183; and sacraments 185; and scripture 185; theory of consubstantiation 275; theory of two kingdoms of Church and State 187–8; *To the Christian Nobility of the German Nation* 185, 186; and Zwingli 188, 271

Mackinnon, Donald 53
Macquarrie, John 56
Maddens 251
Mair, John 91
Manichees 38–9, 40–1
Manneheim, Karl 53
Marburg Colloquy (1529) 275
Marcion 133–4
Martensen, Bishop 172
Marx, Karl 119, 120
Marxist theology 117
Mary Magdalene 242
materialism 117, 120
Melancthon 93
Melitus 33
memory 42, 265
Merton, Thomas 233
Milan, Synod of (355) 30
Milner: *History* 195
Moberley, Walter 53
Moltmann, Jürgen (1926–) 66, 79, 140, 190–5, 207; background 190; and Christology 194; *The Church in the Power of the Spirit* 193; *The*

Coming of God 194; and conception of Church 193–4; *The Crucified God* 191; *God In Creation* 194; and hope 191; *A Theology of Hope* 190–1, 194; *The Trinity and the Kingdom of God* 192; *The Way of Jesus Christ* 194
Moltmann-Wendel, Elizabeth 194
monotheism 120
Montanists 254
Moot 53
moral/morality 133; and Abelard 7; and Baillie 50, 55; of Gnosticism 252; and Kant 165
Mueller, Max 269
Muhammad 156
Murry, John Middleton 53
'Myth of God Incarnate' debate 57
Myth of God Incarnate, The 142

Nazis/Nazism 52, 65, 66, 72, 202
neo-platonism 17, 21, 23, 36, 39, 115, 282
Nero 218
New Testament 158–9, 216, 249, 260
Newman, John Henry (1801–90) 195–8; *Apologia pro Vita Sua* 197; *The Arians of the Fourth Century* 196; background 196; *Essay on the Development of Doctrine* 197; *The Idea of a University* 197; and Oxford Movement 196, 197; *Parochial and Plain Sermons* 197; *Tracts for the Times* 196, 197
Newton, Isaac 112, 195
Nicaea, Council of (325) 25, 26, 28, 281; filoque clause 14, 280; and *homoousios* settlement 29, 30–1, 32, 104, 281
Nicaea, Council of (787) 158
Nicholas of Cusa 265
Niebuhr, Reinhold (1892–1971) 51, 57, 71, 73, 198–202, 256; *The Children of Light and the Children of Darkness* 201–2; and Christian Realism 199–200, 201, 202; and Christology 201; and doctrine of sin 200; *Does Civilisation Need Religion?* 199; *An Interpretation of Christian Ethics* 201; *Moral Man and Immoral Society*

199; *The Nature and Destiny of Man* 200

Niebuhr, H.R. 199, 256

Niebuhr, Ursula 199

nominalism 3–4, 110, 282; *see also* universals

noumenal 136, 147, 163, 282

Old Testament 203, 249

Oldham, J.H. 53

Olsen, Regine 168, 169

Oman, John 141

Origen (185–254) 103, 132, 156, 203–6, 224; *Apologia Contra Celsum* 206; and Bible 204; *Hexapla* 203; *On First Principles* 203, 204; and scriptures 203–4, 205; and Trinity 26, 204, 206

original sin, doctrine of 38; and Augustine 46–7; and Edwards 114–15; and Kant 166

Oster, General 73

ousia 105–6, 285

Oxford Movement 196, 197

pacifism, Barth on 65

Paine, Thomas: *Tracts on the Old Testament* 195

Pannenberg, Wolfhart (1928–) 57, 66, 175, 178, 191, 207–13; and Christology 209, 211–12; commitment to basing his theology on history 209, 210, 213; criticism of 211; and relation between history and gospel 207–8; and resurrection 209–10, 212; and revelation 207–8, 212, 213; and scripture 210, 211; and theological anthropology 211 papacy: and Luther 185

Paul (? –64) 39, 41, 87, 214–20, 242, 249; arrest and imprisonment 217–18; background 214; encounter with risen Christ 214–15; letters 216; missionary journeys and major figure in expansion of early Church 216; and resurrection 219, 220; takes up collection from his churches for church in Jerusalem 217; theology and outlines of thought 218–20Pauline churches 217, 218, 219

Peasants' Revolt (Germany) (1524/25) 187

Pelagius 39, 45–6, 110

penitential theology 14

Perrinists 95

Peter 215, 216

Peter, Bishop of Alexandria 33

Pezel, Christoph 190

phenomenal 147, 163, 282–3

piety 236

Plantinga, Alvin 12–13

Plato 42, 159–60; *see also* neo-platonism

Plerosis 123, 283

Plotinus 203; *Enneads* 40

Polycarp, Bishop of Smyrna 149, 150

polytheism 34–5

Popper, Karl 177

predestination 194, 195, 283; and Augustine 38, 46, 283; and Calvin 98–9, 283; and Edwards 114; and Zwingli 272

Preller, Victor 24

Price, H.H. 146

Protestantism 14

purgatory 181

Rahner, Karl (1904–84) 63, 176, 178, 192, 221–5; and anonymous Christianity 224; anthropological approach to theology 221; background 221; and Christology 222–3; and creation 225; and existentialism 221; and God 223; and Holy Spirit 223–4; and importance of spiritual 224; and incarnation 222; and sin 225

Rauschenbush, Walter 284

realism 3–4, 20, 54–5, 110, 177, 283

redemption 22, 68

Reformation 91, 93, 111, 139, 180, 210

Reimarus, Hermann Samuel (1694–1768) 226–8 ; and Christology 227; *Wolfenbuettel Fragments* 226–8

resurrection 64, 147, 191, 205, 209–10, 212, 219, 220, 227

revelation 16, 18, 207, 230, 283; and
Aquinas 18–20; and Barth 61, 62,
64, 74, 75; and Brunner 64, 80–1;
and Gnostics 150, 251; and history
207–8; and Pannenberg 207–8, 212,
213; and subject-object dichotomy
81; and Tillich 259

Ritschl, Albrecht (1822–89) 122, 132,
167, 229–32, 266, 268; avoiding of
metaphysical concepts 231–2; background 229–30; and concept of
Kingdom 231; *The Early Catholic
Church* 230; and essence of Christianity 230; and God 229; and
history 232; and value judgements
230–1, 232

Robert, Pierre 91

Robinson, J.A.T. 175

Robinson, John (Bishop of Woolwich)
57; *Honest to God* 79

Roman Catholic Church 139

Romans 249

Romantic movement 136, 197

Romero, Arnulfo 194

Roscelin 3, 4

Ruether, Rosemary Radford 233–5;
The Church Against Itself 233; *A
Democratic Catholic Church* 234; *Dis-
puted Questions* 233; *The Radical
Kingdom* 234; *To Change the World*
234

Rule of St Basil 103

'rule of truth' 150–1

Russell, Bertrand 12

Russell, Letty 241

Sabellianism 5, 29

Sabellius 29

Saccas, Ammonius 203

sacraments 180, 182, 221; and Aquinas
23; and Augustine 45; and Barth
65–6; and Calvin 100; and Luther
185; and Zwingli 275–6

Sacred Congregation for the Doctrine
of the Faith 174

Sadoleto, Cardinal 94

salvation 207–8, 213, 219, 283; and
Aquinas 23; and Athanasius 35–6;
and Calvin 98; and Hick 147; and
Irenaeus 152–3; and Kierkegaard

171; and Luther 180, 181; role of
the incarnate Word in 35–6; and
Zwingli 274

sanctification 75, 283–4

Sauter, Gerhard 191

Schelling 135

Schillebeeckx, Edward 224

schismatics 33

Schlatter, Adolf 71

Schleiermacher, Friedrich Daniel
Ernst (1768–1834) 65, 80, 101,
135, 167, 225, 230, 231, 236–9,
244, 261; background 238; *The
Christian Faith* 53, 236–7, 238,
239; and Christology 237, 260;
and hermeneutics 239; as a Prussian
patriot 239; *Religion, Speeches to its
Cultured Despisers* 141, 236, 237,
238; and theme of 'absolute dependence' 237–8; and Trinity 237

Schlink, Edmund 207

Schneider, Paul 194

scholastic(ism) 3, 284

Schüssler-Fiorenza, Elisabeth (1938–)
240–3; *In Memory of her* 240, 241–2

Schweitzer, Albert 228, 247; *Quest for
the Historical Jesus* 248

Scotland, Free Church of 48–9

Scots Confession (1560) 101

Scott, Thomas 195

Scottish Journal of Theology 142

scripture 105; and Barth 96–7; and
Calvin 96–7; and Luther 185; and
Origen 203–4, 205; and Pannenberg 210, 211; tradition of *sola
scriptura* 210, 273; and Zwingli
272–3, 274

Sea of Faith movement 120

Second World War 52

Seeberg, Reinhold 71

Seneca: *De Clementia* 92

Sens, Council of (1141) 8

Serapion, Bishop 36

Servetus, Michael 94–5

sex: linkage with sin 44

Sherrill, Bishop Henry 51

sin 23, 64, 200, 225, 260; *see also*
original sin, doctrine of

Smith, Robertson 122

Social Gospel 50, 132, 199, 284

Socrates 253
Soden, Hans von 89
Soissons, Council of (1121) 5
Spirit-fighters (*Pneumatomachians*) 104
spirituality 224
Stanton, Elizabeth Cady 241
Stoddart, Samuel 112
Stoics 159
Strauss, David Friedrich (1808–74) 118, 228, 244–9; background 244; break with Christianity 248; *Christian Dogmatics* 248; and Christology 245, 246–8; gospels and mythical 244–5, 246; *The Life of Jesus Critically Examined* 244–5, 246–7; *The Old Faith and the New* 248
subject-object dualism 84
synoptic tradition 85–6
systematic theology 229, 230

Tacitus 40
Tertullian, Quintus Septimus Florens (c.160–c.225) 134, 241, 249–54, 282; attitude towards philosophy 253; background 249–50; and Christology 254; fight against heresies 250, 252–3, 254; and Gnosticism 252; as a Montanist 254; *Prescriptions against Heretics* 250–1, 252; and Trinity 254
theism 177
Theissen, Gerd 241
Theoderic, King 67–8
theodicy 123, 124, 284
theological anthropology: and Pannenberg 211
Thirty Years War 186
Thomism 17
Tillich, Paul (1886–1965) 189, 255–62; background 255, 256–7; and Christology 259–61, 262; commitment to socialism 256; *The Courage to Be* 256; definition of God 257–8; method of correlation 258, 262; and revelation 259; *The Shaking of the Foundations* 256; *Systematic Theology* 256; and theology 257, 258, 262
Tomus ad Antiochenos (Athanasius) 36
Tract 90 197

Tracy, David (1939–) 255, 263–6; *The Achievement of Bernard Lonergan* 263; *The Analogical Imagination* 264; background 263–4; *Blessed Rage for Order* 263–4; *Critical Social Theory and the Public Realm* 265–6; and doctrine of God 264–5; and Enlightenment 263, 264; *On Naming the Present* 264–5; *Plurality and Ambiguity* 264; transubstantiation 188, 275, 284
Trent, Council of 174
Trinity/Trinitarian 4, 16, 31, 47, 102, 110, 160–1, 191–2, 195, 284–5; and Abelard 5–6; and Anselm 14–15; and Aquinas 21, 22; and Arius 26–9; and Augustine 5, 38, 43, 47, 108; and Boethius 68; and Cappadocian Fathers 105–7, 108; and filoque 14, 280; and Hegel 139–40; and John of Damascus 157; and Kant 167; and Moltmann 192; and Origen 26, 204, 206; and Schleiermacher 237; and Tertullian 254
Troeltsch, Ernst (1865–1923) 132, 133, 229, 266–9; background 267; on relationship between theology and history 267, 268; *The Social Teaching of the Christian Churches* 268; and world religions 268

Union Theological Seminary (New York) 50, 71
United Church of Canada 50
universals 285; and Abelard 3, 4, 110; and Anselm 20, 110; and Aquinas 20, 110; and Boethius 68, 69; realist versus nominalist 3–4, 20, 110
Urban II, Pope 15

Valens, Emperor 34, 104
Valentinian Gnostics 149, 150, 204
Van Dusen, Henry 51, 57, 199
Vatican Council, Second 174, 225, 263
Vidler, Alec 53
Voltaire 227
Von Balthasar, Hans Urs 174
Von Campenhausen 159
Von Hase, Karl August 70
Von Rad, Gerhard 207

Weiss, Johannes 85–6
Wesley, John 113
Whitfield, George 113
William of Champeaux 3, 4
William II, King 15
William of Ockham 110–11
Wolmar, Melchior 91
women: and Schüssler-Fiorenza 241, 242–3
Word of God see Logos
World Alliance for Promoting International Friendship 71
World Council of Churches (WCC) 51, 54, 279
world religions 147, 178, 268

Yale school 264
Young Men's Christian Association 49

Zwingli, Huldrych (1484–1531) 100, 188, 269–77; background 269–70; on baptism 275–6, 277; influence of 276; and Luther 271; On the Providence of God 274; On True and False Religion 274; 'Plague Hymn' 271–2; and preaching 271; recovery from the plague 271–2; and sacraments 275–6; and scripture 272–3, 274; 67 Theses 273; views on Lord's Supper and eucharist 273, 274–5, 277